Oxford India Studies in Contemporary Society

SERIES EDITOR
SUJATA PATEL

OXFORD INDIA STUDIES IN CONTEMPORARY SOCIETY is a new series of interdisciplinary compilations on issues and problems shaping our lives in twenty-first century India. The Series appears at an opportune time, when the boundaries of social science disciplines are being redefined, and theories and perspectives are being critically interrogated. Using the frameworks developed by social science interdisciplinarity, this Series captures, assesses, and situates social trends in contemporary India. It affirms the necessity of analysing issues and themes that have a direct bearing on our daily lives, and in doing so, brings fresh perspectives into play, integrating knowledge from a variety of unexplored sources in conventional social science practice in India. The Series aims to introduce to a wider audience the central importance of interdisciplinarity in contemporary social sciences. It presents novel themes of investigation and builds a fresh approach towards the long-standing debates on methodologies and methods. With its emphasis on the debates on and about 'society' rather than 'social sciences', this Series should find an audience not only among the students and scholars of conventional social sciences, but also among the students, researchers, and practitioners of fields such as law, media, environment, medicine, policy studies, and business studies.

Sujata Patel is Distinguished Professor, Savitribai Phule Pune University and Kerstin Hesselgren Visiting Professor, Umea University, 2021–2022.

OTHER TITLES IN THE SERIES

Rowena Robinson (ed.)
Minority Studies

Sanjaya Srivastava (ed.)
Sexuality Studies

Ravi Sundaram (ed.)
No Limits: Media Studies from India

Meena Radhakrishna (ed.)
*First Citizens: Studies on Adivasis, Tribals,
and Indigenous Peoples in India*

Kalpana Kannabiran (ed.)
Violence Studies

Purendra Prasad and Amar Jesani (eds)
Equity and Access

OXFORD INDIA STUDIES IN CONTEMPORARY SOCIETY

Sports Studies in India

Expanding the Field

Edited by
MEENA GOPAL AND PADMA PRAKASH

OXFORD
UNIVERSITY PRESS

Great Clarendon Street, Oxford, OX2 6DP,
United Kingdom

Oxford University Press is a department of the University of Oxford.
It furthers the University's objective of excellence in research, scholarship,
and education by publishing worldwide. Oxford is a registered trade mark of
Oxford University Press in the UK and in certain other countries

Published in India by
Oxford University Press
22 Workspace, 2nd Floor, 1/22 Asaf Ali Road, New Delhi 110 002, India

© Oxford University Press 2021

The moral rights of the author have been asserted

First Edition published in 2021

All rights reserved. No part of this publication may be reproduced, stored in
a retrieval system, or transmitted, in any form or by any means, without the
prior permission in writing of Oxford University Press, or as expressly permitted
by law, by licence or under terms agreed with the appropriate reprographics
rights organization. Enquiries concerning reproduction outside the scope of the
above should be sent to the Rights Department, Oxford University Press, at the
address above

You must not circulate this work in any other form
and you must impose this same condition on any acquirer.

ISBN-13 (print edition): 978-0-19-013064-0

ISBN-10 (print edition): 0-19-013064-4

ISBN-13 (eBook): 978-0-19-099310-8

ISBN-10 (eBook): 0-19-099310-3

DOI: 10.1093/oso/9780190130640.001.0001

Typeset in Minion Pro 10/13
by Newgen KnowledgeWorks Pvt. Ltd., Chennai, India

Printed in India by Rakmo Press Pvt. Ltd

Contents

Acknowledgements ix

List of Figures and Table xi

Introduction: A Sporting Engagement 1
Padma Prakash and Meena Gopal

SECTION I. SPORTS AND SPORTS STUDIES: EXPANDING THE FIELD, BREAKING BOUNDARIES

1. The Struggle for Sports Commons: Sports Markets and the Labour Movement 19
   S. Janaka Biyanwila

2. Globalizing Sportscapes: Football in Mumbai's Socio-Spatial Dynamics 36
   D. Parthasarathy

3. India's Olympic Encounter: Sport, Identity and Nationalism 51
   Boria Majumdar

4. Indian Volleyball: From Local Contexts to Global Realities 60
   Bino Paul

5. Sherpas in Himalayan Mountaineering: Identity, Labour and Power in Sport 70
   Vrinda Marwah

6. Women's Cricket in India: Expanding the Inclusionary Possibilities of Sport 89
   Raadhika Gupta

7. Testing the Limits of Science: Sex Difference and Athletic Ability in Elite Sports 114
   Madeleine Pape

SECTION II. REFLECTIONS ON SPORTS STUDIES: TRANSCENDING DISCIPLINES

8. A Sociological Understanding of Sport in India   133
   Elizabeth C.J. Pike

9. Labours of Care in Sport: Relections on Feminist Practice in Athletics   150
   Meena Gopal

10. Perspectives on Sports History in India: Present Challenges and Future Directions   159
    Kausik Bandyopadhyay

SECTION III. NURTURING SPORTS: CRUCIBLES OF GROWTH

11. A City and a Sport: Hockey in Calcutta   175
    Nikhilesh Bhattacharya

12. Goa's Football Story: A Brief Narrative   190
    Frederick Noronha

13. Local Clubs and Sports Culture in Kerala: Community at the Centre   196
    S. Mohammed Irshad

14. Nurturing Sports Talent: What Role Do Academies Play?   205
    Pulasta Dhar

SECTION IV. STATE, SPORTS, AND DEVELOPMENT: POLICY AND REGULATION

15. The Uneven Development of Sport Policy in India: Need for a Coordinated Governance Structure   215
    Kruthika N.S. and Sarthak Sood

16. Mega Sport Events, Development, and Tourism: Case Study of the Commonwealth Games 2010   237
    EQUATIONS

17.	Doping in Sports: Ramifications for India *K.P. Mohan*	251
18.	Performance-Enhancing Substances in Sports: Towards Country-Specific Harm Reduction Strategies *Kaveri Prakash*	266
19.	Sport for Development and Peace: From Global to the Local *S. Ananthakrishnan*	276
20.	Reimagining Play: Football, Muslim Women, and Empowerment *Sabah Khan*	292

SECTION V. MOVIES, MEDIA, AND TECHNOLOGY

21.	The Nationalist Imaginary in the Bollywood Sports Film *Nissim Mannathukkaren*	305
22.	Sports, Celebrity, and the Sports Biopic *Pramod K. Nayar*	322
23.	Breaking into the Press Box and After: A First-Person Account *Sharda Ugra*	334
24.	State, Market, and Media in Indian Cricket *Avipsu Halder*	345
25.	Who Watches Cricket?: The New Spectator in the Sporting-Entertainment Complex *Vidya Subramaniam*	356

Notes on the Editors and Contributors   371
Index   379

Acknowledgements

At the risk of sounding trite, this book stands on the shoulders of giants in the field of sports studies. It is their work that has inspired this broad-based compendium offering a glimpse into the field, which we hope will inspire more work in the area. There is no way we can list them all, but both of us, as social scientists and sports aficionados and sometime practitioners have had the joy of discovering and rediscovering sports through the writings of many. We acknowledge our debt to those stalwarts.

We, at different points of our professional lives, had wanted to knit our passion for athletics and sports with our professional lives that had not given easy opportunities to pursue competitive sports. When Sujata Patel as Series Editor of Oxford India Studies in Contemporary Society accepted our proposal to edit this volume, we thought we had a great opportunity to do just that. At the end of the project the opportunity has turned out to be one of learning and so much more than we expected it to be. Sujata's timely insights, even though in an area that she is not particularly familiar with, have been extraordinarily useful, as was her insistence on a disciplined approach to putting together and editing such a volume. We are most grateful to her for all her inputs, advice and suggestions, even if at times we might have quibbled and procrastinated.

Late A J de Souza of the Don Bosco Athletic Club, Madras, coached Meena in the mid-1980s in heptathlon. I wish to acknowledge and put on record his mentorship, at times stringent but entirely rewarding. He groomed not just me but numerous other local, national and international athletes and was himself an institution that loved sport and built lives around it. Along with A J, the seeds of a life in sports was sown by school principals such as Sr. Joan, sports teachers such as Chellakumari Peters, and sports enthusiasts in those heady years of the eighties and nineties. My friends and co-athletes, Jayashree Venkataraman, M Praveen, R Vasanthy, S Yasmin, Sandra Thomas, Monika & Praveen Fernandes, Ricky Ferrier, Errol Hart, E Ravi, and my brother Keshav Das have through their presence in diverse moments contributed to the making of this volume. My parents, Gowri and Gopal, were quiet but enthusiastic supporters of the new generation of sportspersons in the family. In recent years, my colleagues at the Advanced Centre for Women's Studies,

and Nandini Manjrekar have shared in education, labour and sport playing a part in the making of a new generation of youth. Finally, if it were not for Padma's enterprising self, immense drive and exemplary persistence, this project would not have taken off in the manner it has, and that has to be said!

The first time Padma ventured into sports as an academic exercise was when Maithreyi Krishnaraj then the head of the Women's Studies Centre at SNDT Women's University asked me to write a monograph on women and sports. Until then, I had not ventured to explore the field in detail although I talked about it at every opportunity. Maithreyi, as was her métier, set me on a course and a project so that my ideas could find purchase. I am so very grateful to her for that. A version of that monograph found its way into the pages of the *Economic and Political Weekly*. And for that transition I must acknowledge Krishna Raj's persuasive arguments that overcame my hesitation in submitting a paper to be processed by the prestigious weekly when I was myself a staffer there. In the absence of confidence and skills to pursue academic enquiry into the field of sports, my interest in writing about sports received a great deal of encouragement in writing features for the *Eve's Weekly* on women and sports under the watchful eye of Pamela Philipose. This put me in touch with such inspiring, but not well know sports persona as Violet Peters who represented India in the Manila Asian Games in 1954 winning India a first Asian women's athletic gold in the 4x100 relay.

Padma would also like to register her sincere gratitude to the late Tejeshwar Singh (of Sage) who, way back in the 1980s, was among those who encouraged me to keep alive the idea of working on sports as a field of study, especially sports and the media. This manuscript would not have been completed with so few glitches but for the help from my colleagues at IRIS Knowledge Foundation. I sincerely thank them for their support on a project that did not have anything to do with their work. And appreciation to Prakash, who is never certain what I am working on, but regardless lends support and encouragement. Most of all I owe my enthusiasm for all sporting activities to my mother who herself played tennis in the 1920s.

The volume of course would not have been possible without the participation of all our authors in this project, and their patience and cooperation in keeping to our brief and making our experience as editors of the volume pleasant and fruitful. We also wish to thank Moutushi Mukherjee and others at OUP who also helped us through the production of this volume.

Meena Gopal and Padma Prakash, 2021

List of Figures and Table

Figure 4.1	India's rank in World Volleyball	64
Figure 16.1	Percentage Change in Tourist Arrivals in Delhi	242
Figure 25.1	Richard Giulianotti's Classification of Spectators	358
Table 17.1	NADA Testing Statistics	260

Introduction

A Sporting Engagement

Padma Prakash and Meena Gopal

Sport as a global phenomenon is gaining a cultural and social centrality within countries in different ways and varying pace. Allen Guttmann (1978) defines modern sports as reflecting secularism, equality of opportunity, bureaucratic organization, specialization of roles, rationalization, quantification, and a quest for records. Sports may also be defined in more invested terms of what it does to a society, culture, politics, and economy and how it impacts social relations and economic landscape. Sports has an emancipatory potential that is realized in various ways. A multidimensional perspective on sports allows us to understand in microcosm the operation of embedded forces of patriarchy and capitalism, and of power and resistance in society.

Sports studies is in scope, multidisciplinary and in approach, interdisciplinary. In the literature, a variety of approaches – anthropological, sociological, historical, political economy and gender perspectives – have been applied to sports. For example, the exercise of power and resistance in sports has been explored from the standpoint of conflict theory while functionalist approaches have been applied to the study of resistance to change within sports. Feminist theories help us understand how sport is a gendered activity at every level. Approaches emerging from Marxist and Weberian concepts have been used to look at the emergence of sports as goods for consumer consumption in a new marketplace and the destruction of old community-based forms of sports associations (see Irshad, Paul, Halder, and Subramaniam in this volume). Merton's theory of social structure has formed the basis for understanding the structure of sports and its growth. Tonnies' concepts of *gemeinschaft* and *gesellschaft* on ideal social connections, and Durkheim's notion of 'collective consciousness' have been found useful in understanding

Padma Prakash and Meena Gopal, *Introduction* In: *Sports Studies in India*. Edited by: Meena Gopal and Padma Prakash, Oxford University Press. © Oxford University Press 2021.
DOI: 10.1093/oso/9780190130640.003.0001

2 SPORTS STUDIES IN INDIA

the formation of football clubs and fan clubs. The critique of modern competitive sports using Marxist and feminist theoretical and conceptual constructs, labour studies approaches and a political economy framework has yielded a rich understanding prompting new areas of study (see Biyanwila, Parthasarathy, Gopal, Gupta, Pape in this volume). The concept of subalternity, with an expanded and broader meaning, has been examined in the context of sports providing new insights (Mills 2005). Anthropologists have studied play in traditional societies as a means to understanding those societies. Leisure studies have referenced the theory of play and have sometimes incorporated the study of sports within their disciplinary areas, although in general, study of play has been a distinct interdisciplinary field (Coakley and Pike 2009).

A Brief Survey of the Field

The literature on sports studies in India has been building up over the last decade after a slow start. Cricket, the 'great tamasha' as Astill (2013) describes it, and, to a lesser extent, football have dominated the field. The literature is thinly spread across disciplines, with the pioneering works being social histories of mass sport and biographical accounts. We do not here attempt a systematic review of sports studies literature, but merely draw attention to some significant areas of work that have particularly engaged our attention.

A long-standing focus of sports studies has been historical. Sports as a field of exploration for understanding of the forces in play in the making of the nation and of politics in a colonial setting is much explored. These explorations have looked at power, resistance, the compulsions of politics of the day, the emerging idea of a nation within the field of sports, most often in cricket. So the story of sports in India is heavily invested with the story of the nation in the making. Ramachandra Guha's pioneering work that he describes as 'a history of India told through cricket and cricketers', *A Corner of a Foreign Field* (2004), addresses the transformation of cricket in the subcontinent from a leisure activity for the colonial into a pre-eminently Indian game imbued with the colour and passion of the land. The volume also delves into the interconnected themes of race, caste, religion and nation. Guha (2001, 2004, and several others) has covered a wide scholarly ground on cricket.

It is not surprising that cricket has been a favourite subject of study among historians exploring nationalism, colonialism and modernity and more recently gender in sport. As Arjun Appadurai (1995: 21) points out, 'cricket is

INTRODUCTION 3

the ideal locus for national attention and nationalist passion because it affords the experience of experimenting with what might be called the "means of modernity" to a wide variety of groups within Indian society.'

Published more than a decade after Guha's seminal work is Prashant Kidambi's *Cricket Country* (2019), a fascinating narrative of how the first all-India cricket team's visit to England in the summer of 1911, the year of the coronation of King George, was fashioned. In untangling the numerous threads of this momentous event, Kidambi (2019: xiii) further explores 'how the idea of India took shape on the cricket pitch' in India and England. Here too, in this nuanced story, attention is drawn to how 'patronage, politics and play' became inextricably entwined in the colonial mix. Kidambi, for instance, provides a glimpse of other Indian sportsmen making a mark of their own in England that same summer when the first Indian cricket team was constructed. Other works, for instance, on hockey and football, have explored social tensions that were mirrored in sports. Several scholars have traced how football became a 'cultural weapon' to fight the British, especially after the much discussed Mohun Bagan's historic victory in 1911 over a British team in the Indian Football Association (IFA) Shield, a tournament fashioned by the colonial masters.

Boria Majumdar's (2004, 2018) explorations of the history of sports in India go beyond cricket. Majumdar is among the few who has dug deep into India's early relations with the Olympic agency and how the first Indian contingent emerged under the encouragement of individual Indian businessmen in the period of waning princely influence and colonial apathy. Ronojoy Sen's *Nation at Play: A History of Sport in India* (2015), goes back in time to examine sports, such as archery and wrestling in the medieval era, providing a different perspective to the study of the perception of sports in modern Indian society. Rudraneil Sengupta's short and engaging work on wrestling in Bengal describes how the sport had, by the late nineteenth century, become 'a matter of pride: an indigenous somatic pursuit that stood against the British stereotype of the weakness of Indians' (Sengupta 2016: 187). These political history explorations have documented the formation of modern sport, and the multiple ways that sports played a role in the making of the nation and its struggles for freedom. This literature has underlined the critical importance of studying sports in the context of history, politics, and culture.

There are inevitably many gaps. What role sports played in a community or a region and how that relationship has been affected by the trajectories of growth of modern sports is only now attracting scholarly interest. A seminal work with respect to culture and power is that of James Mills (2005), who

4 SPORTS STUDIES IN INDIA

provides us, in an edited volume, an engaging and thought-provoking insight into the politics of sport in South Asia, exploring issues of power and resistance in various sports and how they may help us understand subalternity.

The lives of those labouring in sports has had no traction at all until recently. A revealing view of elite sports, in this case golf, is provided by the very recently released *Narrow Fairways: Getting By & Falling Behind in the New India* (2019) by Patrick Inglis, an ethnographic study of poor, lower-caste caddies who carry the golf sets of wealthy upper-caste members at golf clubs. Inglis's volume underlines the huge gap in our understanding of the work and lives of those who are part of the sporting world but are not themselves players. Interestingly, Inglis situates the study in a larger context of the widening gap between the rich and poor, and offers the insight that while the gap is real enough, the relationship between the rich and poor contributes in complicated ways to the upward mobility of the poor, even while the master–servile worker status remains intact. The fact that sports may offer a field in which changing social relations can be examined has not yet made an impact in social sciences. The way sports practices may themselves adapt over time to accommodate players from diverse communities and so assist in the assimilation of 'outsiders' into the community is the focus of Stanley Thangaraj, Daniel Burdsey, Rajinder Dudrah's (2014) volume on South Asian basketball clubs in USA. Sports among the diaspora, especially cricket among South Asian immigrant communities, is a fairly new and growing area of interest.[i]

Sociologists in India (and South Asia) have been slow to recognize sports as a potential field of academic enquiry. Veena Mani and Mathangi Krishnamurthi's (2016) substantive review of sociology of sports shows, however, that this might be changing. This text also draws attention to three distinct but intertwined themes in the sociology of sports: modernity and nationalism; sub-nationalisms or regional nationalisms; and gender, masculinities, and culture.

An important hub of sports studies in India has been the set of universities in West Bengal—Jadavpur University, Calcutta University, West Bengal State University, and, to some extent, Rabindra Bharati—that produce path-breaking work concerning the history and culture of sports as well as focusing specifically on gender perspectives in sports. The setting up of a special subarea for sports studies under the Indian Sociological Society (www.insoso.org), web portals, such as www.sportstudies.in, and networks will no doubt create the momentum towards nurturing sports studies within academic disciplines. With this volume, we attempt to understand how scholars

INTRODUCTION 5

from diverse disciplines are framing and understanding sports as a field of enquiry, as a lens to understand society.

Sports Studies for India: An Agenda

It has often been remarked that sports is ubiquitous in India. In the social environment of the recent past, where education and employment were the key words, sports was often positively discouraged even as schools tried hard to embed sports in their curricula. Entire generations lived vicariously through watching cricket, football, and hockey matches and surreptitiously tuning into match commentaries frowned upon by parents and teachers alike, but not playing these games. Nor was sports of significance among the struggling middle class that put jobs above leisure activities like sports (unless, occasionally, it could be turned into a livelihood).

Even today, while cricket matches may enthuse people, even when India is not playing, other sports have much smaller numbers of followers. Occasionally, a badminton victory or a spectacular performance in, say, golf might attract some readership or viewership on television. With the extensive televising of sports, it has even made an entry into living rooms everywhere, urban and rural, rich and poor, drawing more people into watching the game, even if they are quite clueless about its rules. It is hardly the case, however, that sports defines India as a nation. Sports is as yet on the edges of our social life and has not moved to occupy centre stage. Sports does not figure in policy making, nor significantly in the legislative field. Sports continues to be under the full purview of the states without the benefit of an overarching national agenda or budget (see Kruthika and Sood in this volume for a detailed discussion). As important is the fact that sports do not yet provide employment or avenues for professional careers.

Undoubtedly, the increasing commodification of sports is bringing about a change in the way they are played, viewed, and consumed. Even though the state is ostensibly attempting to push sports for development agenda, it is in fact private enterprise, in the form of corporates or as private foundations, that is making an impact on sports—whether it is in the burgeoning sports academies devoted to excellence or the massive investments in packaging sports and players, on technologies that are transforming sports, in rejigging traditional sports for new viewership, and/or in creating a market for the global sports goods industry. The influx of private capital and the simultaneous withdrawal of public investment is a story that has been described

6 SPORTS STUDIES IN INDIA

in many other areas, and the consequences emerge over time and at many levels across social and economic layers, especially in the context of a demographic dividend coming into play and an expanding working-age population. Stories of struggle, resistance, and victory across classes, ethnicities, castes, and genders are bound to be written across sports fields, and an appropriately framed sports studies will be needed to read and make sense of these narratives.

This volume has emerged from the editors' sociological curiosity derived not only from scholarship but from our participation in the world of sports, and as a means of productively sharing widely our exhilarating and liberating sporting experience. Its focus is streamlined, but its spread is wide. The short purposes here are: first, to rejuvenate interest in the field; second, to offer a platform for a wide range of studies on sports, employing a variety of approaches, perspectives, and methodologies to enliven a field of study; and third, equally important, to engender both a scholarly and informed lay readership about serious work and writing on sports.

The question then arises: Should sports studies emerge as a subdiscipline, an interdisciplinary field? Or would it be better that studies of sports occur within various disciplines as the questions emerge, using the frameworks and conceptual understanding of the native disciplines? Our premise is as follows: An interdisciplinary field both creates a challenge to existing disciplines and enriches them while expanding its scope. Given the wide range of studies that deal with sports or that see sports as arena where social, political, and cultural relations play out in the microcosm, sports studies, as a subfield and an interdisciplinary arena, is already upon us. Consequently, our task is only to recognize how scholars from the major disciplines define sports—as an activity, a social endeavour, a cultural entity, or reflecting and refracting social relations and present it.

Towards These Goals, What Should a Sports Studies Agenda Be for India?

While it may be premature to draft such an agenda, we offer an important insight that has emerged from our newly garnered understanding of the world of sports as a field of/for scholarly engagement. The discussion till now has set the stage for a political economy framework with the role of market and state having increasing influence in the development of sports in the global economy. Undoubtedly, an overarching perspective of sports studies in India must involve the recognition of the intersection of class, caste, and gender in Indian society. Questions of body and gender, representation and exclusion have been the central focus of discussion within sociology of sports, and a persistent thread through much of the social science literature on sports. Gender as a mode of analysis in sport studies, especially sociology of sports in India, figures conspicuously, which is not surprising given that masculinity underpins the structure of sport. But this yields a limited, short-sighted understanding of social relations in sports and their operation without considering the intersecting factors of class, caste, race, and community.

The most important, even critical and unavoidable, lens in any work relating to sports would incorporate an acute understanding of intersectionality. It goes without saying then that the central agenda for sports studies ought to be the evolving of conceptual and theoretical frameworks, incorporating intersectionality, that may underpin sports studies. Having said this, we now identify a few of the questions that have been tackled by sports studies scholars and continue to prompt interest.

Nation, Sports, and Identity

Historical writing on sports in India has inevitably focused on the role that sports played in the early part of the last century in the construction of the concept of nation. In large part, the idea of nation and of modernity emerges only in relation to its colonial past. Cricket fields, as we have seen earlier, were where sport, to quote Kidambi (2019: xvii), 'forged the imagined communities of empire and nation'. Today's sports fields are telling many different stories, of how class, caste, and gender are intersecting to inform experiences associated with each other. In the context of India's changing perception of its place in the world, and a redefining of the concepts of nation and nationalism, the role of sports in engendering and fostering feelings of nationalism, subnationalism, regionalism, and a sense of community is being understood in multiple contexts. The field of sports, with its readymade audiences, spectators, and viewers offers a tempting platform for the expression of a variety of agendas. The controversy centring on M.S. Dhoni's novel way of honouring martyred jawans by inscribing the Balidan badge, the insignia of the Indian Para Special Forces, on his wicket-keeping gloves, in defiance of an International Cricket Council (ICC) rule, is a case in point. This is not the first time that an athlete has chosen a sporting arena to publicly express solidarity or protest. But Dhoni's espousal of the newly emerging idea of

8 SPORTS STUDIES IN INDIA

'muscular' nationalism that emphatically prioritizes India's military might is arguably contentious, even though it received overwhelming support from the Board of Cricket Control in India (BCCI). Clearly the ideas of nation and nationalism as they manifest across sports need to be more thoroughly and contemporaneously interrogated in the postcolonial framework.

Does a sportspersons have a responsibility as a public figure to stand up for civil rights or in condemnation of public atrocities and state violence? Or should they keep out of public issues that have nothing to do with sports? These issues have come up recently in the midst of large-scale violence against students and young people who were agitating against certain acts of government (see Ugra's [2020] sharp comments on the issue). The sports figure in a stateman-esque role needs better understanding.

Regional and Subnational Identities and Sport

While national teams may garner support at international arenas, subnational and regional empathies are never too far below the surface. The subsuming of regional identities within sports has been made out to be necessary for the delivery of a national performance. And yet it is these subnational identities that challenge the notion of a monolithic concept of nation. Moreover, the diversity of sports that is rooted in the culture and histories of regions has not received much attention. Whether it is Kalaripayattu from the south or mountain climbing in the north, 'local' sports are gaining national fans aided by television as well as greater mobility among young and upwardly mobile Indians. The interrogation of the regional within the constructed identity of nation poses a challenge to the existing concept of nation.

Law, Governance, and Sports

With expansion of sports organizations, sports governance, legislation, the practice of law in sports, and issues of corruption and politics in sports are emerging areas of interest. India's emerging status in global sports also prompts a number of questions and issues: what are the limits of compliance with international norms? If, as is evident, compliance is forcing a restructuring of sports bodies, what other changes are imminent? On the other hand, does India have the muscle to push through norms that are more suited

INTRODUCTION 9

to it? What does the emerging dynamics within the international sports community say about India's status as a modernizing nation?

The framing of laws and passing of legislation in any field is a recognition of the evolving significance of the field. How these laws impact the sport and how they benefit the athletes and players is not just necessary for the continued development of law, but will lead to other insights. The rights of sports persons and workers in sports has largely been neglected and needs active attention. The case of Dutee Chand and Caster Semenya in the Court of Arbitration for Sports brought in issues of athletes' rights and advocacy. The inclusion of researchers and academics such as Payoshni Mitra in the panel of experts highlights the nature of power wielded against athletes and the need for foregrounding their rights. A recent and exciting work on golf caddies in the context of hegemonic relations in the golfing world is an eye-opener. Nothing like this has been attempted in, say, cricket.

Sports Economy and Technology

With a booming sports market in India, it is surprising that sports economy and industry has not drawn scholarly attention. This is one area in which the paucity of conventional data is a handicap that can now be overcome by the large amounts of data being generated by e-commerce and social media. The intersection of technologies associated with artificial intelligence, big data, market, and sports is already altering the way some sports are played and, even more so, hastening the commodification of sportsmen and women. These technologies are rapidly transforming the way spectators and performers relate to sport. The behaviour of spectators and fans and their influence on sport has long been a focus of scholarly attention in the West and has led to theorizations that have in turn helped to unravel spectator responses and understand fan violence and to uncover class and race elements.

Class, Caste, Gender, and Other Social Locations

Across the world, racism, evident in racist chants in arenas, bias in inclusion, and so on, continues to hold sway in several sports. How do forms of discrimination and exclusion so evident in Indian society affect sporting spaces in India? Historians of sport have written about caste and its play in colonial

10 SPORTS STUDIES IN INDIA

times, not so much in contemporary times. Intersectionality is a lens that is imperative in understanding how existing social hierarchies continue to be reflected in sport even as sport offers a space to break out and offer resistance. The democratic impulse that sports offers is often difficult to surmount given the class barriers that emerge with the expensive investment that sport today requires. As we have noted earlier, complicating the mix is the issue of gender and the persistent and definitive influence of patriarchal practices and masculinist assertions. Religion and caste intertwine with gender in foreclosing options for many while perpetuating stereotypes. Recognizing this and understanding the typically devious ways in which the patriarchal subtext makes its mark is imperative to the delineation of any field of enquiry. The push to encourage women to take up sports as a part of an agenda of 'women's empowerment' does not necessarily involve a critical appreciation of the manner in which patriarchal, caste, communal, and ethnic barriers operate in sports. The grounding of a intersectional and interdisciplinary perspective in sports is urgently needed.

As an illustration, Dutee Chand, India's 100-metre specialist has successfully challenged the Athletic Federation of India's (AFI's) decision to ban her from competition on grounds of unusually high testosterone levels or hyperandrogenism. Her celebrity status notwithstanding, she was denounced and derided, by her mother no less and her village, for coming out as queer. This presents a disturbing picture of the social reality of athletes, especially women and those from marginal social locations, as they catapult to global arenas and social milieus where modernity clashes with social convention.

Contributions in This Volume

Each chapter in this volume addresses specific concerns, issues, or questions and is written in several formats and styles. This diversity is not so much a deliberate choice as it is inevitable in order to fulfil the primary objective of presenting a wide-ranging collective text on sports and society. How these narrative threads are to be woven and what designs emerge is left to the reader.

The broad thematic areas discussed above are reflected in the five sections of the volume. The sections are a combination of themes that are interspersed throughout the volume. Each of the sections thus marks a distinct area in the interdisciplinary field of sports studies while reflecting the dominant themes that the volume attempts to foreground.

INTRODUCTION 11

The first section begins by exploring the intersection of labour, identity, and gender situated with a political economy perspective, locating sports within the larger historical global context setting the tone for the volume. S. Janaka Biyanwila captures the trajectory of sports cultures in the Global South from their emergence in the aftermath of decolonization struggles to their disintegration and transformation post the 1990s wave of globalization. How can these sports structures, dominated by male oligarchies celebrating 'sports spectacles', be transformed to sports commons that encourage participatory democratic sports cultures? D. Parthasarathy deals with these issues with a different scope and perspective, meandering through football as it is played in the streets of Mumbai, Singapore, and Bangkok. He captures the changing politics of class, ethnicity, aspirations, and leisure among the urban working classes using the lens of globalized football. Boria Majumdar steps back into colonial times through newly discovered material and describes the making of India's Olympic moment, connecting it to nationalism and representation, weaving a rich and resonant story. Bino Paul examines international data on volleyball and draws some interesting early linkages between sports performance and changes outside sports, positing his own local lived experience as a starting point in understanding these developments. Vrinda Marwah's deeply perceptive chapter explores the play of labour, identity, power, and modernity in the lives of Sherpas in Himalayan mountaineering. With Raadhika Gupta's essay, the volume steps into cricket via a gender lens locating women's cricket squarely within the larger, 'masculine' world of cricket, where it essays a disruptive path. Madeleine Pape's critical essay puts the issue of gender eligibility regulations in Olympic sports in historical perspective and examines the scientific debates around gender verification, pointing to its formation and continued grounding in the racialized colonial gaze.

The second section dwells on the disciplinary perspectives that have been deployed to study the field of sports demonstrating the necessity of interdisciplinary concepts and tools. Elizabeth Pike's essay explains how theoretical concepts and understandings have been utilized with effect to perceive and understand sports in society, illustrating it with emerging issues in India. She underlines the importance of developing a genuinely post-colonial sociology of sports. Meena Gopal employs a feminist perspective and an autoethnographic method to explore the dimensions of a nurturing, mentoring practice in athletics through an unravelling of school, club, and social intersections, illuminating possibilities of a sports commons even while nurturing competitive excellence. Kausik Bandhyopadhyay's

12 SPORTS STUDIES IN INDIA

account of what a history of sports should mean in India and the travails of establishing it with an academic focus provides a glimpse of an emerging, vibrant sub-discipline.

The next four essays describe regional forces in the making of sports in the face of globalization and pushing privatization, and the struggle to nurture sports. Nikhilesh Bhattacharya takes us on a journey into the past of hockey in Kolkata through the words of hockey stars of the early years of Independence, structuring a history of the city's significance to the game that has been lost in the telling. Frederick Noronha synthesizes an account of the rich social and political history of football in Goa, with the crosscurrents of the influence of the church and the former Portuguese rulers, referencing the economic and political forces that shaped the game in later years. In resonance with the running thread of the disappearing sports commons throughout the volume, S. Mohammed Irshad describes the crumbling of a local sports club in Kerala that was once the heart of a vibrant sports culture and deliberates upon the reasons for the decay. Can the newly emerging sport-specific academies replace the community-based sports clubs of old in nurturing talent? Pulasta Dhar offers a case study of sports academies, visualized through interactions with sportspersons, mentors, and coaches as a possible alternative to the disappearing community-based clubs.

The fourth section examines the interface of state and sports and how discussions on sex and gender in sports have always intersected with race and nation. Kruthika N.S. and Sarthak Sood's is an account of the uneven development of sports policy over time and across states. The chapter makes a case for including sports in the Concurrent List, which would enable a smoother implementation and application of policy, designing of programmes, and administration of international regimes and requirements. But even with regulations in place, mega sports events have had disastrous effect on urban areas. Through a case study of the Commonwealth Games of 2010 and its aftermath, Equations, a non-profit agency actively involved with equitable/green tourism, unravels the destructive impact of mega sports events on labour, urban development, and even tourism that has been much touted as a beneficiary of a mega event.

Elite sports require the reasoned development and fair implementation of rules and regulations across nations. K.P. Mohan's detailed account of how doping regulations are applied and misapplied in India underlines the disarray in sports administration. India needs to devise better programmes of educating athletes and implementing regulations. Given that the current strategies focusing on deterrence and punishment are increasingly ineffective worldwide, Kaveri Prakash cautiously argues for adopting a relatively new approach under wide discussion, centring on a harm reduction strategy, that would allow performance enhancing substances to be administered under supervision, given of course that ethical frameworks in the practice of medicine in sports are strengthened.

In the rapidly globalizing environment of sports, what is the impact of international regulations and codes? S. Ananthakrishnan describes in detail the progressive incorporation of sports in the United Nations (UN) development agenda and discusses the limits and possibilities for member countries like India. Sabah Khan's essay is an intersectional recount of how football has been instrumental in enabling young Muslim women from a ghettoized suburb of Mumbai to engage with community- and society-imposed boundaries, illustrating the sports-for-development agenda.

The fifth and last section meanders into the realm of movies, media, and technology. Nissim Mannathukkaren argues that the genre of sports films, by mirroring the limited notion of nationalism that is in sync with the logic of the market, is as yet a disappointment. It papers over the fissures and the complications within the current hegemonic nationalism but carries the potential of reimagining it. Pramod K. Nayar, describing the fashioning of the celebrity through the cinematic medium, unpacks the factors that make a sports celebrity worthy of a biopic and thereby expands his/her marketability. Sports celebrities and cultures may once have been local, but today, the very articulation of national pride demands the cooperation of global media forces and personalities. The third chapter moves the reader into the realm of reportage, telecasts, and the state–market–media dimension in sports. Who are the people who create the images and reportage we consume? What 'makes' a journalist in the sporting field? And even more specifically, what drives a woman to break into the all-male citadel of sports media? Sharda Ugra's perceptive and illuminating first-person account of her journey through the media boxes of cricket fields is not just fascinating, but it opens up a Pandora's box where conflicting notions of gender, sports, and media interact. The last two chapters address the interplay of the state and market forces with sports media. Avipsu Halder's essay distils a watershed moment when big private broadcasters muscled out state media, and sports became vulnerable to global market forces. Vidya Subramaniam explores the role of media, technology, and market in more recent times in the continuing transformation of cricket into its current form as a hugely marketable, visible entertainment entity.

14 SPORTS STUDIES IN INDIA

With a burgeoning youth population, India and South Asia are on the cusp of change. The emergence of a genuinely postcolonial sports studies field is perhaps imminent and has already begun to take shape. This volume attempts to amplify interest in the field and also to draw attention to the new themes that are seeking an entry into the realm of sports studies. It is possible that the merging, even clashing of approaches and perspectives will make possible a paradigm nudge, even if not a shift, in the realm of studies of sport in India. If the volume throws up more questions than it deliberates upon, then it will have achieved its purpose.

Note

i. 'Beyond the Boundary: Cricket and Community in England, c.1965–2015' is one such project headed by Prashant Kidambi and James Moore.

References

Appadurai, Arjun. 1995. 'Playing with Modernity: The Decolonization of Indian Cricket'. In C.A. Breckenridge (ed.), *Consuming Modernity: Public Culture in a South Asian World*, pp. 23–48. Minneapolis: University of Minnesota Press.

Astill, James. 2013. *The Great Tamasha: Cricket, Corruption and the Turbulent Rise of Modern India*. Bloomsbury, UK: Wisden Sports Writing.

Coakley, Jay and Elizabeth Pike. 2009. *Sports in Society: Issues and Controversies*. London: McGraw-Hill.

Guha, Ramachandra. 2001. *The Picador Book of Cricket*. Basingstoke, Hampshire, England: Pan Macmillan.

———. 2004. *A Corner of a Foreign Field: The Indian History of a British Sport*. Gurgaon, India: Allen Lane.

Guttmann, Allen. 1978. *From Ritual to Record: The Nature of Modern Sports*. New York: Columbia University Press.

Inglis, Patrick. 2019. *Narrow Fairways: Getting By & Falling Behind in the New India*. New Delhi: Oxford University Press.

Kidambi, Prakash. 2019. *Cricket Country: The Untold History of the First All India Team*. Gurgaon, India: Penguin Random House India.

Mani, Veena and Mathangi Krishnamurthy. 2016. 'Sociology of Sport: India'. In Kevin Young (ed.), *Sociology of Sport: A Global Subdiscipline in Review (Research in the Sociology of Sport, Volume 9)*. Bingley, UK: Emerald Group Publishing Limited.

Majumdar, Boria. 2004. *Twenty-Two Yards to Freedom: A Social History of Indian Cricket*. Gurgaon, India: Penguin Viking.

———. 2018. *Eleven Gods and A Billion Indians: The On and Off the Field Story of Cricket in India and Beyond*. New York: Simon and Schuster.

INTRODUCTION 15

Mills, James H. (ed.). 2005. *Subaltern Sports: Politics and Sport in South Asia*. London: Anthem Press.

Sengupta, Rudraneil. 2016. *Enter the Dangal: Travels Through India's Wrestling Landscape*. New York: HarperCollins.

Sen, Ronojoy 2015. *Nation at Play: A History of Sport in India*. Gurgaon, India: Penguin-Viking.

Thangarajan, Stanley, Daniel Burdsey, and Rajinder Dudrah (eds). 2014. *Sport and South Asian Diasporas: Playing Through Time and Space*. Oxfordshire, UK: Routledge.

Ugra, Sharda. 2020. 'Why Aren't Our Sports Celebrities Speaking Out?'. *The India Forum: A Journal-Magazine on Contemporary Issues*. 17 February. Available at https://www.theindiaforum.in/article/why-aren-t-sports-celebrities-speaking-about-caanrc-protests; accessed on 1 March 2020.

SECTION I
SPORTS AND SPORTS STUDIES
Expanding the Field, Breaking Boundaries

1

The Struggle for Sports Commons

Sports Markets and the Labour Movement

S. Janaka Biyanwila

The expansion of sports markets in South Asia, particularly in India, has been dramatic following the launch of the Indian Premier League (IPL) in cricket in 2008. Since then, new markets in sports consumer culture has emerged (in badminton [2013], hockey [2013], and kabaddi [2014]), while revitalizing existing professional leagues (football). This extension of making profits from sports takes place in a geographically uneven process of neo-liberal capitalism promoted through state strategies of deregulation of markets and privatization of public goods.

While absorbed into global, regional, and national sports markets as con-sumers of audiences or 'fans', the workers in the region are also a significant labour force, engaged in global production networks of sports cultures. The workers in India, Sri Lanka, Bangladesh, and Pakistan produce a range of sports goods (balls, bats, shoes, shirts, shorts, and other merchandise); pro-vide care labour as migrant domestic workers for urban middle-class sports consumers; build sports venues as construction workers; and grow food as farmers for 'sports nutrition' markets. Of course, there are a multitude of other workers in the region absorbed within global production networks of sports.

The emergence of sports consumer markets illustrates an element of a growing middle class in the region, which also includes a few celebrity sports workers, mostly men playing cricket. A significant feature of the labour markets in South Asia is that majority of workers are in the informal sector with limited legal protection and low wages. Even in the formal sector, the deregulation of labour markets along with privatization has meant increas-ingly insecure employment while depleting household capacities to care for one another and maintain life (Elson 2012). Not only are workers spending longer hours at work and more intensely, the wages earned are often inade-quate to escape poverty. The South Asian region is one of the poorest regions

S. Janaka Biyanwila, *The Struggle for Sports Commons* In: *Sports Studies in India*. Edited by: Meena Gopal and Padma Prakash, Oxford University Press. © Oxford University Press 2021.
DOI: 10.1093/oso/9780190130640.003.0002

in the world and over the next two decades, the number of people living in slums is expected to double (United Nations [UN] Habitat 2016).

The struggles of organized workers are fundamental to shaping sports cultures, which is also the realm of social reproduction involving leisure. The organized workers' struggles for eight-hour work days in core capitalist economies in the mid-1800s were significant for carving out a notion of well-being that included rest and leisure for workers. In the Global South, the decolonization struggles for cultural self-determination, encompassing a range of social movements, was instrumental for democratizing elitist sports cultures and expanding state social provisioning for sports. In elaborating citizenship, the increasing access to sports as a public good is mainly related to the expanding public sector education and state enterprises and services (for example, railways). However, the emergence of sports markets in the region since the mid-1990s illustrates a disembedding of sports markets from local communities, weakening access to actual sports participation while promoting passive consumer audiences for sports entertainment.

The reframing of sports from a public good or a common cultural property into a private good relates to emphasizing identities of consumers as opposed to citizens. The capture of sports cultures by market ideologies involve romanticizing competitive individualism while denigrating the public sector and recasting notions of interdependence and mutuality in terms of ethnic communal identities. Thus, the emergence of sports markets re-articulates notions of belonging within sports cultures in terms of a 'sportive nation', reinforcing tendencies of ethno-nationalist (communal) politics in the region while undermining citizenship, at multiple levels (national, regional, and local). This coupling of sports markets with the sportive nation harnesses enduring authoritarian masculine cultures while expanding the militarization of the state. The expansion of sports markets in the subcontinent takes place in what the US Department of State (2015) describes as the 'front-line region in the battle against terrorism'. This integration of sports markets with regional and global dynamics of militarism, legitimized through a discourse of 'national security', overlaps with processes of urbanization and securing safe spaces for urban consumer markets.

Locating the celebration of dominant sports markets in the region, in a context of inequality, hyper-masculine ethno-nationalist communal politics and militarism, is significant for considering an alternative notion of sports and play. How can enduring cultures and institutions of sports sustained by authoritarian male oligarchies, celebrating 'sports spectacles', be transformed into alternative 'sports festivals' or the 'sports commons' encouraging participatory democratic sports cultures?

Evangelical Sports and Sportive Nationalism

The dominant discourse of sports illustrates an 'evangelical sports' narrative, where sports represent a secular sacred realm with a sense of inherent goodness (Giulianotti 2004). For the devoted sports fan, this is a realm of self-transcendence, of spiritual communion with others. It reproduces a notion of 'sports exceptionalism' or a 'mystique of sports', suspending judgement and any critical analysis of actual practice. Thus, sports enter a sacred, value-free, cultural space, transcending the concrete reality of sports production based on authoritarian hypermasculine sport cultures and institutions.

A range of actors in sports markets, such as corporations, governments, and global institutions of economic and sports governance, along with civil society organizations (non-governmental organizations [NGOs]), nurture this evangelical sports discourse. Thus, sport is seen as a catalyst for development, education, health promotion, the empowerment for young people, particularly for girls and women, while facilitating social inclusion, conflict prevention, and peace building (UN 1993).

This evangelical sports narrative couples with a 'sport and development' agenda, which is committed to a notion of sportive nation. The sportive nation translates into 'sportive nationalism', where the state strategies focus primarily on elite athletes for gaining international recognition as a form of cultural capital. In turn, sports mega events, such as the Olympics, Commonwealth Games, Asian Games, (Fédération Internationale de Football Association) FIFA World Cup and the International Cricket Council (ICC) World Cup, are not only sporting events but also brands that can enhance the cultural capital of nation-states, which mainly relates to a concentration of sports resources (sports workers and facilities) in specific cities and processes of urbanization.

The discourse of sportive nation is directly linked with issues of national security in terms of securing safe spaces for hosting sports mega events. The military also has an enduring relationship with local sports in terms of cultivating attitudes, dispositions, and bodily practices of disciplined soldiers compliant with cultures of command and control. The military and police forces remain integrated with local sports cultures in various ways, such as providing employment for elite athletes, participation in local sports events (including the promotion of disabled soldiers), and performing opening and closing ceremonies at sports events. Securing safe spaces for urban sports consumers also relates to the deployment of latest surveillance technology reframing urban development while criminalizing peaceful protests.

The dominant discourse on 'sports and development' in the Global South is integrated with UN conventions on human rights and sustainable development (David 2005; Donnelly 2008; Kidd and Donnelly 2000). In terms of sports, Article 24 of the Human Rights Convention highlights leisure as an entitlement, where '[e]veryone has the right to rest and leisure, including reasonable limitation of working hours and periodic holidays with pay.' (UN 2016). The recognition of the right to rest and leisure also overlaps other UN conventions specifically targeting women, children, people with disabilities, and indigenous people. However, the actual implementation of these rights remains shaped by national, regional, and local institutional dynamics.

The sports and development agenda is deployed at two main levels. The main priority is to develop elite athletes capable of competition in sports mega events. The sports mega events are seen as significant for asserting comparative advantage of city, region, and nation, as well as enabling investment and advertising opportunities for the city through global media. Sports mega events, promoted by key actors within sports–media–tourism institutional complex, are notorious for corruption, waste of public resources, displacement of urban poor, and environmental destruction, which includes abandoned sports stadiums and infrastructure after the event. A second priority of sports and development is to foster local- (community-) level sports for youth engagement, which is aligned with education and health. However, competitive sport is primarily about 'performance', where education and health remain a lesser priority (Theberge 2007). This relates back to the limitations of sustainable development grounded in carbon-intensive economic growth strategies based on privatization and deregulation. These strategies not only restrain state social provisioning for local sports cultures along with health and educational services, but also encourage authoritarian institutions and sports cultures.

In terms of developing local sports cultures, the institutional architecture of sports at the nation-state level depicts a mix of dependence on markets and state social provisioning. While a few national-level sports federations are embedded in sports markets (cricket, football, badminton, field hockey, and athletics), most depend on state social provisioning. The affluent sports federations in the region (primarily cricket) increasingly function as competitive firms driven by profits (and providing global sports audiences for the advertisers and the nation-state), where community-level sports is reduced to a form of charity sustained by NGOs in partnership with 'corporate social responsibility' of private firms. While the financial benefits of the richer sports federations have the potential to develop local sports cultures, the logic of markets (commercial values) overrides the interests of communities (social provisioning values). In effect, the sportive nation, under a veneer of 'sport for development', mystifies how the profit extraction from local sports markets are integrated with global production networks of sports.

Production of Sports Cultures and Sports Workers

The social practice of sports illustrates the production of a cultural good. Cultural goods involve a spectrum of activities from arts, theatre, music, and cinema to architecture, which shapes localized ways of life, heritage, collective memories, and affective communities (Harvey 2002). Profits extracted from cultural goods combine two distinct domains. Profits are gained through 'the culture of the product to the cultural practices that surround its consumption' as well as 'the cultural capital that can evolve alongside among both producers and consumers' (Harvey 2002: 100). In other words, revenue is extracted from the actual sports entertainment produced in the field of competition as well as the symbolic or cultural capital through 'intellectual property rights'. The carving out of intellectual property rights, in terms of patents, trademarks, and broadcasting rights, is a central feature of commodification of cultural goods such as sports (Andrews and Jackson 2001; Brookes 2002; Wenner 1998).

The spread of sports markets depends on the reproduction of multiple fan cultures (or affective communities), which invent a sense of belonging linked with identities and self-esteem. Strategies for winning hearts and minds through sports involves 'reinventing sports' (Rein, Kotler, and Shields 2006) by selling notions of cultural 'uniqueness' and 'authenticity' of experience. The driving logic is to extract profits through monopoly rent (branding) as well as processes of urbanization (sports venues). Branding that express the trade in symbols and experiences is a key component of the 'sales effort' in the production process of sports. Branding of cities, such as 'smart cities', reflects forms of inter-urban competition for capital or urban entrepreneurialism, encompassing policies of urban beautification, regeneration, and redevelopment, which also displace and re-segregate the urban poor.

24 SPORTS AND SPORTS STUDIES

The commercialization of sports and global trade in services is shaped by transnational corporations (TNCs) in diverse sectors (media, sports clubs, and leagues), international financial institutions (such as the World Bank, International Monetary Fund, and the Asian Development Bank), and the World Trade Organization (WTO). The General Agreement on Trade in Services (GATS), initiated in 1994, provides the basis for a range of Free Trade Agreements (FTAs). In 2013, the Trade in Services Agreement (TISA), negotiated among states in the Global North, was placed outside the WTO in a non-transparent manner. The Trade-Related Aspects of Intellectual Property Rights (TRIPS), also part of GATS, limits state capacities to protect their citizens' rights to a range of essential services. Similarly, the development of sports markets is less about access of citizens to organized sports and more about the accumulation of profits by male oligarchies or cartels in media and sports governing institutions (Biyanwila 2010).

The production of sports and sports labour relates to the service sector of an economy, which is integrated with other economic sectors. Within the services sector, sports workers overlap with other workers in education, health, finance, media, telecommunications, construction, entertainment, and social services. While these are important domains of employment for sports labour in competition as well as post competition, they also reflect different shared occupational identities for the formation of collective interests and mobilization.

The production of elite competitive sports spectacles depends on a stratified and differentiated global labour force integrated within global production networks. This illustrates a new international division of sports labour (Miller et al. 2001; Mirrlees 2013). In effect, the sportive nation is sustained by skilled migrant sports labour force (athletes, coaches, and trainers) that engages in sports markets beyond the nation-state, often delinked from local community-level sports cultures.

The articulation of sports labour as cultural workers is grounded in ideologies of competitive individualism and enterprising workers. The ideology of individualism draws on aspects of artisanal producers where the professional 'enterprising worker' is projected as a flexible worker, multi-skilled and self-motivated towards his or her own career development. This prioritization of having control over one's work and relative freedom from hierarchical control, a key feature of a 'professional's' identity, often subordinates the complex power dynamics within organizations and the labour process.

THE STRUGGLE FOR SPORTS COMMONS   25

While sports labour functions within stratified and differentiated organizational settings, the dominant sports organizations are mostly controlled by patriarchal bureaucratic oligarchies. And the sports labour process is increasingly intensified owing to the temporary nature of participation in competitive sports. Most 'professional' sports workers are compromised within diverse authoritarian labour regimes, which also involve rationalizing elements of self-exploitation and subservience. While this self-exploitation involves absorbing risks of sports injuries and performance enhancement (doping), the subservience relates to navigating systems of patronage that enable access to resources, national teams, and international competitions, which in turn relates to aspirations of class mobility.

The sports labour regimes can be viewed within a spectrum of regimes: from despotic (in which coercion prevails over consent) to hegemonic (in which consent prevails along with coercion) (Burawoy 1985). Many professional players work without a contract, frequently delayed wages, no provisions for pension, and no support for education (or employment pathways). Other restrictive practices include: high incidence of harassment and discrimination; invasion of privacy by drug testing away from the workplace; increase in evening work; insufficient notice for changes to work schedule; and a low awareness of disciplinary rules. Most professional players have been exposed to various unwanted physical acts, threats, and bullying and discrimination on the grounds of ethnicity, gender, sexuality, disability, language, religion, region, and age (UNI Sport PRO 2013). Despite the high risks of injuries, which included effects of doping involving biotechnology (pharmaceuticals), there is limited support and insurance, particularly against career-ending injuries.

A significant feature of sports labour regimes is violence against oneself and others. The hyper-competitive masculine sports cultures sold as 'entertainment' foregrounds a 'culture of risk' over 'culture of precaution' (Theberge 2007). In terms of sports labour, violence in sports relates to risk-taking behaviour, pain and injury, and the use of performance-enhancement drugs (Giulianotti 2005). Sports violence is also part of sports entertainment in terms of combat sports, but also in terms of aggressive play and intensity of competition. The male-dominated sports media nurtures and normalizes sports violence in order to enhance the consumer (or spectator) pleasures. This violence in sports overlaps with the militarization of the state in terms of sportive nationalism, reproducing enduring patriarchal masculine sports cultures (Fuller 2006; McKay and Sabo 1994; Messner 1992, 2007).

26 SPORTS AND SPORTS STUDIES

Organizing and Mobilizing Sports Workers

The difficulty in organizing sports workers encompasses a broader context of challenges faced by services sector workers to self-organize. The workplaces in services sector are small and decentralized, scattering workers in different spaces and time scales. Along with complex patterns of ownership, shifting lines of control means challenges in determining the place and space in which corporate decisions are made and where pressure may be applied. An emerging tendency among unions is to organize workers across the value chain or the global production network. For sports labour, this entails organizing within and across the sports–media–tourism complex while integrating workers in the global production networks of sporting goods (Palmer 2016).

Trade unions represent an organized nucleus of workers amongst a sea of unorganized workers. The spread of neoliberal flexible markets represents a direct attack on unions' and workers' capacities to collectively organize. The labour movement, which encompasses unions as well other worker organizations, highlights the fundamental contradiction of capital accumulation within capitalist systems revealing aspects of class exploitation, class struggle, as well as class compromise.

As agents of the politics of redistribution, trade unions go beyond workplace issues of wages, conditions, and workplace democracy, into issues of social protection, equity, as well as social justice. Trade unions depict a spectrum of strategies from creating consent to actively resisting or contesting hegemonic labour regimes. In South Asia, most dominant unions are incorporated within political party systems in varying degrees. This subordination of unions within political parties prioritizes the realm of representative politics aimed at re-regulating labour markets and strengthening workplace protection. Nevertheless, a range of independent unions and worker networks oriented towards building alliances and mobilizing workers has also emerged, foregrounding movement politics. The unions' capacities to mobilize workers to engage in contentious collective action is significant not only for building class consciousness amongst workers but also for asserting the movement dimensions of unions as agents of social justice (Gillan and Biyanwila 2009).

The stratified and differentiated nature of sports labour is significant for understanding the functioning of sports markets and the challenges of organizing sports labour. The class relations in the economic realm (politics of distribution) interact with enduring power relations of gender, ethnicity, caste, disability, sexuality, and age (politics of recognition). The dominant sports institutions are mostly based on middle-class, heterosexual, able-bodied, patriarchal cultures, with regionally shaped ethnic and caste privileges. While Hindu nationalism in India is compatible with Sinhala-Buddhist nationalism in Sri Lanka, there are sub-national regional variations of ethnic and caste dynamics in sports cultures. The interaction of class relations (politics of distribution) with multiple forms of cultural discrimination (politics of recognition) is significant for understanding inclusions and exclusions (politics of representation) within the sports–media–tourism institutional complex and how to transform them.

Sports markets are sustained and coordinated by sports associations or the governing bodies, sports clubs, private firms including media firms which own or sponsor clubs, sports labour, and fans. Each of these actors can influence the functioning of sports markets in diverse ways. The sports markets also vary in terms of geography and temporality. Sports leagues along with local clubs can emerge and dissolve owing to multiple factors, but mainly owing to speculative financial flows. Specific sports markets, such as men's cricket and football, with established institutional and social networks, can be more enduring than others. Advanced sports labour markets, mostly in the North America and European Union (EU), are characterized by governance mechanisms that include varying degrees of collective bargaining, dispute settlement mechanisms, and freedom of association (Khan 2000). However, in the dominant cricket sports market in South Asia, Indian and Pakistani players' associations are yet to form, while Sri Lanka has maintained a fragile association for nearly two decades.

Nevertheless, sports labour engages in multiple forms of resistance both individually and collectively. This resistance or activism within sports includes athletes, coaches, officials, support staff (sports doctors, trainers), as well as workers maintaining sports facilities (fields, tracks, sports halls, and swimming pools). Much of this resistance within sports is invisible in the mainstream sports media, owing to ideologies of evangelical sports and sportive nationalism. More importantly, the relative lack of self-organization among sports labour in the region highlight that majority of athletes are not sustained by wages but by in-kind support and the care labour of families and communities.

28 SPORTS AND SPORTS STUDIES

Social Provisioning of Sports and Sports Commons

Labour markets, including sports labour markets, intersect both the realms of production and reproduction (Elson 1999). While paid work relates to the realm of production, the realm of social reproduction relates to the everyday unpaid care work of maintaining life. The public realm of production is integrated with the private household realm of social reproduction through hierarchies of gendered and sexualized labouring bodies. The production of sports entertainment, while nurturing masculine sports cultures, also incorporates labouring bodies of women as sports producers, consumers, as well as carers. The labouring body is also a body needing rest, care, and pleasures. The body as a site of pleasure overlaps the crucial interdependence between the market economy and the care economy or the reproductive economy along with the entire human (economic) system and the ecosystems (Fraser 2016; Salleh, Goodman, and Hosseini 2015; Shiva 2016).

Expanding sports consumer cultures are based on sports mega events (disney-fication of sports), reinforced by nation-state policies focused on elite competitive sports. This culture of 'sports spectacles' is parasitic upon local sports cultures and household capacities to participate in sports. In 2007, according to the Indian state (the Ministry of Youth Affairs and Sports), only around 6 per cent of those below thirty-five had access to organized sports. In order to address this misallocation of resources, the Indian state expressed the need to reframe sports in terms of 'national development'.

> Parliament recognises the need to shift the emphasis on sports from its present Constitutional position where it is clubbed with 'entertainments' and 'amusements' to treating sports as a key instrument of youth development for accelerated and inclusive national development. (Government of India 2007)

However, the notion of 'national development' is focused on elite competitive sports and sports mega events extending a consumer culture of sports. The following year, in 2008, the Indian cricket-governing institutions launched the IPL and, in 2010, India hosted the Commonwealth Games. The Indian sports minister at the time, who was dismissed for disagreeing with the hosting of the 2010 Games, later articulated his position:

> By having a 11-day jamboree in New Delhi, the idea that you can become a sporting nation is nonsense. We had the Asian Games in 1951 and 1982, did

THE STRUGGLE FOR SPORTS COMMONS 29

they make us a sporting nation? Even if a percentage of the money spent on the CWG had been pumped into real sport, we would have been producing champions. But we have put the money into these tamashas. (Vats 2010)

In 2014, the Indian sports minister, who was simultaneously the chair of the 2010 Commonwealth Games and the president of Indian Olympic Association (1996–2011), Suresh Kalmadi, was charged with corruption, along with five other officials from the Commonwealth Organising Committee.

The promotion of consumer culture of sports illustrates the disembedding of sports markets from society, limiting access to sports to many involving a maldistribution of economic resources (including theft), cultural discrimination, and political exclusion. Despite the evangelical sports narrative of health and well-being benefits of sports, dominant sports cultures are embedded in 'violence, corruption, discrimination, hooliganism, nationalism, doping and fraud' (UN 2014). Re-embedding sports markets in local communities is about re-asserting social provisioning values of sports articulating a notion of sports commons. Sports commons suggests cooperative, non-market, sports cultures that foreground social provisioning values of love, solidarity, and care as the grounds for developing human capacities for cultural flourishing (Biyanwila 2018).

Sports commons, or the re-embedding of sports markets in society, relates to democratizing institutions and cultures governing sports (Biyanwila 2018). This involves nurturing multiple forms of individual and collective resistance within and outside sports. The resistance within sports, involving direct producers of sports (discussed in the previous section), overlaps with resistance outside. This outside-sports resistance includes: fans; other workers in the sports value chain such as workers in sports apparel and equipment manufacturing factories; sports journalists; and urban activist networks engaged in a range of issues such as housing, education, transport, water, and urban ecology. Given that sports markets are primarily located in urban centres, catering mostly to affluent sports consumers, sports commons also relates to transforming processes of urbanization where struggles for social justice are inseparable from ecological justice.

The articulation of sports commons in the contemporary context requires reframing sports and play from the discourse of 'development' towards a notion of 'living well'. This involves revealing the contradictions of sustainable development, which intersect carbon-intensive growth strategies of unlimited capital accumulation with militarism. The dominant sports markets

30   SPORTS AND SPORTS STUDIES

located mainly in cities vandalize the ecology in multiple ways, from development of sports venues in fragile ecosystems and pollution (air, water, waste, and noise) to the depletion of the ozone layer (UNEP 2015). The global production network of sports is intertwined with the global production network of oil and 'resource wars'. The processes of urbanization reproducing masculine sports cultures in the subcontinent rely on a 'car culture' amidst inadequate public transport. Auto companies sponsor a range of sports including motor sports, while projecting a car-culture romance, which also consists of violence, disabilities and fatalities, and environmental degradation. Particularly in terms of cricket and football markets in the subcontinent, the petro-monarchies or autocratic regimes in West Asia play a significant role in sports finance, governance, and hosting of events. Locating the struggle for sports commons in terms of an eco-friendly, non-militarist alternative points to democratizing sports governing institutions, including the media.

In the South Asian region, the democratization of sports governing institutions and expansion of actual participation in sports was instigated mainly by the labour movement and working-class parties within anti-colonial movements. Following political independence, the expansion of public education system along with public enterprises and services were instrumental in contributing to the development of local level sports organizations. This phase of early sports commons which expanded notions of citizenship, based on public provisioning of sports, began to erode by the early 1990s, with the spread of sports consumer markets accompanying state strategies of privatization and deregulation. Along with the uneven deregulation of services sector in the global economy in the mid-1990s, the changes in information and communication technology (ICT) ushered in a new phase of sports markets influenced by the interests of privately owned media companies.

The articulation of sports commons is interdependent with media commons, where media and telecommunication services are driven by public interest (Barnett 2003; McChesney 2008, 2013). Revealing the complicity of media in maintaining authoritarian hypermasculine sports cultures, or the media–sports nexus, is significant for democratizing sports journalism that primarily focus on male elite sports, results, and winners. The socialization and democratization of media markets foregrounds the transformation of self-censorship and encourages forms of collective ownership of media and communication. The effort towards 'media commons', which couples with sports commons, involves prioritizing voices of those struggling against economic exploitation, cultural discrimination, and political exclusion.

THE STRUGGLE FOR SPORTS COMMONS   31

The re-embedding of sports markets within local/community sports cultures promoting sports commons suggests a movement orientation towards notions of 'living well'. This involves mobilizing sports and play as a form of resistance to hegemonic hyper competitive masculine sports cultures as well as work cultures. Redefining *work* is about democratizing the realm of work, contesting authoritarian employment relations, and despotic labour regimes (on the basis of expanding rights of workers, meaningful work, and dignity). The democratization of work implies redefining work in terms of 'producing differently, producing other things and even working less' (Waterman 1998).

Deconstructing the cultural myth of 'the more each works, the better off all will be' is central to rethinking well-being in an ecological civilization. The articulation of an alternative notion of *work* and *play* depends on transforming the relationship between the wage labour (production) and non-wage household labour (reproduction). The search for decent paid work also concerns decent (unpaid) care work within the households and communities, adequately supported though state social provisioning.

Developing a broad counter movement, overlapping the realm of production as well as social reproduction of sports, suggests articulating complex solidarities, which incorporate experimentation and play in building solidarities and in repertoires of collective action. The notion of 'complex solidarities' highlights 'diversity in unity', enabling a multiplicity of marginalized subjects and acknowledging diverse temporal and spatial contexts of collective knowledge production and engagement. This also concerns deconstructing oppressive power relations within communities while reconstructing notions of citizenship. The coupling of sports commons as a movement towards enhancing citizenship, relates back to the revitalization of labour movement by encouraging new conversations around work and play that enables new forms of organization, alliances and collective action.

***

The flourishing of sports markets in a few sports (cricket, football, badminton, hockey, and kabaddi) in South Asia takes place in a context of enduring structure of poverty and inequality, multiple forms of cultural discrimination (ethnicity, gender, sexuality, disability, caste, language, and region), and exclusion from political representation. The emergent sports consumer culture, mostly dominated by competitive male sports, is sustained

32 SPORTS AND SPORTS STUDIES

by the combined interaction of key actors within sports governing bodies, along with media and tourism companies (the sports–media–tourism complex). This expansion of profit making through sports is rationalized by overlapping discourses of evangelical sports, the sportive nation, and sport and development.

Locating sports in terms of the realm of production and social reproduction reveals how most sports labour is working within despotic labour regimes (experiencing exploitation and violence) while most households and communities are depleted of their capacities to participate in sports. The promotion of neoliberal markets as 'development' involving privatization and deregulation not only expands forms of insecure work while undermining worker rights, but also exacerbates household capacities to care for people by increasing costs of maintaining life.

Sports-governing institutions, in local, national, regional, and global spatial scales, are dominated by male oligarchies reproducing systems of patronage. The emergent aggressive masculine cultures, which overlap with the state and ethno-nationalist militarism, are not only intolerant of diversity and democracy, but also destructive of local communities and nature, including human nature. Nevertheless, there is resistance within and outside sports that suggests the re-embedding of sports markets in communities, where identities of sports consumerism are grounded in substantive citizenship.

The articulation of sports commons involves reinforcing social provisioning values of sports as opposed to the commercial values of sports. This relates to encouraging the collective organization of sports workers (athletes) across the value chain or the global production network sports. Recasting sports workers as a part of the labour movement requires revealing the concrete reality of 'professional' sports work, their shared experience with other workers in different despotic labour regimes, and the desire for an alternative mode of sports production. Emphasizing the overlap between the realm of production and social reproduction suggests the need for a broad counter movement encouraging a range of complex alliances that reframes sports and development as well as citizenship in terms of 'sports and living well'.

References

Andrews, D.L. and S.L. Jackson (eds). 2001. *Sport Stars: The Cultural Politics of Sporting Celebrity*. London: Routledge.
Barnett, Clive. 2003. *Culture and Democracy: Media, Space and Representation*. UK: Edinburgh University Press.

THE STRUGGLE FOR SPORTS COMMONS   33

Biyanwila, S.J. 2010. *The Labour Movement in the Global South: Trade Unions in Sri Lanka*. London: Routledge.

———. 2018. *Sports and the Global South: Work, Play and Resistance in Sri Lanka*. UK: Palgrave.

Brookes, Rod. 2002. 'The Globalization and Commodification of Sport'. *Representing Sport*. London: Arnold, pp. 49–82.

Burawoy, M. 1985. *The Politics of Production: Factory Regimes under Capitalism and Socialism*. London: Verso.

David, P. 2005. *Human Rights in Youth Sport: A Critical Review of Children's Rights in Competitive Sports*. London: Routledge.

Donnelly, Peter. 2008. 'Sport and Human Rights', *Sport in Society* 11 (4): 381–94.

Elson, Diane. 1999. 'Labour Markets as Gendered Institutions: Equality, Efficiency and Empowerment Issues'. *World Development* 27 (3): 611–27.

———. 2012. 'Social Reproduction in the Global Crisis: Rapid Recovery or Long-Lasting Depletion?'. In P. Utting, S. Razavi, R.V. Buchholz, and R. Varghese Buchholz (eds), *The Global Crisis and Transformative Social Change*, pp. 63–80. Palgrave UK and UNRISD.

Fraser, Nancy. 2016. 'Contradictions of Capital and Care'. *New Left Review* 100: 99–117.

Fuller, Linda K. (ed.). 2006. *Sport, Rhetoric, and Gender: Historical Perspectives and Media Representations*. New York: Palgrave Macmillan.

Gillan, M. and Biyanwila, S.J. 2009. 'Revitalising Trade Unions as Civil Society Actors in India, South Asia'. *Journal of South Asian Studies* 32 (3): 425–47.

Giulianotti, R. 2004. *Sport and Modern Social Theorists*. Basingstoke, UK: Palgrave Macmillan.

———. 2005. *Sport: A Critical Sociology*. Cambridge, UK: Polity Press.

Government of India. 2007. *Comprehensive Sports Policy*. New Delhi: Ministry of Youth Affairs and Sports. Available at http://yas.nic.in/sites/default/files/File371.pdf; accessed on 11 July 2017.

Harvey, David. 2002. 'The Art of Rent: Globalization, Monopoly and the Commodification of Culture'. *Socialist Register* 38. Available at http://socialistregister.com/recent/2002/harvey2002; accessed on 12 July 2017.

Khan, Lawrence M. 2000. 'The Sports Business As a Labor Market Laboratory'. *Journal of Economic Perspectives* 14 (3): 75–94.

Kidd, B. and Peter Donnelly. 2000. 'Human Rights in Sports'. *International Review for the Sociology of Sport* 35 (2): 131–48.

McChesney, R.W. 2008. *Media: Enduring Issues, Emerging Dilemmas*. New York, NY: Monthly Review Press.

———. 2013. *Digital Disconnect: How Capitalism is Turning the Internet Against Democracy*. New York: New Press.

McKay, Jim and D. Sabo (eds). 1994. *Sex, Violence and Power in Sports: Rethinking Masculinity*. Freedom, CA: Crossing Press.

Messner, M. 1992. *Power at Play: Sports and the Problem of Masculinity*. Boston, MA: Beacon Press.

———. 2007. *Out of Play: Critical Essays on Gender and Sport*. Albany: State University of New York Press.

34 SPORTS AND SPORTS STUDIES

Miller, T., J. McKay, G. Lawrence, and D. Rowe. 2001. *Globalization and Sport: Playing the World*. London, UK: SAGE.

Mirrlees, T. 2013. 'Producing Entertainment in the New International Division of Cultural Labor (NICL)'. In T. Mirrlees (ed.), *Global Entertainment Media: Between Cultural Imperialism and Cultural Globalization*, pp. 147–78. New York: Routledge.

Palmer, Walter. 2016. 'It Is Time for a Global Framework Agreement in World Sport'. *Global Labour Column*. Available at http://column.global-labour-university. org/2016/08/its-time-for-global-framework-agreement.html; accessed on 11 July 2016.

Rein, Irving, Philip Kotler, and Ben Shields. 2006. *The Elusive Fan: Reinventing Sports in a Crowded Marketplace*. London: McGraw-Hill.

Salleh, Ariel, James Goodman, and Hamed Hosseini. 2015. 'From Sociological to Ecological Imagination: Another Future is Possible'. In Jonathan Marshall and Linda Connor (eds), *Environmental Change and the World Futures*, pp. 96–109. London: Routledge.

Shiva, Vandana. 2016. *Earth Democracy: Justice, Sustainability and Peace*. London: Zed Books.

Theberge, Nancy. 2007. ' "It's Not About Health, It's About Performance": Sports Medicine, Health and Culture of Risk in Candian Sport'. In J. Hargreaves and Patricia Vertinsky (eds), *Physical Culture, Power and the Body*, pp. 176–94. London: Routledge.

United Nations (UN). 1993. *International Year of Sport and the Olympic Ideal*. Available at http://www.un.org/wcm/content/site/sport/home/resourcecenter/ resolutions/pid/19431; accessed on 11 July 2017.

———. 2014. *Sports and Development*. Available at https://www.un.org/sport/con-tent/why-sport/overview; accessed on 26 September 2016.

———. 2016. *UN Human Rights Convention*. Available at http://claiminghumanrights. org/holidays_definition.html; accessed on 11 July 2017.

United Nations Environment Programme (UNEP). 2015. *Sports and the Environment*. Available at http://www.unep.org/sport¬env/impactEnv_Sport.aspx; accessed on 12 July 2017.

UNI Sport PRO. 2013. *UNI Europa/EU Athletes Working Conditions Survey*. Available at http://www.euathletes.org/uni-europaeu-athletesworking-conditions-survey-published/; accessed on 12 July 2017.

UN Habitat. 2016. *Slum Almanac 2015/2016: Tracking Improvement in the Lives of Slum Dwellers*. Available at http://www.worldurbancampaign.org/sites/default/ files/subsites/resources/Slum%20Almanac%202015-2016%20EN_16.02_web_ 0.pdf; accessed on 2 January 2019.

US Department of State. 2015. *Investment Climate Statement—Sri Lanka, Bureau of Economic and Business Affairs*. Available at http://www.state.gov/e/eb/rls/othr/ics/ 2015/241750.htm; accessed on 12 July 2017.

Vats, Vaibhav. 2010. 'The CWG Will Actually Be Remembered as the Common Whore Games'. *Tehelka*, 11 September. Available at http://www.tehelka.com/

2010/09/the-cwg-will-actually-be-rememberedas-the-common-whore-games/   ;
accessed on 12 July 2017.

Waterman, Peter. 1998. *Globalisation, Social Movements and the New Internationalisms*. London and Washington, D.C.: Mansell/Continuum.

Wenner, Lawrence A (ed.). 1998. *MediaSport*. New York: Routledge.

2

Globalizing Sportscapes

Football in Mumbai's Socio-Spatial Dynamics[*]

D. Parthasarathy

Since the early 1990s, Asian ownership of European league football clubs has seen a rapid increase. A large number of clubs are foreign-owned, including some by Middle East Sheikhs and Russian oil tycoons. But a significant number are also owned by tycoons from other parts of Asia including from India, Singapore, Thailand, Malaysia, and Indonesia.[i] Steel magnates and real estate moguls, poultry and chicken feed entrepreneurs and industrialists, airline operators, and mining/ automotive interests are all part of the global capital from around the world channelled via Asia into European soccer. This, in turn, has set off a chain of global cultural and economic flows that have implications for political, social, and even spiritual processes in the respective national contexts. Globalization is not merely about flows across diverse scapes (Appadurai 1996) from one part of the world to another but involves multiple and reverse flows in ways that challenge their conventional understanding that restrict them largely to those from the Global North to the Global South. While ownership of clubs may rest formally with some of Asia's richest businesspersons, they operate transnationally, receive investments from around the world, service customers in multiple parts of the world, and act to make European soccer clubs truly global—beyond their cultural reception in other countries. The complex web of flows that Appadurai describes as ideoscape, mediascape, and financescape have consequences for ethnoscape and technoscape (Appadurai 1996), as new media technologies, the politics of aspiration, and migratory flows of people temporarily and permanently create a new global sportscape of football citizens owing allegiance

---

[*] This is a revised version of a paper presented at the conference, 'Soccer as a Global Phenomenon', organized by the Weatherhead Initiative on Global History, Harvard University, 14–16 April 2016. The author is thankful to the participants of the conference for comments and suggestions, in particular Roland Robertson.

D. Parthasarathy, *Globalizing Sportscapes* In: *Sports Studies in India.* Edited by: Meena Gopal and Padma Prakash, Oxford University Press. © Oxford University Press 2021.
DOI: 10.1093/oso/9780190130640.003.0003

to different soccer clubs, nations, and players united by fandom, spectatorship, and consumption.

Such global connections however are different from other kinds of globalization, which are perceived to have originated in the Global North, especially North America. As a global cultural form and practice, football links Europe to other parts of the world in specific ways as the powerhouse of the sport. As an aspect of cultural globalization, football 'recenters globalization' (Iwabuchi 2002) with Europe as its chief node; however, the global flows are not simply one-way or two-way flows between Europe and, say, Asia. New nodes emerge, such as China as the manufacturer and supplier of fake and genuine football merchandise, Singapore and Thailand as bases for global illegal betting and match fixing, and the ownership and financing of football clubs located across the world by Asian tycoons.

This chapter is based on ethnographic field research in Mumbai, Singapore, and Bangkok during 2007–9 and 2013–14. The central focus of the research was to describe and interpret the changing politics of class, ethnicity, aspirations, and leisure, especially in, but not restricted to, the urban working classes in the formal and informal sectors of these cities, using the lens of globalizing football. Locating itself within the framework and analysis of urban public spaces, the research centred on the ways in which public spaces are used and contested by different classes, migrant and ethnic groups; the uses of football in a political economy of leisure and aspirations that are simultaneously local and global was also a key concern. The research began with a dual focus on informal economy and informal uses of public spaces in these three Asian cities by migrants and the working class for sports and recreation, cultural expression, celebration of festivals, and political and religious purposes. Ethnographic research involved transect walks in selected localities, participant observation, and informal in-depth interviews with fans, merchandise producers, consumers, traders, players in public spaces, and organizers of formal and informal sports in public spaces. For reasons of space, and to better contribute to the overall objective of constructing sports studies for the Indian subcontinent, this chapter mainly focuses on the Mumbai case. A brief outline of the Bangkok and Singapore cases are, however, presented in order to strengthen the argument about the regional scope of global sportscape and to adduce support for some of the analytical frames used in exploring and explaining the Mumbai case.

A key analytical lens that is deployed is time-space, the transformation and use of public spaces across and within different time scales by diverse groups both as a matter of routine and as an aspect of urban socio-spatial

38   SPORTS AND SPORTS STUDIES

contestation. Rather than positing camps and heterotopias against each other as Foucault and Miskowiec (1986) were wont to do, public time-space in the three South and Southeast Asian cities studied were simultaneously or alternately camps and heterotopias especially where sports, and more particularly football as a sport, was concerned. Political protest camps were also spaces where elite dominance was challenged, with football as a source of both inspiration and leisure during lengthy protests that would stretch for weeks and months. Male street vendors in the informal sector would play small games of football in small enclosed spaces to while away time as they waited for customers. Migrant workers would occupy open fields and *maidans*[ii] in the evenings and weekends to escape their cloistered and suffocating dormitories and slum housing conditions. Heterotopic uses of public spaces demonstrated not just a counter strategy to the proliferation of urban camps in the form of slums, worker dormitories, and homeless dwelling places, but reflected ways in which the urban poor and working classes attempted processes of othering—both as political beings and as humans with aspirations, as persons who seek to humanize themselves from the disciplining effects of alienating work—through sport.

Unlike David Harvey's (2000: 539) critical view of heterotopia as a banal idea which critiques Foucault's and Kant's spatial and geographic thinking as necessarily and 'always local, regional, and contingent', and hence may not be emancipatory, this research attempts to show (by using football in Asian cities as an example) that the spaces of European football in Asia are both camps and heterotopias, that they are locally contingent and globally articulated at the same time, and that they are to be viewed as an illustration of urban processes and phenomena that evolve and transform within 'a network of relationships that are irreconcilable with each other and absolutely impossible to superimpose' (Foucault and Miskowiec 1986).

European soccer clubs and Fédération Internationale de Football Association (FIFA) have for some years embarked on an ambitious strategy to expand their global reach into territories outside of Europe and Central and South America—the traditionally strong soccer countries. Asia has been an important market, with its population exceeding four billion. Apart from Japan and South Korea, and the countries of the Middle East to some extent, Asian national football teams have been perceived to be weak, and the market for consumption of football in the media and via merchandise was considered to be inadequately developed. Over the last two decades, there have been attempts to redress these: European clubs make pre-season tours of Asian countries, playing friendlies with national teams and local clubs;

several of the top clubs have started football academies in cities like Mumbai and Bangkok; and tie-ups with elite private schools and local soccer academies have been established to train students both in their own countries and in Europe. The FIFA is organizing its next World Cup in Qatar, and the 2017 Under-17 World Cup was in India, all with a view to developing the market for global football, along with increasing live telecast of football matches. Football in Asia has now been placed within a global network. However, it would be a mistake to assume that globalization of soccer in Asia is only about club and world football seeking to accumulate more capital, that it is solely about economic networks, even though the global production of football merchandise and commercial profits of electronic media constitute an important aspect of this phenomenon.[iii]

In Asia, there are subtler inter- and intra-Asian urban and national networks that emerge and develop, and football gets linked to local political movements, class politics, and contestations between migrants, natives, and ethnic groups. Football is also about short- and long-term claims of empowerment; aspirations for emancipation; struggle to retain a sense of being human under conditions of extreme alienation, precariousness, and vulnerability; and contestations over urban public space. (The rapid rise of football in Jammu Kashmir reflects all of these, and more.) These claims and contestations are not always successful, but soccer and public participation in sporting activities in general constitute the 'experience of living men and women' (Thompson 1978: 21); their participation in and performance of global football culture are material and exemplify ways in which workers of all hues seek to escape the discipline of capitalist labour regimes, which does not spare the informal sector. Self-exploitation is an aspect of both informal and formal work in modern capitalist labour processes, and football offers an opportunity to free oneself from the disciplining effects of capitalist work. Football as leisure activity provides an excuse to perform 'useless' bodily actions, and participation in football fan culture enables participants to express themselves in terms of identities that may not derive from their participation in capitalist labour processes but are subsumed by larger capitalist accumulation tendencies. In the following sections, these are illustrated using examples from field work in Mumbai, one of Asia's large urban metropolises with significant a migrant population and exposure to global football cultures. This case of Mumbai is preceded by brief explorations of the sociospatial dynamics of football in Bangkok and Singapore. The concluding section seeks to develop a cogent argument about understanding these

40   SPORTS AND SPORTS STUDIES

dynamics against broader processes relating to the politics of class, ethnicity, and globalization driven aspirations of urban and urbanizing populations.

Football and the Global–Local Intra-Asian Dynamics in Bangkok and Singapore

Playing short games of street-side football, or even just joining for a few minutes in longer games, is common among informal sector workers in Bangkok, such as motorcycle taxi drivers. The game itself is not taken seriously: no strict rules are enforced and the purpose is mainly to 'relax', get one's feet moving, and do something other than change gears or apply the break on a motorcycle with one's feet. The motorcycle taxi parking stations are camps which function as everyday spaces of friendship; they are spaces of affect and affinity, providing a place for food, rest, recreation, and emotional rejuvenation before they go off into Bangkok's mad traffic. In his study on Bangkok's motorcycle taxi drivers, Claudio Sopranzetti (2013) makes similar observations: While waiting for customers or relaxing at a station, motorcycle taxi drivers fill up illegal soccer betting slips; during a negotiation with the state, the Association of Motorcycle Taxis of Thailand met with government officials in a room in the military base where a large flat screen television set was broadcasting a British football game.

In Benglumphoo and Chakraphong neighbourhoods of Bangkok, street children at work play football at varying times of the day and night, even as upper- and middle-class kids are in pool parlours, gaming shops, clubs, malls, and stadiums, formally learning and playing a variety of sports. As dusk falls in Sanam Luang, the large open 'Royal Field' and public square, a fair number of the city's homeless gather and find a place to settle for the night on the pavements around the ground. Children and youth begin impromptu football games. The homeless spread out their assorted ware of filched, salvaged, second-hand, and used goods around Sanam Luang. Among this assortment are second-hand 'fake' football merchandise relating to European clubs—T-shirts, badges, posters, keychains, and other memorabilia. Among the wide range of counterfeits and fakes that one can buy on Bangkok's streets, club football souvenirs are prominent. In the infamous Patpong area, well-known for its night clubs, streets magically transform every night into a market for counterfeits, largely catering to foreign, western tourists, with whom football merchandise is a hot item. In the Fortune Town shopping plaza, it is possible to buy T-shirts of almost every famous club from the major leagues in

GLOBALIZING SPORTSCAPES 41

Europe and South America. In Iron Bridge and Khlong Thom markets, counterfeit football merchandise is easy to get, notwithstanding the frequent raids on such shops by officials of the Economic and Cyber Crime Division of the Royal Thai Police. Most of these are made in China, Hong Kong, or Thailand itself.

In the Red Shirt protest camps that were a regular feature of Bangkok life in the past decade, football is not just a way of passing the time by rural and urban working-class protesters who camp for long weeks and months; it is an important source of political mobilization. Their populist leader Thaksin Shinawatra's short-lived ownership of one of the biggest clubs in European football—Manchester City—in 2007–8, is often used in political imagery, both by protesters loyal to Thaksin, and by Thaksin's own trusted lieutenants who organized public protests. There is a certain pride in projecting Thaksin's association with Manchester City Football Club, reflected also in the current performance of Leicester City owned by a fellow Thai, Vichai Srivaddanaprabha, which has shifted loyalties of thousands of Thais from other English football clubs to Leicester City.

These are not just illustrations of the multiple registers of football as an aspect of cultural globalization with local resonances, but reflect larger contextualizations of the global, of the 'local life of global forces' (Coombe 2001: 298). The Chinese dominance of global markets for all kinds of products reflects a process whereby Chinese manufacturers understand cultural symbols and flows, and the demand for cheap products emanating from such flows; kinship and long-term trade linkages between China and Thailand and the presence of a significant Chinese diaspora in Thailand contribute in significant ways to the flow of Chinese goods (including counterfeits) into Bangkok's streets. The use of Thaksin's images associated with Manchester City is part of a larger project of constructing Thaksin as a grand, heroic figure to take on the King, who is the powerful symbolic figure of the yellow shirt Royalists; opposing the invocation of the monarchy as a powerful symbol by the yellow shirts requires such a construction of a populist, alternative symbolic figure who has mass appeal, with football as one of the symbols which is drafted into this project.

The numerous public informal games of football by informal sector workers and children across a series of 'camps' express 'city life as a sidewalk ballet' in Jane Jacobs's (1961: 50) evocative phrase. Or, as Lefebvre (2004) would put it, they reflect the 'temporal order of rhythms in everyday life' (Meyer 2008: 147), rhythms that derive from the global popularity of football, but also draw from work patterns, leisure needs and the time available

42   SPORTS AND SPORTS STUDIES

for leisure, and recreational preferences of the urban poor and working-class young males in Bangkok.

In Singapore, where the migrant working classes are barricaded into dormitories with strict controls on where they can assemble and socialize outside of the workplace, football in informal public spaces reflects the well-known ability of sports to bring people together. This is not unique or strange by itself, but in a rigidly enforced context of segregation of migrant work-force by ethnicity, race, and nation, football has a greater ability than other sports or cultural activities to bring together workers of different nations and ethnicities. On Desker Road in the Little India precinct of Singapore, oppo-site the hugely popular and always crowded twenty-four-hour supermarket, Mustafa, South Asian workers congregate on weekends and in the evenings on weekdays to buy ethnic products and groceries, meet with friends, and just hang out. The increasing number of Bangladeshi workers in this hangout has resulted in enhanced interaction between Indian and Bangladeshi workers, some of whom bond over beer and football in the roadside cafes. Football on TV in the streets is itself fairly new as local respondents men-tioned, but Bangladesh's longer and more popular association with football compared to the relative absence of a football culture among South Indian migrants creates new possibilities of affinity and friendship.

As open spaces are increasingly being developed for real estate in Singapore or barred for informal and impromptu sports events, there is increasing frustration among workers about the lack of access to recre-ation and sports facilities. Beyond the need for and preference for football grounds, the point to note is the nature of informal public physical exertions of migrants which are different from native Singaporeans—Chinese, Malay, and Indian who play various sports including football in highly regulated environments and not in the open, not in public, and not informally or as impromptu games. As in other cities, there is a clear class distinction in the case of football in Singapore; the middle class and elites largely relate to foot-ball through informal and formal club-specific fan clubs and in sports bars, buy genuine merchandise at a high price online or in sports retail shops, and their youth attend football matches and training camps/clinics conducted by European clubs both in Singapore and in Europe. The migrant workers,[iv] on the other hand, play in open fields often without the requisite permissions and watch football either in their dormitories where televisions are shared and decisions on what to watch are jointly made or in small street side cafes in ethnic enclaves. This class divide is further aggravated as a result of urban transformation and cultural gentrification. In one of the streets of Little India,

GLOBALIZING SPORTSCAPES 43

which has become popular for its backpacker hostels, the large presence of young European and American tourists has transformed the street from its erstwhile 'Indian' character to a more 'hip' one. Bars and cafes have sprung up which play league football continuously on their television screens.

Ethnic preferences mixed with class issues and their implications for football in Singapore are also the subject of the late Pattana Kitiarsa's *The 'Bare Life' of Thai Migrants* (2014). Outlining the resources, time, and effort invested by precariously placed Thai male workers in Singapore to organize football tournaments and other events, he describes how such events enable Thai migrant workers to assert their identity and culture. Historical ethnic relations and working and living together in dormitories in Singapore play a role in bringing Thai, Malay, Indonesian, and Burmese workers into collective games of football, infrequently observed among migrant workers of other nationalities.

If, as Lefebvre states (2004: 51), 'capitalism . . . constructs and erects itself on a contempt for life, and from their foundation: the body, the time of living', then football for the migrant worker in Singapore is part of a larger effort to cope with their loss of agency, overcome and deal with a break in ties with kin groups and families, and recover some control over their bodies, time, and life itself. Gradually, as Kitiarsa's (2004) work also shows, the migrant worker's footballing efforts get linked to global football through corporate sponsorship of community events, player identification with European and South American football icons, and enhanced fan following among the migrant worker class for global football nations and clubs.

Mumbai

In India and in Mumbai, historians show that football was more popular in the pre-independence period, lasting upto the 1950s and 1960s, when hockey also began to compete for popularity owing to India's global dominance of the sport (Majumdar and Bandyopadhyay 2006). In a poor country with easy access to open public spaces, football was not only popular and easy to play, but was seen by sections of the colonized as a key mechanism to assert their masculinity, contra efforts by the colonial rulers to project the 'natives' as lazy, effeminate, and physically weak. Despite the fairly strong historical work on football in India in general, and in Mumbai in particular, there is very little research on contemporary football practices, even though it has become popular and re-emerged among certain demographics, especially the youth, as a preferred sport for playing and spectatorship in post-economic liberalization India (from the early 1990s).

Notwithstanding the city's shrinking public spaces, Mumbai is currently witnessing a spurt in the number of people playing football informally in some of its historic maidans, school playgrounds, and stadiums. It is competing with cricket, which still retains its number one status, but gradually slipping in popularity among the younger generation. New corporate sponsorship has entered Indian football in a big way with its base in Mumbai. The emergence of the Indian Super League (ISL) with an entirely different financial structure has upended the traditional power structure of Indian football; the creation of new football infrastructure and the renovation of existing ones in Mumbai have generated new aspirations among the youth for soccer-related careers. Mumbai and Maharashtra based political leaders (Praful Patel and Aditya Thackeray, for instance) have found ways to use these transformations to elicit more support for their political careers. Several national-, state-, and city-level football leagues have emerged and been formed to become more television friendly, which in turn raise the aspirations of younger people playing football as a leisure sport in schools and colleges. European football clubs such as Manchester United opened their first ever India-based Soccer School in Mumbai at one of its historic and iconic football venues newly refurbished with corporate sponsorship—the Cooperage. Mumbai's two premier school sports bodies—the Mumbai School Sports Association and the District Sports Organization—conduct arguably the most competitive sports events in football, hockey, and cricket, and going by media reports, football is gaining more popularity than cricket in the city's schools in recent years. There is an explosion of city-wide and neighbourhood-level school sports tournaments, including many for school girls, hitherto not very prominent. New leagues at district, city, and neighbourhood levels vie with each other to attract finances, footballing talent, and publicity. Media and corporate houses including the Times of India and Reliance Industries Ltd jostle to organize soccer leagues with significant support for talent spotting, training, and career management.

Are these transformations a reflection of what is sometimes referred to as a demotic turn in popular culture (Turner 2010) prompted by global promotion of football by the sports-media complex, and by European soccer clubs and FIFA? Or are they simply a manifestation of an increasing weariness with cricket among the youth, a sport which does not have global icons and whose stars are mostly home-grown? In other words, is it an attempt by

GLOBALIZING SPORTSCAPES   45

Indian youth to seek global (read Western) iconic figures for emulation, aspiration, and fandom?

On the one hand, as in Bangkok and Singapore, there are attempts by the Mumbai's urban poor to occupy and claim public spaces increasingly for football games, something that was seen earlier only for games of cricket. Such occupation is happening not just in the streets but also in its historic public spaces, its maidans, which are usually used for public meetings and protests, political rallies, and myriad games of cricket played simultaneously. On the other, the urban poor increasingly express themselves in school sports, as beating elite schools become significant events for schools that predominantly admit children from poorer and working-class backgrounds. Class issues are evident in the pride and hullaballoo that surrounds even minor victories of municipal and minority schools (Christian, Muslim) over elite schools. However, there are class divisions evident within the convent schools as well. Christian missionary-run 'convents schools' have historically dominated school sports, and they also play a prominent role in organizing school sports events and tournaments in the city.[v] This is due to historical reasons relating to the origins of mass schooling, and India's status-oriented caste system which defines how many activities including sports are regarded, with physical activities generally not preferred in the past by upper castes. Depending on their urban location, these may cater to children of the rich and elites, or the urban poor and migrant worker class. Increasingly, there is competition within missionary-run schools. Schools in poorer neighbourhoods largely have children from religious minorities and lower castes, whereas schools in elite localities mostly have children from upper caste and Hindu families. Competition is stiff, and in Mumbai's school sports (especially football and cricket), coaches are often paid more than other subject teachers, and there is frequent poaching of coaches from other schools. Given its strong class inequalities and historical class struggles, as well as ethnic conflicts, football carries much larger meanings both for school staff and for children from working class and ethnic minority populations.

Globalization of football, in this scenario, creates new aspirations for such children. While European football clubs largely cater to elite children due to their high fees and their tie-ups with elite schools, some scholarship programmes and corporate sponsorship as well as support from minority run institutions and non-government organizations (NGOs) create opportunities for poorer children to aspire for a career in football with local clubs and at the national level, if not at the international level. This has implications for the use of public spaces. A mapping exercise of the uses of public spaces in Mumbai revealed that minority localities have more football games being played in such spaces than other residential areas. Political parties with a clear Hindu majoritarian agenda rarely sponsor neighbourhood football tournaments or poorer children for training. Political parties with a more open agenda and community-based organization working in ethnic minority areas are more likely to support football-related events. This is, however, changing with the enhanced interest in football exhibited by new generation leaders such as Aditya Thackeray of the Shiv Sena. Contestations inevitably take place over how public space and playgrounds are to be used, sometimes becoming the cause of political conflicts and violence. The attempted suppression of ethnic minorities in Mumbai by majoritarian and nativists/chauvinist forces leads to new football and sports-related claims made in public, over public spaces, and these mark attempts by marginalized social groups to gatecrash the opportunities that are opening up in the realm of football.

The situation is particularly poignant among the minorities and working classes. Unlike cricket where talent spotters pick up and mould young cricketers across all communities and class backgrounds and a relatively smooth transition occurs for talented cricketers to move up from age group and school cricket to higher levels, football has still not developed such institutions, structures, and organizations. Hence, while it is predominantly the religious/ethnic minority and working-class children who do well in school sports, they soon lag behind. Even as they try to inch their way upwards to play for clubs, states, and national teams, they find opportunities closed or not encouraging enough, or simply do not have the financial resources to make the upward struggle. With football in India increasingly being taken over by corporate-led private tournaments, it is the few elite children and young men of Mumbai who find opportunities to play in such leagues. Corporate sponsors make claims that the new leagues help unearth and train new talent from the margins, but these initiatives are yet to have mainstreaming effects. Owing to the higher status of formal education and white-collar jobs, as well as the uncertainty and nepotism surrounding sports careers in India, even middle-class and elite households tend to focus less on sports as an aspiration and career option, and instead encourage children in other directions.

Partly, then, as a consequence of thwarted ambitions, young people shift towards consumption as a vicarious way of playing football: consumption of games, soccer as a spectator sport, becoming a part of fandom subcultures, and so forth. Neighbourhood, workplace, and school peer groups form around fandom for specific clubs; some of these interestingly are

GLOBALIZING SPORTSCAPES   47

cross-gender groups. They meet, watch matches, organize events around tele-vised matches; some of these become large events in educational institutions, housing complexes, and neighbourhoods, as well as pubs and bars, as large screens are put up to enable mass participation vicariously in premium foot-ball matches such as Champions League finals. These have their counterparts in smaller events in slums and poorer localities. With football merchandise a must at these events, a sizeable retail market has spread from high-end malls to neighbourhood stores, selling both genuine and counterfeit football mem-orabilia once again linking Chinese, Thai, and Hong Kong production units (including via business-to-business [B2B] online sites such as Alibaba) to local economies of consumption. Mumbai itself is also a major production location for counterfeits.

A thriving economy also develops around sports for the middle classes and elites: short- and long-term coaching camps in schools and gated complexes; tie-ups with ex-players of European soccer leagues; tourist trips that coincide with European football tournaments with guaranteed seats for the engagements; and private coaching for aspiring footballers. The shifts towards football and football spectatorship is thus an aspirational goal, keeping up with peers in globalized workplaces and schools where families have more exposure to European cultures through regular tourist trips. It is also a way of allowing young people to partially participate in the global cul-ture of football without permitting them to abandon family centric career objectives and paths. Ironically, the coaching, tourist, production, and retail industry around global football for the elites in Mumbai largely employ the urban poor through whom the cultural globalization of football spreads into their families, communities, and localities.

***

These case studies of global–local linkages around the globalization of soccer or football have highlighted the complexities of studying processes of cultural globalization that are both rooted in and seek to assert autonomy from global-izing economic and cultural impulses. As the sports–media–industry com-plex (particularly strong in Mumbai), aided by the accumulative impulses of national and global capital, penetrates Asian markets, football is not imper-vious to this impulse. However, the actual ramifications of these new global thrusts of world and European football clubs need to be interpreted against a context of large-scale, dense urbanization and increasing global linkages and

48 SPORTS AND SPORTS STUDIES

influences in the work place, in schools, through tourist flows, media, and collective consumption in cities like Mumbai. Urban space is more than just a geographical territory in which events take place. Space is a resource; individuals, groups, and communities imbue space with agency by attempting to convert the constraints of space into social and political advantages that advance their lives, aspirations, and give meaning to the 'bare lives' of the urban poor, the migrant working class, and marginalized ethnic minorities. Football, in its new globalizing avatar, offers a social field, creates new transnational spaces, and makes communities use public space as a strategic resource, whether these are public grounds, temporarily available open spaces, stadiums, school playgrounds, pubs and sports bars, or private clubs.

In addition, the spaces of global football in Mumbai reflect processes, local contingencies, and forces that give meaning to the ways in which diverse classes and communities relate to and engage with global football. These transnational and translocal spaces enable the participation of the rich and the poor in consumer modernity through playing, spectatorship, fandom sub-cultures, and buying and flaunting football merchandise. Across low-income, middle-class, and high-consumer modernity enclaves, the city of Mumbai displays diverse spaces that reflect how people, particularly the young, experience socio-spatial inclusion and exclusion that affect their aspirations, leisure practices, and futures. Inclusion and exclusion also apply to how they consume football modernity, and the streets, malls, and retail outlets reflect how urban desires are met and how the global market meets such demands through monopolistic production and sale of high-end, expensive football merchandise and their counterpart counterfeits. The significance of schools in feeding into and expanding football culture and its linkages with the global soccer sportscape is a significant phenomenon that requires further research, not just for understanding the global–local linkages in football better but for achieving a larger sociological understanding of contemporary socio-spatial dynamics around sports.

Richard Sennett (2011) establishes a concern with popular struggles around the meaning that people strive to give to their everyday lives. The rising popularity and transformation of football as a game, as a site of new corporate–political–media nexus, and as an emerging social field of spectatorship/fandom in Mumbai, goes to the very heart of sport: the appeal of its sheer physicality both for men and women; its ability to bond people with diverse and shared interests and struggles; its capacity to generate aspirations; and the possibility of linking local contexts to global cultural flows. In highly cosmopolitan Mumbai, Singapore, and Bangkok, with large

GLOBALIZING SPORTSCAPES 49

migrant populations, exposure to forces of globalization, and an everyday engagement with the global in schools, workplaces, streets, markets, media, and spaces of consumption, soccer as a global phenomenon has to be understood in two ways. It is an outcome of the global push of soccer through the sports–industry–media complex, which itself is influenced by the exigencies of capital accumulation. But it is also a response to, and expression of, local anxieties and aspirations around issues of place, community, class, work, leisure, and status—hence the increasing interest of local political leaders to get involved in football leagues in Mumbai. The meanings that people construct everyday around soccer as a global phenomenon derives as much from their everyday struggles as from global mediascapes and ideoscapes, and it is in these meanings that one can find the true essence of the global appeal of soccer or football. It is in the search for and interpretation of these meanings that one can also find new directions for understanding urban dynamics and the politics of class-, ethnicity-, and globalization-driven aspirations of diverse groups and classes. Thereby, and in this case, through a study of the Global South, it is possible to derive analytical frameworks that are evidence based and challenge Global North theoretical perspectives to become more expansive and inclusive.

Notes

i. These include: Queens Park Rangers F.C. owned by Tony Fernandes (Malaysian) and Lakshmi Mittal (Indo-British); Cardiff City F.C. and FK Sarajevo F.C. owned by Vincent Tan (Malaysian); Inter Milan F.C. owned by Erick Thohir (Indonesian); Valencia CF and Salford City F.C. owned by Peter Lim (Singaporean); Leicester City F.C. owned by Vichai Srivaddanaprabha (Thai); Manchester City F.C. owned by Sheikh Mansour bin Zayed Al Nahyan (Qatari); Paris Saint-Germain F.C. owned by Nasser Al-Khelaifi (Qatari); Blackburn Rovers F.C. owned by Anuradha Desai, Venkatesh Rao, and Balaji Rao (Indian); Fulham F.C. owned by Shahid Khan (Pakistani-American); Birmingham City F.C. owned by Carson Yeung (Hongkonger); and Sheffield United F.C. owned by Abdullah bin Musa'ed bin Abdulaziz Al Saud (Saudi Arab).

ii. 'Maidan' is a term of Persian-Urdu origin that refers to open spaces in cities that are used for public events, sports, political gatherings, or informal collective get-togethers.

iii. The historian Dipesh Chakrabarty (2004) refers to this media-led sports capitalism growth as 'sports-media complex'.

50 SPORTS AND SPORTS STUDIES

iv. Majority of the working-class people in Singapore are migrants from other parts of South and Southeast Asia.

v. One of the major organizations running school sports in Mumbai is the Christian Sports and Cultural Association,

References

Appadurai, Arjun. 1996. *Modernity at Large: Cultural Dimensions of Globalization*, Volume 1. Minneapolis: University of Minnesota Press.

Chakrabarty, D. 2004. 'Introduction: The fall and rise of Indian sports history'. *The International Journal of the History of Sport* 21 (3-4): 337–43.

Coombe, Rosemary J. 2001. 'Anthropological Approaches to Law and Society in Conditions of Globalization'. In Nick Blomley, David Delaney, and Richard T. Ford (eds), *The Legal Geographies Reader: Law, Power and Space*, pp. 298–318. Singapore: Blackwell.

Foucault, Michel, and Jay Miskowiec. 1986. 'Of Other Spaces'. *diacritics* 16 (1): 22–7.

Harvey, David. 2000. 'Cosmopolitanism and the Banality of Geographical Evils'. *Public Culture* 12 (2): 529–64.

Iwabuchi, Koichi. 2002. *Recentering Globalization: Popular Culture and Japanese Transnationalism*. Durham and London: Duke University Press.

Jacobs, Jane. 1961. *The Death and Life of Great American Cities*. New York: Vintage.

Kitiarsa, Pattana. 2014. *The 'Bare Life' of Thai Migrant Workmen in Singapore*. Chiang Mai: Silkworm Books.

Lefebvre, Henri. 2004. *Rhythmanalysis: Space, Time and Everyday Life*. London: Continuum.

Majumdar, Boria, and Kausik Bandyopadhyay. 2006. *A Social History of Indian Football: Striving to Score*. London: Routledge.

Meyer, K. 2008. 'Rhythms, Streets, Cities'. In K. Goonewardena, S. Kipfer, R. Milgrom, and C. Schmid (eds), *Space, Difference, Everyday Life: Reading Henri Lefebvre*, pp. 147–60. London: Routledge.

Sennett, Richard. 2011. *The Corrosion of Character: The Personal Consequences of Work in the New Capitalism*. London: WW Norton & Company.

Sopranzetti, C. 2013. 'The Owners of the Map: Motorcycle Taxi Drivers, Mobility, and Politics in Bangkok'. PhD Diss., Harvard University, Cambridge, USA.

Thompson, Edward Palmer. 1978. *The Making of the English Working Class*, 2nd edition with new postscript. Middlesex: Harmondsworth.

Turner, Graeme. 2010. *Ordinary People and the Media: The Demotic Turn*. London: SAGE.

3

India's Olympic Encounter

Sport, Identity, and Nationalism[i]

Boria Majumdar

India's Olympic encounter, which dates back close to a century now, has been a fertile playing ground for the myriad internal battles of an emerging nation. Ranging from issues of national representation, colonial and postcolonial resistance, women's empowerment, the north–south divide, and sports diffusion to the fight for control of sporting organizations, the Olympic journey documents the compelling struggles of an emerging nation striving to break out of colonial rule.

This chapter, on the origins of this encounter, explores the complex relationship between sport, identity, and nationalism in India. At the same time, it is a conscious effort to come to terms with the philosophical debates that emerged in the course of India's engagement with Olympic ideals. In documenting the Indian story, since its origins in the 1910s to now, and locating it in specific historical contexts and timeframes, the chapter has attempted to resurrect India's Olympic journey from its position as a mere footnote in most Olympic tomes and integrate it within the global story of Olympism and the Olympic movement. Led by nationalist elites and princes, the early story of the Indian Olympic movement is also a narrative of a global league of upper-class elites, connected through patronage networks in Europe that passionately pushed the Olympic ideal. Until the 1920s, the Olympics were largely a Eurocentric enterprise. India's embrace of Olympism in the 1920s was simultaneously accompanied by a powerful push to diffuse the Olympic ideal in Latin America and Southeast Asia. In all three areas, the same strategy was followed: The use of the global network of

Boria Majumdar, *India's Olympic Encounter* In: *Sports Studies in India*. Edited by: Meena Gopal and Padma Prakash, Oxford University Press. © Oxford University Press 2021.
DOI: 10.1093/oso/9780190130640.003.0004

the Young Men's Christian Association (YMCA) and the co-option of local elites with enough private resources and European contacts to liaise with the Olympic movement's centre. In that sense, the origins of Olympic sport in India documented in this chapter is a missing piece in the global story of Olympism.

In a Europe divided by War, the International Olympic Committee (IOC) pushed this expansion as a strategy for survival. In India, the ideal was appropriated by elite nationalists as a new avenue for self-respect, modernity, and identity politics in the sporting arena. Olympism came to India as part of the processes of globalization, decades before the term itself became fashionable. But once it was initiated, it was appropriated by, and became inseparable from, both the forces of nationalism at first, to the centrifugal regional tendencies later.

This chapter seeks to understand the true nature of the Olympic movement by first looking briefly at Olympic histories in certain countries or regions: area studies, as it were. It then alludes to the fact that the story of India's engagement with Olympism is acutely political and provides a unique prism to understand the complex evolution of modern Indian society through the lens of sport. In this context, it has tried to grapple with the impact of the Indian nationalist movement on Olympic sport in the decades before Independence.

Another point that runs through the narrative is that India's Olympic story is not a unilinear one. Rather, it is a conflux of many stories and undercurrents, making the task of striking a scholarly balance between archival research and critical analysis in the writing of a meaningful story a rather difficult one. Add to this the paucity of written material and the almost non-existent tradition of record keeping and it is evident why no work on India's Olympic history can claim to be compellingly comprehensive in its range.

Ultimately, across historical contexts and timeframes, the Olympic Games have played a critical role in shaping modern societies. In doing so attention has been drawn to the numerous experiences and experiments from India's Olympic past. In the course of this exercise, the IOC, which has managed the Olympic Games for over a century, emerges as a composite meeting point of people, power and national interests: a global parliament with all its attendant intrigue, power machinations and high stakes manoeuvring.

The chapter has sought to demonstrate that the essence of Olympism and the Olympic movement does not reside in medals won, records broken, or television rights sold as ends in themselves. The Olympics and its relevant records and statistics are primarily important because of the way they can affect societies. So, when the Puerto Ricans march in the Olympic opening ceremony although they do not have a representative in the United Nations, or when an unknown Anthony Nesty of Surinam wins a gold, defeating the favourite Matt Biondi of USA, or when, in 1928, an Indian hockey team wins gold, the significance of such acts stretches far beyond the narrow confines of sport.

The 'Political' Origins

Olympic scholarship has traced the history of India's Olympic encounter back to 1920. It was at Antwerp in Belgium that India first participated in the Olympic Games. This was made possible by the generosity of Dorabji Tata, the first president of the Indian Olympic Association, who funded the participation of three Indian athletes in the 1920 Olympics. The Indian Olympic Association was formed in 1923, and India sent a reasonable team of athletes to Paris in 1924 and won its first Olympic medal in field hockey in the 1928 Amsterdam Olympic Games.

> There are so many communities, so many different religions, so many languages and dialects, so many different customs and ideals, that it is almost impossible to select a national team.[ii]

To Sir Dorab Tata goes the credit of starting systematic Olympic activity on Indian soil in 1920. Son of the pioneering nationalist steel baron Jamsetji Tata, Dorabji was intimately involved in fulfilling his father's idea of creating an indigenous and modern steel industry in India. He is widely credited with the establishment of the Tata Steel Company in Jamshedpur that became India's largest private enterprise of the time. Simultaneously, in the great tradition of Parsi philanthropists in colonial India, some of his most valuable contributions came as a benefactor for sport, culture, and education.[iii] Before taking an interest in Olympism, Sir Dorabji had already played a key role in the establishment of school and college cricket in Mumbai in the 1880s. Till the 1890s, the structure of cricket in Mumbai educational institutions was irregular. It was under Sir Dorabji's initiative that the move to form the Bombay High School Athletic Association gathered momentum. Determined to eliminate differences of caste and creed on the sporting field, he wished to unite local clubs and inculcate notions of 'fair play' among young boys.

54   SPORTS AND SPORTS STUDIES

At first, the success of the scheme seemed uncertain, as there was a question mark over whether European schools would join such a union. However, with the elite Cathedral School joining hands with Sir Dorabji, the Association came into existence in 1893 and initiated the famous Harris Shield tournament in 1896. This is now the oldest surviving inter-school cricket tournament in India and has been the nursery for many Indian cricketers, most prominently Sachin Tendulkar and Vinod Kambli. The Association also prompted the formation of cricket clubs in schools with regular coaches, which served the dual purpose of providing employment to veteran cricketers while also promoting the game.

A principal obstacle that Sir Dorabji faced was the paucity of playgrounds in late nineteenth- and early twentieth-century Mumbai. To redress this, a games fee was levied in most high schools, but in order to safeguard the interests of poorer students, students from modest backgrounds were exempt. With aristocratic and upper-class patronage coming their way, many schools revoked the levy in course of time (Majumdar 2004: 93–4).[iv]

Sir Dorabji was largely educated in England, and his interest in sport was a product of his Western upbringing, which exposed him to the period ideology of athleticism and the 'Games Ethic'. The Games Ethic saw sports as a form of moral education and was central to the ideology of English education at the time, in public schools and in universities. It was the key to the socialization in metropolitan Britain of the future administrators and conquerors of the Empire.[v]

This was the underlying philosophy grounding the colonial policy of most sports. In Sir Dorabji's words:

> Having been educated in my youth in England I had shared in nearly every kind of English Athletics and acquired a great love for them. On my return to India I conceived the idea of introducing a love for such things there. I helped set up with the support of English friends, as General Secretary, a High School Athletic Association amongst numerous schools of Bombay, in the first place for cricket, and then for Athletic Sports Meetings which embraced nearly all the events which form part of the Inter-University contests every year in London.[vi]

Adopting a game also meant adopting the entire paraphernalia of modernity that went with it. It did not just mean playing a foreign game, it also meant adopting European clothes, European rules, and European notions of order and 'fair play'.

INDIA'S OLYMPIC ENCOUNTER   55

Sport became the playing field where tradition and modernity met, clashed, and fused. A good example here is that of the Deccan Gymkhana. After the successful start of the Harris Shield, the idea was modified in Pune with the creation of the Gymkhana. The committee, which ran the Gymkhana, was not conversant with the details of managing athletic meets on European lines and wanted to develop their sports programme more in line with established Indian traditions. Sir Dorabji, who was nominated the president of the Gymkhana, played a central role in the merging of foreign and indigenous cultures that ensued. At the first athletic meet the Gymkahana organized, Dorabji found that the competitors were 'all boys of the peasant class working in the fields and living off poor fare'.[vii] Naturally, they had no idea of European rules or modern training of any kind. On attending a meeting of the Gymkhana, Sir Dorabji found that they were proposing to run their 100-yard heats round a bend without strings. This was because their sports ground was very small, and the track was part of a rough unrolled grass field. To the peasants, running was running, but now it had to be undertaken under standardized and controlled conditions. In Sir Dorabji's letters on the subject, preserved at the International Olympic Museum, the one thing that strikes the reader most palpably is his sense of wonder at this clash of 'peasant' and Western cultures in the races at the Deccan Gymkhana.[viii]

Other popular events included the long-distance race of about twenty-five miles, rightly designated the Marathon. The peasants who participated were used to running barefoot on hard macadamized or dirt roads. Despite their lack of training and primitive conditions, the first three or four men ran the distance in fair time. As Sir Dorabji observed, their time 'would compare well with the times done in Europe or elsewhere'.[ix] In 1919, some of their times were close to those clocked in the Olympics. Suitably impressed, the Tata scion decided to send three of the runners, at his own expense, to the Antwerp Games of 1920. This was the birth of India's Olympic encounter and nationalist sentiment was at its core. Dorabji Tata described his motives in a personal letter to the IOC president, Count Baillet Latour, in 1929:

I therefore offered to arrange for the sending of three of the best runners to Antwerp to run the Olympic Marathon at the next meeting, when I hoped that with proper training and food under English trainers and coaches they might do credit to India. This proposal fired the ambition of the *nationalist element* in that city to try and send a complete Olympic team.[x]

Going Further Back

Interestingly, however, documents at the Public Records Office in Kew Gardens in London trace India's Olympic history back to 1912, almost a decade before India sent a team to Antwerp. These documents and letters demonstrate that there was a series of letters exchanged between the British Olympic Association, the International Olympic Committee, and the India Office discussing prospects of Indian participation at the 1912 Stockholm Olympics. Had such participation taken place, India would have become the first Asian country to embrace Olympism alongside Japan, which established a national Olympic Committee in 1911 and participated in the 1912 competition as the first Asian country.

The exchange of letters did not abate after the 1912 Games. Rather, the correspondence only increased, discussing prospects of Indian participation at the proposed 1916 Olympic Games in Berlin, which did not eventually take place on account of the outbreak of the First World War. In fact, the trail of documents on the subject demonstrates that India would surely have sent a team to the 1916 Games had it not been cancelled. This is borne out by the Indian request to have advance intimation of the dates of the 1916 Olympics to enable requisite funding to send a team.

Of significance is the discussion on the nomenclature of the team. Would the athletes participate under the India banner or would they represent Britain? If they represented British India what would that mean for the Olympic Games in general? Chances are that the success of the all-India cricket team's tour to Britain in 1911—a tour organized by the Maharaja of Patiala, the leading patron of Indian sport—acted as a catalyst for India's Olympic participation. Patiala's tour received widespread support among the sporting community both in India and the UK and is considered a turning point in the history of Indian sport.

In the many dispatches discussing India's participation, it is evident that funding was a key issue and a constant thread of discussion. Who would fund the team and how many of the athletes were entitled to receive support from the Olympic host city? That nothing came of this effort does not minimise the significance of this exchange because this is where the foundation was laid. It was on this base that the superstructure to send an Indian team to the 1920 Olympic Games was built. The discovery of these documents adds a new chapter to the history of India's Olympic encounter and helps date the story back to 1911–12.

INDIA'S OLYMPIC ENCOUNTER   57

Eventually, however, India first sent a team of athletes to the Antwerp Games of 1920, an effort that was due, to a large extent, to the munificence of Sir Dorab Tata. India's embrace of the Olympic movement in 1920, while still a British colony, was no mere coincidence. It was intricately linked to the forces of nationalism, the politics of self-respect, and indeed the inculcation of what has been called the British 'Games Ethic' among Indian elites. Colonial India's early Olympic encounter was born out of a complex interplay of all three factors and it also forms a crucial missing link in the story of Indian nationhood. It was in Indian hockey, and in the Olympic Games, that the nationalist aspirations of colonial India found full expression.

The IOA as we know it today was formed in 1927 and a strong Indian contingent participated in the Amsterdam Games of 1928, winning India its first gold medal in hockey in the very first year of official participation.

A precursor to the IOA, as referred to earlier, had been formed in 1923 with the same name and it had served the Olympic cause for three years until 1926 before being shut down. At a time when nationalist sentiment in India was gaining pace, the Olympics were the only international arena where Indianness could be projected on the sporting field.

In fact, India's participation in the Olympics from the 1920s was an important watershed for the politics of colonialism. Indians participated in the Olympics on equal terms with the British, at a time when the colony was not even invited to the first British Empire Games (1930; later Commonwealth Games) in Canada. Apart from Bermuda, British Guyana, and Newfoundland, other invitees were only the white settler dominions of Australia, South Africa, and New Zealand. The organizers even funded the athletes from the white settler dominions. The exclusion of non-white athletes from big colonies, despite India's success at the Olympic Games, meant that the Empire Games were fraught with tension. The decision to prohibit India from competing at the first British Empire Games ignited angry demonstrations from both the pro-British aristocracy and the nationalist middle classes. (In fact, it has been argued that it was partly the chance to participate in the Games that later persuaded Prime Minister Nehru to allow India to remain in the Commonwealth.) The Games helped provide an arena for nationalist ambition and anticolonial sentiment, and while they extended imperial cultural power, they also offered an opportunity for the once subordinate and colonized to beat the master at his own game. This was now true for the African, Asian, and Caribbean Commonwealth as it already was for the white settler dominions such as Australia, Canada, and New Zealand.

58 SPORTS AND SPORTS STUDIES

In sum, the early story of Indian Olympism was structured by the movement of nationalist elites converging with global elites that were keen to establish the Olympic ideal. After 1920, with the Indian presence, the Olympic movement also drew support in Latin America and Southeast Asia. While in Europe, divided by tensions and war, the movement was pushed as a means of bringing together nations, in India, the nationalist elite grasped the Olympic movement as a means of furthering the emerging ideals of nationhood, self-respect, and modernity. The Olympic movement was appropriated by nationalist elite and became broadly integrated with the ideals of nationhood and the forces of nationalism.

Notes

i. The chapter, a product of meticulous and thorough research, would have been impossible to write without access to the International Olympic Committee (IOC) archives at Lausanne, Switzerland. In fact, the fundamental motivation for this chapter had arisen from an interest in developing a corpus of writing on India's Olympic encounter enriched by access to hitherto little-used archives.

ii. Personal letter from Dorabji J. Tata to the IOC President Count Baillet Latour, 21 May 1929. ID Chemise 7334 CIO 3535 MBR-TATA-CORR, Correspondence de Dorabji Tata 1926–1930. International Olympic Museum, Laussane, Switzerland.

iii. For instance, the Sir Dorabji Tata Trust provided the seed money to fund the setting up of one of India's premier scientific and engineering research institutions, the Indian Institute of Science, Bangalore.

iv. Also see Polishwala (1921: 11).

v. For details on the impact of the 'Games Ethic' on the colonies, see Mangan (2001) and Stoddart (2006).

vi. Personal letter from Dorabji J. Tata to the IOC President Count Baillet Latour, 21 May 1929. ID Chemise 7334 CIO 3535 MBR-TATA-CORR, Correspondence de Dorabji Tata 1926–1930. International Olympic Museum, Laussane, Switzerland.

vii. Personal letter from Dorabji J. Tata to the IOC President Count Baillet Latour, 21 May 1929. ID Chemise 7334 CIO 3535 MBR-TATA-CORR, Correspondence de Dorabji Tata 1926–1930. International Olympic Museum, Laussane, Switzerland.

viii. See the letters in ID Chemise 7334 CIO 3535 MBR-TATA-CORR, Correspondence de Dorabji Tata 1926–1930. International Olympic Museum, Laussane, Switzerland.

ix. Personal letter from Dorabji J. Tata to the IOC president, Count Baillet Latour, 21 May 1929. ID Chemise 7334 CIO 3535 MBR-TATA-CORR, Correspondence de Dorabji Tata 1926–1930. International Olympic Museum, Laussane, Switzerland.

x. Personal letter from Dorabji J. Tata to the IOC president, Count Baillet Latour, 21 May 1929. ID Chemise 7334 CIO 3535 MBR-TATA-CORR, Correspondence de Dorabji Tata 1926–1930. International Olympic Museum, Laussane, Switzerland.

References

Mangan, J.A. 2001. *The Games Ethic and Imperialism.* London: Frank Cass.

Majumdar, Boria. 2004. *Twenty-Two Yards to Freedom: A Social History of Indian Cricket.* New Delhi: Penguin-Viking.

Polishwala, P.N. 1921. *School and College Cricket in India.* Mumbai.

Stoddart, Brian. 2006. 'Sport, Colonialism and Struggle: CLR James and Cricket'. *Sport in Society* 9 (5): 914–30.

4

Indian Volleyball

From Local Contexts to Global Realities

Bino Paul

Volleyball as a creative human activity in India seems to have been traversing a journey of progress and regress. While volleyball is not as widely subscribed to as is cricket or hockey, the game is well-grounded mainly in southern and north-western India and is also played in a few other regions in India. Volleyball does not require as much space as football or hockey. Narrow beach strips or undulating hillocks alike may be adapted to the basic needs of the game and matches to be organized. Moreover, volleyball is a socially intensive activity with every game involving at least a dozen of players. These features of volleyball meet the social expectations about participative recreation,

In the emerging global scenarios, participative sports tend to be embroiled in virtual networks that harness contents of diverse formats to create customized entertainment or information products. More succinctly, participative activities that are bound by socio-physical-cultural domains do not necessarily isomorph smoothly into global networks. While some games are adaptive, many struggle to align with these changes. This chapter first looks at the trajectory of volleyball on the global stage and tries to unravel the intertwining factors that promote success and failure in the game. A close personal look at volleyball at the village/local level leads to some understanding of how changes in global factors, both related to the game and external to it, impact on the local that in turn influences the global country-level standings in the sport.

Historic Context

Volleyball as a sporting system originated in 1895 and was invented by William G. Morgan, a US-based physical education academic. The game

Bino Paul, *Indian Volleyball* In: *Sports Studies in India*. Edited by: Meena Gopal and Padma Prakash, Oxford University Press. © Oxford University Press 2021. DOI: 10.1093/oso/9780190130640.003.0005

evolved from its prototype version 'mintonette' to metamorphose to 'volleyball'. While designing the game, the inventor seems to have envisaged it as a competitive recreational sport, suitable not only for young people but older age groups as well. Over time, spanning a little more than a century, this sport has been growing in scale and scope. Since the beginning, there have been endeavours to codify the rules of the game. Under the patronage of the Young Men's Christian Association (YMCA), Frank Wook and John Lynch were the first movers to frame the system of rules for the game that seem to have made the sport more pliable for global adoption. The sport became a 'demonstration event' in the 1924 Paris Olympics. In the following two decades, the sport spread to nearly eighty countries across the globe. During this phase, volleyball emerged as a pan-continental sport, with nations that adopted it forming respective federations to organize and regulate the sport. Rules of the game were changing over these decades and these changes were adopted across the globe. To a great extent during 1895–1948, volleyball as a sport became a more organized, pan-continental sport that grew in terms of adopting countries, players, organizing agencies such as federations, events, and spectators.

In the first five decades, notwithstanding two World Wars and other upheavals in socio-political-economic spheres, volleyball grew from being a US-based college/club recreation to a pan-continental institution, having its formal constituents (for example, rules) and informal constituents (for example, norms and cultures) (North 1990). Propitious factors, emerging from the global power alignments, probably tacitly bolstered the trajectory of its growth, particularly in a colonial global system. In the postcolonial period, during 1950–90, the sport witnessed more discernible proliferation, culminating in continent-specific championships for men and women and the formation of the global federation.[1] In 1964, volleyball became an Olympic event and 1994 saw the launch of the world championship for volleyball. Over the years, across continents, volleyball has been growing quite vividly in scale, with ever expanding amateur communities along with an upsurge in professionalism. A variant of volleyball, called 'beach volleyball' with a different format was introduced in 1915. For this stream of sporting, competition is between two teams, each having two players. This variant, too, has been gaining major traction in terms of spectators, media interest, broadcasting rights, events, and players. In 1996, beach volleyball became an Olympic event in Atlanta. Another interesting variant of volleyball, snow volleyball, is gaining worldwide interest.

Structures and Performance

Global context

While volleyball has been evolving as a global sport, its institutional frame seems to share features of long-extant dominant structures prevalent in many popular or prestigious human activities such as sport, art, and scholarly pursuits. On the global scale, taking the Olympics as a case in point, volleyball portrays the chronicle of cumulative opportunities translating to discernible gains for a few countries. During 1964–2016, combining men and women, there seemed to be a positive relation between success rate of a country in Olympic volleyball matches and the number of matches played by the country. This pattern resembles a non-linear curve. While the relation between these variables looks direct for a range of values, beyond this range, the curve falls. Does this demonstrate 'success begets success'?[2] Since the inception of volleyball in Olympics, nearly 70 per cent (fifty-eight medals) of the eighty-four Olympic medals won were claimed by six countries (Soviet Union/Russia [18], Brazil [10], USA [10], Japan [9], China [6], and Cuba [5]).[3] More succinctly, what this graph shows is that success in Olympics volleyball tends to be visibly impacted by cumulative experiences in playing Olympics matches. Maybe 'learning by doing' translates to wins.

Quite importantly, during 1964–2016, nearly two-fifths of the competing national teams in the Olympics played no more than twenty matches and just one-fourth played at least fifty Olympic matches. The corresponding graph depicts a pattern showing accolades accruing to a few countries while the vast majority of countries account for very few favourable outcomes (here, participation in the Olympics volleyball).

However, this is far from a core–periphery global order considering that the 'elite' in the order have heterogeneous ideological, political, economic, social, and cultural legacies and contexts. It is possible that the skewed distribution of cumulative advantages might have emanated from the institutional design and evolved praxis (in particular vision, mission, governance, and incentive) of volleyball federations in these countries. Does institutional design and evolved praxis tend to have significant sway on the persistence of success, culminating in a sort of path dependency[4] of favourable outcomes?

Now, we move from matches to wins. Here, the skewness of favourable outcomes is more evident. Plotting the count of wins with wins as a proportion of matches played generates a steeply declining curve. A large majority of competing countries (nearly 80 per cent) won not more than twenty matches during 1964–2016, while very few countries (8 per cent) won at least 50 matches. This means that winning frequently tends to a rare possibility, reinforcing the earlier pattern of accumulation of favourable outcomes to a few.

Is this pattern static over time, being locked in peculiar institutional contexts? If we let the mean count of participation in Olympic matches (treating the mean count of one as a reference point[5]) change upwards, this curve transforms to a bell-shaped pattern with a long tail towards the right, indicating improved chances of participating in more than one Olympic match. This cannot happen unless the Olympics provides more berths for the volleyball. This structure seems to repeat itself even for the World Cup and continental games like Asian Games.[6] Put simply, a progressive change in average count of participation may fetch more opportunities for the teams to participate in Olympic volleyball. On the other hand, a stagnant average count over a period makes the structure more tenacious than the level it is supposed to evolve.

Moreover, tallying the laurels in Asian Games (men [1958–2018] and women [1962–2018]), only four teams, men or women, ever won at least a gold (Japan [16], China [11], South Korea [5], and Iran [2]). Other than countries from the East Asia, Iran is the only country to have won at least a gold medal. The silver also appears to follow a pecking order (South Korea [18], China [6], Japan [5], Iran [3], India [1], and Thailand [1]). Nevertheless, the bronze is distributed more evenly than the other two. Again, this pattern also tells the story of accumulation of laurels for a few, mimicking the global structure.

Indian Context

Volleyball in India has been evolving as sport in terms of popularity and laurels. Indian men won bronze in 1958 Asian Games when volleyball was first introduced. In 1962, Indian men, were placed second. India's next stellar performance was in 1986, winning the bronze by defeating a global elite team like Japan. Apart from this and a few wins in international tournaments at discrete intervals, Indian teams (either men or women) never participated in pan-continental events like Olympics or World Cup. Indian senior men are placed 131 according to the latest ranking, reporting a drop of 92 positions from the previous rank order (Figure 4.1). For senior women, India's rank is 117, descending 62 positions from the last rank order.

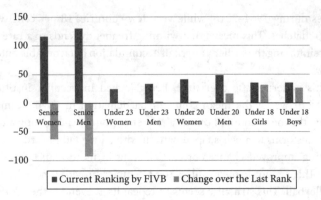

Figure 4.1 India's rank in World Volleyball

Source: Tabulated from http://www.fivb.org/en/volleyball/Rankings.aspames; accessed on 23 March 2019.

Note: FIVB: Federation Internationale de Volleyball. Ranking is as per latest updates (Senior Men [October 2018], Senior Women [October 2018], and the rest [January 2019]). In this rank order, lower the number, better the position is, and vice versa.

However, in the junior groups (under 23, under 20, and under 18), across gender, ranks vary in the range of 23 (under 23 women) to 49 (under 20 men). It is important to note that across junior categories, except under 23 women, positions in the rank order improved (in the range of 3 to 32) from the last declared rank order.

Why has this change in rank order for Indian senior men and women, a hugely disruptive one, occurred? Intuitively, sporting performance is unlikely to plummet to extreme margins within a span of two years. This scale of disruption seems to be related to the ban imposed by the Fédération Internationale de Volleyball (FIVB) in 2016 on Volleyball Federation of India (VFI) due to the crisis in the governance of the VFI. However, the ban was lifted in 2018.[7] Thereafter, a major change was the start of Professional Volleyball League in 2019 under the auspices of VFI and Baseline India Ventures Private Limited, a sports marketing firm.[8] The league features six teams with independent owners: Ahmedabad Defenders, Calicut Heroes, Chennai Spartans, Hyderabad Black Hawks, Kochi Blue Spikers, and U Mumba Volley. The first edition of the league was won by Chennai Spartans. The new professional league is a visible departure from the earlier system of clubs being owned by public sector companies or government departmental enterprises such as railways. More importantly, the relationship between the

INDIAN VOLLEYBALL   65

club and the player has changed from the previously prevalent framework of employee–employer to the players of different nationalities being auctioned by resorting to varying bids. Thus, the compensation or wage, paid to the players who were in an employment relation, was substituted by the price at the auction.[9] How far reaching is this change? On 25 April 2019, the Indian League Champions Chennai Spartans became the first Indian club to qualify for Asian Men's Volleyball Championship.[10] Does the new league herald disruptive changes? Quite vividly, money plays a pivotal role in this format, akin to the global structure of any popular sport. How is this emergent order aligned with the life of people, who have been avid followers of the game? Stories may vary across contexts. In the next section, one story of disrupted human engagement with volleyball is narrated.

Lived Experience: Towards an Epilogue

Before drawing to an epilogue on the future of volleyball, with India as a case in point, I discuss my experience as an avid spectator of volleyball and how I relate to the sport. When I was a child, I watched the youth of my village playing this sport. This was in the early 1980s in central Kerala where I was born and brought up. Volleyball required relatively fewer facilities than did other sports. I used to watch the game with avid interest from afternoon to sunset. I yearned for a floodlit space in my village so that the game would go on until a fiduciary limit. That remained a wish. However, the zest created match after match was a gratifying continuum.

Our village did not have an all-season court that fulfilled the minimum standards of the game. All that existed was an open space, owned by one family. This space was used for multiple purposes, as if it was dancing to the rhythm of seasons. Throughout the monsoon months and a few thereafter, the space was engaged for diverse farming-related functions, ranging from pre-sowing to post-harvest. Then, post the industrious phase came the lull and weariness of the peak summer. Now, the young men flocked here to play volleyball.

Nobody taught me the rules of game. While watching it, being immersed in it, and living with it, I began internalizing the rules and the system. There was no formal instruction. Many things were learnt by spectators like me: number of players each team has; service, smash, and block; fouls; and sets and points. For me, the core of the game was players, referee, court, ball, net, and the system of scoring. The place where I grew up to be a young man

66 SPORTS AND SPORTS STUDIES

had the rare distinction of hosting an all India Volleyball Tournament in the 1980s. My panchayat,[11] Koratty[12] in Thrissur District, Kerala, India, was the location of a textile plant, Madura Coats,[13] directly and indirectly employing nearly 3,000 people. This firm was interested in promoting volleyball. In the early 1980s, the company launched an all India tournament for men and women. The events were held during February–March. The company was not merely a sponsor but built a stellar women's team that competed in the tournament.

For me, this tournament was not just a sporting event but a cherished season of thrills and enduring moments. I had my iconic stars whose indomitable acts fused my passion and experience together, making me earnestly wait for the morning newspaper to read the review of the match and black and white photos of critical moments in the game. This was not just a cursory read, but more with a piercing attention to the favourable reporting of 'my team' and 'my player/s'.

My experience with the tournament was a special one. I was connecting the tournament with my experience in the neighbourhood court. Unlike the tournament, our neighbourhood did not have opportunities for women to play. There, it was a man's space, excluding women from playing, perhaps an evolved praxis of gender discrimination. We had benchmarks for those who would play in the tournament, perfect in smashing, services, cuts, and blocks. We were mimicking stalwarts like Jimmy George,[14] the legendary international volleyball player, who spearheaded Indians to win the bronze in Asian Games Men's Volleyball in the Tokyo Asian Games, beating the star-studded Japanese team. In this tournament in Thrissur, he represented the Kerala Police team for many years and became the heartthrob of spectators.

Over the years, the tournament brought diverse teams from all over India: Indian Railways, Travancore Titanium, Premier Tyers, Kerala Police, Haryana State Electricity Board, Andhra Pradesh State Transport Corporation, Indian Overseas Bank, Madura Coats, Kerala State Electricity Board, Services, Hindustan Photo Film Company, Tirupur Textiles, Southern Railways, and South Central Railways. Except a few, most were clubs owned by public sector organizations.

The tournaments, over the years, were held outdoors. Matches were played on a special mud court that was temporarily laid out on the football field. Spectators were seated in a gallery made of whip tree logs. For me, this was nothing short of an Olympic arena. This was the time India had just won the Cricket World Cup. Down a few years, television broadcasting began proliferating, featuring global sporting events along with other entertainment.

INDIAN VOLLEYBALL   67

I never imagined in all those years that any power would disrupt the tournament. Towards late 1980s, I was completing my schooling, envisaging hitherto unexplored life of university education. There came the news that stunned us: The tournament would not be held that year. How was this possible? How would spectators endure this loss? Clueless and in a spiral of anguish, I affirmed and reaffirmed to myself that the 'show must go on'. It was not just that year that the tournament was cancelled; it was never organized again. Soon afterwards, the company shut down due to industrial unrest.

In essence, this process of local tournaments disappearing or being absorbed by larger 'global' initiatives, has happened to volleyball everywhere in India. In the glittering glamour of globally connected formats and competitions, will volleyball be a sport of collective purposes that espouses shared and decentralized contexts? Both of these—shared local contexts and global structures—are realities that need mutually beneficial ties (Andrews and Ritzer 2007). On the other hand, commentators like Donnelly (1996a) see the divergence between global structures and local sporting cultures in the frame of contrasting ideologies of Olympism and professionalism, positing emerging sporting monocultures that create opportunities, but also problems.[15]

A more intense exploration through the dynamics of a participative sport like volleyball may help to unravel the complex patterns of the embedding of creative human activities within socio-economic-political-techno structures. This, in turn, throws up cues about the non-linear trajectory of human performance, particularly in the context of a neo-liberal global system.

Notes

1. Federation Internationale de Volleyball was founded in 1947. See http://www.fivb.org/EN/FIVB/FIVB_History.asp; accessed on 24 March 2019.
2. Lotka (1926) observed a pattern of this sort emerging from the frequency distribution of journal publications. Frequency distribution of this nature is called the power laws. Sylvan Katz and Katz (1999) examine the application of power laws to the athletics.
3. Data available at https://en.wikipedia.org/wiki/Volleyball_at_the_Summer_Olympics; accessed on 23 March 2019. Andreff (2001) points to the correlation between development of the country and performance in sports.
4. Path dependency refers to the long prevalence of processes or outcomes principally due to strong dominance of certain legacies. If the path dependence is

strong, even if there are alternatives, the order of outcomes (here, the Olympic medal) may prevail over a long period (see David 1985, 2000). Put simply, across events over the years, laurels accrue to the same pack of countries. This is often applicable to product standards, for example, QWERTY keyboard.

5. This is not very unrealistic since there are 176 ranked countries in VIFB ranking. From this pool, only 12 teams march to the Olympics. See http://www.fivb.org/en/volleyball/VB_Ranking_M_2018-10.asp; accessed on 23 March 2019.

6. Here, 'isomorph' means institutional isomorphism, referring to similarity of the processes or structure of one organization to those of another (DiMaggio and Powell 1983). Slack and Hinings (1994) discusses isomorphism in the context of sports.

7. https://sportstar.thehindu.com/other-sports/fivb-lifts-volleyball-federation-of-india-suspension/article23896419.ece; accessed on 23 March 2019.

8. https://sportstar.thehindu.com/volleyball/pro-volleyball-league-2019-season-teams-auction-date-telecast-news-volleyball-federation-india/article25598316.ece; accessed on 23 March 2019.

9. Vrooman (1995) provides a general theory of professional sports leagues. Also, see Szymanski (2003).

10. https://sportstar.thehindu.com/other-sports/avc-championship-chennai-spartans-enter-semifinals/article26936937.ece; accessed on 26 April 2019.

11. Panchayat is the grass root unit of democratic governance in India.

12. http://lsgkerala.in/korattypanchayat/; accessed on 23 March 2019.

13. https://www.moneycontrol.com/company-facts/maduracoats/history/MC18; accessed on 23 March 2019.

14. https://web.archive.org/web/20080514040141/http://sportal.nic.in/legenddetails.asp?sno=667&moduleid=&maincatid=59&subid=0&comid=55; accessed on 17 November 2020.

15. Also see Donnelly (1996b). As argued by Washington and Karen (2001), the organizational power systems create convincing narratives to convince the society to incur the cost of infrastructure while privatizing all the benefits that accrue from the sporting.

References

Andreff, W. 2001. 'The Correlation between Economic Underdevelopment and Sport'. *European Sport Management Quarterly* 1 (4): 251–79.

Andrews, D.L. and G. Ritzer. 2007. 'The Grobal in the Sporting Glocal'. *Global Networks* 7 (2): 135–53.

David, P.A. 1985. 'Clio and the Economics of QWERTY'. *The American Economic Review* 75 (2): 332–7.

INDIAN VOLLEYBALL 69

———. 2000. 'Path Dependence, Its Critics and the Quest for "Historical Economics"'. In P. Garrouste and S. Ioannides (eds), *Evolution and Path Dependence in Economic Ideas: Past and Present*, pp. 15–40. Cheltenham, England: Edward Elgar Publishing.

DiMaggio, P.J. and W.W. Powell. 1983. 'The Iron Cage Revisited: Institutional Isomorphism and Collective Rationality in Organizational Fields'. *American Sociological Review* 48 (2): 147–60.

Donnelly, P. 1996a. 'Prolympism: Sport Monoculture as Crisis and Opportunity'. *Quest* 48 (1): 25–42.

———. 1996b. 'The Local and the Global: Globalization in the Sociology of Sport'. *Journal of Sport and Social Issues* 20 (3): 239–57.

Lotka, A.J. 1926. 'The Frequency Distribution of Scientific Productivity'. *Journal of the Washington Academy of Sciences* 16 (12): 317–23.

North, D.N. 1990. *Institutions, Institutional Change and Economic Performance.* Cambridge: Cambridge University Press.

Slack, T. and B. Hinings. 1994. Institutional Pressures and Isomorphic Change: An Empirical Test. *Organization Studies* 15 (6): 803–27.

Sylvan Katz, J. and L. Katz. 1999. 'Power Laws and Athletic Performance'. *Journal of Sports Sciences* 17 (6): 467–76.

Szymanski, S. 2003. 'The Economic Design of Sporting Contests'. *Journal of Economic Literature* 41 (4): 1137–87.

Vrooman, J. 1995. 'A General Theory of Professional Sports Leagues'. *Southern Economic Journal* 61 (4): 971–90.

Washington, R.E. and D. Karen. 2001. 'Sport and Society'. *Annual Review of Sociology* 27 (1): 187–212.

5

Sherpas in Himalayan Mountaineering

Identity, Labour, and Power in Sport

Vrinda Marwah

For the last few years, Mt Everest has been in the news for the wrong reasons. On 18 April 2014, an avalanche swept the area between base camp and camp one on Everest, killing sixteen climbers, thirteen of whom were Sherpas. The surviving Sherpas went on a strike, bringing the 2014 climbing season—the deadliest season till then in the history of Everest—to an abrupt close. The striking Sherpas demanded that, among other things, the Nepalese government pay higher compensations for death and disability on Everest. The fatalities of 2014 would be trumped only by 2015, when a 7.8 magnitude earthquake hit Nepal, killing seventeen people at Everest base camp, including seven Sherpas. In 2019, the Nepalese government issued a record 381 climbing permits for Everest; photographs from this season show hundreds of climbers lined up on a steep ridge, attached to a single fixed rope and waiting for hours to reach the summit. Eleven climbers died that year. As a corrective to the overcrowding, the Nepalese government in August 2019 announced new safety rules to reduce the number of permits issued for Everest.

The fatalities on Everest reflect the organization of the sport.[i] A third of Everest deaths are Sherpas (Preiss 2018). Dying on Everest is an occupational hazard for Sherpas; most die from avalanches while fixing ladders and ropes across very risky parts of the mountain, like the Khumbu icefall.[ii] And this is an occupational hazard unlike most others. According to one estimate, the death rate for Sherpas on Everest from 2004 to 2014 was twelve times higher than the death rate for US military personnel deployed in Iraq during 2003–7 (Ogles 2014). The pattern of who dies where on the mountain has a lot to do with who does what on the mountain. Paying climbers—called 'members' in mountaineering parlance, to distinguish them from hired Sherpas—are shielded from the mountain's dangers before the summit. Thanks to the work of Sherpas, they typically move through avalanche-prone zones of Everest

Vrinda Marwah, *Sherpas in Himalayan Mountaineering* In: *Sports Studies in India.* Edited by: Meena Gopal and Padma Prakash, Oxford University Press. © Oxford University Press 2021.
DOI: 10.1093/oso/9780190130640.003.0006

SHERPAS IN HIMALAYAN MOUNTAINEERING   71

quickly, and save time and energy for summit bids. Around the summit, the air is thin and falls are more likely. Between 1950 and 2009, 40 per cent of member deaths were attributed to falls (Himalayan Database, cited in Narula 2014). What is more, this mortality divide between Sherpas and members is widening. Climbing Everest is much safer for members today than in the past; they can use bottled oxygen and altitude sickness-minimizing steroids far more liberally than Sherpas can, and with the commercialization of climbing, they routinely pay their way to the top despite lacking the training and experience that climbing Everest once demanded.[iii]

Recent media coverage of Everest has brought into sharp focus the dangerous conditions under which Sherpas climb, particularly given the commercialization of the mountain that attracts tourists without adequate mountaineering experience. Some media reports detail the various kinds of labour that Sherpas perform on Everest and ask angrily: Why should they climb? The unfortunate answer often is, for the money. Everest is a lucrative business. Nepal, one of the poorest countries in Asia, charges US$ 11,000 for every permit to climb Everest. Foreign climbers pay anywhere from US$ 50,000 to US$ 90,000 to be guided up Everest. Sherpas make anywhere between US$ 2,000 to US$ 8,000 per climbing season and are insured for approximately US$ 10,500 if they die on the job; these sums may be disproportionate to the risks of Everest, but they are much higher than US$ 600, which is the median annual income in Nepal (Karkauer 2014).

However, in this chapter, I am interested in going beyond the common refrain of 'they do it for the money', to deepen our understanding of how and why Sherpas climb. I want to situate Sherpas within the particular history and dynamics of Himalayan mountaineering, especially in the Everest region, to investigate how Sherpa labour and Sherpa identity inflect each other. Sport provides a fertile avenue through which dynamics like labour, identity, power, and modernity can be interrogated. The position of Sherpas in Himalayan mountaineering presents a particularly illuminating case for the sociology of sport, and can fill several lacunae in the study of sport. As Belinda Wheaton (2010) notes, lifestyle sport research has yet to first, examine how systemic global forces shape the practices and structure of the sporting 'glocal', and second, move beyond insider accounts of the experiences of Western, male, white-privileged participants. Wheaton (2010: 1071) points out that 'research to date that examines participants' racialized experiences or explores how "race" articulates with class and gender, age and sexuality in the construction of identity, inclusion and exclusion, is extremely limited'. Ben Carrington (2007) similarly notes that while extant scholarship on

72 SPORTS AND SPORTS STUDIES

identity has been very insightful, it needs to be more grounded in everyday lived contexts. He argues that because identity is a strategic intervention by marginalized communities for cultural, political, and economic recognition, it must be studied in conjunction with inequality.

A study of Sherpa identity and positionality in Himalayan mountaineering has the potential to further these, and other, important lines of inquiry in the study of sport. In this chapter, I examine scholarship on Sherpas in Himalayan mountaineering. I consider the three key texts that constitute contemporary scholarship on the subject of Sherpas and mountaineering, namely, James Fisher's (1990) *Sherpas: Reflections on Change in Himalayan Nepal*, Vincanne Adams's (1996) *Tigers of the Snow and Other Virtual Sherpas*, and Sherry Ortner's (1999) *Life and Death on Mt Everest*. Through my reading of these texts, I explore the limits and possibilities of both, this particular field of climbing as well the scholarship on it.

In the first section, I begin with a brief description of Sherpas and short summaries of these texts. In the next two sections, I bring Fisher, Adams, and Ortner in conversation with each other, through what I see as two shared concerns that run across their texts: the search for authenticity and the search for motive.

By 'search for authenticity', I mean the common concern that Fisher, Adams, and Ortner have of countering distorted Western representations of Sherpas. Fisher and Adams understand Sherpa authenticity through competing frames, whereas Ortner demonstrates how cultural images of Sherpas stem from material conditions, in this case the labour that Sherpas do in Himalayan mountaineering. 'Search for motive' refers to the shared aim that Fisher, Adams, and Ortner have of understanding why Sherpas climb. Here I explore the racialized labour of Sherpas in climbing, and demonstrate that the question of *why* Sherpas climb is inseparable from *how* they climb. Using Ortner, I discuss how Sherpa labour is also gendered and sexualized.

In the final section, I undertake a critical discussion of Fisher, Adams, and Ortner. I argue that although they set out to decentre Western narratives about the Sherpas, each of them ends up in their own way privileging the relationship of the Sherpas with the West. I then build on this critique to discuss ways forward for scholarship on Sherpas and Himalayan mountaineering that can illuminate new directions not just for Himalayan studies, but for our understanding of identity, mobility, and the sporting field.

SHERPAS IN HIMALAYAN MOUNTAINEERING   73

Sherpas and Scholarship

Who Are the Sherpas?

Sherpas are an ethnic group that migrated from Eastern Tibet to Solu Khumbu in northeast Nepal in the sixteenth century. Today, many Sherpas have settled outside of Solu Khumbu, in places like Kathmandu (Nepal) and Darjeeling (India). As a result of both, the parcelling of land that created fraternal competition in Sherpa society and the raising of taxes by Nepal's ruling Ranas, some Sherpas began migrating to Darjeeling for work in the late 1800s (Ortner 1999). By the early 1900s, Sherpas had distinguished themselves as porters on mountaineering expeditions, and, in 1953, Tenzing Norgay Sherpa became the first man to summit Mt Everest along with New Zealander Edmund Hillary. Himalayan mountaineering has always relied on Sherpas for portering and general expedition support like cooking.[iv] With time, Sherpas have also become members of the climbing party. Today, they occupy many roles in Himalayan mountaineering, as porters, climbers, expedition leaders, owners of private trekking agencies, and so on. The term 'Sherpa' has come to stand for both the ethnic group as well as the role/status of a high-altitude porter with climbing expertise (Ortner 1999).

Key Texts
The analyses that these three texts arrive at are significantly different. But they have a common interest: they each want to recover the story of the Sherpas. I pick these texts because together they comprise the body of contemporary Western anthropological writing on Sherpas that seeks to understand the relationship of Sherpas with Himalayan mountaineering.

James Fisher (1990) in *Sherpas* presents an account of change in the Nepal Himalayas through the Sherpas. He aims to move beyond what he calls two dominant but unhelpful representations: accounts that are either nostalgic romanticizations of the region and the ones that pronounce 'expert' solutions to the region's problems. Instead, Fisher's (1990) work aims to foreground the Sherpa view, which he sees as missing from both academic and development narratives. Fisher (1990) describes himself as an anthropologist writing for a general audience. His book covers distinct periods of time over three decades (1964, 1974 and 1978, and 1985–6 and 88) spent by him in Solu Khumbu. This part memoir begins with Fisher's involvement in the Edmund Hillary Schoolhouse Expedition of 1964. Expedition members did not know it at the time but their efforts, such as building an airstrip to bring in supplies for

74 SPORTS AND SPORTS STUDIES

schools, would soon spark a burgeoning tourist economy in the area. Fisher (1990) notes that while anthropology has recently paid attention to the impact of the field on the observer, the question of what impact the anthropologist has on the long-term development of a society is rarely raised. In his case, he was directly part of 'cataclysmic events that changed the face of Khumbu forever' (Fisher 1990: 1). His book discusses a wide range of subjects, from Sherpa history and religion to an evaluation of student learning. It also studies the impact of tourism through a comparison of three Khumbu villages and the monastery that serves them, Tengboche, and ends with an account of ethnographic futures gleaned through interviews with adult Sherpa men about how they imagine life twenty years hence (Fisher 1990).

In *Tigers of the Snow and Other Virtual Sherpas*, Vincanne Adams (1996) examines the impact of Westerners on Sherpas and vice versa. Her book is an ethnography of encounters and draws on fieldwork in Khumjung through the 1980s and in 1993. She notes that there is something hyperreal about the representations of Sherpas, and yet, the term 'Sherpa' has come to enjoy a certain currency through these images and meanings. Adams (1996: 13) asks, 'By what mechanisms and with what profits have Sherpas become self-willed "Tigers of the snow"?', a title given to them by Western climbers in the 1930s. Through an examination of tourism, charitable aid, Buddhism, and Shamanism, Adams argues that Sherpas are engaged in a relational process of mutual seduction with the West. Sherpas are expected to be both similar to and different from Westerners; they have to remain attractive enough in positive ways to be saved by the West, and needy enough in negative ways to legitimize Western presence. Sherpas in turn recruit Westerners to be their sponsors through this play of seduction and impermanence, that is, multiple and shifting ways of being Sherpa. In a word, she insists that we cannot presuppose an essential Sherpa identity that is not inextricably bound up with the West (Adams 1996).

Finally, in *Life and Death on Mt Everest*, Sherry Ortner (1999) explores Sherpa perspectives on Himalayan mountaineering. Despite the immense contribution of Sherpas, the sport continues to be defined and imagined from the standpoint of Western, and recently international, climbers. Ortner (1999) presents the complex relationship between Sherpas and Himalayan mountaineering as a dialectical one, and animates the Sherpas as active participants in this relationship. To this end, Ortner (1999: 21) uses the metaphor of 'serious games'. 'Serious' emphasizes the constant play of power in which a great deal is at stake, but also that 'human experience is never just "discourse", and never just "acts", but is some inextricably interwoven

SHERPAS IN HIMALAYAN MOUNTAINEERING 75

fabric of images and practices, conceptions and actions in which history constructs people and the games that they play, and in which people make history by enacting, reproducing, and transforming those games' (Ortner 1999: 23–4). As her account demonstrates, Sherpas have made significant gains, both material and non-material, in their position vis-à-vis the sport of mountaineering and its 'sahibs' over the years. Ortner (1999) wants to understand Sherpas in the fullness of their real, complex lives, and to counter any one-sided representation of them, whether positive or negative. In studying the encounter between two groups with unequal material and symbolic power, Ortner (1999) situates herself within a trend in scholarship that emphasizes the co-production of the histories of the West and the rest. She uses the method of deconstructing sahib representations of Sherpas, and ethnographically establishing Sherpa perspectives. She locates her work between, on the one hand, Clifford Geertz—understanding how people make meaning of their worlds—and, on the other, Edward Said and Michel Foucault—understanding the power of discourse over people's worlds (Ortner 1999: 292–3).

In the next two sections, I bring these three texts into conversation with each other. To grasp the ways in which they build on each other, I suggest that we understand these texts through their differential treatment of what I see as two shared concerns: the search for authenticity, seeking to capture/ represent the 'truth' of Sherpa-ness, and the search for motive, trying to understand why Sherpas climb.

The Search for Authenticity: Understanding Western Representations of Sherpas

Fisher, Adams, and Ortner agree that there is a distorted Western representation of Sherpas. According to Fisher (1990), Westerners admire in Sherpas qualities that Westerners feel they themselves should embody but conspicuously lack. The Western image of Sherpas as peaceful, hardy, cheerful, and heroic is based on literary representations, and is reinforced when everything goes well in the course of a trek or climb (Fisher 1990). For Fisher (1990), this image captures only one side of Sherpa personality. He argues that Sherpas wear masks: the 'public onstage' that they want the world to see, and the 'private backstage' that is truer to themselves. He gives the examples of alcoholism and contraband smuggling, which are a part of Sherpa life but are not part of what he calls the official Sherpa image on display. He notes that

76   SPORTS AND SPORTS STUDIES

'successful trekking Sherpas realise that they are, in part, paid professional actors and entertainers' (Fisher 1990: 125).

Adams (1996) is opposed to this casting of Sherpas as impression managers. She argues that the view that Sherpas are staging performances for Westerners and that their real selves only emerge 'backstage' is one that denies Sherpa modernity any legitimacy. According to Adams, the attempt to access and understand a 'backstage' presupposes an authenticity that is being wilfully concealed when commercialized through tourism. She references the scholarship on tourism to suggest that all cultures, and not just the touristed ones, are staged and inauthentic to an extent. In this respect, Adams (1996: 25) problematizes the notion of locating 'truth' in a world 'where truth is made impermanent by seduction—a seduction through which Sherpas become visible to westerners and through which westerners come to know themselves through Sherpas'.

Adams's (1996) project then is to deconstruct the idea that there is a singular authentic Sherpa. She suggests that Western narratives thus far have been flawed in their implication that there is a more authentic Sherpa story to be told; this includes the insistence that Sherpas should be allowed to speak for themselves. She points out that there is also Sherpa investment in showcasing one culture type. Rather than looking for 'authentic' Sherpa-ness, she deploys a notion of 'virtual identities' (Adams 1996: 11). Adams argues that through mountaineering tourism, development aid, and anthropology, a process of identity construction takes place for the Sherpas. She calls this 'mimesis' (Adams 1996: 9). It involves the imitation of what is 'taken to be one's "natural" self by way of the Other, through whom one's constructed identity is made visible to oneself' (Adams 1996: 17). As such, Sherpa mimesis comes to reflect Western imagination, signifying difference in all the ways Westerners desire and making Sherpas larger than life (Adams 1996).

Accounts of Himalayan expeditions speak of the physical endurance and skill of Sherpas, their love and respect for the mountain, and their desire to climb irrespective of fear. Adams (1996) suggests that the Sherpas of these representations are highly capable, rugged, loyal, and skilled, to the point that the term 'Sherpa' has come to enjoy a certain currency through these meanings. She illustrates what she means by currency here: 'modern' Sherpas[v] present in their writings about themselves a version of identity that reiterates notions of Sherpa-ness already perceived as praiseworthy by Westerners and already determined by the tourist gaze (Adams 1996). Also, scholarly texts have become founding texts in a way, with Sherpas using Western accounts of themselves to talk about who they are. Thus, Adams (1996) describes this

SHERPAS IN HIMALAYAN MOUNTAINEERING   77

representational relationship between Sherpas and Westerners as a two-way mirror, one that calls into question both identity and its authorship. She concludes that 'modern seductions are not only *of* Sherpas, they are also *by* Sherpas' (Adams 1996: 237). Sherpas speak in a Western tongue today, she says, and seem to have 'mastered the canon and the strategy', turning it back on the West, and reproducing both a rhetoric of intervention (neediness) as well as a rhetoric of authenticity (Sherpa-ness) (Adams 1996: 235).

Adams (1996) captures important elements of the production and circulation of cultural images. However, even though she seeks to tackle the problem of how deeply power is bound up in the representation of otherness, the power differential between Sherpas and Westerners quickly slips away from her analysis. We see how Sherpas can, and do, capitalize on Western representations of themselves, but we do not get an adequate sense of how selective or stratified this capitalization is or how unequal the relationship between Sherpas and Westerners continues to be.

Ortner (1999) helps us understand how the cultural representations of Sherpas are tied to their material position vis-à-vis mountaineering. She undertakes an examination of the fabled 'good nature' of Sherpas, and by denaturalizing it, demonstrates how this particular cultural representation in early mountaineering accounts stemmed from Sherpa labour in Himalayan mountaineering then (Ortner 1999).

First, Ortner (1999) argues it was no coincidence that Sherpas were being characterized as cheerful in the early expedition years. She points out that Sherpas competed with the Tibetans for sahib attention and distinguished themselves as the more willing and able group for high-altitude portering. They did the hard work of not only making themselves indispensable to Himalayan expeditions, but also of endearing themselves to sahibs. Ortner (1999) also demonstrates how Sherpas fought to establish and preserve the recognition that the work they did was more skilled, dangerous, and valuable than that of ordinary porters. In this regard, she reminds us that Sherpas have resisted on mountains—from refusing to climb further to striking for better food, equipment, and toilet facilities. Ortner (1999) locates Sherpa agency in this active and continuous shaping of the conditions that made their work more rewarding. She argues that both the money as well as their successes in bettering their working conditions contributed to Sherpa 'cheerfulness'.

Second, Ortner (1999) also shows that the kind of hardiness and reliability that Western climbers find so praiseworthy in Sherpas did not spring from an essential nature. She excavates accounts of the disciplining of Sherpas from sahib narratives, which reveal that early mountaineering accounts by sahibs

78 SPORTS AND SPORTS STUDIES

constructed the Sherpas as childlike, possessing the physicality but not the mentality to climb. Sherpas were 'in need of discipline'. This disciplining into an expedition ethic that would serve Western climbers well took place, Ortner (1999) points out, in both more and less benign forms. It ranged from Western climbers ensuring there were no drunken brawls between Sherpas on expeditions to forcing unwilling Sherpas to proceed up the mountain under difficult circumstances. The British, in particular, also used paternalism to instil 'the right spirit'—from caring for their Sherpas and asking after them to conferring awards (the tiger medal, for instance, was instituted in 1939).

Ortner (1999) also discusses how sahibs read the responses of surviving Sherpas in the event of the death of fellow Sherpas on the mountains; this is perhaps the starkest manifestation of the orientalism of sahib accounts. She discusses several early Western writings that mentioned the 'stoicism' of the surviving Sherpas and rationalized this in terms of their faith: Buddhist religion made Sherpas 'more fatalistic' and 'less affected' by death. Ortner (1999) insists that it was simply not true that the reactions of surviving Sherpas to Sherpa deaths were always stoic; many were deeply and visibly upset. But often they tried to focus on and fulfil the obligation of the expedition job they had taken on—a job that was an opportunity to make more money than any other available avenue—while often mobilizing non-Western cultural resources to cope, like the religious injunction to control one's emotions and let go of attachments (Ortner 1999).[vi] Overall, by taking the material conditions of their production into account, Ortner (1999) is able to present a more complete analysis of the cultural representations and images of Sherpas.

Search for Motive:
Racialized Labour of Sherpas

Another common theme that ties Fisher, Adams and Ortner together vis-à-vis Himalayan mountaineering is their attempt to understand why Sherpas climb.

Fisher (1990) states that Sherpas climb for money, and are usually mystified that Westerners come to Khumbu at such great expense and in such great numbers. In their eyes, climbing is dangerous, and deaths in the community are a grim reminder of this danger. While Ortner (1999) agrees that most Sherpas climb for money (and some climb for sport and some for fame), she also insists that money as a motive is not easy to understand. To

SHERPAS IN HIMALAYAN MOUNTAINEERING 79

say that Sherpas climb for money is the beginning and not the end of understanding why they climb. She reminds us that money is not just money; it is
all the desires and meanings that money can fulfil, such as sending children
to school or building a monastery. Money also has very different meanings
for sahibs who have it and can afford to reject it, and for Sherpas who aspire
to it (Ortner 1999).[vii]

If we are to take this search for motive seriously, I argue that we cannot
understand *why* Sherpas climb in isolation from *how* they climb. It is what
climbing entails that makes climbing both risky and rewarding in unique
ways. In other words, there is a particular racialized labour that Sherpas perform in climbing, which produces certain possibilities and motives while
precluding others. Let us now turn to a closer examination of this racialized
labour.

Ortner (1999) reminds us that British activity in the Himalayas was always
an amalgam of the economic, political, scientific, orientalist, and sporting
interests that characterized the Raj. The colonial project of exploring and
climbing the Himalayan peaks that began in the 1850s was predicated on
the labour of the natives. However, there is no record of how many natives
died in this enterprise. Ortner (1999) notes that nearly every one of the
early expeditions had a fatal accident, and in nearly every case one or more,
Sherpas died. The tasks performed by Sherpas on early mountaineering
expeditions ranged from acts of generosity towards sahibs (voluntarily giving
up their oxygen or sleeping bag and making extra trips to ferry supplies) to
acts of outright heroism (risking and often losing their own lives to rescue
stranded or sick sahibs). As noted previously, Sherpas were valued not only
for their physical strength and stamina, but also for their cheerful good nature (Ortner 1999). As such, their labour was both physical and affective.

Importantly, as all three scholars point out, then and now, Westerners
come out of Himalayan treks feeling immense trust and respect for Sherpas.
According to Fisher (1990), this is because the Sherpa–climber relationship
is long and intense, and the exigencies of high-altitude trekking break down
barriers. Adams (1996) agrees with this assessment. She notes that contemporary Himalayan adventures are like 'sacred journeys'. They involve physical and emotional endurance, expectations of 'the exotic', and ritual spiritual
performances. These experiences leave tourists feeling a sense of limi-
nality and unusual achievement. She argues that there occurs a reversal in
Himalayan adventures wherein tourists, instead of following the footsteps of
'great white explorers' of the past, find themselves entirely dependent on the

80   SPORTS AND SPORTS STUDIES

heroism and expertise of Sherpa guides. Thus, they come away with a feeling of unfulfilled gratitude for Sherpas (Adams 1996).

According to Adams, these positive feelings towards Sherpas become a form of symbolic and cultural capital for Sherpas. Sherpas do what she calls 'culture work', which can be loosely understood as doing work to put culture to work for them (Adams 1996: 226). Sherpas host the tourists they have become particularly close to, and through dinner, drinking, dancing, and gift exchange, they draw these tourists into a relation of sponsorship. In this way, Sherpas are able to use Western clients to derive more long-term material benefit. They make them their *zhindak*. A zhindak[viii] is a cultural schema for Sherpas: a protector and mentor whom you serve and who also serves you back by fulfilling the promise of upward mobility. One illustration of this is the fact that between 1986–7, when Adams was writing, over one-third of the families in the Sherpa village of Khumjung were receiving some kind of foreign sponsorship (Adams 1996).

Further, Ortner (1999) provides insights about how the racialization of Sherpas is also gendered and sexualized. This highlights not just the co-constitutive character of race, gender, and sexuality, but also its unique interplay in the context of Himalayan mountaineering. According to Ortner (1999), the adventure involved in mountaineering was a twentieth-century phenomenon, constructed in binary opposition to modernity as a 'dropping out of the continuity of life' (Simmel 1971: 187). Even though everything about it—from the colonialism to the equipment that enabled it—was engendered by modernity, mountaineering was seen as the antidote to the problem of modernity. For early climbers, she argues, mountaineering came to embody spirituality, romanticism, and adventure that was absent in the crass materialism and humdrum routine of everyday life. And even as sahibs questioned the mechanical aspects of modernity, they embraced certain other values associated with modernity, such as strength, courage, leadership, aggression, and paternalism. Therefore, Ortner (1999) demonstrates how mountaineering represented both the dominant culture of masculinity, as well as the challenge to it. She suggests that as mountaineering/modernity mapped on to the nature/culture binary, the 'innocent' and 'childlike' Sherpas got coded with the mountains in the realm of nature.

In the 1950s and 1960s, the military approach[ix] to mountaineering gained strength. Ortner (1999) notes that the heightened machismo of this period was epitomized by an unabashed sense of competition, a certain raunchiness in interactions, and sexualization of the mountaineering conquest. However, in the 1970s, Nepal became a hippie magnet, and many sahibs brought a countercultural perspective to mountaineering that had more in common with pre-War romanticism than with the machismo of the 1950s and 1960s. This is manifest in the resultant rise in environmentally sensitive and technologically minimalistic mountaineering (Ortner 1999). Although there were a few instances of both memsahibs and sherpanis climbing in the 1950s, Ortner (1999) points out that it was in the 1970s that women really began to enter the field of Himalayan mountaineering. These women faced generalized disrespect and dismissal from fellow male climbers, as well as some instances of sexual harassment. However, even though it did not disappear, Ortner (1999) argues that machismo began to be problematized in this phase; this is illustrated by the self-reflexivity regarding sexism in the mountaineering literature of the time. Importantly, Ortner (1999) notes that Sherpas were coded as female and it took the entry of female climbers to truly underscore their maleness. She instantiates this by drawing attention to some of the debates that emerged during this time: For Western women, would a women's expedition be a success as a women's expedition if the Sherpas had assisted? How were sexual relations, specifically instances of Sherpa men getting involved with both Sherpanis and memsahibs, to be managed (Ortner 1999)?

In sum, Adams demonstrates how the Sherpa economy is an economy not only of cash but of meanings and depends on what she calls 'culture work' for the cultivation of relations of sponsorship with Westerners. Here we see how the dangerous conditions on the mountain that make adventure possible also create the space for dependence, gratitude, and repayment, turning, as I argued, the 'why' and 'how' of climbing—the motive and the labour—into inseparable enquiries. Further, Ortner (1999) helps us understand historically how the racialization of Sherpas and their labour has been simultaneously gendered and sexualized; this was so even before women themselves climbed, but women's entry into and experiences of climbing now provide a whole new register through which to understand the sport.

Discussion: Sherpa Identity, Mobility, and the Sporting Field

Further study of Sherpa identity and positionality in Himalayan mountaineering can make important contributions to the sociology of sport. In this section, I critically discuss Fisher (1990), Adams (1996), and Ortner (1999). All three set out through their respective texts to deconstruct Western representations and decentre Western narratives about the Sherpas. And yet,

82 SPORTS AND SPORTS STUDIES

each of them ends up in their own way privileging the relationship of the Sherpas with the West.

Adams (1996) argues that while the West cannot be erased from the Sherpas, it is not totalizing either. However, she is interested only in the relationship of Sherpas with Westerners. She does not consider Sherpa relationality, sociality, and the construction of Sherpa-ness vis-à-vis any other non-Sherpa, non-Western group. She critiques both Western and Nepalese scholarship on the Sherpas as containing a yearning for cultural difference and taking for granted the notion of Sherpas. However, she too appears disproportionately invested in Sherpa difference. Her book does not focus on cultural schemas of the West, which forms one half of the encounter between Sherpas and the West. Instead, she discusses an undifferentiated West in relation to an undifferentiated Sherpa, thus reifying the two poles of her analysis even as she attempts to capture a shifting mimetic relationship between them.

Fisher escapes this problem of a West-centric paradigm to an extent. He argues that there is a 'tradition of change' in Sherpa society (Fisher 1990: 64). Ever since the departure from Eastern Tibet, he argues, Sherpa society has not been static. Fisher (1990) is interested in how, and to what effect, the Sherpas of Khumbu have changed. He notes a distinction between the cumulative, compounding change of the past and the fundamental realignment represented by the change that began in the 1960s.[x] As a result, he concludes that the transformation of the Sherpa economy from one of mixed farming, animal husbandry, and trading to one with heavy dependence on tourism has been accomplished. He states that 'the Sherpas had a long tradition of dealing with and profiting from foreigners; tourists and mountaineers are only the latest variety of outsider to do business with' (Fisher 1990: 163).

While Fisher (1990) manages to elide a West-centric understanding of Sherpas, he nonetheless demonstrates a problematic objectification of Sherpa identity. He undertheorizes both Sherpa identity and that of his own[xi] in relation to Sherpas. He argues that while Khumbu Sherpas are being Westernized through markers like language and clothing, Sherpa identity is so positively reinforced by outsiders that it is, in fact, intensifying. Sherpas are coming to value their traditions more than they did before tourism.[xii] He concludes that if a loss of Sherpa identity occurs, it will be amongst the generation of Sherpas growing up in Kathmandu. They will become 'the Nepalese equivalent of the second- and third-generation Sherpas who live in Darjeeling—still ethnically Sherpa but so far removed from the social and religious traditions of their homeland that they have become marginal to them'

SHERPAS IN HIMALAYAN MOUNTAINEERING   83

(Fisher 1990: 176–7). Here we see that Fisher (1990) regards Sherpas as a group in advance of its relations. Fisher is interested in the effects of changes on Sherpas and how outsiders and institutions act on Sherpas. This, I argue, has the effect of fixing Sherpa identity rather than treating it as processual and dynamic.

In contrast, Ortner (1999) is conscious of neither reifying nor objectifying Sherpas. Her attempt is to recover the meaning that mountaineering has for both Sherpas and sahibs, without losing sight of the role of cultural, political, and economic power in constructing and justifying difference and inferiority. Ortner (1999) understands sahibs and Sherpas in mountaineering as an encounter. She examines what each group has brought to and taken from this encounter. In doing so, she situates both groups within the contexts from which they come. For instance, the sahibs in early mountaineering were largely educated upper middle-class Western men; expeditions could be long and personally expensive, which made them unaffordable for working-class men. Climbing Sherpas, also mostly men, came from a position of less privilege within their societies at the time (Ortner 1999).

Not only does she point to differences between Sherpas, she also problematizes the category of Sherpa itself. For instance, Ortner (1999) notes that within Solu Khumbu, class differences between the Sherpas grew after the 1960s, with Khumbu Sherpas hiring Solu Sherpas to work their fields while they themselves went off to pursue lucrative trekking jobs. She also notes, albeit in passing, that a certain competitive divide emerged between the Sherpas from Darjeeling and the ones from Nepal. Within Nepal, Ortner (1999) suggests that the category Sherpa is in flux, in part because the Nepali state has forced it on other Tibetan-derived northern border groups in Nepal and in part because non-Sherpas sometimes try to pass as Sherpas since tourists now want 'Sherpas'.[xiii] Therefore, she reminds us that all ethnic Sherpas are not climbing Sherpas, and also today, not all climbing Sherpas are ethnic Sherpas (Ortner 1999).

Significantly, Ortner (1999) is mindful that Sherpas have a life outside of Everest as well. She states categorically that while it is not inaccurate to define Sherpas in terms of mountaineering, it certainly is incomplete. Of all three authors, she is most able to demonstrate that Sherpa lives in the twentieth century and onwards are just as contradictory and complex as anyone else's.

Identity

However, although Ortner (1999) points to the differentiation within Sherpa identity, she does not take this line of enquiry far enough. She mentions Darjeeling Sherpas but does not incorporate them into her analysis. Sherpas in Nepal and Darjeeling today are living in variegated political contexts. We have to take these political contexts much more seriously if we are to illuminate *the kind of Sherpa it is possible to be* in different times and places.

Indeed, the question of Sherpa identity is a vast one. Sherpas are apprehended in nation-building projects in—and conflicts between—India and Nepal; for instance, Tenzing Norgay accepted Indian citizenship after his ascent of Everest. More recently, how might ethnic consciousness for mountain groups like Sherpas be heightened in Nepal since the *janajati* (Adivasi/ tribal) movement for indigenous rights in the 1990s? Similarly, how might the Gorkhaland agitation in Darjeeling (for separate statehood within the Indian nation) have divided ethnic consciousness more along Nepalese versus Tibetan or Hindu versus Buddhist lines? Sherpa identity, like any ethnicized/racialized identity, is evolving and contextual, and can only be studied adequately by attending to the many variables of place, gender, class, citizenship status, and so on that matter for identity, from Darjeeling to Delhi, from Solu Khumbu to Kathmandu, and beyond.

Mobility

How can we understand Sherpa resistance as both constituted by, and in opposition to, the racialized labour in climbing? What kinds of Sherpa mobility are both enabled *and crucially disabled* by the organization of the sport? The Nepalese state profits from mountaineering but does not institute adequate protections and compensations for the labour that mountaineering requires; the 2014 strike is the most recent example of collective action by Sherpas to get the Nepalese state to act. Meanwhile, the enlisting of a grateful client as a sponsor is an avenue that is available to Sherpas because of the nature of mountaineering; this avenue is also more immediately effective for improving their material status. It would be illuminating to ask: At what points and for what reasons do individualized forms of mobility become more salient versus collectivization for Sherpas and vice-versa?

In fact, we have an inadequate sense of what mobility through mountaineering really means for Sherpas. This is because there is scholarship focused on Sherpas who climb, but there is no simultaneous focus on Sherpas who do not climb or more importantly, on Sherpas who have moved away from climbing. For instance, Sherpas in India have had Scheduled Tribe status since 1950. Future research can compare Indian and Nepalese Sherpas across generations to tease out how mechanisms, from mountaineering to reservations, compare when it comes to lifting families out of poverty. It can also investigate which Sherpa families continue in mountaineering, and which do not, and why. Even when Sherpas go from being porters to members, what remains unattainable and what is this transition predicated on? After the 1953 expedition that made Tenzing Norgay Sherpa and Edmund Hillary the first men in the world to summit Mt Everest, Edmund Hillary and expedition leader John Hunt were knighted, but Tenzing Norgay was not. It appears that even when porters become climbers, the ideal abstract climber of mountaineering continues to be coded white male, and the climber versus porter binary, which makes portering riskier and less rewarding, is still preserved.

Sporting Field

Since Simmel (1971), sociologists have been interested in the dual nature of adventure and in the conditions of its production broadly defined. For Simmel (1971), the most enticing feature of adventure is its ability to synthesize categories of life: activity and passivity, strength and luck, certainty and uncertainty, what we conquer and what is given to us. Adventure is also both part of, and apart from, the rest of our lives; it is 'certainly a part of our existence, directly contiguous with other parts which precede and follow it; at the same time, however, in its deeper meaning, it occurs outside the usual continuity of this life' (Simmel 1971: 188). Wheaton (2010: 1059) describes the meaning of lifestyle sport as lying in its 'creative and self-actualization potential, through which the individual loses him/herself in "transcendence of the self"'. How might we think about the conditions under which adventure, self-actualization, and transcendence are produced and achieved, and how might that vary within the same sporting field depending on one's positionality as porter or member? Caddies and golfers are perhaps the only other example in which labour and sport form a binary capable of being collapsed like porter/member. Given the sharp differences in risk and reward for porters and members, how might we understand the field of Himalayan mountaineering as a sport, and for whom?

86 SPORTS AND SPORTS STUDIES

Building on the writings of Fisher, Adams, and Ortner, these inter-related questions of identity, mobility, and the sporting field are enquiries that can be fruitfully conducted into Sherpas and Himalayan mountaineering. Past scholarship provides important perspectives using which more empirical research can be conducted, to begin to answer some of these questions.

Notes

i. From 1922 to 2017, 288 people have died on Everest, while 4,833 have summitted during the same period, with the first summit of Everest in 1953 by Tenzing Norgay Sherpa and Edmund Hillary (Himalayan Database, cited in Desai 2018).

ii. The Khumbu icefall is a shifting expanse of glacier that extends from 17,600 to 19,500 feet on Everest, and can open with little warning, causing blocks of ice to collapse. A team of Sherpas open Everest season each year in April by figuring out the best way through Khumbu icefall. These 'ice doctors', as they are informally known, fix ropes from base to summit for others to climb the world's highest mountain. While most climbers pass through the icefall just a few times per season, Sherpas might make 15–30 trips, carrying heavy loads and fixing equipment.

iii. In 2017, Everest recorded the highest number of commercial summiteers in its history: 319 paying clients and 329 high-altitude guides who supported them. In 1997, when commercial climbing was still nascent, these figures stood at 54 and 31, respectively (Desai 2018).

iv. This is different from local porters who do low-altitude portering, as well as from expedition members. A Sherpa who is a high-altitude porter on an expedition can be picked for a summit attempt, making him/her a member of the climbing party.

v. Adams identifies 'modern' Sherpas as ranging from tourist industry types to the rimpoche, or head lama, of the Tengboche monastery.

vi. However, this relationship of Sherpas to their religion cannot be exceptionalized as an over-determining one that can fully explain their responses to life (and in this case, death) situations. In fact, as Ortner details in her other books (1978, 1989), Sherpa religion is studiedly non-monochromatic; it is flexible, and comprises the active participation of Sherpas, such as the reshaping of monastic elements of their faith and the embedding of monasteries in the life of communities.

vii. In the early years, the commonly-held sahib idea was that Sherpas were not participating in mountaineering for the money. Ortner (1999) reads this as sahib desire to not see Sherpas as modern, and to deny their own economic power over the Sherpas. She also notes that sahib accounts today take the opposite view; they note with some anguish that Sherpas have become 'too materialistic', climbing only for money.

viii. According to Ortner (1999), it is this zhindak relationship that makes Sherpas obliging but not servile. It characterizes their selflessness as a subordinate loyalty, but one that is nonetheless built on an egalitarian base.

ix. This style and discourse of climbing was one of military assault, with camps set up and stocked like a supply chain up to the final summit assault.

x. According to Fisher (1990: 64), previous changes were 'a piece with the Tibetan cultural cloth from which Sherpa culture had been cut'. But since the 1960s, there has been a fundamental realignment of the ecological, economic, and political pillars of Sherpa society: schools have brought literacy in Nepali and English; hospitals have eliminated thyroid deficiency diseases and reduced fertility through contraception; the Lukla airstrip has accelerated tourism; and the Nepali state has established a panchayat system and a national park (Fisher 1990).

xi. Fisher (1990) is also inattentive to his own positionality vis-à-vis Sherpas. His book is sprinkled with many lay observations which are not seriously substantiated or analysed. These include: the 'forward' nature of Sherpa women compared to their counterparts in the lower hills; the 'cocky' and 'brazen' nature of Sherpa children (he notes that young children in Sherpa society are not raised so much as merely lived with); and the 'mainstreaming' of people with mental disabilities in Sherpa and Nepalese family and community life (Fisher 1990).

xii. For Fisher this 'Sherpaization' counters the momentum of 'Sanskritization' (emulation of higher castes) that has characterized upward mobility in the Indian subcontinent.

xiii. Ortner also discusses the general playing out of identity politics in contemporary climbing by nation, ethnicity, and other markers like age.

References

Adams, V. 1996. *Tigers of the Snow and Other Virtual Sherpas: An Ethnography of Himalayan Encounters*. Princeton, NJ: Princeton University Press.

Carrington, B. 2007. 'Merely Identity: Cultural Identity and the Politics of Sport'. *Sociology of Sport Journal* 24 (1): 49–77.

Desai, S. 2018. 'How Do You Solve a Problem Like Everest?'. *Livemint*. Available at https://www.livemint.com/Leisure/Onl0j5Qdjx7IZDswOjlqjL/How-do-you-solve-a-problem-like-Everest.html; accessed on 5 May 2018.

Fisher, J.F. 1990. *Sherpas: Reflections on Change in Himalayan Nepal*. Berkeley: University of California Press.

Krakauer, J. 2014. 'Death and Anger on Everest'. *The New Yorker*. Available at https://www.newyorker.com/news/news-desk/death-and-anger-on-everest; accessed on 5 May 2018.

88 SPORTS AND SPORTS STUDIES

Narula, S.K. 2014. 'Charting Deaths on Mount Everest'. *The Atlantic*. Available at https://www.theatlantic.com/international/archive/2014/04/mortality-on-mount-everest/360927/; accessed on 5 May 2018.

Ogles, J. 2014. 'Everest Deaths: How Many Sherpas Have Been Killed?'. *Outside*. Available at https://www.outsideonline.com/1922431/everest-deaths-how-many-sherpas-have-been-killed; accessed on 5 May 2018.

Ortner, S.B. 1978. *Sherpas Through Their Rituals*. Cambridge: Cambridge University Press.

———. 1989. *High Religion: A Cultural and Political History of Sherpa Buddhism*. Princeton, NJ: Princeton University Press.

———. 1999. *Life and Death on Mt. Everest: Sherpas and Himalayan Mountaineering*. Princeton, NJ: Princeton University Press.

Preiss, D. 2018. 'One-Third of Everest Deaths Are Sherpa Climbers'. *NPR*. Available at https://www.npr.org/sections/parallels/2018/04/14/599417489/one-third-of-everest-deaths-are-sherpa-climbers; accessed on 5 May 2018.

Simmel, G. 1971. *On Individuality and Social Forms: Selected Writing*. Chicago: University of Chicago Press.

Wheaton, B. 2010. 'Introducing the Consumption and Representation of Lifestyle Sports'. *Sport in Society* 13 (7): 1057–81

6

Women's Cricket in India

Expanding the Inclusionary Possibilities of Sport[1]

Raadhika Gupta

Cricket occupies a powerful social and political space in India. While men's cricket has almost entirely dominated the cricketing space, the past few years have witnessed women's cricket gradually carving out its share in the glory, attention, and recognition that the sport receives in India. As a sex-segregated group sport of vast national importance, cricket offers an interesting site to observe how women's participation can influence gender dynamics in highly gendered spaces as well as the implications of such influence on gender equality in general.

This chapter examines cricket as a case study on how women have been able to progressively make a mark in a sport that has largely remained a male territory. Once reserved for the colonial rulers and the affluent, cricket developed as an inclusionary space for men from all classes. Today, men's cricket has become the established form of cricket, with women's cricket occupying an outsider status. However, there have been shifts towards women's inclusion within the sport. The chapter will analyse the factors leading to such inclusion and examine the implications of such changing gender dynamics within cricket for gender equality in the wider field of sports and society in general. An understanding of the influencing factors in cricket can help understand the inclusionary and exclusionary practices involved in other sports, especially sex-segregated sports that are largely male-dominated.

India is considered a cricket-crazy nation. Cricket is a site of national, social, and political importance. Cricket had the largest share of viewership in India in 2017 (Sharma 2018). India sees a match victory as national triumph, and players as national heroes. The sport is used to influence political

---

Raadhika Gupta, *Women's Cricket in India* In: *Sports Studies in India*. Edited by: Meena Gopal and
Padma Prakash, Oxford University Press. © Oxford University Press 2021.
DOI: 10.1093/oso/9780190130640.003.0007

relations. Cricket also brings the nation together, constructing a feeling of 'unity in diversity'. Cricket is even described as the common religion of Indians. However, this status and glory is largely limited to men's cricket, although women's cricket has been gaining popularity with women participating in increasing numbers.

The British brought cricket to India during the colonial era but excluded the locals from participation. Men's cricket developed in a top-down fashion through a process of elite imitation, where each excluded group aspired towards a higher social status by entering a hitherto elite reserve. Today, men's cricket became so widespread among the Indian masses that the sport is said to have become 'indigenized and decolonized' (Appadurai 2015: 2).

Women's organized cricket in India started much later. An Australian teacher is credited for introducing cricket at a school in Kerala in 1913. It is believed that women's cricket was gaining popularity in Delhi in the 1950s, and some women's cricket clubs started developing in the 1960s in some cities (Oborne 2014: 422). Women's cricket officially began at the national level with the establishment of the Women's Cricket Association of India (WCAI) in 1973, recognized by the Indian government in 1978, more than 200 years after cricket entered India as a man's sport, and almost half a century after the formal organization of men's cricket at the national level. This led to inter-state tournaments, where an increasing number of states participated, and eventually to many other tournaments (Kulkarni 2000). International women's cricket was played for the first time in India in 1975 and has grown since then (Duncan 2013).

Women's cricket has undergone various transitions, which may be attributed to a range of factors. While women's cricket has grown over the years, it is men's cricket that continues to represent the cricketing domain, with women's cricket occupying only an outsider space. While many factors have enhanced women's cricket, they have also either contributed to the outsider status of women's cricket, or the outsider status has remained despite the existence of these factors. This chapter examines factors that have enabled women's cricket to carve out its space in the male-dominated cricketing world. The study is based on both desk research and interviews carried out with women cricketers and others associated with women's cricket in India. Interviewees were selected through snowball sampling.

Exclusionary and Inclusionary Processes within Cricket

Cricket evolved as a global sport through a process of exclusion and inclusion, and developed in a manner that reinforced masculine virtues, limiting women's participation.

Othering and Emulation in Cricket

The history of men's cricket demonstrates a continuous process of 'othering' of excluded groups, challenges to such exclusion, and an eventual inclusion. The British brought cricket to India during the colonial era, excluding Indians from participation. The moral superiority associated with cricket allowed the elite group to maintain dominance over the sport and exclude others from participation. But it also emerged as a space where upward mobility was sought and power norms were challenged and redefined. Initially played exclusively by the Europeans, men's cricket first reached the affluent and elite Indians, then the urban population, and is now widespread among the masses (Appadurai 2015: 2).

Philosopher Iris Young's analysis of the faces of oppression provides a useful lens to understand these power struggles, and how excluded groups face marginalization, cultural imperialism, and powerlessness. Young describes marginalization as a situation where one group is 'expelled from useful participation' (Young 2004: 50), facing 'uselessness, boredom, and lack of self-respect' (Young 2004: 51). Excluded groups in cricket were denied participation, being rendered useless and not worthy of cricket. They also faced cultural imperialism, which involves universalizing and normalizing the experience of the dominant group, and rendering perspectives of a particular group invisible, while at the same time stereotyping and marking it out as the 'other' (Young 2004: 54). The oppressed group has little opportunity to allow its experience to influence the dominant culture, while the dominant culture imposes its experience and interpretation on the oppressed group (Young 2004: 56). In cricket, the excluded groups were rendered invisible in participation and, at the same time, marked out as lazy, uncivilized and not worthy of playing cricket. Lastly, as per the frame of 'powerlessness', the powerless have power exercised over them, and they themselves lack authority or decision-making powers. As cricket emerged, the dominant group held power over the meanings and resources related to cricket, excluding other groups from sharing such power.

92   SPORTS AND SPORTS STUDIES

Even while various classes experienced such exclusion within cricket, the sport also provided space to challenge such exclusion. In India, men's cricket has now become a site of expression of nationalism and solidarity.[2] The diversity in the team has played a unifying role for Indians, for example, by representing communal solidarity (Majumdar and Bandopadhyay 2004: 1453). Indian men's cricket today strongly influences the dynamics within world cricket. For example, the Board of Control for Cricket in India (BCCI) pioneered the Indian Premier League (IPL)[3] based on the fast-paced Twenty20 (T20)[4] format of cricket, which gained quick and widespread popularity in international cricket (Majumdar 2011: 173–9). India is considered as 'the new cricketing superpower' (Majumdar 2011: 173), and the BCCI has even been accused of wielding excessive power and dominance (Jones 2013). Thus, Indians are no longer powerless or marginalized in cricket, and have gradually occupied a dominant position where they are part of decision-making and have control over key resources. In fact, cricket has got so indigenized that sociologist Ashish Nandy famously said that cricket is an 'Indian game accidentally invented by the English' (Veera 2016).

It can be said that women are the excluded group within cricket today. Sociologist Philippa Velija uses the established outsider framework to analyse the relationship between men's and women's cricket. According to Velija (2015: 17), the way cricket developed in various countries, an established-outsider figuration emerged. Men could monopolize the key power resources and set men's cricket as the established form of cricket, while women's game occupied the outsider position. The position of women's cricket as an outsider also embodies the characteristics of Young's faces of oppression. Women's cricket holds a marginalized position with lesser opportunities for participation and recognition; women's game does not receive much coverage and is rendered invisible, while also being marked out as 'other' or an outsider and not a 'real' form of cricket; and women hold little, if any, power over key decisions within the sport.

Masculinity

An important aspect that limits women's access to cricket is the linkage between cricket and the notion of masculinity, both in terms of the values associated with cricket and the way the sport came to be organized.

Across various nations, cricket was diffused as a male sport reflecting a type of English masculinity and became established as a male sport (Velija

2015: 86). The code of conduct associated with cricket governed masculine sportsmanship, which included fair play, team loyalty, and suppression of strong sentiments on the field (Appadurai 2015: 3). Cricket was seen as a 'gentleman's game', played by the respectable nobility. Despite there being no explicit ban on women playing cricket, and despite the rules of the game being same for both sexes, except for a minor difference in the ball dimension to suit women's smaller hand size[5] and a difference in the boundary dimensions,[6] strong notions of cricket as a masculine sport and the social norms for femininity ensured that it continued to develop as a male reserve (Velija 2015: 48).

While attributes associated with cricket have changed over time, it still represents masculinity—it has evolved from 'gentlemanly' to a more aggressive masculinity. As cricket got tied up with national identity, it became an aggressive, passionate, and commercialized sport where victory became more important than civility (Appadurai 2015: 17). The game evolved from a sport featuring five-day long Test matches[7] with no guaranteed result to limited-overs matches where a decision was expected (Ismail 1997: 35), featuring greater aggression, adrenalin, and competitiveness (Ismail 1997: 36). For example, Virat Kohli, a record-breaking cricketer and the captain of Indian men's cricket team, is known, and even commended, for his aggression (Dey 2017; Kumar 2017). Further, the BCCI developed the IPL league to commercialize the game, raising and cashing in on its entertainment value. The IPL involves fast-paced matches, high on entertainment, involving suspense until the end, riding on the passion and emotions of the crowd waiting for their team to win. Even the selection of players takes place through auctions, called as the 'death knell' of the gentleman's game by a politician (Majumdar 2011: 174). There have been changes in perception within women's cricket as well. The US player Anahita Arora mentions that while women cricketers have been traditionally expected to fit 'gentlemanly' behaviour, these perceptions are now loosening (Arora 2018). But notably, while the meanings of manliness may have changed, the sport is still largely characterized as masculine.

The association of sports with masculinity plays an important role in women's exclusion. Sports in general play a key role in creating and maintaining conceptions of hegemonic masculinity, which represents the ideal masculinity that all men must strive towards (Brake 2000: 92–107; Glass 2008: 2). An important aspect of hegemonic masculinity is defining masculinity as 'not feminine' (Cohen 2010: 525). The construction of cricket as 'male' also requires establishing the sport as 'not female'. Thus, relating

94   SPORTS AND SPORTS STUDIES

cricket to masculine attributes goes hand in hand with othering of women, allowing men to continue to protect the hegemonic spot.[8]

The exclusion of women was justified on various grounds, for example, using medical discourses to establish that the sport was not suited to women, as was done in New Zealand (Velija 2015: 70) or because of social norms, such as dress codes. For example, in England, women players and umpires were required to adhere to dress codes, such as wearing skirts, which ensured that they maintained their femininity even as they played this masculine sport. (Velija 2015: 105). Historically, the support towards women's game was only to the extent of letting it develop in an outsider position, without threatening the position of the men's game (Velija 2015: 48).

Stretching the Boundaries: Limits to Inclusionary Processes

It is widely acknowledged that women's cricket in India has significantly developed over the years. Like inclusion within men's cricket, there is scope for women's cricket to stretch the existing boundaries and expand the inclusionary spaces within cricket. In this section, I examine some factors that influenced women's participation in cricket in India and the world, and how the inclusionary and exclusionary forces have played out. The intention is to present these factors from the point of view of women in the sport, without necessarily making a judgement on the soundness of the practices or policies involved.

Early Training and Grassroots Facilities

Availability of and accessibility to good training and other grassroots facilities is crucial for any sportsperson's career. Most women in India and abroad began their cricketing journeys playing with boys. According to Velija, while this may have been a form of support for some women, it may make others feel excluded. Male dominance in the sport can create ideological beliefs about the capabilities of boys and girls. It may make females perceive themselves as outsiders and internalize the belief that cricket is a male sport. It also allows men to control women's access to the sport (Velija 2015: 122–3). However, for many women, this was a natural way to start playing. Many women cricketers in India started playing at home or streets with family,

WOMEN'S CRICKET IN INDIA 95

neighbours or friends (for example, Arora 2018; Bhaskar 2018; Kohli 2018; Nagarajan 2018; Vijaikumar 2018). Even training academies were common for boys and girls, being mostly boys' camps with a few girls (Vijaikumar 2018). According to former Tamil Nadu player Vyshali Vijaikumar (2018), playing with boys was not necessarily a disadvantage. It challenged girls to match up to the boys' level.

Women cricketers have expressed the need for grassroot-level reform (Upendran 2013). Although there have been improvements, girls find it difficult to find coaches or training academies and opportunities to play cricket at school level.

However, the facilities and opportunities for girls at local levels has improved over the years. For example, earlier there was more resistance towards the intake of girls into coaching centres and academies because of the assumption that girls could not handle playing with boys (Bhaskar 2018), but there is more acceptance today for girls (Vijakumar 2018). The facilities available to girls have also greatly improved (Nagarajan 2018).

However, women still get less hours of practice and access to facilities than men (Vijaikumar 2018). It is not always easy for girls to figure out how to start a cricketing career. Girls face difficulty in finding the right academy having the facilities they need (Yadav 2018). The number of playing years and the extent of exposure to cricket makes a huge difference to how a person develops as a cricketer later in life (Arora 2018). Vijaikumar (2018) notes that while international cricket is important, it is even more critical to develop grassroots cricket. Grassroots facilities can determine both the quantity and quality of women players, and impact the overarching position of women's cricket compared to men's cricket.

Number of Matches

Women cricketers have consistently said that greater number of matches is key to further development of women's cricket (for example, Vijaikumar 2018; Yadav 2018). Mere practice and training are not enough. Unless the players come together as a team and play competitively, they will not be prepared enough to win tournaments (Vijaikumar 2018).

However, women play much fewer matches than men, across all formats and age groups (Anupriya 2014a, 2015). Frequent inter-school matches and club-level tournaments for girls, usually organized for boys, will allow talent in women's cricket to develop (Anupriya 2014a). There is a dearth of domestic cricket opportunities for women in India, with almost no local leagues. The US player Shebani Bhaskar (2018) explains how local leagues can be significant by contrasting the Indian scenario with that of Sydney. Sydney organizes a local city league, which has eight teams and around three grades. This allows a hundred players to play just in a local league, providing immense exposure in terms of the number of matches and engagement with other players. However, even at an international level, opportunities for women are limited. For example, only eight women's teams compete in One-Day Internationals (ODIs)[9] and ten in T20, compared to twelve to fourteen for men. This limits opportunities for teams from nations where women's cricket, or cricket in general, is not highly developed, and disadvantages women players from those nations even further. In fact, according to Bhaskar (2018), disparity among teams in terms of skills and performance level is not as high in women's cricket as it is in men's cricket, which will make it easier to have a greater number of nations participating in a global league for women.

Women players have also complained about limited opportunities to play Test cricket. Interestingly, due to lack of time and facilities, the ODI format became more accepted in women's cricket, as opposed to men's cricket where the Test format used to dominate. Because of this, the first World Cup for women was played in 1973, later copied in men's cricket, which had its first World Cup in 1975 (Velija 2015: 97). However, Test cricket is still considered 'the premier form of cricket', for which Indian women cricketers get limited opportunities (Anupriya 2014a). According to Karnataka player Akanksha Kohli (2018), Test matches are important for a player to develop cricketing skills and stay in the sport for a long period of time. However, there is a perception that five days may be too much for women to handle, and matches may last only three or four days. Right now, there are only T20 and 50-over matches in domestic cricket for women.

There are limited opportunities for Indian women to play even T20 matches. Many players desire to see an IPL in India (Bhaskar 2018; Kohli 2018; Nagarajan 2018; Vijaikumar 2018). Some countries are already running similar leagues, like the Big Bash League in Australia and Kia Super League in England. An IPL for women will provide domestic cricketers a platform to showcase their talent and can boost women's cricket (Kohli 2018). While women's IPL has been in the pipeline for a while, it has not materialized yet due to, as the BCCI claims, insufficient funds. However, in a move towards this direction, the BCCI launched the Women's T20 Challenge, starting with one exhibition match in 2018 that was played before the men's IPL qualifiers, followed in 2019 by the first multi-team women's T20 challenge, with three teams playing four matches over six days (Acharya 2019).

The lack of opportunities to play matches strengthens the perception of women's cricket as an outsider form of cricket, good enough to be played in non-competitive atmospheres but not professionally. It is argued that the BCCI has missed opportunities to launch tournaments. For example, immediately after the 2017 World Cup, where Indian women's team ended as runners-up, the BCCI could have launched the IPL (Bhaskar 2018) or organized a tour (Kohli 2018), allowing women's cricket to ride the wave that was generated post the World Cup. However, no such steps were taken, and the game lost that momentum (Bhaskar 2018). Such reluctance and resistance towards increasing playing opportunities for women is a further indication of the outsider position of women's cricket.

Performance

Indian women's cricket team has been performing well since the early days. Indians have consistently won the Asia Cup—both ODIs and T20s—since 2004, when it first started (except the T20 Asia Cup in 2018, which was won by Bangladesh). Indian players have held numerous international records, including having the highest score in a Test match;[10] highest runs in ODI cricket;[11] best bowling figures in a Test match innings;[12] most wickets in ODI cricket;[13] and most catches by a fielder.[14]

While top performances have attracted more players and spectators to women's cricket, they have not been enough for the game to get its due recognition. In contrast, men's cricket interestingly became popular in India despite the lack of remarkable performances. At the time of Independence, both hockey and cricket were popular in India. But hockey was popular mainly because of India's international performances, and its popularity declined with dwindling performances. On the other hand, men's cricket gained popularity, even when the team was not very successful, largely due to the process of imitation that caused the followers to shadow the leaders (Joseph 2004: 122). However, for women's cricket, the exclusionary processes played out in a manner that denied them due recognition as well as financial and other resources, despite spectacular performances. This phenomenon has also been seen in other countries, such as Australia, where despite cricketing success, the women's governing body was not able to sustain itself financially and merged with the men's board in 2001 (Velija 2015: 107–8).

That said, it would be wrong to deny the role performance played in giving momentum to the sport. According to former cricketer Shantha Rangaswamy, great performances during the pioneering days in the 1970s enabled women's cricket to survive until later, unlike many other women's sports that were starting up at that time but could not last (Pradhan 2017). Indian women's team performance in the 2017 World Cup undoubtedly led to much greater recognition and popularity of the sport in India (Nagarajan 2018; Yadav 2018). According to Kohli (2018), the platform where a good performance was delivered also matters. For example, beating Australia in the 2017 World Cup semi-finals gave Indian women's cricket wide popularity and acknowledgement on social media. Recognition at the international level also boosted domestic cricket. There was a different feeling altogether post the World Cup even at the domestic level; it was more competitive and seemed to have moved a level up. But this momentum can be sustained only if the team continues throwing in good performances.

Organizational Structure and Support

Cricket for men and women was initially governed separately. Internationally, since its formation in 1909, the International Cricket Council (ICC) has been responsible for governing men's cricket. The International Women's Cricket Council (IWCC) was formed in 1958. There is little evidence of interaction between the two bodies. The IWCC was not able to develop as a strong governing body and struggled financially. Tours and tournaments were sporadic and not well scheduled (Velija 2015: 93–100). In 2005, the IWCC merged with the ICC (Asian News International 2016) to enable the women's game to survive financially. Women's cricket picked up pace after the merger, and the game spread to more countries. This merger set the trend for the governance of women's cricket across nations, with the ICC mandating all nations to have a single governing body. The boards had already merged in England in 1998 and in Australia in 2001, and other countries followed suit (Velija 2015: 102–3).

Merging of governing bodies has had both pros and cons. While mergers give access to better financial resources, facilities, and coaching, women tend to lose out on the administrative autonomy they had earlier (Velija 2015: 106). The mergers in England and Australia, which took place before the ICC–IWCC merger, were primarily triggered by resource constraints. Many women had concerns, such as whether the merger would benefit elite-level cricket at the expense of grassroots cricket and whether there would be a loss of identity for the women's game and loss of autonomy for the women. In both countries, men's boards seemed silent about the mergers and seemed to be 'bailing' women out (Velija 2015: 106–8). Overall, while mergers gave women access to physical resources, the organizational change did not result in a change in the attitude. A systematic approach towards gender equality within these organizations is still missing (Velija 2015: 129).

In India, the BCCI and the WCAI came together in 2006 (Engineer 2012), albeit with some apparent reluctance on the BCCI's part (Kotian 2005). The merger is credited to have contributed greatly to the growth of women's cricket (Bhaskar 2018; Kohli 2018). Earlier, while the level of cricket was high, the grounds, facilities, and compensation were not as good. Players often had to pay out of their pockets to travel and play in tournaments. But the BCCI had the money and television (TV) rights, which greatly helps the sport (Bhaskar 2018). Infrastructure and facilities, even at local levels, have improved (Vijaikumar 2018). The pay has also improved (Nagarajan 2018). There have been other developments, such as starting of under-twenty-three category for women, and conversion of zonal matches from fifty-over games to three-day games (Kohli 2018).

However, it is alleged that the BCCI's support has been half-hearted and has not led to the level of progress that could have been achieved, especially considering its affluence and influence. In the early years after the ICC–IWCC merger, many boards scheduled more tours for women (Anupriya 2014b). But for India, there were fewer international matches, especially Test matches, and domestic tournaments. In fact, women's playing schedule shrunk so much that cricketer Mithali Raj famously said, 'We attend more camps than play matches' (Patnaik 2014). Further, despite the merger, many cricket academies remain exclusive to men (Velija 2015: 63). There is also a wide disparity in terms of salaries, perks, and match fee (Kohli 2018). Vijaikumar (2018) further pointed out that merely merging is not enough; it is also important for the managing team to be gender-sensitized and unbiased in order to achieve equality.

The established outsider relationship remains within the merged body, and women's cricket continues to face 'othering'. Men as the established group continue to control financial aspects and opportunities. Even in England and Australia, mergers increased involvement of men in the women's game, without an equal partnership emerging. Ultimately, women's cricket had to fit in with the men's game (Velija 2015: 142). These mergers presented men with the opportunity to develop women's cricket in line with the established group, whether intentionally or not, even if this were at odds with the desires and needs of the outsider group (Velija 2015: 142–3). However, despite the differences, the merger increased organizational interdependency between women's and men's cricket, which itself becomes a power resource for women

100 SPORTS AND SPORTS STUDIES

'as women's cricket cannot be ignored by those who organise and run the game' (Velija 2015: 63).

Pay Structure

Financial support has been a major hurdle for women cricketers and associations globally. Historically, elite-level women players played international matches voluntarily, paying for their own travel and expenses. There have been wide differences in the remuneration structure and amount, match fee, benefits, and prize money for women and men, both in India and abroad. The mergers with the ICC and national associations brought more funding to women's cricket, but huge disparities remain, limiting participation and growth opportunities for women (Anupriya 2014a).

Many women cricketers in India have expressed the need for better pay structures, including contractual payments. When male players are on tour, they get a retainer or base fee under a contract, match fee per match, and daily allowance per day of the tour. But in the absence of a contract, when women players, for example, represent their state, they get only the match fee and daily fee, but not a base fee. There is also disparity in the amount of match fee and daily allowance. Moreover, men usually get to play more matches, and are able to draw more money just through match fees and daily allowances. These arrangements put professional women at a disadvantage in terms of their earning potential from cricket (Bhaskar 2018).

In India, the BCCI introduced central contracts for men in 2001 (Basu 2015). For women, India introduced central contracts for the first time during the 2015–16 season, becoming the last cricket board to do so. These contracts covered eleven players across two categories. The BCCI took this step again recently in March 2018, covering nineteen players across three categories. There has also been a significant increase in the amount (Swaminathan 2018).[15] However, women continue to earn relatively much less than men. For example, even at Grade A, a category that includes the likes of Mithali Raj and Harmanpreet Kaur, a female player will get a base fee only half of what a Grade C male player gets.[16] At the domestic level, male domestic reserve players would be paid more than a playing member of a domestic women's team (Swaminathan 2018).[17]

The re-introduction of contracts for women is no doubt significant, but domestic cricket cannot be left ignored. Lack of funds is a primary reason why girls drop out of cricket in India, failing to meet even their basic needs of a cricket kit and bowling shoes (Anupriya 2014a). In contrast, most boys who play for the state at junior level get sponsorships for equipment. If the player plays at the level of Ranji Trophy,[18] these commercial contracts sometimes provide income as well (Upendran 2013). But women do not get contracts even at the state level (Nagarajan 2018), making it hard to sustain. For example, a cricketer with no other job may have to undergo a year-long training without pay, just to play in some five matches where she gets some match fee (Kohli 2018).

Due to the lack of financial support, many female players need to be otherwise employed. Most cricketers who make it to the Indian team are employed by the Indian Railways. According to cricketer Niranjana Nagarajan (2018), a Railways player, the management gives the players time off to play, while also being a source of income, which was especially vital in times when women were hardly getting paid for playing. In fact, India is the first country to employ professional female players in companies like the Indian Railways that have their own cricket clubs (Duncan 2013). But it is not easy to find a job (Kohli 2018). It also leaves players limited time to practice. For example, there have been times where some senior players have not got enough leave to attend their state camps (Bhaskar 2018).

There is also a vast difference in the prize money. According to a 2017 study, in the World Cup, men drew prize money that was almost seven times that for women.[19] And even this is a significant change since 2014, when prize money for men was fifty-three times that for women (*BBC Sport* 2017).[20]

A common argument in favour of maintaining such financial differences is the low capacity of women's cricket to generate revenue (Anupriya 2014b). However, to the extent that greater support can lead to an increased interest in the sport, this seems to be a self-fulfilling prophecy. For example, the telecast of women's World Cup in 2017 made a huge difference to the fan-following for women's cricket, thus impacting the revenue-generation ability of the sport.

Media

Media coverage for women's sports in general has traditionally been poor in India and abroad. For example, a 2013 study concluded that women's sport in the UK accounted for only 7 per cent of total sports coverage.[21] Another study in 2017 on Indian newspapers' coverage of the 2014 Incheon Asian Games concluded that the accomplishments of women players did not merit coverage on the front pages of magazines. But this trend has been slowly changing, with one study on the 2016 Rio Olympics reporting that female athletes received significantly higher coverage than their male counterparts in the leading newspapers of Bengal (Chakraborty and Sil 2016: 11–13).

102   SPORTS AND SPORTS STUDIES

There is no doubt that media plays an important role in developing the popularity of a sport and changing perceptions about it. Media had earlier played a crucial role in indigenization of men's cricket in India and in taking the sport to the masses through radio commentaries, first in English and later in regional languages (Appadurai 2015: 10–11). Later, television intensified the national passion for cricket and turned cricketers into national heroes (Appadurai 2015: 11–12). Other forms of media, including books, newspapers, and magazines, also gave a wide coverage to men's cricket, adding to its popularity and recognition (Appadurai 2015: 12). In general, men's cricket has dominated Indian sports media coverage (Akoijam 2012).

Media has played an important role in the growth of women's cricket as well, although the support has been much less extensive. 'To get women playing, it is important to show that women are playing' (Bhaskar 2018). This shift had happened in other sports, such as lawn tennis, and is now visible in cricket as well (Bhaskar 2018). There has been an increase in the telecast of women's matches (Vijaikumar 2018), which is an important factor in changing people's mindsets. For example, when Vishal Yadav, founder of an online platform on women's cricket, started working in this field in 2016, there was greater resistance from parents towards girls joining the sport. But seeing women play in the 2017 World Cup on television changed their perspective. While cricket was earlier largely considered a game one pursues out of passion, now it is being seen as a career option as well (Yadav 2018). When Yadav started his online platform, he realized that a fan base already existed, keen to know more about women's cricket. Thus, the role of media goes both ways: While media increases fan base, the fans also need media to get access to the sport (Yadav 2018).

Despite these developments, coverage of men's cricket continues to be much higher (Banerjee and Kakade 2016). Media coverage of the 2013 Women's Cricket World Cup held in India was criticized as 'barely befitting of the name' (Shemilt 2017). There was non-existent publicity and the scheduled matches were cancelled at the last moment to make way for men's matches (Shemilt 2017). More recently, the South Africa–India women's series held in February 2018 instantiates the same. Being held as part of the ICC Women's Championship, the series gave an opportunity to directly qualify for the Women's Cricket World Cup. It, however, coincided with the men's India–South Africa bilateral series. While men's matches received extensive coverage, women's matches were not broadcast. Only women's T20 matches received telecasting, but that was likely because they took place on the same day as men's game with the recording instruments and other setup already in

WOMEN'S CRICKET IN INDIA   103

place (Bhaskar 2018). Various critics claimed that the non-airing of this tournament has been a missed opportunity to consolidate women's fan-following by continuing the momentum gained in viewership on the account of the women's 2017 World Cup (*The News Minute* 2018; *Scroll* 2018).

This incident demonstrates how the events of the established group were prioritized. In fact, many women's matches in the recent past have been conducted at odd times (around 9 a.m.) as compared to prime-time men's cricket matches (*Indian Express* 2018). Subsequently, the March 2018 Australian women's tour of India was covered on television (*FirstCricket* 2018), but England's tour of India in April 2018 was again not telecast. The Indian team emerged as winners in the latter (Press Trust of India 2018), and the absence of television coverage hurt the chances to gain traction (Karhadkar 2018). However, the BCCI live-telecast the match on its website, and other websites like *Scroll* and *Cricbuzz* posted regular updates. Social media has played an important role in the growth of women's cricket (Hariharan 2017), though social media updates do not substitute the experience or impact of viewing the matches on live screens. The May 2018 T20 Challenge exhibition match, which took place before the men's IPL qualifiers, was telecast live. But it started at 2 p.m., contributing towards half the stadium being empty (Acharya 2019). Notably, for the 2019 T20 Challenge, three of the four matches were scheduled for nights, which is rare for Indian women's cricket (Ghosh 2019). The tournament had a more robust coverage than usual, with live telecasting, live streaming on the popular streaming platform Hotstar, and live and regular media updates (*Hindustan Times* 2019).

One of the reasons posited for the poor coverage of women's cricket is the lack of interested advertisers (Bhushan and Verma 2016), who do not find women's cricket a lucrative investment. The present trend, therefore, puts pressure on the teams to perform well to garner attention from governments, media, and viewers. Considering that media plays a huge role in developing spectatorship, this is a circular argument. Indian Captain Mithali Raj pointed out that the lack of audience in stadiums can be attributed to the scanty media coverage (Press Trust of India 2017). Further, as described earlier, the Indian team has been performing well internationally for a long time. In addition, despite the poor coverage of the 2013 World Cup, its viewership broke world records and reached 23.7 million viewers (Press Trust of India 2013). This was further surpassed by the 2017 World Cup, which was watched by 156 million people in India alone (ICC 2017; Tirkey 2017). This shows that the interest in women's cricket in India has been increasing, and there is scope for its development in this cricket-crazy nation. In fact, according to

104   SPORTS AND SPORTS STUDIES

Bhaskar (2018), men's cricket seems to have reached saturation in terms of the number of people to reach within the country, and women's cricket can become the next big thing. But unbalanced coverage inhibits women from reaching their full potential, cements the belief that cricket is not a promising career for women, and discourages talented women from taking up this sport, further contributing to the outsider status of the sport.

The Equalizing Potential of Cricket

The analysis in this chapter shows that while various inclusionary processes are supporting the development of women's cricket, it still occupies a marginalized and outsider position. While these forces work towards creating gender equality within cricket, the relationship of cricket to the broader social structure also deserves attention. Broader societal development related to gender equality influences changes within cricket, while at the same time, cricket holds an equalizing potential in society. For example, England's Women's Cricket Association (EWCA) was formed in 1926, around the same time when governing bodies of other women's sports, such as netball and lacrosse, were developing (Velija 2015: 38). Globalization and greater recognition of women's rights had an impact on the growth of women's cricket (Velija 2015: 88). The general trends towards equalization in the broader society and in sports influenced the mergers in the ICC, England, and Australia (Velija 2015: 117). These mergers were also influenced by moral arguments in support of women cricketers (Velija 2015: 118).

General trends towards gender equality has led to increasing pressure on the BCCI to justify gender-biased practices, thus influencing the growth of the sport in India. For example, mergers in other countries put pressure on India to follow suit. According to Arora (2018), society has a lot to do with how a sport evolves. People today are more conscious of the gender divide. Women are also more educated, financially independent, and empowered. The awareness created through other means, such as popular Bollywood movies on women sportspersons in masculine-perceived sports like boxing or wrestling, also have a wider effect leading to changed perceptions about women in sports in general.

Simultaneously, the growth of women's cricket has influenced the participation of women in cricket and other sports. Men's cricket has taken on a persona as something more than sports, symbolizing national pride and unity and influencing politics, entertainment, and business. Development of

WOMEN'S CRICKET IN INDIA   105

women's cricket can also have spill-over effects for gender equality in society at large. Kohli (2018) points out that national-level women cricketers are now acquiring celebrity status like their male counterparts, which can also bridge the gap between men and women. Arora (2018) explains how the more people see women as role models, especially in non-traditional domains, the more it encourages women to participate, and men to respect them as equals. Giving her own example, she said that around twenty years ago, most boys would dismiss her until she bowled to them and got a chance to showcase her talent. Even then, a woman playing well would either shock the boys or hurt their egos. But greater participation of women in cricket leads to greater acceptance of girls in the sport, making it easier for girls to play and contribute towards gender equality.

Another area where such change is visible is in the parental support for girls. Parents are now more open to allowing girls to take up the sport and can view this as a career option (Bhaskar 2018), making it easier for girls to take up the sport (Kohli 2018). The 2017 World Cup particularly attracted girls to the sport and gave their parents confidence that there is scope for girls to succeed in cricket (Nagarajan 2018; Yadav 2018). Parental support is crucial for girls because often their major decisions are dependent on the family's approval, much more than is in the case for boys (Yadav 2018). There is also greater acceptance of female students among coaches and academies (Bhaskar 2018).

Growth of women's cricket also opened other career options for women, such as coaching, sports psychology, video analysis, sports nutrition, and media. Although the awareness of these options is limited in India (Bhaskar 2018), many have become umpires, coaches, mentors, physiotherapists, and commentators (Nagarajan 2018; Vijaikumar 2018). Former women cricketers are now pursuing commentating, refereeing, and other related careers (Kohli 2018), thus lending further comfort to aspiring players in viewing cricket as a viable career option.

There are other ways as well in which cricket is helping bridge the gender gap. For example, Yadav uses women's cricket as a means to generate awareness and sensitize people around issues related to gender, such as girls' education and physical fitness. In Africa, tournaments are conducted to spread awareness about female genital mutilation and girls' education (Yadav 2018). In Australia, the McGrath Foundation organizes Pink Stumps Day, on which cricket clubs, schools, companies, and others are encouraged to play cricket using pink cricket gear, raising awareness and generating funds for breast cancer care.[22]

106 SPORTS AND SPORTS STUDIES

In fact, the wider relationship between women and sport has undergone a transformation in India. Women in India are now more empowered in terms of sports in general. According to Bhaskar (2018), an increasing number of women are now participating in sports, even if for recreation. For example, more women are running in events such as marathons, half-marathons, and 10K races, joining running groups, going to gyms, playing football with men recreationally, and so on. While all of this cannot be attributed to the growth of women's cricket, or considered to be influencing women's cricket, there has been a discernible change in the relationship of women to sports in general (Bhaskar 2018), including cricket.

***

This chapter has discussed that while men's cricket has clearly set itself as the established form of the sport, women's cricket occupies an outsider position. However, women's cricket has gradually been carving out its own space in cricket. It would be useful to refer to Velija's (2015: 109) observations on moving towards equality between the established and outsider groups:

> Outsider groups are more likely to be successful in challenging power if they are able to organise themselves and disrupt wider chains of interdependence, and over time, denser chains of interdependency create more reciprocal dependency . . . processes of equalization do not result in equality, and inequalities still exist, but crucially reciprocal dependency enables the outsider group to have a power resource which may enable power imbalances to become more equalized.

She further states that greater interdependence leads to greater mutual identification and new expectations around conduct and behaviour from the two groups. The outsider group may keep requesting greater involvement, and while the established group may ignore many of these requests, it will at least have to consider the needs of the outsider group. Moral arguments are also used as a further source of power for women in cricket (Velija 2015: 114–15). The growth of women's cricket in India and the world reflects these trends. With the mergers of the governing bodies, the space for interdependency has increased. The support for and recognition of women's cricket has also been on the rise and an equalizing trend is visible.

WOMEN'S CRICKET IN INDIA   107

While women's cricket has largely been operating within the established group's framework, gradually women's cricket itself has the power to influence such framework. Velija (2015: 35, 42) argues that by not challenging masculinity and male superiority in cricket, and not participating in the organization of the sport, women were able to play cricket without much challenge. She talks about a 'harmonious inequality', which allowed women in England to develop women's cricket on their own initially in a quiet, although invisible and marginalized, way, without challenging the superiority of the established group, and men continued to provide the much-needed resources to women. However, gradually, women's cricket necessitated the mergers of various governing bodies. Other subtle changes are also visible more often, such as use of gender-neutral terms like 'batter' as opposed to 'batsman'. These changes suggest how the outsider groups can not only make a mark within the established frameworks, but also influence such frameworks to move towards more equal relationships.

While equality within sport is critical, it is important to recognize the relationship between sports and wider society. Sports can act as strong equalizing force in society. Cricket has been used in the past to make statements; for example, some countries declined to play against Zimbabwe to respond to human rights abuses within the country (Dabscheck 2005). At the same time, existing social relationships can influence the development of a sport. The development of cricket in India shows both these trends: Cricket was often used to make social, political, or other statements; at the same time various sociological factors influenced the growth of cricket and people's access to cricket in India. We can now witness how women's cricket holds and is exploiting its potential to bring equalizing trends within the broader society. It remains to be seen how much the various equalizing factors within and outside cricket can work to bring women's cricket on par with men's cricket, and how such parity can then influence gender dynamics within the broader Indian society.

Notes

1. I am very grateful to the following persons for candidly sharing their experience with me and contributing greatly to my research: Akanksha Kohli, Karnataka women's cricket player; Anahita Arora, women's cricket player, USA; Niranjana Nagarajan, women's cricket player, India; Shebani Bhaskar, women's cricket player,

108   SPORTS AND SPORTS STUDIES

USA; Vishal Yadav, founder, *Female Cricket*; and Vyshali Vijaikumar, former Tamil Nadu women's cricket player.

I am also grateful to Apoorv Madan, Isha Malik, and Rishabh Bajoria, students at Jindal Global Law School, Sonipat, India, for their support with research and transcription.

2. In another article, I discuss how men's cricket in India shapes Indian nationalism in powerful ways, but the exclusion of women from equal participation and recognition leads to the construction of a gendered nationalism. See Gupta (2013).

3. The IPL is a cricket league in India that began in 2008, where teams representing different cities in India compete. The teams consist of players from both India and abroad.

4. T20 is a format of cricket where each team faces a limited number of maximum twenty six-ball overs. One match may last for up to around three hours.

5. The ball used in women's cricket is slightly lighter than the one used in men's cricket and slightly heavier than the one used in junior cricket. While the ball used in men's cricket weighs not less than 155.9 grams and not more than 163 grams, the ball used in women's cricket ranges from 140 to 151 grams. The difference in the circumference is of only around one centimetre.

6. In women's cricket, the boundary is between 55 to 65 yards from the centre of the pitch, while in men's cricket, the boundary is between 65 to 90 yards from the centre of the pitch.

7. Test cricket is a format of cricket where there are no limitations on the number of balls each team faces. Each team gets the opportunity to bat twice. Generally, one match may last for a maximum of five days.

8. In another article, I examine in further detail the application of masculinities theory to cricket in detail and its impact on exclusion of women from cricket. See Gupta (2013).

9. The ODI is a format of cricket where each team faces a limited number of maximum fifty six-ball overs. One match may last for up to around eight hours.

10. Sandhya Agarwal, with 190 runs, held this record from 1986 to 1987 (Eyre 2001).

11. Mithali Raj holds this record with 6,720 runs and is also the only woman to score 6,000 runs. See http://stats.espncricinfo.com/ci/content/records/284264.html; accessed on 10 October 2020.

12. Neetu David holds this record with her bowling spell of 53 runs for 8 wickets on 24 November 1995. See http://stats.espncricinfo.com/ci/content/records/283972.html; accessed on 10 October 2020.

13. Jhulan Goswami holds this record with 218 wickets and is also the only woman to take 200 wickets. See http://stats.espncricinfo.com/ci/content/records/283976.html; accessed on 10 October 2020.

14. Jhulan Goswami holds this record with 63 catches, sharing this record with Suzannah Bates from New Zealand. See http://stats.espncricinfo.com/ci/content/records/283644.html; accessed on 10 October 2020.

WOMEN'S CRICKET IN INDIA   109

15. INR 50 lakh per year for Category A players as opposed to INR15 lakh earlier.

16. INR 50 lakh per year for Grade A female cricket player versus INR 1 crore per year for Grade C male cricket player; Grade B and Grade C women players get INR 30 lakh and INR 10 lakh, respectively.

17. INR 17,500 for male reserve players compared to INR 12,500 for female players part of the team.

18. Ranji Trophy is a prestigious domestic-level men's cricket tournament in India where teams representing regional and state cricket associations compete.

19. Men got around GBP 3.1 million (INR 27.3 crore) as prize money, and women got only around GBP 470,000 (INR 41.4 lakh).

20. Prize money for men was around GBP 2.5 million (INR 22.1 crores) as compared to around GBP 47,000 (or Rs. 41.4 lakh) for women.

21. See https://www.womeninsport.org/wp-content/uploads/2015/04/Womens-Sport-Say-Yes-to-Success.pdf; accessed on 10 October 2020.

22. See https://www.pinkstumpsday.com.au/about/; accessed on 10 October 2020.

References

Acharya, Shayan. 2019. 'Women's T20 Exhibition Matches to Be Held during IPL Playoffs'. *Sportstar*, 9 April 9. Available at https://sportstar.thehindu.com/cricket/womens-t20-exhibition-matches-to-be-held-during-ipl-playoffs-2019-chennai-bengaluru/article26770829.ece; accessed on 10 October 2020.

Akoijam, Indira. 2012. 'Skewed Sports Coverage in Top Dailies'. *The Hoot*, 23 July. Available at http://www.thehoot.org/research/books/skewed-sports-coverage-in-top-dailies-6110; accessed on 10 October 2020.

Anupriya. 2014a. 'More Money and More Matches Please, BCCI'. *ESPN Cricinfo*, 23 August 23. Available at https://www.espncricinfo.com/story/_/id/21460018/measures-bcci-take-improve-health-women-cricket-india; accessed on 10 October 2020.

———. 2014b. 'Indian Women's Cricket Languishes under the BCCI'. *ESPN Cricinfo*, 13 August. Available at http://www.espncricinfo.com/magazine/content/story/769515.html; accessed on 10 October 2020.

———. 2015. 'Contracts for Indian Women: Better Late than Never'. *ESPN Cricinfo*, 27 May. Available at http://www.espncricinfo.com/magazine/content/story/881199.html; accessed on 10 October 2020.

Appadurai, Arjun. 2015. 'Playing with Modernity: The Decolonization of Indian Cricket'. *Other Modernities* 14: 1–24. Available at https://dialnet.unirioja.es/descarga/articulo/5911056.pdf, accessed on 10 October 2020.

Arora, Anahita. Interview. 14 February 2018.

Asian News International. 2016. 'Charlotte Edwards Terms ICC's Merger with IWCC "Significant"'. *Cricket Country*, 6 June. Available at http://www.cricketcountry.com/news/charlotte-edwards-terms-iccs-merger-with-iwcc-significant-456013; accessed on 11 May 2019.

110 SPORTS AND SPORTS STUDIES

Banerjee, Shourini and Onkargouda Kakade. 2016. 'Coverage of Women's Sports in Two English Dailies of Karnataka: A Comparative Study'. *Amity Journal of Media & Communication Studies* 6 (1). Available at http://amity.edu/UserFiles/asco/journal/ISSUE34_12.%20Shourini.pdf; accessed on 10 October 2020.

Basu, Souromitro. 2015. 'Indian Women's Cricketers Offered Central Contracts by BCCI after Nine Year Wait'. *Sports Keeda*, 6 October. Available at https://www.sportskeeda.com/cricket/indian-womens-cricketers-offered-central-contracts-bcci-after-nine-year-wait; accessed on 10 October 2020.

BBC Sport. 2017. 'Prize Money in Sport—BBC Sport Study', 19 June. Available at https://www.bbc.com/sport/40300519; accessed on 10 October 2020.

Bhaskar, Shebani. Interview. 29 February 2018.

Bhushan, Ratna and Ravi Tej Verma. 2016. 'With Women's ICC World Twenty20 Failing to Get Advertisers, Star India Stalls Marketing Plans'. *Economic Times*, 15 March. Available at https://economictimes.indiatimes.com/industry/services/advertising/with-womens-icc-world-twenty20-failing-to-get-advertisers-star-india-stalls-marketing-plans/articleshow/51402987.cms; accessed on 10 October 2020.

Brake, Deborah. 2000. 'The Struggle for Sex Equality in Sports and the Theory Behind Title IX'. *University of Michigan Journal of Law Reform* 34 (1, 2): 13–149.

Chakraborty, Mitrali and Pintu Sil. 2016. 'Women Empowerment in Sports: An Analysis of the Sports Coverage of Leading Newspapers in Bengal with respect to Rio Olympic'. *International Journal of Physical Education, Sports and Health* 3 (6): 11–13. Available at http://www.kheljournal.com/archives/2016/vol3issue6/PartA/3-5-97-639.pdf; accessed on 10 October 2020.

Cohen, David. 2010. 'Keeping Men "Men" and Women Down: Sex Segregation, Anti-Essentialism, and Masculinity'. *Harvard Journal of Law and Gender* 33: 509–53.

Dabscheck, Braham. 2005. 'Of Human Rights and Contracts: International Cricket and the Problem of Zimbabwe'. *Australian Quarterly* 77 (2): 7–14.

Dey, Prasanjit. 2017. 'Passion, Aggression, Consistency: Virat Kohli's Secret to Success'. *The Quint*, 3 November. Available at https://www.thequint.com/sports/cricket/virat-kohli-road-to-200-odi-india-cricket; accessed on 10 October 2020.

Duncan, Isabelle. 2013. *Skirting the Boundary: A History of Women's Cricket.* London: The Robson Press.

Engineer, Tariq. 2012. ' "Don't Know What I'd Do without Cricket"—Goswami'. *ESPN Cricinfo*, 26 January. Available at http://www.espncricinfo.com/women/content/story/551087.html; accessed on 10 October 2020.

Eyre, Rick. 2001. 'Two World Records for Michelle Goszko'. *ESPN Cricinfo*, 26 June. Available at http://www.espncricinfo.com/ci/content/story/103693.html; accessed on 10 October 2020.

FirstCricket. 2018. 'India Women vs Australia Women: When and Where to Watch ODI Series, Coverage on TV and Live Streaming'. *Firstpost*, 11 March 11. Available at https://www.firstpost.com/firstcricket/sports-news/india-women-vs-australia-women-when-and-where-to-watch-odi-series-coverage-on-tv-and-live-streaming-4385617.html; accessed on 10 October 2020.

Ghosh, Annesha. 2019. 'Women's T20 Challenge a Step towards an IPL for Harmanpreet, Mandhana and Co'. *ESPN Cricinfo*, 5 May. Available at http://www.espncricinfo.com/story/_/id/26677961/women-t20-challenge-step-towards-ipl-harmanpreet-mandhana-co; accessed on 10 October 2020.

Glass, Courtney. 2008. 'Gender, Sport & Nationalism: The Cases of Canada and India'. MA diss., University of South Florida, USA. Available at http://scholarcommons. usf.edu/etd/262/; accessed on 10 October 2020.

Gupta, Raadhika. 2013. 'Bowled Out of the Game: Nationalism and Gender Equality in Indian Cricket'. *Berkeley Journal of Entertainment and Sports Law* 2 (1): 89–120. doi: https://doi.org/10.15779/Z38B934

Hariharan, Shruti. 2017. 'Meet Mamatha Maben, the Unsung Hero of India Women's Cricket'. *Cricket Country*, 4 October. Available at http://www.cricketcountry.com/ articles/meet-mamatha-maben-the-unsung-hero-of-india-womens-cricket-648260; accessed on 10 October 2020.

Hindustan Times. 2019. 'Women's T20 Challenge Live Telecast, Trailblazers vs Velocity: When and Where to Watch, Online Streaming'. 8 May. Available at https://www.hindustantimes.com/cricket/women-s-t20-challenge-live-telecast-trailblazers-vs-velocity-when-and-where-to-watch-online-streaming/story-TI9SeJC2unavy70ePvfK7M.html; accessed on 10 October 2020.

Indian Express. 2018. 'India Women vs England Women T20: England Beat India by Seven Wickets', 25 March. Available at http://indianexpress.com/article/sports/ cricket/india-women-vs-england-women-live-score-live-cricket-streaming-online-5110552/?#liveblogstart; accessed on 10 October 2020.

International Cricket Council [ICC]. 2017. 'Record-Breaking Global Reach of Women's World Cup', 10 August. Available at https://www.icc-cricket.com/media-releases/447432; accessed on 10 October 2020.

Ismail, Qadri. 1997. 'Batting against the Break: On Cricket, Nationalism, and the Swashbuckling Sri Lankans'. *Social Text* 50 (Spring): 33–56.

Jones, Dean. 2013. 'India the New World Provider for Cricket'. *The Sunday Morning Herald*, 23 February. Available at https://www.smh.com.au/sport/cricket/india-the-new-world-provider-for-cricket-20130222-2ex1x.html; accessed on 10 October 2020.

Joseph, Manu. 2004. 'An Unnatural Cricketing Nation'. In Boria Majumdar and J.A. Mangan (eds), *Cricketing Cultures in Conflict*, pp. 116–77. London: Routledge.

Karhadkar, Amol. 2018. 'India vs England Women's ODI Blacked Out'. *The Hindu*, 6 April. Available at http://www.thehindu.com/sport/cricket/womens-odi-blacked-out/article23454840.ece; accessed on 10 October 2020.

Kohli, Akanksha. Interview. 14 February 2018.

Kotian, Harish. 2005. 'WCAI Optimistic of Merger with BCCI'. *Rediff*, 13 April. Available at http://www.rediff.com/cricket/2005/apr/13merger.htm; accessed on 10 October 2020.

Kulkarni, Shubangi. 2000. 'The History of Indian Women's Cricket'. *ESNP Cricinfo*, 8 September. Available at http://www.espncricinfo.com/ci/content/story/94140. html; accessed on 10 October 2020.

Kumar, Amit. 2017. 'How an "Aggressive" Virat Kohli Became Team India's Strength, Explains Sachin Tendulkar'. *NDTV*, 24 October. Available at https://sports.ndtv. com/cricket/how-aggressive-virat-kohli-became-team-indias-strength-explains-sachin-tendulkar-1766169; accessed on 10 October 2020.

112 SPORTS AND SPORTS STUDIES

Majumdar, Boria. 2011. 'The Indian Premier League and World Cricket'. In Anthony Bateman and Jeffery Hill (eds), *The Cambridge Companion to Cricket*, pp. 173–86. Cambridge: Cambridge University Press.

Majumdar, Boria and Kausik Bandopadhyay. 2004. 'Cricket as Everyday Life: World Cup 2003'. *Economic and Political Weekly* 39 (14/15): 1450–4.

Nagarajan, Niranjana. Interview. 25 February 2018.

News Minute, The. 2018. 'No Country for Women's Cricket: India vs SA Match Not Aired, BCCI Passes the Buck', 6 February. Available at https://www.thenewsminute. com/article/no-country-women-s-cricket-india-vs-sa-match-not-aired-bcci-passes-buck-76019; accessed on 10 October 2020.

Oborne, Peter. 2014. *Wounded Tiger: A History of Cricket in Pakistan*. London: Simon & Schuster.

Patnaik, Sidhanta. 2014. 'Women's Cricket in India: A Progressive Journey'. *Wisden India*, 12 August. Available at https://www.wisdenindia.com/cricket-article/ womens-cricket-india-progressive-journey/121014; accessed on 11 May 2019.

Pradhan, Snehal. 2017. 'Shantha Rangaswamy, a Pioneer on and off the Field, Who Helped Shape Women's Cricket in India'. *Firstpost*, 1 March. Available at http:// www.firstpost.com/firstcricket/sports-news/shantha-rangaswamy-a-pioneer-on-and-off-the-field-who-helped-shape-womens-cricket-in-india-3308684.html; accessed on 10 October 2020.

Press Trust of India. 2013. 'ICC Women's World Cup 2013 Breaks Viewership Record'. *Firstpost*, 12 February. Available at https://www.firstpost.com/sports/icc-womens-world-cup-2013-breaks-viewership-record-622663.html; accessed on 10 October 2020.

———. 2017. 'Mithali Raj Blames Scant TV Coverage of Women's Cricket for Poor Attendance in Stadiums'. *Firstpost*, 23 May. Available at https://www.firstpost.com/ firstcricket/mithali-raj-blames-scant-tv-coverage-of-womens-cricket-for-poor-attendance-in-stadiums-3469774.html; accessed on 10 October 2020.

———. 2018. 'India Women vs England Women 3rd ODI: Hosts sign Off Home Season with 2–1 Series Win'. *Deccan Chronicle*, 12 April. Available at https://www.deccanchronicle.com/sports/cricket/120418/india-women-vs-england-women-3rd-odi-hosts-sign-off-home-season-with.html; accessed on 10 October 2020.

Scroll. 2018. 'No TV for Women's Cricket: India vs South Africa Not Telecast, BCCI Says Onus on CSA', 5 February. Available at https://scroll.in/field/867615/no-tv-for-womens-cricket-india-vs-south-africa-not-telecast-bcci-says-onus-on-csa; accessed on 10 October 2020.

Sharma, Rajender. 2018. 'Cricket Undisputed Leader in Indian TV Viewership In 2017'. *Inside Sport* 8 January. Available at https://www.insidesport.co/cricket-undisputed-leader-indian-tv-viewership-2017-508012018/; accessed on 10 October 2020.

Shemilt, Stephan. 2017. 'England's World Cup Win: The Transformation of Women's Cricket'. *BBC Sport* 24 July. Available at https://www.bbc.com/sport/cricket/ 40701196; accessed on 10 October 2020.

WOMEN'S CRICKET IN INDIA   113

Swaminathan, Swaroop. 2018. 'BCCI Annual Contracts for Women: Where Ranji Reserves Earn More Than Domestic Cricketers'. *New Indian Express*, 8 March. Available at http://www.newindianexpress.com/sport/cricket/2018/mar/08/bcci-annual-contracts-for-women-where-ranji-reserves-earn-more-than-domestic-cricketers-1783863.html; accessed on 10 October 2020.

Tirkey, Joy. 2017. 'ICC Women's World Cup Generates Massive Hike in TV Viewership in India'. *NDTV Sports*, 10 August. Available at https://sports.ndtv.com/icc-womens-world-cup-2017/icc-womens-world-cup-generates-massive-hike-in-tv-viewership-in-india-1736025; accessed on 10 October 2020.

Upendran, Ananya. 2013. 'The Problem with Women's Cricket in India.' *ESPN Cricinfo*, 13 February. Available at http://www.espncricinfo.com/magazine/content/story/604617.html; accessed on 10 October 2020.

Veera, Sriram. 2016. 'Cricket, Religion, and Nationalism: Once bitten, Twice Smitten'. *The Indian Express*, 20 March. Available at http://indianexpress.com/article/sports/cricket/cricket-religion-and-nationalism-once-bitten-twice-smitten/; accessed on 10 October 2020.

Velija, Phillipa. 2015. *Women's Cricket and Global Processes*. New York: Palgrave Macmillan.

Vijaikumar. Vyshali. Interview. 1 February 2018.

Yadav, Vishal. Interview. 9 January 2018.

Young, Iris. 2004. 'Five Faces of Oppression'. In Lisa M. Heldke and Peg O'Connor (eds), *Oppression, Privilege, and Resistance: Theoretical Perspectives on Racism, Sexism, and Heterosexism*, pp. 37–63. Boston: McGraw-Hill.

7

Testing the Limits of Science

Sex Difference and Athletic Ability in Elite Sports

Madeleine Pape

The Court of Arbitration for Sport (CAS) announced in May 2019 that it would uphold regulations for international track and field aimed at excluding women athletes with naturally high levels of testosterone from middle-distance events.[i] The appellant was Caster Semenya, a black South African woman and double Olympic gold medallist in the 800 metres. Her legal team argued that the Eligibility Regulations for Female Classification of the International Association of Athletics Federations (IAAF) were not supported by scientific evidence demonstrating a clear link between natural testosterone levels and athletic ability. Following the CAS decision, various researchers and organizations, including the World Medical Association (WMA), expressed concern about the integrity of the scientific research presented by the IAAF (WMA 2019). A similar debate around the scientific basis of regulating women with high testosterone had unfolded during an earlier appeal brought to the CAS in 2015 by Indian sprinter, Dutee Chand. In this instance, however, Chand's appeal was successful. Taken together, the two cases illustrate the increasing pressure on sports governing bodies to justify exclusionary eligibility rules that have long been part of elite women's sport (Henne 2014).

The organization of the vast majority of sports competition around binary sex/gender categories—male/female, men/women, boys/girls—may at first glance appear a relatively straightforward endeavour. It mirrors, after all, the organization of social life across a whole range of institutional spheres, including education and the family. Yet, sport has emerged as a key institutional sphere where the biological bases of a binary sex/gender system have been called into question (Kane 1995; Pieper 2016; Wackwitz 2003). Identifying the physiological traits that contribute to athletic ability,

---

Madeleine Pape, *Testing the Limits of Science* In: *Sports Studies in India*. Edited by: Meena Gopal and Padma Prakash, Oxford University Press. © Oxford University Press 2021.
DOI: 10.1093/oso/9780190130640.003.0008

TESTING THE LIMITS OF SCIENCE   115

or to average differences between male and female athletes, has consistently proven an elusive task for the medical experts affiliated with leading international sports governing bodies (Henne 2014; Karkazis et al. 2012; Pape 2017). In addition, efforts to define which women are eligible to compete in the female athlete category have often been characterized by dynamics of race and nation. Efforts to maintain binary sex and gender on the sporting field, and the regulatory instruments that sports-governing bodies have relied on to do so, are alleged to target the bodies of non-Western women and, most recently, women of colour from the Global South (Bohuon 2015; Henne and Pape 2018; Karkazis and Jordan-Young 2018).

The purpose of the present chapter is to consider the history of gender eligibility regulation in Olympic sports with particular attention to the sport of athletics, the key sport both historically and in more recent years where debates have unfolded over the regulation of women with variation in their sexual development. Focusing on how such efforts have changed and been contested over time, and the global context within which they have emerged, I draw on primary and secondary sources to consider the following questions: First, how can we put gender eligibility regulation in *historical perspective* in order to see how the science of sex difference is deeply subjective? Second, how can we put such efforts in *global perspective* in order to see how gender is implicated in the ideological and material relations between nations, which are still dominated by Western interests and perspectives? To answer these questions, I trace the scientific debates surrounding the gender verification efforts of the International Olympic Committee (IOC) and IAAF, from the chromosome-based testing regime enforced by the two organizations from the 1970s to the 1990s, to the 2015 suspension of testosterone-based regulations by the CAS. I end with the 2016 Rio Olympic Games, where public scrutiny focused on the bodies of three women of colour from Sub-Saharan Africa. In doing so, I reveal how definitive scientific evidence linking the biological bases of sex difference to athletic performance has always eluded governing bodies in international sport. Moreover, I show how discussions of sex, gender, and intersex bodies in sport have always intersected with projects of race and nation, with the geopolitical focus of these projects changing over time.

116   SPORTS AND SPORTS STUDIES

Theoretical Context: Gender and Race in Subjective Science

Gendering Subjective Science

Both sport and science are highly gendered institutions (Pape 2017). To begin, sports governance is gendered both in terms of the predominance of men in leadership positions and the decisions taken by sports leaders that affirm masculine superiority and constrain the representation and partici-pation of women (Adriaanse and Claringbould 2016; Burstyn 1999; Messner 1988; Schull, Shaw, and Kihl 2013). The overwhelmingly male-dominated leadership of the IOC and IAAF have been slow to grant participation rights to women and abandon ideas about their alleged physical frailty in com-parison with men. Indeed, only in very recent years have women begun to approach parity in terms of the numbers of athletes competing at major sporting events like the Olympic Games (Smith and Wrynn 2013). In the sport of athletics, for instance, the 3,000-metre steeplechase first became an Olympic event for women in 2008, compared to 1920 for men. The relatively recently won place of women in elite track and field aids in understanding contemporary anxieties amongst some female athletes about the participa-tion of women with high testosterone, which they experience as threatening their precarious place in elite international sport (Henne and Pape 2018).

Science as a broad institution is also demonstratively gendered at mul-tiple levels, beginning with *who* is producing scientific knowledge. It is well documented that women are both under-represented and devalued within scientific workplaces and educational fields (Fox, Sonnert, and Nikiforova 2011; Smith-Doerr 2004; Traweek 1988). The *content* of scientific knowledge claims is also gendered, particularly scientific and medical knowledge about sex difference, women's bodies, and reproductive processes. A central project for scholars in feminist science studies has been to reveal how the produc-tion of binary sex—or the reduction of sex-based variation to two distinct male and female categories—relies on scientists making particular decisions throughout the research process. The commitment of researchers to 'proving' the existence of binary and biological sex as a scientific fact informs the re-search questions they deem worth pursuing, the design of experiments, and the interpretation and reporting of data (Fausto-Sterling 2000; Lorber 1993; Sprague 2005; Tuana 1988). For example, geneticists may discard data that does not fit within a binary sex framework when attempting to identify sex-determining genes in mice (Fujimura 2006).

The imposition of binary sex categories onto far more complex natural variation also occurs in the work of medical professionals tasked with 'treating' infants and children with differences of sexual development, such as sexual and reproductive anatomy and/or chromosomal patterns that do not fit typical definitions of male and female. Rather than allow their bodies to develop naturally, medical practitioners across many countries, particularly in the Global North, have preferred to perform 'corrective' and irreversible surgeries on such individuals in order to align their bodies with expectations of binary sex.[ii] Such interventions are also accompanied by socialization practices aimed at ensuring the gender identities and (hetero-)sexual preferences of such children align with their assigned sex category (Davis 2015; Rubin 2012). The urgency with which medical practitioners intervene to 'fix' intersex bodies reveals the fragility of binary accounts of sex and gender and the social and expert work needed to bolster them (Fausto-Sterling 2000). In other words, though intended to naturalize the heteronormative alignment of binary sex, gender, and sexuality, the medical response to intersex people in fact reveals how very *unnatural* such models of sex difference are (Fausto-Sterling 2000; Karkazis 2008; Kessler 1990; Rubin 2012).

Race and Nation in Subjective Science

In the words of Shohat (1991: 55), 'colonial discourse [posits] the colonized "other" . . . as an uncontrollable, savage, wild native whose chaotic, hysterical presence requires the imposition of law'. Such discourse underlies the production of scientific knowledge about differences of sexual development that, as feminist scholars have shown, is intertwined with histories of racialization, colonialism, and Western imperialism. The case of Sarah Bartmann is one of the most shocking example of such practices: a 'Hottentot' woman transported from the Dutch colonies at the Cape of Good Hope to London and then Paris, where she was exhibited to fuel the fascination of white Westerners—and men in particular—with the allegedly large and abnormal buttocks and breasts of so-called savage and primitive women (Fausto-Sterling 1995). This same impulse to construct Black women's sexual anatomy as abnormal is found in the nineteenth- and twentieth-century medical textbooks (Magubane 2014). For example, US medical texts published as recently as the 1980s have alleged the over-representation of sex-based abnormalities among women of colour in non-Western contexts,

118   SPORTS AND SPORTS STUDIES

such as 'an enlargement of the clitoris' (Beck and Beck 1863: 176) and 'ambig-uous genitalia' (Ramsay et al. 1988: 4).

Today still, dominant constructions of femininity in Global North deny women of colour the 'pure' femininity associated with white women (Collins 1990). The racialized construction of gender may explain why certain women athletes appear to be over-represented amongst those believed to have high levels of testosterone at the elite level of track and field and accused of 'unfair' advantage (Bohuon 2015; Henne and Pape 2018; Karkazis and Jordan-Young 2018). A key aspect of recent regulatory efforts is that only those women athletes deemed 'suspect' by medical officials are made to undergo testing, a departure from earlier regimes from the 1950s to the 1990s that required all female athletes to verify their eligibility (Erikainen 2017; Pieper 2016). In a context of discretionary application, it becomes possible for hidden biases to shape which bodies become designated as 'suspect' (Pape 2017).

In sum, both sport and science are marked by legacies of gender inequality, racialization, and colonialism, with implications for opportunities to partic-ipate in women's sport. In what follows, I trace this history and deconstruct two moments in the story of gender eligibility regulations in particular—one historical, and one more contemporary—in order to further reveal the sub-jectivity and politics of these scientific practices.

1936–99: Mandating Gender Verification at Any Cost

> Rules should be made to keep the competitive games for normal
> feminine girls and not monstrosities.
>
> Avery Brundage[iii]

The 1936 Olympic Games in Berlin marked the beginning of anxieties around the presence of women with differences of sexual development in the female athlete category. Concerns were expressed about the eligibility of suc-cessful women athletes like Stella Walasiewicz of Poland, and Dora Ratjen of Germany (Carlson 1991). As documented by Anais Bohuon (2015: 965), it is no coincidence that these two women, whose legacies continue to shape attitudes about regulating women athletes today, represented nations as-sociated with the Eastern European side of what would later become Cold War antagonisms. The disdain of Western officials for the muscular bodies of dominant women athletes emerging from the Eastern Bloc in the 1960s underpinned and provided the impetus to leverage advances in genetic

TESTING THE LIMITS OF SCIENCE 119

science and institute a chromosome-based regime for determining women's eligibility in Olympic sports (Carlson 1991).

The technology identified for this purpose was the 'Barr body' or buccal smear test. Using a cheek smear to test for chromosomal deviations from the standard XX for women, the test was considered both less invasive and more scientifically accurate than the gynaecological examinations (or 'nude parades') required of women athletes in preceding years (Bohuon 2015; Pieper 2016). The original technology, developed outside of sport, was not intended for the purposes of defining binary sex categories. In fact, according to the scientist who created the test, Dr Murray Barr, it had 'diagnostic value' for clinicians but 'the presence or absence of sex chromatin . . . [should be considered] a minor detail in the femaleness or maleness of the whole person' (Barr 1956, cited in Pieper 2016: 66). For the IOC Medical Commission, however, the technology offered a relatively simple way to identify women with atypical variations in their sex chromosomes, who were assumed to have 'unfair' athletic abilities relative to other women (Ljungqvist 2000: 184). The Barr body test became mandatory for all women competitors beginning at the 1968 Olympic Games in Mexico City and remained so until the 1990s. During that period, women who 'passed' the test by a sanctioned body were granted a femininity certificate that was valid for life, known also as a 'femininity card' (Wackwitz 2003: 554). For three decades, the eligibility of women athletes was reduced to the absence of a Y chromosome, despite the lack of evidence for a link between chromosomal variation and athletic ability.

The problematic use of the Barr body test did not go unnoticed by the scientific community, which repeatedly raised their objections with the IOC Medical Commission. From the early 1970s onwards, the records of the IOC Medical Commission reveal a growing international chorus of voices critiquing the use of the test on scientific grounds. In 1972, a group of five Danish researchers working in various medical and scientific fields at the University of Aarhus, Denmark, released a memorandum in which they called for the IOC to stop their use of the sex chromatin test for the purposes of femininity control, arguing that the method was 'open to severe criticism for scientific reasons' (p. 6).[iv] They considered the test to be wrongly excluding women with rare chromosomal conditions who otherwise had no physiological characteristics typically associated with men.[v] In 1979, such concerns even appeared in the IOC publication *Olympic Review*, with Dr Elizabeth Ferris writing:

Sex testing was originally instituted to ensure that males were not entering female competition with an unfair advantage. What has in fact happened is that women with rare, anomalous chromosome conditions have been the unfortunate victims of this weeding-out process. (Ferris 1979: 338)

Ferris also attempted to contact members of the IOC Medical Commission directly to discuss her concerns. The response in 1981, however, was that an imperfect method was better than no method at all. The IOC Medical Commission maintained that although they did not have 'the complete answer to the problem', *some* form of femininity control was necessary 'to protect the woman athlete in competitions reserved for female competitors'.[vi]

Even Dr Barr expressed direct concern about the use of the test for gender eligibility purposes. Writing to the president of the Canadian Olympic Committee in 1987 ahead of the Winter Olympic Games in Calgary, he wrote, 'scientists and clinicians known to me . . . agree that buccal smear testing in the area of athletics is totally inappropriate. In fact, its use in this way has been an embarrassment to me and I request that it be stopped'.[vii] Geneticist Dr Albert de la Chappelle wrote repeatedly to the IOC Medical Commission throughout the 1980s, arguing in 1983 that 'the present screening method [was] scientifically unfounded, nearly totally ineffective and sometimes harmful'. In this instance, the IOC Medical Commission acknowledged that 'the procedure [was] not an absolute safe method, but [was] a practical and economic one'. Similarly, at a 1988 review of 'femininity control' protocol by the IOC Medical Commission, it was noted:

The Barr test with X and Y chromatin has since been widely criticized for its inaccuracies, but although the test was not 100 per cent sure, he felt that for sports purposes, where the athletes were not patients, it was to date the most feasible method available.[viii]

Thus, just as would be repeated in later decades when the IOC and IAAF turned from chromosomes to testosterone, fear rather than science drove the regulation of female athletes with differences of sexual development.

In their effort to retain gender eligibility regulation but satisfy the concerns of the scientific community, the IOC shifted to a new technology in 1991, called the polymerase chain reaction (PCR) method. However, this new method continued to receive criticism from the scientific community, such as from Spanish researchers who reported following the Barcelona Olympic Games that the PCR method to identify 'genetic sex might lead to errors in the classification of samples, at least in sports competitors' (Serrat and de Herreros 1996: 312). Scientists active in international sports governance also opposed the method. For example, Arne Ljungqvist, then-chairman of the IAAF's Medical Committee, and Joe Leigh Simpson wrote in 1991 that although 'superficially attractive', 'using polymerase chain reaction (PCR) . . . could well prove disastrous' because of the high risk of contamination and the wrongful detection of women with 'rare disorders of sexual development' with a Y chromosome but 'no physical attribute relevant to sports performance that is not attainable or present in other (46,XX) women' (Ljungqvist and Simpson 1991: 4). Importantly, however, such experts were not opposed to the concept of regulating women's eligibility. Rather, they called for different methods. Geneticists like de la Chappelle, for instance, claimed that 'as many as 90% of those hypermuscular women who should probably not compete in the female events' were currently avoiding detection.[ix]

When, in 1999, the IOC finally abandoned chromosome-based screening for female athletes, a new and far-less transparent regime was immediately adopted, one that abandoned the universal testing of women athletes and instead gave the IOC Medical Commission the 'right to intervene in any suspicious individual case, and then conduct a scientifically proper investigation'.[x] As recalled by Ljungqvist, the decision was not 'widely announced by the IOC' and 'passed relatively silently in [the] media', likely to 'save the face of certain people'.[xi] Politicized from the beginning, a scientific controversy that grew from an 'East/West antagonism' (Bohuon 2015: 965) ended with a selective testing regime that continued underground and made testosterone levels its primary focus. As has increasingly been documented, this new regime has entailed geopolitical dimensions of a different kind, with a return to the racialized construction of sex difference that preoccupied Western medical experts during periods of colonial conquest (Bohuon 2015; Henne and Pape 2018; Karkazis and Jordan-Young 2018).

1999–Present: The Gendered 'Science' of Testosterone in Postcolonial Perspective

> I was born a woman, reared up as a woman, I identify as a woman and I believe I should be allowed to compete with other women.
>
> Dutee Chand, cited in CAS (2015: 8)

122   SPORTS AND SPORTS STUDIES

At the 2009 World Championships in Berlin, a decade of silence around the regulation of women athletes was brought to an abrupt end when the IAAF announced their plans to investigate the biological sex of rising South African superstar Caster Semenya, prompting intense public scrutiny of her body and ushering in a new era of public debate about the legitimacy of such practices. It was not the first time in this era that the eligibility of a woman of colour from Global South had been publicly questioned. In 2006, Indian 800-metre athlete Santhi Soundarajan had been investigated by Indian authorities following her silver medal at the Asian Games on 'suspicion' of having differences of sexual development, the results of which were leaked to the media. In 2008, some members of the athletics community expressed similar suspicions about Olympic gold medallist in the women's 800 metres, Kenyan Pamela Jelimo.[xii] As documented below, in subsequent years, such accusations would expand to include several other Black women from Sub-Saharan African nations. But it was the controversy surrounding the IAAF's handling of Semenya in 2009 in particular that prompted an overhaul of the organization's existing gender eligibility regulations, leading to the 2011 release of the Hyperandrogenism Regulations, which were also adopted by the IOC shortly thereafter.

The Hyperandrogenism Regulations of the IAAF and IOC formalized the focus of regulatory efforts on endogenous (or naturally occurring) testosterone in female athletes, which they claimed was the key factor compromising the 'fairness and integrity' of women's competition (IAAF 2011b: 1). In the case of the IAAF, the limit to the amount of functional endogenous testosterone in female athletes was defined as the start of the 'normal male range' or 10nmol/L (IAAF 2011a: 12).[xiii] Women singled out for testing and found to have testosterone above this limit were then clinically assessed to determine the extent of 'virilization' (development of masculine characteristics), which was assumed to provide a measure of the extent to which they enjoyed 'unfair' athletic abilities.[xiv] Put differently, the IAAF and IOC believed that the development of certain physical characteristics, such as deepness of voice, body hair, and acne, could be used as evidence that such women also have 'male-like' athletic abilities.

The legitimacy of this claim was brought into question in March 2015, when Dutee Chand brought her appeal to the CAS. Chand had been investigated by the Athletics Federation of India (AFI) at the age of eighteen. Found to have testosterone above the specified limit, but unwilling to undergo treatment to alter her body, Chand opted to contest the Regulations and challenge, in particular, their scientific basis. In assessing the legitimacy of the

Hyperandrogenism Regulations, the CAS determined in 2015 that a clinical assessment of virilization could not be considered a precise measure of the performance advantage gained by women with higher than 'normal' testosterone levels, leading them to suspend the Regulations for a two-year period.

Nevertheless, the CAS adjudicating panel was confident that the experts representing the IAAF could generate the 'scientific' evidence needed to have the Hyperandrogenism Regulations reinstated in the future, stating that while there was 'presently no available evidence', the IAAF's 'assumption [of a male-sized advantage] may well be proved valid' (CAS 2015: 155). Thus, though favourable to Chand in the short-term, the decision to suspend the Hyperandrogenism Regulations did not reject the regulation of gender eligibility in elite sport, nor did it reject the reliance on testosterone to do so. Although scientific experts testifying on behalf of Chand pushed for a more complex conceptualization of sex difference and athletic ability, and provided scientific evidence in support of their claims, their efforts were not recognized by the adjudicating panel (Pape 2019). Instead, the problematic aspects of the IAAF's science went unrecognized, as did Dutee Chand's experiences of mistreatment and trauma. These considerations, along with the racialized dynamics underpinning implementation of the Regulations (Karkazis et al. 2012; Karkazis and Jordan-Young 2018), were cast by the adjudicating panel as irrelevant to their decision (Pape 2017).

The real impacts of the Hyperandrogenism Regulations emerge most clearly in their implementation, with Dutee Chand's story particularly illustrative. Just as has been observed in the experiences of other women athletes singled out for investigation (Karkazis et al. 2012), Chand's case included violations of her right to confidentiality and informed consent. As stated during the CAS appeal, without Chand knowing the purpose, she was 'subjected to a "humiliating" examination by a male doctor, who asked intrusive questions about her body hair, menstrual cycle, surgical history and her hobbies. Several doctors carried out physical examinations of the Athlete body, including on her genital area' (CAS 2015: 108). Chand also reported feeling vulnerable and as having no choice but to submit to the procedures. Alarming stories have also emerged about other unnamed women singled out for scrutiny. In one peer-reviewed article, the authors described the treatment of four elite women athletes with high testosterone, all aged twenty-one or younger and from 'rural or mountainous regions of developing countries' (Fenichel et al. 2013: 2), who each consented to a gonadectomy, clitoral surgery, and a 'feminizing vaginoplasty' (Fenichel et al. 2013: 3–4). None of these surgical interventions are relevant to athletic ability or required

124   SPORTS AND SPORTS STUDIES

under the Regulations. It is highly questionable whether athletes, faced with the prospect of never returning to elite competition, could truly provide informed consent to such interventions (Henne and Pape 2018). Indeed, an IAAF witness conceded during the Chand appeal 'that it was "questionable at best" whether young women in that position can give informed consent' (CAS 2015: 97).

Following Chand's appeal to the CAS, and the suspension of the Hyperandrogenism Regulations, the suspicion levelled at women of colour—from Sub-Saharan African nations in particular—has reached new heights. At the 2016 Olympic Games in Rio de Janeiro, all three medallists in the women's 800 metres were described by some media commentators and even experts tied to the IAAF as having high testosterone.[xv] Stakeholders at the elite level of athletics, including athletes and coaches who were present at the Rio Games, have alleged that women with high testosterone are over-represented in rural 'tribal' areas of Sub-Saharan Africa and that managers and national coaches may even be attempting to recruit and train these women because of assumptions about their athletic abilities (Henne and Pape 2018). Olympic gold medallist in 2016, Caster Semenya has continued to be the focus of the IAAF's efforts to develop new rules that meet the scientific standards of the CAS. Their preoccupation with Semenya became clear in September 2017, when the IAAF released revised regulations that would only apply to women's events over distances between 400 metres and one mile (CAS 2018). In other words, the IAAF has introduced Regulations that will apply only to those events where Caster Semenya has been (or has threatened to be) dominant in recent years.

Importantly, the 'restricted events' to which the revised regulations apply are inconsistent with the IAAF's own research, which has since been widely discredited. This research asserted that the women's events most impacted by testosterone levels were the hammer throw and pole vault (Bermon and Garnier 2017). As claimed by scientists who had formerly supported the regulation of women with high testosterone, the absence of hammer throw and pole vault from the IAAF's latest Eligibility Regulations for Female Classification reveals the deeply subjective 'scientific' basis of efforts to regulate gender eligibility in sport (Vilain and Martinez-Patiño 2019). However, when Semenya appealed these regulations in 2019, the CAS ruled that they were not able to assess the legitimacy of the IAAF's heavily critiqued scientific evidence (CAS 2019).

Implications for Sport and Gender Scholarship

In this chapter, I have traced change over time in the regulatory practices of international sports governing bodies to show how their claims about sex difference have consistently drawn scientific critique. This in turn reveals the considerable institutional work that goes into maintaining the belief that the exclusion of women with certain physiological traits is 'fair' and can allegedly be scientifically justified. I have also explored how constructions of sex and gender in sport continue to be influenced by legacies of imperialism and colonial conquest. Bohuon (2015) has referred to this as a shift from an 'east-west' to a 'north-south' antagonism: Whereas initially sports governing bodies were preoccupied with the deviant muscularity of Eastern Bloc women, more recently, the regulation of gender eligibility has been characterized by the racialized colonial gaze that had also been part of the initial emergence of medical knowledge about differences of sexual development.

The implications of such insights for the work of gender scholars and activists operating outside of Global North nations, such as in India, are worth elaborating. As argued by Raewyn Connell (2009) in her concept of Southern theory, and as Kathryn Henne and I have discussed elsewhere (see Henne and Pape 2018), Southern feminist perspectives are necessary to produce fully elaborated postcolonial critiques of the regulation of gender eligibility. Such perspectives could further specify precisely how such efforts reflect a Western gaze and differently impact women of colour in the Global South. Further research is also needed on the perspectives of athletes and officials in such contexts: How do they make sense of the regulation of gender eligibility and its relationship to race and nation, and what are the implications for activism? The project of deconstructing the geopolitical dimensions of such regulatory regimes remains relatively underdeveloped, especially when compared to the more established literature on their *gendered* dimensions. Here, Western feminism has its limits, pointing to the importance of elevating the work of Southern scholars and activists, whose research can contribute in vital ways to the project of holding governing bodies and their scientific experts to account (Henne and Pape 2018).

Notes

i. The restricted events to which the Regulations apply are: 400 metres, 400-metre hurdles, 800 metres, 1,500 metres, and the mile.

126 SPORTS AND SPORTS STUDIES

ii. However, definitions of intersex are 'context specific' (Dreger and Herndon 2009: 200).

iii. Letter from Avery Brundage, president of the American Olympic Committee, to Count Henri de Baillet-Latour, president of the IOC, 23 June 1936.

iv. Letter from Danish National Olympic Committee to Monique Berlioux, 18 February 1972, Memorandum on the Use of Sex Chromatin Investigation of Competitors in Women's Divisions of the Olympic Games.

v. According to the president of the Danish Olympic Committee, the release of the memorandum had led to 'a very extensive newspaper discussion about testing of our girls at the Olympic Games and other large sports arrangements' (Letter dated 18 February 1972, Archives of the Olympic Studies Centre, Lausanne, Switzerland). Berlioux notified the president that the memorandum would be forwarded to Prince de Merode, chair of the Medical Commission, who would 'take care of this matter' (Letter dated 24 February 1972, Archives of the Olympic Studies Centre, Lausanne, Switzerland).

vi. Letter to Elizabeth Ferris, 4 March 1981, Archives of the Olympic Studies Centre, Lausanne, Switzerland.

vii. Letter from Barr to Jackson, 2 June 1987, pp. 1–2, Archives of the Olympic Studies Centre, Lausanne, Switzerland.

viii. Meeting of the IOC Medical Commission Working Group on Gender Verification, 2 July 1988, p. 1, Archives of the Olympic Studies Centre, Lausanne, Switzerland.

ix. Letter from Albert de la Chappelle to Juan Antonio Samaranch, 7 May 1987, p.1, Archives of the Olympic Studies Centre, Lausanne, Switzerland.

x. Letter from Arne Ljungvist, chairman of the IAAF's Medical Committee, to 'the members of the gender verification fax club', 23 June 1999, p.1.

xi. Letter from Arne Ljungvist, chairman of the IAAF's Medical Committee, to 'the members of the gender verification fax club', 23 June 1999, p.1.

xii. Based on interview data collected from 56 elite stakeholders in track and field as a part of the author's dissertation research.

xiii. The IOC policy specified a limit of 8 nmol/L.

xiv. An assessment of virilization is specified as including an examination of 'physical appearance, deepness of voice, body hair' and 'genital characteristics' (IAAF 2011a: 11).

xv. Joanna Harper stated in an interview that 'it is very possible that we could see an all intersex podium in the 800 in Rio, and I wouldn't be surprised to see as many as five intersex women in the eight-person final' (Tucker 2016).

References

Adriaanse, J.A. and I. Claringbould. 2016. 'Gender Equality in Sport Leadership: From the Brighton Declaration to the Sydney Scoreboard'. *International Review for the Sociology of Sport* 51 (5): 547–66.

Beck, T.R. and J.B. Beck. 1863. *Elements of Medical Jurisprudence*, Volume 1. Philadelphia: Lippincott.

Bermon, S. and P.Y. Garnier. 2017. 'Serum Androgen Levels and Their Relation to Performance in Track and Field: Mass Spectrometry Results from 2127 Observations in Male and Female Elite Athletes'. *British Journal of Sports Medicine* 51 (17): 1309–14.

Bohuon, A. 2015. 'Gender Verifications in Sport: From an East/West Antagonism to a North/South Antagonism'. *The International Journal of the History of Sport* 32 (7): 965–79.

Burstyn, Varda. 1999. *The Rights of Men: Manhood, Politics and the Culture of Sport*. Toronto: University of Toronto Press.

Carlson, A. 1991. 'When Is a Woman Not a Woman?' *Women Sport Fitness* 13: 24–9.

Collins, P.H. 1990. *Black Feminist Thought*. Boston: Unwin Hyman.

Connell, R. 2009. *Southern Theory: The Global Dynamics of Knowledge in Social Science*. Cambridge: Polity.

Court of Arbitration for Sport (CAS). 2015. CAS 2014/A/3759 Dutee Chand v. Athletics Federation of India & The International Association of Athletics Federations. Interim Arbitral Award. Available at http://www.tas-cas.org/fileadmin/user_upload/award_internet.pdf; accessed on 30 July 2015.

———. 2018. 'The Application of the IAAF Hyperandrogenism Regulations Remains Suspended.' Media release, 19 January. Available at http://www.tas-cas.org/fileadmin/user_upload/Media_Release_3759_Jan_2018.pdf; accessed on 6 May 2019.

———. 2019. Semenya, ASA and IAAF: Executive Summary. May 5, 2019. Available at: https://www.tas-cas.org/fileadmin/user_upload/CAS_Executive_Summary__5794_.pdf; accessed on 6 May 2019.

Davis, G. 2015. *Contesting Intersex: The Dubious Diagnosis*. NYU Press: New York.

Dreger, A.D. and A.M. Herndon. 2009. 'Progress and Politics in the Intersex Rights Movement: Feminist Theory in Action'. *GLQ: A Journal of Lesbian and Gay Studies* 15 (2): 199–224.

Erikainen, S. 2017. 'Hybrids, Hermaphrodites, and Sex Metamorphoses: Gendered Anxieties and Sex Testing in Elite Sport, 1937–1968'. In V. Demos and M.T. Segal (eds), *Advances in Gender Research 24: Gender Panic, Gender Policy*, pp. 155–76. Bingley, UK: Emerald Books.

Fausto-Sterling, A. 1995. 'Gender, Race, and Nation: The Comparative Anatomy of "Hottentot" Women in Europe, 1815–1817'. In J. Terry and J. Urla (eds), *Deviant Bodies: Critical Perspectives on Difference in Sex and Popular Culture*, pp. 19–48. Bloomington, IN: Indiana University Press.

———. 2000. *Sexing the Body: Gender Politics and the Construction of Sexuality*. New York: Basic Books.

128 SPORTS AND SPORTS STUDIES

Fenichel, P., F. Paris, P. Philibert, S. Hiéronimus, L. Gaspari, J.Y. Kurzenne, P. Chevallier, S. Bermon, N. Chevalier, and C. Sultan. 2013. 'Molecular Diagnosis of 5α-Reductase Deficiency in 4 Elite Young Female Athletes through Hormonal Screening for Hyperandrogenism'. *The Journal of Clinical Endocrinology and Metabolism* 98 (6): 1055–9.

Ferris, E. 1979. 'Sportswomen and Medicine'. *Olympic Review* 140: 332–9.

Fox, M.F., G. Sonnert, and I. Nikiforova. 2011. 'Programs for Undergraduate Women in Science and Engineering: Issues, Problems, and Solutions'. *Gender & Society* 25: 589–615.

Fujimura, Joan. 2006. 'Sex Genes: A Critical Sociomaterial Approach to the Politics and Molecular Genetics of Sex Determination'. *Signs* 32: 49–82.Henne, K. 2014. 'The "Science" of Fair Play in Sport: Gender and the Politics of Testing.' *Signs* 39: 787–812.

Henne, K. and M. Pape. 2018. 'Dilemmas of Gender and Global Sports Governance: An Invitation to Southern Theory'. *Sociology of Sport Journal* 35 (3): 216–25.

International Association of Athletics Federations (IAAF) 2011a. *IAAF Regulations Governing Eligibility of Females with Hyperandrogenism to Compete in Women's Competition*. Monaco: IAAF.

———. 2011b. *HA Regulations: Explanatory Notes*. Monaco: IAAF.

Kane, M.J. 1995. 'Resistance/Transformation of the Oppositional Binary: Exposing Sport as a Continuum.' *Journal of Sport and Social Iss*ues 19: 191–218.

Karkazis, K. 2008. *Fixing Sex: Intersex, Medical Authority, and Lived Experience*. Durham, NC: Duke University Press.

Karkazis, K. and R. Jordan-Young. 2018. 'The Powers of Testosterone: Obscuring Race and Regional Bias in the Regulation of Women Athletes'. *Feminist Formations* 30 (2): 1–39.

Karkazis, K., R. Jordan-Young, G. Davis, and S. Camporesi. 2012. 'Out of Bounds? A Critique of the New Policies on Hyperandrogenism in Elite Female Athletes'. *American Journal of Bioethics* 12 (1): 3–16.

Kessler, S.J. 1990. 'The Medical Construction of Gender: Case Management of Intersexed Infants'. *Signs* 16 (1): 3–26.

Ljungqvist, Arne and Joe Leigh Simpson. 1991. 'Medical Examination for Health of All Athletes Replacing Gender Verification in International Sports: The International Amateur Athletic Federation'. 20 May. IAAF Gender Verification Working Group.

Ljungqvist A. 2000. 'Women in sport'. In Drinkwater B. L. (ed), *Olympic Encyclopedia*, vol. 111. pp. 183–19. Oxford: Blackwell Science.

Lorber, Judith. 1993. 'Believing is Seeing: Biology as Ideology'. *Gender & Society* 7: 568–81.

Magubane, Z. 2014. 'Spectacles and Scholarship: Caster Semenya, Intersex Studies, and the Problem of Race in Feminist Theory'. *Signs* 39 (3): 761–85.

Messner, M.A. 1988. 'Sports and Male Domination: The Female Athlete as Contested Ideological Terrain.' *Sociology of Sport Journal* 5: 197–211.

Nyong'o, T. 2010. 'The unforgivable transgression of being Caster Semenya.' *Women & Performance: A Journal of Feminist Theory*, 20(1), 95–100.

Pape, M. 2017. 'The Fairest of Them All: Gender Determining Institutions and the Science of Sex Testing.' In V. Demos and M.T. Segal (eds), *Advances in Gender*

Research: Gender Panic, Gender Policy, pp. 177–200. Bingley, UK: Emerald Publishing.

———. 2019. 'Expertise and Non-binary Bodies: Sex, Gender and the Case of Dutee Chand'. *Body & Society* 25 (4): 3–28.

Pieper, L.P. 2016. *Sex Testing: Gender Policing in Women's Sports*. Champaign, IL: University of Illinois Press.

Ramsay, M., R. Bernstein, E. Swane, D.C. Page, and T. Jenkins. 1988. 'XX True Hermaphroditism in Southern African Blacks: An Enigma of Primary Sexual Differentiation'. *American Journal of Human Genetics* 43 (1): 4–13.

Rubin, D. 2012. 'An Unnamed Blank that Craved a Name: A Genealogy of Intersex as Gender'. *Signs* 37 (4): 883–908.

Schull, V., S. Shaw, and L.A. Kihl. 2013. ' "If a Woman Came in . . . She Would Have Been Eaten Up Alive": Analyzing Gendered Political Processes in the Search for an Athletic Director'. *Gender & Society* 27 (1): 56–81.

Serrat, A. and A. García de Herreros. 1996. 'Gender Verification in Sports by PCR Amplification of SRY and DYZ1 Y Chromosome Specific Sequences: Presence of DYZ1 Repeat in Female Athletes'. *British Journal of Sports Medicine* 30 (4): 310–12.

Shohat, E. 1991. 'Imaging Terra Incognita: The Disciplinary Gaze of the Empire'. *Public Culture* 3 (2): 41–70.

Smith, M.M. and A.M. Wrynn. 2013. *Women in the Olympic and Paralympic Games: An Analysis of Participation and Leadership Opportunities*. Ann Arbor, MI: SHARP Center for Women and Girls.

Smith-Doerr, L. 2004. *Women's Work: Gender Equality vs. Hierarchy in the Llife Sciences*. Boulder, CO: Lynne Rienner Publishers.

Sprague, J. 2005. *Feminist Methodologies for Critical Researchers*. Walnut Creek, CA: AltaMira Press.

Traweek, S. 1988. *Beamtimes and Lifetimes: The World of High Energy Physicists*. Cambridge, MA: Harvard University Press.

Tuana, N. 1988. 'The Weaker Seed: The Sexist Bias of Reproductive Theory'. *Hypatia* 3: 35–60.

Tucker, R. 2016. 'Hyperandrogenism and Women vs Women vs Men in Sport: A Q&A with Joanna Harper'. *The Science of Sport*. Available at http://sportsscientists. com/2016/05/hyperandrogenism-women-vs-women-vs-men-sport-qa-joanna-harper/; accessed on 6 May 2019.

Vilain, E. and M.J. Martinez-Patiño. 2019. 'Science's Place in Shaping Gender-Based Policies in Athletics'. *The Lancet* 393: 1504.

Wackwitz, L. 2003. 'Verifying the Myth: Olympic Sex Testing and the Category Woman'. *Women's Studies International Forum* 26 (6): 553–60.

World Medical Association (WMA). 2019. 'WMA Reiterates Advice to Physicians not to Implement IAAF Rules on Classifying Women Athletes' Available at https://www.wma.net/news-post/wma-reiterates-advice-to-physicians-not-to-implement-iaaf-rules-on-classifying-women-athletes/; accessed on 3 May 2019.

SECTION II
REFLECTIONS ON SPORTS STUDIES

Transcending Disciplines

8

A Sociological Understanding of Sport in India

Elizabeth C.J. Pike

The sociological study of sport in India is a relatively recent, albeit emerging, development. In part, this is because sport remains a subject considered unworthy of serious academic attention (Bandyopadhyay 2005). This is not new or unique to the Indian context. In 1982, John Hargreaves berated the blindness of the academic community to the social significance of sport, referring to this as cultural chauvinism. He argued that while academics would attend to traditional forms of culture, popular culture such as sport was not taken seriously by them. Indeed, the association of sport with forms of leisure and play means that sport is often considered to be the opposite of work (despite the industry that surrounds many sports) and, therefore, not worthy of analysis (Hargreaves 1982).

The marginality of the sociology of sport may also be attributed to the relative prioritization of disciplines in the emergent nation-state of independent India. Academic attention at this time was directed toward those disciplines that might contribute to the building of the new nation-state and, in this context, primacy was given to economics, political science, international relations, and history. When the discipline of sociology did emerge, its focus was also on social and economic development, and a sociological study of sport remained a marginal area (see McDonald 2000; Srivinas 1987).

This chapter reflects an emerging discipline and will explain how a sociological approach to studying sport in Indian society enables an understanding of the ways in which sport is connected with history, culture and society. The chapter will outline several key sociological theories which provide the frameworks for asking research questions about social issues as they relate to sport, interpret the available information, and uncover deeper meanings associated with sport.

Elizabeth C.J. Pike, *A Sociological Understanding of Sport in India* In: *Sports Studies in India*. Edited by: Meena Gopal and Padma Prakash, Oxford University Press. © Oxford University Press 2021.
DOI: 10.1093/oso/9780190130640.003.0009

134   REFLECTIONS ON SPORTS STUDIES

The main social theories that will be examined in this chapter are: functionalism, conflict theory, critical theory, feminism, interactionism, and figurational theory. For each theory, there will be an overview of the approach and indications of some of the limitations of the theory, based on the work of Coakley and Pike (2014). This will be followed by a case study of a social issue related to sport in India in order to illustrate how a sociological examination of sport helps us to understand how individual experiences of sport are connected with broader social, economic, political and environmental issues. First, some contextual information is provided regarding the discipline of sociology in India and the biographical position of the author.

Context

Much of the focus of sociological research in India is contextualized within its status as a postcolonial nation (primarily as a former British colony) and the simultaneous connection and conflict with its colonial past. As such, it is important to note at the outset that this chapter is written by a scholar who is a British national and resident, whose only shared cultural heritage with the country of India is grounded in the historical exploitation of India by the British Empire. The content of this chapter is, therefore, presented from the perspective of an interested outsider, who is mindful of the complex relationship of her ancestors with India. Furthermore, there remains some debate regarding the 'Indian-ness' of sociological studies of India, and particularly the implications of Western intellectual influence (see Deshpande 2001). In writing this chapter, the main sociological theories presented are Western in origin, presented by a white Western woman, and should be read and critically analysed for their relevance to a sociological understanding of sport in India in that context.

At the time of writing this chapter, India was described as being one of the five 'BRICS' nations—a term that is used to describe the nations with the largest emerging economies, geopolitical status, and power to rival the developed world (Brazil, Russia, India, China, South Africa). The term 'BRICS' was adopted following the attacks on the World Trade Center in USA in recognition of the complexity of economic globalization and decreased dominance of Americanization. The BRICS nations have now established means of cooperation for sustainable and mutually beneficial development. It is worthy of note that India, along with other BRICS nations, has recently hosted several mega sports events, which is indicative of these social changes and the economic development of these countries.

Take, for example, the fact that India hosted the Cricket World Cup in 1987, 1996, 2011, and will do so again in 2023. The sponsorship in 1987 totalled the equivalent of approximately US$ 1.5 million; in 1996, it had increased to nearly US$ 13 million; and by 2011, it was estimated that the sponsorship was worth approximately US$ 320 million (see McDonald 2000; Mercer 2015). The main sponsor was Moneygram International, with other sponsors including PepsiCo as the official beverage and snacks partner, and LG Electronics, which was a long-term sponsor of the Cricket World Cup. More recently, the International Cricket Council (ICC) has moved towards long-term brand partnership deals so that the ICC, rather than the hosts, manage the sponsorship.

In contrast to the economic success of hosting the Cricket World Cup, the 2010 Commonwealth Games held in Delhi had to deal with criticisms of the infrastructure and living conditions of athletes. Many of these criticisms appeared to be grounded in stereotypes about the poverty, organizational inadequacies, and political corruption that are supposedly rife in a developing nation such as India (see Carter 2011; Curi, Knijnik, and Mascarenhas 2011). The final cost of the Delhi Commonwealth Games increased from a projected US$ 1.3 billion to approximately US$ 15 billion, making these Games the most expensive to date. It has been argued that the amount of funds invested into hosting major sporting events is indicative of a view that BRICS and other countries in the Global South feel under pressure to outperform those events hosted in the Global North by way of demonstrating their economic development on the global stage that is offered by major sporting events (see Palmer 2013).

In order to better understand the social significance of sport in India, the following sections in this chapter will outline a range of sociological theories. Theorizing is a process of describing and analysing why social worlds are the way they are, as well as reflecting on how they might be changed. According to Coakley and Pike (2014), theories enable people to understand and make informed decisions about the relationship between sports and social life. In what follows, six different sociological theories will be outlined, acknowledging the limitations of each approach, and their relevance for a deeper understanding of sport in India.

136 REFLECTIONS ON SPORTS STUDIES

Functionalist Theory

Functionalist theory starts with the premise of whether aspects of society (including sport) are functional—in other words, whether they can meet their goals. In sport, this may be whether an athlete or team performs in such a way that they win and whether equipment improves performance. If this is not the case and the players or equipment are deemed to be 'dysfunctional', then the athlete may be dropped from the team or the equipment changed. Functionalist theory is based on the assumption that society is an organized system of interrelated parts held together by shared norms and values. In sport, the 'interrelated parts' could be the players, the coaches, and scientists, the agents, and so on. In order for these parts to be held together, players need to follow the rules imposed by management and coaches so that norms and values are shared for the good of the team or club.

Functionalists generally focus on the positive aspects of sport and, in particular, consider the ways that sport contributes to the organization and stability of society by socializing people into shared values, develop valued aspects of character, and enhance social bonds (Coakley and Pike 2014). Stevenson and Nixon (1972) identified five general functions of sport: (*i*) a socio-emotional function, providing opportunities for communities to bond and resolve conflict; (*ii*) socialization and the learning of cultural values through sport; (*iii*) social integration by providing opportunities for diverse groups of people to interact with each other; (*iv*) political functions through the wearing of national uniforms, the singing of anthems, and the presence of political leaders at events; and (*v*) social mobility and the opportunity to improve one's social status through sport.

When functionalism is used to inform policy and social action, it seeks to develop and expand sport programmes that promote traditional values, use sport to build the type of character that is valued in society, and see the potential of sport to contribute to social order and stability (see Coakley and Pike 2014).

Weaknesses of Functionalist Theory

Delaney (2015: 27) claims that 'the functionalist perspective has been attacked by proponents of nearly every other theoretical perspective.' Functionalist theory can overstate the positive effects of sports in society and understate its negative effects, including issues related to discrimination and exploitation. Functionalists can also overlook the diversity of sports and the possibility that sports may reproduce social outcomes that disrupt the smooth functioning of society. Furthermore, functionalist theory may overlook the differences and conflicts of interest in society and the fact that sports often promote the interests of powerful people over others (Coakley and Pike 2014). Despite these criticisms, it is argued that functionalist theory helps to explain the social institution of sport and how it reflects the key values and norms of society (Delaney 2015).

Functionalist Theory: Case Study

Mani and Krishnamurthy (2016) describe how football was introduced in Kashmir by missionaries, seeking to inculcate values such as being energetic, courage, and willpower among schoolboys. These values conform to the social norms of muscular Christianity, which symbolizes a particular type of muscular body that is in the highest state of physical health and so capable of performing religious devotion. As such, an activity that was promoted by way of teaching these attributes was valued by the missionaries, and so football was seen to serve a 'function' to promote valued norms.

However, football was simultaneously able to challenge traditional notions of privilege and otherness as they were defined by the powerful missionary colonizers, particularly intervening with ideas regarding backwardness as they play out within the conceptualization of caste and other social norms in Kashmir. In this way, the development of football in Kashmir represents the 'functions' of sport, and also enables an analysis of norms, citizenship, and migration when considering the relative roles of the indigenous population and the colonizers.

Conflict Theory

Conflict theory is based on the work of Karl Marx and the belief that societies are primarily shaped by economic factors. In particular, conflict theorists are interested in the relationships between social classes, which is often assumed to be an exploitative relationship between those who have economic power and the workers who are compelled to accept economic inequalities.

When conflict theorists undertake research in relation to sport, they primarily focus on the ways that sports are shaped by these economic forces and

138 REFLECTIONS ON SPORTS STUDIES

can be used by economically powerful people to increase their wealth and in-fluence. It is argued that sports are generally organized by wealthy people and large corporations because they perpetuate capitalist values. When people are employed to work in sports, they may be paid for their job, but conflict theorists argue that they often risk their bodies for their sporting achieve-ment (illustrated in the high injury rates, concussions, and drug usage in some sports), and that sport merely serves as a means to distract them from their exploitation (see Coakley and Pike 2014; McDonald 2015).

The implications of conflict theory for policy and social action lie in its ability to raise class-consciousness and make people aware of their own al-ienation and powerlessness. If conflict theorists informed sports develop-ment, there is the potential to eliminate the profit motive in sports replacing this with a focus on fostering expression, creativity, and physical well-being (see Coakley and Pike 2014).

Weaknesses of Conflict Theory

Conflict theory is criticized for the fact that it overemphasizes the repressive and exploitative culture of sports and, in so doing, can ignore the possibility that sports in capitalist societies may involve experiences that empower indi-viduals and groups. The focus on the economic forces in society also means that conflict theorists often assume that all aspects of social life are economi-cally determined, whereas not all sports are completely shaped by economic factors and not every sport is controlled by economically powerful people. As a result, conflict theory has been critiqued for failing to consider the pos-sibility that power and inequalities in society are based on factors other than social class and economic differences (see Coakley and Pike 2014).

Conflict Theory: Case Study

The Indian Premier League (IPL) is a professional league for men's Twenty20 cricket, contested by eight teams in a franchise system. When it held its in-augural tournament in 2008, it was argued that it changed the face of na-tional and international cricket, focused as it was on a spectator-friendly and spectator-focused version of the game (Pike and Coakley 2010). The devel-opment of the IPL saw a move away from the original version of the game

A SOCIOLOGICAL UNDERSTANDING OF SPORT IN INDIA   139

steeped in its colonial history with Britain to being based on the franchise system used in many professional sports in USA.

When the IPL is considered from a conflict theory perspective, those with the economic power would be considered as those owning the franchises. The Board of Cricket Control for India (BCCI) owns the infrastructure and loans this to the franchise. The franchises ultimately were sold collectively for US$ 723.6 million, and by the second season in 2009, it was estimated that the IPL's net worth was close to US$ 5 billion. By 2009, on-air advertising had also increased through the introduction of timeouts during games, as a result of which 118 two-and-a-half minute slots were sold to advertisers. This may be illustrative of the ways in which sports can create pleasurable feelings that encourage spectators to engage with the sport and not challenge the corporate interests of the owners.

Some clubs will pay in excess of US$ 1 million for players, who will play only six weeks of cricket in a season. While this may appear to be to the benefit of the players, it is also possible to argue that these players are themselves subject to the sort of exploitation that concerns conflict theorists. For example, while the IPL has an anti-doping code which aims to prevent the use of performance-enhancing substances, Mohammad Asif, a Pakistan fast bowler, was the first player to test positive in the inaugural 2008 IPL season. There also have been concerns that the increased opportunity for players to compete year-round in different countries may increase the risk of injuries. In the first tournament, the Australian player Matthew Hayden was injured while playing in the IPL and, controversially, Cricket Australia subsequently deducted his pay because he was unable to complete an international tour (see Pike and Coakley 2010). In 2013, the consequences of commercialism and economic forces also became evident when three bowlers were arrested for match fixing and two of the franchises were suspended (see Houlihan and Malcolm 2016).

Critical Theory

The two theories outlined earlier, functionalist and conflict theories, have a shared belief that societies can be understood as 'systems'. Critical theory developed in recognition of the complexity and fluidity of societies and, instead of focusing on society as a whole, it focuses on diversity, complexity, contradictions, and changes of social life. As a result, critical theory is based on assumptions that societies are characterized by both shared values and

140   REFLECTIONS ON SPORTS STUDIES

conflicts of interest; that social life involves continuous processes of negotiation, compromise, and coercion; and that social organization changes due
to the shifts in the power balance between groups of people in society (see
Coakley and Pike 2014).

One of the most influential critical theorists is Pierre Bourdieu. Bourdieu
believed that people internalize the patterns and norms of the world in which
they live, which influences their actions and thoughts about society, but that
their choices are limited by the practices and structures of their social world.
He described this in terms of a person's habitus or system of predispositions
of how to behave in different situations with different people and used the
term field to describe the different social contexts in which we live our lives,
each of which has their networks of relationships and traditions of behaviour
(see Coakley and Pike 2014).

Bourdieu (1986) also adopted the term capital to identify the resources
available to people that generate power and influence or control specific
situations. He identified four types of capital: economic, cultural, social,
and symbolic. Economic capital are those resources that are convertible to
money; cultural capital refers to a person's social status and cultural competence which may be due to their skills, knowledge, and behaviour; social
capital is a complex and contested concept but there is some consensus that
it emphasizes the role of social connections, networks, and civic norms; and
symbolic capital refers to the resources available to an individual as a result of
some recognition, prestige, or reputation.

When critical theory informs the sociological study of sports, it can help
to answer research questions regarding the ways that sports reproduce and/
or challenge patterns of privilege in society; how sports are related to social
categories such as gender and sexuality, race, and ethnicity as well as physical
ability and disability; and the ways in which sports may become sites where
people challenge, resist, and change prevailing ideas about society.

If critical theory is applied to inform policy and social action, sports could
be developed as sites for challenging the voices and perspectives of those
with power and transforming exploitative and oppressive forms of social
relations. Furthermore, critical theory asks questions that could lead to an
increase in the range and diversity of sport participation opportunities (see
Coakley and Pike 2014).

Weaknesses of Critical Theory

Critical theory has been criticized for its failure to clarify when sports reproduce culture and social organization and when they become sites for resisting and transforming them. In part, this is because critical theorists do not always provide the criteria needed to identify the characteristics of effective forms of opposition and resistance. Furthermore, it is argued that some critical theories use confusing vocabularies that undermine its potential to inform strategies that are most likely to produce progressive change and transform sports and society (see Coakley and Pike 2014).

Critical Theory: Case Study

Mani and Krishnamurthy (2016) describe the ways in which cricket in India is a product of the colonial times when India was a British colony. This means that Indian cricketers have negotiated identities that are both in line with colonial expectations but are also steeped in nationalist values; in other words, they are simultaneously with and against the British.

They provide two examples of Indian cricketers who demonstrate this process and, in turn, Bourdieu's conceptualization of the ways in which a person's habitus illustrates how they have internalized the patterns and norms of their social world or field in which they live and the relevance of the different forms of capital available to them. The first example they provide is of Ranjitsinhji, who was an Indian prince who used cricket to solidify his identification with the colonizing British. Ranjitsinhji identified as an English cricketer and was representative of the Indian elite in the early twentieth century who wished to identify themselves with the British middle class while simultaneously distinguishing themselves from the native Indians. For Ranjitsinhji, the habitus of an upper-class Indian meant embodying Englishness, and cricket was one means by which this could be achieved. This was available to him due to his access to capital and, in turn, could offer him access to additional forms of capital. In contrast, Dinkar Deodhar learned cricket in India, and believed that Indians should devise their own ways of playing cricket that represent the Indian social field, partly in practical terms regarding issues such as the country's climate but also other cultural variations from English culture. These two examples illustrate the ways in which cricket can be seen as both a colonial product while also serving as a medium for decolonization and as

142   REFLECTIONS ON SPORTS STUDIES

a site of intense nationalist expression. This is particularly the case when the Indian team beat the English team in international competitions.

Feminist Theory

Feminism is premised on a belief that in order to understand society, it is necessary to understand gender and gender relations. Feminist theories explain the ways that women have been systematically devalued and oppressed in many societies, and seek equality for men and women in all aspects of life. There are many different branches of feminism, including liberal feminism, which seeks to enable women to have the same opportunities as men, and radical feminism, which argues for fundamental changes in society to challenge and eliminate the cultural norms that allow for male supremacy. Sociologists of sport have tended to draw on critical feminism, which focuses on issues of power and seeks to explain the origin and consequences of gender relations, especially those that privilege men over women and some men over other men. Critical feminists argue that sports are grounded in the values and experiences of some men and celebrate attributes associated with dominant forms of masculinity in society (see Coakley and Pike 2014).

When feminist thinking informs policy and social action, sports can become sites for challenging and transforming oppressive forms of gender relations. Feminist theorists often expose, and so enable resistance to, homophobia and misogyny in sports. Radical and critical feminists seek to go beyond merely offering equal opportunities to men and women, to find ways to transform sports such that they emphasize partnership over competition and domination (see Coakley and Pike 2014).

Weaknesses of Feminist Theory

The fact that there are so many different forms of feminist theory can make this approach challenging to understand and draw on to inform understanding of society. In addition, feminism should not be used to homogenize the experiences of all men and all women as if they are the same, and therefore, some research needs to focus more on the sports-related experiences of men and women of different ages, abilities, religions, and nationalities.

Feminist Theory: Case Study

It is important to note that there is little mention of female sports or players in the sociological research on sport in India. This in itself arguably reflects the cultural marginalization of many women in aspects of Indian society (Majumdar 2003). However, McDonald (2003) presents two different forms of sporting practice, which reflect a diversity of possibilities for the presentation of masculinities in sport.

According to McDonald (2003), the sports-related training offered by the Hindu right-wing organization Rashtriya Swayamsevak Sangh (RSS) remasculinizes Hindu people to build a competitive strong nation. The training takes the form of Western-style military exercise with indigenous games. These are used to create a sense of attachment to, and starting point for the creation of, a new Indian nation-state. The RSS is a uniformed all-male organization, and the exercises extol the virtues of masculinity, strength, and warfare. Here, a feminist perspective helps to understand that the building of a nation is deemed to be dependent on masculine norms, values, and attributes, which explains the marginalization of women from these specific activities and more generally from Indian sporting culture.

The second example provided by McDonald is the martial art of Kalaripayattu, which imagines a unity of body and mind, enabling a masculine performance of exotic culture. The common elements of this system are physical, breathing, and meditative exercises, which are designed to prepare the body and mind for combat. While women are not excluded from Kalaripayattu, it is a male-dominated activity that witnessed a resurgence as part of a revival of sport and physical culture during the 1920s as part of a reaction against British colonial rule. In particular, this interest in physical activities for males was to counteract the perception that there was colonial discourse that Indian men were effeminate and lacking in Victorian masculine virtues. Feminist theory informs an understanding that a fear of effeminacy is grounded in a belief of male superiority and female inferiority, and this underpins the development of particular types of sporting activities which reflect masculine, rather than feminine, norms.

Interactionist Theory

Interactionist theory focuses on the idea that as people interact with one another, they give meanings to themselves, other people and the world around

144   REFLECTIONS ON SPORTS STUDIES

them. These meanings are then used as a basis for making decisions and taking action in people's everyday lives, as the meanings inform what might be the consequences of any decisions or actions. A key element of this is the development of a sense of identity, or the sense of who an individual is and how they are connected to other people and the social world. One well-known interactionist is Erving Goffman, whose work has informed many sociologists of sport. His research attempted to develop an in-depth understanding of social worlds from the inside by spending time observing and speaking to people in order to gain their perspectives and understand how they create, maintain and change their social worlds.

When interactionist theory is applied to sport, it enables sociologists to address issues such as what the social processes through which people become involved in sports are, how people come to be defined and identified as an athlete, what meaning is derived from sports experiences, and what happens when athletes retire from competitive sports (see Coakley and Pike 2014).

The implications of interactionist theory for policy and social action is that it offers the potential to allow individuals to shape sports to fit their definitions or reality. In focusing on the culture and organization of sports, the consequence can be that sports may become more open and democratic (see Coakley and Pike 2014).

Weaknesses of Interactionist Theory

Interactionist theory is often criticized for its failure to explain the ways in which social interactions and the construction of meaning are influenced by power dynamics. As a result, it has been argued that interactionist theory needs to be combined with critical theory to develop analyses beyond simply describing social worlds to consider what power issues may be at play, and also to consider how sports might be organized.

Interactionist Theory: Case Study

Mills (2001) describes the development of football in Goa in terms of the way that participation in football enabled the expression of a distinct Goan identity during the period that Goa transitioned from a Portuguese colony to independence and integrated into the Indian Union. A critical interactionist perspective informs an understanding of the ways in which sport enabled

A SOCIOLOGICAL UNDERSTANDING OF SPORT IN INDIA   145

people to give meaning to their social world during a time of significant up-heaval, and to develop a personal sense of identity within this social context and through interactions with others. Mills (2001) outlines the ways that some Goan workers based in Bombay (now Mumbai) formed their own communities based on the sport of football, so that they could continue to maintain a Goan identity while displaced to a different part of India. This case study demonstrates how Goan people were able to give meaning to their world during complex times, through interactions with other people, and to negotiate the power dynamics at play while imagining a different life.

Figurational Sociology

Figurational theory, also known as process sociology, is based on the belief that social life consists of networks of interdependent people (or 'figurations'). According to figurational sociologists, people are believed to be dependent on each other as a result of socialization, education, and reciprocal needs. The focus of many figurational theorists is on the long-term processes through which the relatively autonomous actions of people can influence and constrain each other (see Coakley and Pike 2014). Figurational theory is grounded in European intellectual traditions, in particular in the work of German sociologist, Norbert Elias, who is argued to be unique among major social theorists in both developing a sociology of sport and developing his sociological theory through sport (Malcolm 2015).

When figurational theory is used to inform studies of sport, sociologists often study the social and historical processes through which sports have developed, and the ways that sports become increasingly serious in people's lives. Elias's (2000) central theory was that of the civilizing process, a process by which people in western Europe came to consider themselves to be more civilized than others, creating what he calls 'the established' and 'the outsiders', and so contributing to discussions of the western European colonization of India and the role of sport in colonial relations. This also helps explain how manners and customs became increasingly regulated: in the way that people eat, control their bodily functions, and express violence. The latter is particularly significant in sport, and Elias and Dunning (1986) argue that the civilizing process led to sports that became more regulated and controlled in terms of violence, but also that sports provided an outlet for excitement in increasingly routine societies.

146 REFLECTIONS ON SPORTS STUDIES

When figurational sociology is used to inform policy and social action, this provides a resource of valid knowledge that can be used to enable people to control expressions of violence, exploitation, and abuse of power. A figurational sociological perspective also contributes to an understanding of the processes by which people have access to, or are denied, power and, hence, provides an opportunity to increase access to sport participation among those who have lacked power through history (see Coakley and Pike 2014).

Weaknesses of Figurational Sociology

The primary criticism of figurational theory has been that its focus on long-term, historical interconnections between people minimizes attention to more immediate issues. Furthermore, traditional figurational theory focused so much on the emerging dynamics of social interdependence between people that it understated the consequences of oppressive power relationships and the need for political actions to change the balance of power in social life (see Coakley and Pike 2014). However, Malcolm (2015) argues that more recent figurational sociologists of sport have given greater attention to a breadth of issues including race relations, sport and drugs, and gender relations.

Figurational Sociology: Case Study

Bandyopadhyay (2008) describes how the partition of Bengal into West Bengal and what is now known as Bangladesh created communal and regional tensions between the natives and the migrant Hindus who were leaving East Bengal for West Bengal. The two groups formed their own interdependent networks, and football became a focus for the assertion of their identities in terms of who each faction considered to be the established and the outsiders. It is worthy of note that the divide was based on region rather than religion, as both groups were Hindus, demonstrating the complexity of interdependence and the formation of figurations. This was not only the case for the players but also for the supporters. The support of the East Bengal and Mohun Bagan (West Bengal) teams reflected the social divide, such that spectator violence became a part of the sporting culture indicative of the

A SOCIOLOGICAL UNDERSTANDING OF SPORT IN INDIA   147

kinds of sport-related violence that figurational sociologists have examined elsewhere as an integral dimension of the civilizing process.

Future Directions for the Sociology of Sport in India

Mani and Krishnamurthy (2016) have identified that as a post-colonial country, the future sociology of sport research in India will benefit from an interdisciplinary and multi-method approach to uncover the rich cultural heritage and social significance of sport. This means drawing on traditional sources such as academic papers and official documents, alongside life histories and ethnographic data.[i]

At this stage, it may be relevant to consider what a 'post-colonial' sociology of sport might look like in a post-colonial country such as India. Carrington (2015) defines what he terms 'post/colonial' as the period following the Second World War after the formal demise of western European colonial regimes (for example, the independence of India from Britain in 1947). Post/colonial theory is the attempt to understand how some countries were able to control and exploit others through the process of colonialism; how these regimes were sustained and resisted; and how colonialism affected the culture, language, and identity of the 'non-Western' nations as well as to interrogate the very belief systems of Western nations. Of course, there remains an argument that Western regimes are still dominant and, as such, we are not yet in a post/colonial era.

In applying post/colonial theory to sports, Carrington (2015) argues that there is limited work in this area and, too often, the focus is on analyses of sports in societies that were formerly colonized rather than a critical examination of the ways in which countries might be 'post/colonial' in different ways and what this means for a sociology of sport. Furthermore, colonialism provides the foundations for a logic that sport started in Europe and was diffused through the colonies, which means that so much of the sociology of sport focuses on sporting forms and culture that are recognized in Western nations. There is much merit in developing a sociology of sport in India that focuses on understanding the role of traditional Indian sports as well as the commercial professional sports that may be more widely recognized on the global sporting stage (see Mani and Krishnamurthy 2016).

It is encouraging that there have been significant advances in the sociological study of sport in India, reflected in the development of a research group for the sociology of sport within the Indian Sociological Society, the website

148 REFLECTIONS ON SPORTS STUDIES

'Beyond the Scoreboard: Sports Studies Hub' and, indeed, the publication of this book. Future research, which critically analyses Western sociological theories, considers the relevance of post/colonial thought, and draws on the wealth of expertise within the Indian academic community, will further enrich the understanding of sport in Indian society but, perhaps more importantly, will enable the Indian sociology of sport to further enrich a global understanding of sport and the international sociology of sport community.

Note

i. In the context to the chapter, it was identified that the author of this paper is not Indian. In reflecting on the theories outlined in the chapter, it may be worth considering whether: an Indian scholar might have a different, or better, understanding of the 'functions' of sport in India if drawing on a functionalist perspective; someone who has never lived in India should be commenting on the economic power and exploitation in sport in the country from a conflict theoretical framework; a non-Indian scholar might have a complete critical theoretical understanding of the field and habitus of Indian sport and sports people; a white Western woman can realistically draw on her own feminist perspective to fully appreciate the situation for Indian sportswomen and marginalized sportsmen; it is possible to understand the interactions within the Indian sporting social world without having spent time with the participants. These are considerations for the readers of this chapter to reach their own conclusions.

References

Bandyopadhyay, K. 2005. 'Sports History in India: Prospects and Problems'. *The International Journal of the History of Sport* 22 (4): 708–21.

———. 2008. 'The Nation and its Fragments: Football and Community in India'. *Soccer and Society* 9 (3): 377–93.

Bourdieu, P. 1986. *Distinction*. London: Routledge.

Carrington, B. 2015. 'Post/colonial Theory and Sport'. In R. Giulianotti (ed.), *The Routledge Handbook on the Sociology of Sport*, pp. 105–15. Abingdon: Routledge.

Carter, T. 2011. 'Interrogating Athletic Urbanism: On Examining the Politics of the City Underpinning the Production of the Spectacle'. *International Review for the Sociology of Sport* 46 (2): 131–9.

Coakley, J. and E. Pike. 2014. *Sports in Society: Issues and Controversies*. Maidenhead: McGraw Hill/Oxford University Press.

A SOCIOLOGICAL UNDERSTANDING OF SPORT IN INDIA   149

Curi, M., J. Knijnik, and G. Mascarenhas. 2011. 'The Pan American Games in Rio de Janeiro 2007: Consequences of a Sport Mega Event on a BRIC Country'. *International Review for the Sociology of Sport* 46 (2): 140–56.

Delaney, T. 2015. 'The Functionalist Perspective on Sport'. In R. Giulianotti (ed.), *The Routledge Handbook on the Sociology of Sport*, pp. 18–28. Abingdon: Routledge.

Deshpande, S. 2001. 'Disciplinary Predicaments: Sociology and Anthropology in Postcolonial India'. *Inter-Asia Cultural Studies* 2 (2): 247–60.

Elias, N. 2000. *The Civilising Process.* Oxford: Blackwell.

Elias, N. and E. Dunning. 1986. *Quest for Excitement: Sport and Leisure in the Civilising Process.* Oxford: Blackwell.

Hargreaves, John. 1982. 'Sport, Culture and Ideology'. In Jennifer Hargreaves (ed.), *Sport, Culture and Ideology*, pp. 30–61. London: Routledge and Kegan Paul.

Houlihan, B. and D. Malcolm. 2016. *Sport and Society.* London: SAGE.

Majumdar, B. 2003. 'Forwards and Backwards: Women's Soccer in Twentieth Century India'. *Soccer and Society* 4 (2–3): 80–94.

Malcolm, D. 2015. 'Norbert Elias and the Sociology of Sport'. In R. Giulianotti (ed.) *The Routledge Handbook on the Sociology of Sport*, pp. 50–60. Abingdon: Routledge.

Mani, V. and M. Krishnamurthy. 2016. 'Sociology of Sport: India'. In K. Young (ed.) *Sociology of Sport: A Global Subdiscipline in Review (Research in the Sociology of Sport, Volume 9)*, pp. 37–57. Bingley: Emerald Publishing.

McDonald, I. 2000. 'India'. In J. Coakley and E. Dunning (eds), *Handbook of Sports Studies*, pp. 539–41. London: SAGE.

———. 2003. 'Hindu Nationalism, Cultural Spaces, and Bodily Practices in India'. *American Behavioral Scientist* 46 (11): 1563–76.

———. 2015. 'Marxist and Neo-Marxist Approaches'. In R. Giulianotti (ed.), *The Routledge Handbook on the Sociology of Sport*, pp. 40–9. Abingdon: Routledge.

Mercer, P. 2015. 'Cricket World Cup hosts Australia and NZ to reap rewards?' *BBC News*, 12 February.

Mills, J. 2001. 'Football in Goa: Sport, Politics and the Portuguese in India'. *Soccer and Society* 2 (2): 75–88.

Palmer, C. 2013. *Global Sports Policy.* London: SAGE.

Pike, E. and J. Coakley. 2010. 'The Social Significance of Sport'. *eSocialSciences*, 21 February.

Srinivas, M. 1987. 'Development of Sociology in India: An Overview'. *Economic and Political Weekly* 27 (4): 135–8.

Stevenson, C. and J. Nixon. 1972. 'A Conceptual Scheme of the Social Functions of Sports'. *Sportwissenschaft* 2: 119–32.

9

Labours of Care in Sport

Reflections on Feminist Practice in Athletics

Meena Gopal

This chapter lays out some of the core aspects of the practice of sport from a feminist perspective. The essence of the essay is to demonstrate how the endeavour of sport, in this instance track and field sport or athletics, a non-contact sport that is practised at diverse levels of competitiveness, can be seen as participatory, inclusive, and emancipatory. It tries to delve into these principles adopting the feminist lens of care labour.

What appears to be a contradiction, that of practising care in the context of competition and aggression, is sought to be unpacked through a discussion on the role of mentoring, nurturance, and development of sport where aspiring athletes are groomed through the stages of fun and play into levels of gruelling competition at regional, national, and international arenas of sport.

Feminist Framing

Using an autoethnographic approach,[i] the author presents a personalized narrative that is interwoven with other contextual evidence to sketch the role that mentoring plays in keeping the core of sporting practice ongoing. Through this qualitative approach, the role of the labour of care is attempted to be placed on a continuum in the understanding of sport. Sport strives to achieve excellence through training and competition. However, the basis for this routine and rigour are nurturance and mentoring. It is these two impulses that the chapter tries to integrate for the realization of an emancipatory imaginary and a democratic community using a feminist lens.

Earlier feminist perspectives have foregrounded the inequality in opportunities and lack of visibility to women in sport, moving later to unravelling the discourses of masculinity and femininity that influence power relations, along with the intersections of gender and other social locations (Scraton and

Meena Gopal, *Labours of Care in Sport* In: *Sports Studies in India*. Edited by: Meena Gopal and Padma Prakash, Oxford University Press. © Oxford University Press 2021.
DOI: 10.1093/oso/9780190130640.003.0010

Flintoff 2013). In addition, recent literature challenges the dominance of the Global North in the production of knowledge that relegates the experiences and theorizing that emerges from the global periphery. These emphasize how voice and representation need to be nuanced, reflecting local contexts, and how issues of empowerment and emancipation challenge a global script, some of which reflect an ambivalent attitude towards femininity, albeit implicitly feminist in its practice. These emerging literatures also offer insights into methodologies of eliciting knowledge from the diverse standpoints (Toffoletti, Palmer, and Samie 2018). There is also scholarship on sport and leisure cultivating values, feelings, capacities for care, strength of will, compassion, and human relationships that suggests further enquiry (Duquin 2000). Further, the need is to also reclaim sport, especially in South Asia, from the realm of sports markets to that of sport commons, as communities where sports is nurtured have greater claim to participation than sport being a vehicle of just profits for industry (Biyanwila 2018: 1–10).

Moving beyond while also incorporating these above feminist articulations, the paper focuses on the labour of care, or nurture, of mentoring as the key vehicle for the development of athletics. Feminist analyses and discussions on sexual division of labour bring out its gendered nature, and makes visible the unpaid and unacknowledged care labour done by women. Such devaluation of care labour further erases the contribution of anyone performing nurture. Such care labour, that builds the institutions of sport, is evident when women nurture young children into play, families support sportspersons, community organizations contribute to building young sporting careers, and finally institutions, such as the school, college, and state bodies, encourage, sustain, and fund individuals, groups, and their endeavours. Much of the labour that goes into the nurture of sport comes under this realm. Within this critical domain of care, the voluntary efforts of those individuals who nurture and support the evolution of sporting cultures, its participatory and inclusive reach, and its emancipatory ideals is placed. Mentoring young people in schools and community organizations, such as sports clubs, thus forms the terrain on which these questions are explored in this chapter.

The chapter discusses the layers of mentoring, both experienced and observed, that enveloped the sporting phase in the author's life beginning with the experience of competing in school, university, and later national-level track and field events, beginning in the city of Madras (now Chennai), in Tamil Nadu. In this experience, the school and the sports club, which is

152   REFLECTIONS ON SPORTS STUDIES

community based, form noteworthy trajectories of mentorship, nurture, and support.

Schools and Their Priorities:
A Brief Overview

In India, the skewed nature of the development of schools means poor infrastructure is the lot of public schools that is mostly accessed by the poorer classes, with an uneven spread of private schools managed by trusts, religious institutions, missionaries, and others that could boast of some semblance of avenues for creativity and the development of bodily cultures for children. While not attempting a review of the literature in the field, this section draws on the experience of the author. In the 1980s, this was evident in the difference in the spread of curricular and extra-curricular education among the schools, with its impact being felt on the lack of priority given to sporting activities within the school system. Physical education or PT was mundane compulsion that children were put through, but often in a chaotic manner that neither enhanced their potential for emancipation nor built any form of bodily cultures.

Some of the states in India did nurture what are known as sports schools, attempting to follow but ending up poor and corrupt imitations of the East European model of beginning the nurture of sports among young people in schools, and sports hostels which then feeds into the higher education system, expecting continued support from the state. For instance, Kerala has a proactive Sports Council that has under its structure numerous school sports hostels to cater to the needs of school children and nurture them into promising players. One of the most prominent among them, set up in the 1970s, was the G V Raja Sports School (Sreekumar 2004).[ii]

But the environment of patronage that dominated the functioning of state associations and federations in our context meant that nurturing talent among youth by organizing competitions and coaching camps, eliciting dedicated coaches, and maintaining sports facilities and infrastructure was less of a priority while the competition among the officials was in seeking favours in the form of opportunities to travel abroad, creating groups to advance their agenda within the associations and federations. Those states such as Kerala where the network of the schools, hostels that are set up by the state sports council were more widespread, some of the talent was tapped and it emerged in the form of the sports stars such as P.T. Usha and Shiny Abraham (Wilson).

Given the sad story of the public nurture of sports in schools, the role of nurture and mentoring in the private and the not-so-private realm of the sports club deserve mention. In the late 1980s, there were thriving sports clubs in Bangalore (now Bengaluru) and Bombay (now Mumbai) that produced track and field athletes such as Ashwini Nachappa and Reeth Abraham, and Adille Sumariwalla and Bakhtawar Khambatta, respectively.

From School to Club

The following autoethnographic account of the author will discuss the transition from the school to the sports club as a space to nurture talent, and the creative role of the mentor who sought the best interests of the athletes while also nurturing networks of institutions that would bring in young people from a vast pool rather than only nurture those from elite and privileged backgrounds. Some of the clubs recognized the important relationship between schools and subsequent nurture of sport. The school as a cradle of the nurture of sport was evident in the special care taken by some of the heads of institutions in Madras such as the Salesians of the Don Bosco, the Franciscan Missionaries of Mary, and the Presentation Order, who formed part of the pool of 'convent' educational institutions.

It was 1981, and the annual Don Bosco Athletic Club's (DBAC) Kiddies Meet was announced. The Irish nun, the energetic principal of St. Ursula's Anglo-Indian Higher Secondary School of the Presentation Order, selected a few of the young girls who had just won several top spots in the school's annual sports competition to participate in the Meet. Among them was I, just fifteen. The principal urged me along with a batch of girls to attend the weekend practice sessions that the coach from DBAC had informed the school about. He had reached out to several school principals to send young girls and boys who displayed interest, and not necessarily talent, for practice sessions.

Among the other competitions that the DBAC organized was the innovative annual Pentathlon Meet, where the all-round ability of the participants was on display, including a sprint or hurdle race, a jump and a throwing event, and a middle-distance run. These were thrown in for good measure for a variety of age groups beginning from under nine, progressing till under sixteen and nineteen years for girls and boys, respectively, and above that onto women's and men's categories. The year I joined the DBAC in its practice sessions, the Pentathlon Meet was in its twenty-fifth year. It was no coincidence

154   REFLECTIONS ON SPORTS STUDIES

that I would later go onto creating the All-India Inter-University Athletics Heptathlon (an extension of the pentathlon) record for women and holding it for a while. There would be other national and regional competitions for which the athletes of the club would train along with its own local competitive events. Thus, the DBAC as a community-based organization both conducted competitions to encourage talent while democratising its own reach as a training organization extending itself to diverse schools to attract their young sporting talent.

Networks of Nurture

In the club itself, the practice sessions would go on every weekend all year round, with the competition season ensuring more sessions during the week, and the off-season being a bit lean in attendance. The summer months would witness vigorous routines with special camps in the city or even short trips to some exciting place where rigorous tests of endurance were enacted. The main driving force of the Don Bosco Athletic Club was its coach A.J. de Souza, who was a salesman in explosives for a chemical production company, but whose passion was track and field athletics, which he pursued as a voluntary vocation. A.J., as he was known among the athletic community as well as sporting officialdom, founded the club in 1960 with Ken Bosen, who later became one of the established athletic coaches at the National Institute of Sports, Patiala, and Father McFerran of the Salesian order that founded the Don Bosco institutions (see *The Hindu* 2005).

The core of the mentoring regimen was directed at achieving excellence in competition. A.J. had meticulously charted out training schedules for everyone in the practice session. It was utterly democratic; everybody, the youngest participant in the Kiddies Meet to the average university- and college-level athlete to the Asian medallist in triple jump, were equitably tutored. There was seriousness to the various drills, short packages prescribed, and a trial run or event to be clocked for timings and distance covered for each of the training sessions. A.J. also made it a point to bring fun and play into the three-hour training sessions. A day or a session missed was noted with annoyance, indicating that the labour put into the attention of the athlete was being slighted. A stickler for punctuality, his wards would scuttle around to begin the warm-up, which ought to have been completed before his arrival, on hearing the sputter of his Yezdi motorbike entering the grounds. Gazing from a distance across the field, his sharp eye would keep account of every movement, every interval, and every culmination of practice; although terse in his communication, the outcomes of dedicated care of each person's routine was evident in the progress seen in competitions.

It was not just the entry into the portals of the club from the school that kept up the link of nurture, but attention was paid to the space of the training. The initial couple of years of training after I enlisted in the DBAC in 1981 was at the grounds of a school in Central Madras, St. George's Anglo-Indian Higher Secondary School. Athletes of the club from all parts of Madras, North, Central, and South would congregate every weekend for the practice sessions from 3 to 6 p.m. Thus, schools would extend their patronage by lending their spaces as well, to nurture the club's attention to young athletes. After a few years, A.J. befriended a professor at the YMCA College of Physical Education located in South Madras, who later went on to become its principal and sought permission for the training of the club's athletes. For several years thereafter, the cool environs of the YMCA College at Nandanam was the training grounds for several of us. Thus, not just private schools but state institutions were also enlisted in this development of athletes and their care. Additionally, sports facilities such as stadiums that had the patronage of the city police, the Rajarathnam stadium in Egmore, for example, were also a part of the club's repertoire of spaces in organizing sporting events or in encouraging the athletes to participate in the state schools' meet, city's intercollegiate athletic meets, and inter-university athletic meets.

The Don Bosco Athletic Club and its coach and chief administrator, A.J. thus had this vision of modifying and incorporating the East European model of development of athletics in his own way, incorporating several institutions into creating a generation of competitive athletes but also committed social individuals. His approach was to generate sustained interest in school authorities and patrons among state associations as well as be connected with some of those within the coaching fraternity. Thus, the club formed a bridge between the school as a source of athletic potential and the broad set of institutions that formed the community space for the development of the sport. This ensured that sport remained within the common pool into which newer talent was added to develop the competitive thrust or an expansion of the space with the potential for young people to have fun and play. Thus, the labour of care nurtured diligently added to a democratization of the sport and avoided elitist inclinations. The state was constantly made accountable and present even as schools generated the pool of young people.

An extension of the labour of grooming athletes was A.J.'s passion for writing about sport. All through his own sporting and subsequent coaching

156 REFLECTIONS ON SPORTS STUDIES

career, A.J. was a prolific writer. Thus, the knowledge generated was documented with care, absorbing the visions learnt through international experiments that were customized for local use and application. A regular contributor to *The Hindu* and its sports columns, A.J. disseminated the knowledge gathered over the years, authored four books titled, *Handbook of Professional Sport Management* (2005), *Track Geography and Field Sites* (1995; inspired by Ken O. Bosen), *Total Fitness for Higher Performance Sports* (1985; co-authored with V.R. Beedu, Bangalore), and *Romancing the Decathlon* (2005) (Nair 2005).

Social Relations, Self, and the Body

The significance of the club space was its inclusivity, attracting flocks of young people from schools, including wards brought by parents to be specifically coached and others who just wandered in. Communities did not envelop just the athletes but incorporated an enthusiastic parent or sibling, who would then be invited to be part of some camp or competition that the club participated in with a bunch of athletes young and old. Thus, members of families accompanying their wards did not deter the professional expectations that the coach had of his athletes. My peers included a bunch of Anglo-Indian youngsters, a couple of Brahmins, a few Other Backward Class (OBC) and Dalit men and women from local colleges, and a couple of Bohra Muslims, all of whose names alone alluded remotely to their social location. Nothing in the way the coach treated them and the social interaction within the athletic arena indicated favour or discrimination. A.J.'s journalistic talent and wry sense of humour only added to the general bonhomie through his penchant for cartoons, where all of us became objects of hilarious depictions. His favourite appellation was 'coconut oil' to refer to the Malayalis among us! Most importantly, men and women were on par. It was a matter of chance that the bunch of women among us performed well in the competitive arena, be it the national level school games, the university competitions, the national camps, and international selections.

The labour of mentoring proceeded to be equitable whatever body you possessed, awkward, sleek, bulky, light. Everybody had similar routines if your levels of competence were similar, be it the school star, the university champion, or the Asian medallist. All of us participated in the gruelling bounds up the St. Thomas's mount steps, the beach games with medicine ball, or the morning runs by the sea in the summer months, in teams formed earlier with names such as 'cool cats' and 'hot dogs' comprising all athletes, stars, and newcomers alike. The preparations in the off season and the competitive season were challenging as they were exciting; we watched ourselves coming into our own, our 'forms' evident as we felt our bodies perform effortlessly, while at times be suffering from injury.

For several of us women, this coming into our own was a movement into another domain, of liberation experienced through the body as it transcended height, distance, and speed, and brought relief from shame. We joyously resisted sexualized cultures of bodily display and those of heterosexist wifehood and motherhood, grabbing our freedoms felt through sporting gear such as shorts, spikes, singlets, all of which offer women of all classes an equitable space among other athletes and professionals. The atmosphere in the athletic club gave neither preferences nor exclusions but offered an emancipatory community, free from barriers of participation, much like a community space that women sought outside the home and the hearth. Of course, things were not all hunky-dory or without dissonance, but the common feel of a sports community was clearly nurtured and not inhibited. Most of all, menstruation and hygiene did not appear as barriers to us as young women who trained and competed alongside one another. It was, of course, my specific experience that my performance, for instance, in competing in a high jump event on the day that I menstruated enhanced my effort helping me cover a greater height than usual.

The labour of care is incrementally built, with the school being the catchment area of youthful energies, which are then groomed subsequently within the sports club. Other institutions are enlisted along the way, democratizing the arena of sport while keeping fun and play alive for children across classes and channelizing specific talent into competition. A feminist view on this labour, however, notes that such effort by consistent sports workers is not devalued as gendered labour is within social reproduction. Here, a successful but delicate democratic balance is maintained between keeping the sports commons alive while maintaining the rigour of sports excellence in competition. In addition to participation in a community of sports persons, which is the result of labours of care and practices of mentoring, the latter integrates various institutions and broadens inclusion, offering spaces of liberation for women specifically, and working to be emancipatory to all who venture into it.

158   REFLECTIONS ON SPORTS STUDIES

Notes

i. Autoethnography as a method was found most appropriate to think about the formative role that individuals and institutions play in sustaining care and nurture in sport. See Ellis, Adams, and Bochner (2011).
ii. See also details of the G V Raja Sports School, available at https://www.sportskerala.org/GV_RajaSportsSchool; accessed 18 April 2019.

References

Biyanwila, S.J. 2018. *Sports and the Global South: Work Play and Resistance in Sri Lanka*. Cham, Switzerland: Palgrave Macmillan.

Duquin, M. 2000. 'Sport and Emotions'. In Jay Coakley and Eric Dunning (eds), *Handbook of Sports Studies*, pp. 477–89. London: SAGE.

Ellis, Carolyn, Tony E. Adams, and Arthur P. Bochner. 2011. 'Autoethnography: An Overview'. *Forum: Qualitative Social Research* 12 (1). Available at https://www.qualitative-research.net/index.php/fqs/article/view/1589/3095; accessed 18 April 2019.

Hindu, The. 2005. 'Ken Bosen Passes Away', 17 February. Available at https://www.thehindu.com/2005/02/17/stories/2005021703681900.htm; accessed 18 April 2005.

Nair, Shashi. 2005. 'A Guide to Professionally Managing Sport'. *Madras Musings*, 1–15 September, p.8. Available at http://madrasmusings.com/older-archives/Vol%2015/Vol%20XV%20-%20No%2010.pdf; accessed 20 April 2019.

Scraton, S. and A. Flintoff. 2013. 'Gender, Feminist Theory and Sport'. In David L. Andrews and Ben Carrington (eds), *A Companion to Sport*, pp. 96–111. Chichester, UK: Blackwell Publishing Ltd.

Sreekumar, P. 2004. 'Sports Council Picks Up Speed'. *Kerala Calling*, p.16.

Toffoletti, K., C. Palmer, and S. Samie. 2018. 'Introduction: Sport, Feminism and the Global South'. *Sociology of Sport Journal* 35 (3): 193–6. doi: https://doi.org/10.1123/ssj.2018-0077.

10

Perspectives on Sports History in India

Present Challenges and Future Directions[*]

Kausik Bandyopadhyay

I was only four when my father first took me to Kolkata *maidan*[1] to watch a football match. After that followed many more matches—football, cricket, and hockey—through my school days. He was full of stories and anecdotes on Indian football and cricket, which inspired me to look upon sport as an integral part of my life. My passion for the game drove me to take up the social history of Bengali football as the subject of my doctoral research in the late 1990s. I also started teaching in universities from 1998, and since then, I have concentrated on understanding the significance of sport, particularly football and cricket, in South Asia. Sport became an intriguing lens to look upon the histories of colonialism, nationalism, communalism, decolonization, international relations, popular culture, and so on in the South Asian context.

However, the road to study and teach the history of sport in India has been challenging, often against heavy odds.

When I first wrote on the status of sports history in India (Bandyopadhyay 2005), the subject was only in its infancy. The quality and quantity of scholarly work since 2010s have significantly increased, even though the number of scholars seem still only a few.[2] The horizontal growth of sports history in India as well as in South Asia, still seems quite limited, and we are quite behind the task of overcoming 'that deep and abiding intellectual suspicion which is so commonly manifested towards the very concept of sports history

---

[*] This chapter has been developed following two of my earlier writings on the same subject, namely, K. Bandyopadhyay, 2005, 'Sports History in India: Prospects and Problems', *The International Journal of the History of Sport* 22 (3–4): 708–21 and K. Bandyopadhyay, 2017a, 'Fighting Against Heavy Odds: An Indian Perspective on Sports History', *The International Journal of the History of Sport* 34 (5–6): 320–5. It may, therefore, resonate some of the arguments and discussions offered in those writings. On a different note, this article may be seen as a broad and discursive sequel to the same.

Kausik Bandyopadhyay, *Perspectives on Sports History in India* In: *Sports Studies in India*. Edited by: Meena Gopal and Padma Prakash, Oxford University Press. © Oxford University Press 2021.
DOI: 10.1093/oso/9780190130640.003.0011

160   REFLECTIONS ON SPORTS STUDIES

or sports sociology' (Walvin 1984). The problems and prospects facing sports history in India need to be addressed immediately if the study of sport has to develop as a serious intellectual discipline.[3] In this chapter, drawing on my experiences of doing research on and teaching the history of sport over the past two decades, I intend to identify and address the present challenges confronting sports history in India and look forward to its future potential.

Sport in Indian History: A Historiographical Note

The Indian academia's tryst with sports history dates back to 1988 when Soumen Mitra, a graduate of the Presidency College, Kolkata, and an MA in history from Calcutta University, submitted an MPhil dissertation at Jawaharlal Nehru University, New Delhi, on the theme of sport in colonial India (Mitra 1988).[4] It was also late 1980s onwards that cricket was considered seriously by Indian writers such as Mihir Bose (1990), Ashis Nandy (1989), Ramachandra Guha (1992, 1994, 1998, 2002), and Arjun Appadurai (1995). Little attention, however, was paid to either historical studies of other sports or to sport in general.

Non-Indian specialists on sport in India have mostly focused on the games introduced by the British in the colonial period. Much of this work has dealt with cricket (see for instance, the works of Edward Docker [1976] and Richard Cashman [1979]) Some of the studies on colonial Indian sport focus on the colonial introduction of modern sports and explore deeper imperial motives behind this and their impact upon Indian life.[5] Some European scholars have also studied indigenous sports and games of India (see, for example, Alter [1992, 2000] and Zarrilli [2004]).

The recent major Indian contributions to the history of sport have come mostly from a few noted Indian sports historians (Bandyopadhyay [2011, 2012, 2015, 2017b]; Majumdar [2004a, 2004b, 2018]; Majumdar and Bandyopadhyay [2006]; Majumdar and Mangan [2005]; Majumdar and Mehta [2008, 2010]; Mitra [2006]; R. Sen [2015]; S. Sen [2004]).[6] These works have concentrated on histories of various sports, particularly cricket and football in India, India's engagement with the Olympics and the Commonwealth Games, and the evolution of sports culture in India in relation to the diverse forces and factors such as colonialism, nationalism, communalism, regionalism, postcolonialism, commercialism, identity, gender, and so on. Although most of the scholarly writing has focused on modern

PERSPECTIVES ON SPORTS HISTORY IN INDIA   161

sports in India, a few have tried to explore sports in ancient and medieval India (Pearson 1984; R. Sen 2015).[7] There is, of course, no dearth of popular and journalistic writings on diverse aspects of Indian sport, including autobiographies and biographies, with cricket receiving the greatest attention.

Doing Sports History:
The Researcher's Battle

Like many other forms of social behaviour, as James Walvin (1984: 8) rightly noted, sporting activity is largely socially and historically determined. Hence, the prime purpose in the academic exercise of research in the history of sport should not aim at a descriptive study of a particular sport, but try to understand and explain what it says about the society of a particular period. There have been, as Ramachandra Guha (1998: 157) has suggested, two approaches to the Indian history of sport. The first has focused narrowly on its practice, the background of its patrons and players, the evolution of its associations and tournaments, and how it pays or does not pay for itself. The second approach, which Guha himself prefers, uses sport to illuminate themes of wider interest and relevance.

> It views sport as a *relational idiom*, a sphere of activity which expresses, in concentrated form, the values, prejudices, divisions and unifying symbols of a society. (Guha 1998: 157)

However, Guha's (1998: 158) assertion that the sociology and politics of cricket 'presumes no technical knowledge of the game itself' is not tenable because changes in its rules, rituals, and vocabulary are intimately related to and highly influenced by the politics, culture, and economy of the game.

The study of sport as history offers major correctives to our understanding of the social and economic history of late nineteenth- and twentieth-century India. There has also been a quite irrational yet popular belief that only the 'committed', the insiders or the practitioners, are qualified to pursue sports history. This is certainly a flawed assumption. Personal experience or membership of course can be useful at times in understanding 'certain distinct sensibilities which outsiders could never experience' (Walvin 1984: 7). But that should never be considered a deciding factor in pursuing academic research on sport. Walvin (1984: 7) is again pertinent in his comment:

162   REFLECTIONS ON SPORTS STUDIES

[S]uch claims to exclusivity are intellectually crippling and depend ultimately for their *rationale* on the belief that there is, or ought to be, only
one particular approach or interpretation of historical experience. It is to
be hoped that sports history will avoid such factional fights, although this is
not to claim that sporting practitioners have *nothing* to tell us. Far from it.
What is quite clear however is that one does not need to be player, spectator
or *aficionado*—of any sport—to appreciate its broader social, or historical
significance.

Social historians, therefore, should not feel obliged to describe events or
matches that they never saw or engage in discussions of the tactics employed.
It is less important for our purposes to understand the genius of Virat Kohli[8]
and P.V. Sindhu[9] than to analyse what sport means and why it matters.[10]
Nevertheless, as noted earlier, it can be useful to have some knowledge of
the evolution of a game's technicalities, which sometimes proves crucial in
understanding its social history. It is also important to look at a sport's local
origins, developments, and specificities, without which the construction
of its wider national history can be a flawed exercise. To again use Walvin's
(1984: 10) words, 'more emphasis needs to be placed on local studies without
losing sight of the broader context' or, for that matter, 'general structures do
indeed have a place, but they will inevitably be subjected to the qualifications
of specific and local peculiarities'. To achieve this end, the study of sport in
India from the perspective of social history should put a strong emphasis on
vernacular sources. This has not been true of the past.

Finally, to establish sport as a legitimate part of historical studies and other
social sciences in India (and across the world) may sometimes raise the question of the autonomy of sports history. There are two ways to approach the
question: using sport as a lens to illuminate wider issues of society, politics,
culture, or economy; and/or using a host of contexts (social, political, cultural, or economic) and perspectives (of the social sciences) to understand
the importance of sport. Hence, an interdisciplinary framework and a comparative perspective in convergence may be a useful methodology to study
sport as a historical experience and subject. In this context, it is important to
remember what Walvin (1984: 13) stated more than three decades ago:

In the determination to establish legitimacy there is the basic danger of
overstatement and exaggeration. This, however, is not the most seductive
danger, for in seeking to stake out an autonomous historical empire, it is all
too easy to wrench sports history from its determining social and economic

context. There is no single model upon which the sports historian ought to proceed but in the last resort the viability and even the respectability of sports history must rest upon the quality of the work produced. Unless the traditional canons of historical research and reconstruction are applied to this relatively new field, it will not—and ought not to—gain acceptance. Like sport itself, sports history will ultimately depend on the skills and imagination of its practitioners.

The problems faced by a sports historian in India are often frustrating and challenging: frustrating because the essentially 'non-academic' character of sports authorities, personalities, and spectators in India makes the task of collecting primary materials hopelessly difficult, with journalists preferring to keep valuable sources with themselves than to share with researchers; and challenging because researchers still find it difficult to convince academic bodies and funding agencies in India of the credibility and relevance of research in the history of sport, often depriving them the best of academic supervision and funding.[11]

The long-standing academic negativity and myopia towards accepting sport as worthy of serious research often makes the quest of the researcher much more critical. I faced this attitude while pursuing my research in the late 1990s, and was often ridiculed by established Indian academics for working on a 'trivial' aspect. This remained the trend for long despite the fact there have been efforts to institutionalize sports history research in India and, occasionally, create research facilities. India became the first non-European country to have an Annex of the International Research Centre for Sport, Socialization and Society (IRCSSS), situated at the De Montfort University, England.[12] The Annex centre was expected to offer an institutional space including a quality research infrastructure to all those interested in sports history. It also had plans to act as an interdisciplinary forum to promote future research in sports studies in general.[13] The publishing successes of IRCSSS in the West ensured a positive response from publishers such as Oxford University Press (India), Penguin India, Yoda Press, Harper Collins (India), and Marine Sports of Mumbai.[14] In addition, Ananda Publishers, Kolkata, agreed to publish the most important IRCSSS works in Bengali.[15] A sports library centre for excellence was also founded in the Cricket Association of Bengal at the Eden Gardens in 2005. Unfortunately, none of these ventures have progressed well, as both the centres have become non-functional.[16]

164   REFLECTIONS ON SPORTS STUDIES

Teaching Sports History:
The Teacher's Struggle

At the turn of the twentieth century, I found it hard to include sport as part of postgraduate studies in history simply because of the absence of sufficient quality research and publications. But I believed that teaching sports history at the postgraduate level within the broader discipline of historical studies would help dispel the erroneous views about the relative unimportance of sport in the shaping of modern Indian society and culture and make students aware of the extent to which entertainment and leisure have a compelling influence on their lives.

It is relevant here perhaps to provide my contrasting experiences of teaching sports history in the two departments of history where I have taught to date—North Bengal University and West Bengal State University.[17] I first started teaching sports history at North Bengal University in 2000, not as a part of social history but as a part of the political history of modern India after 1857.[18] I found it useful to present sport as a novel political tool in the analysis of a redefined relationship between the British and the native princes in the aftermath of the Revolt of 1857. Students showed immense interest and excitement in the early lectures on the importance of sport in the politics of reconciliation in the context of aristocratic reaction in British policy in the post-Revolt period. Later, I developed a perspective in tune with J.A. Mangan's widely acclaimed *The Games Ethic and Imperialism* (1998) in order to impress upon them sport's political and social importance beyond leisure or entertainment by means of a discussion of the significance of public-school sports like cricket as moral tools of the Empire as well as essential cultural instruments in the Anglicization of the native aristocracy. Students with modern India as their specialization chose these topics for their seminars with considerable enthusiasm.[19] A few students with Mughal India as specialization offered the games and sports of that age as their seminar presentations.[20] For project papers based on students' field work, I tried to break the mould by suggesting that they consider the growth and impact of modern sports in colonial India under the supervision of an interested colleague and I.[21]

Despite my efforts, popularizing sports history research proved to be an uphill task. The moderation board for the final question papers rejected the questions I set for the postgraduate final examinations on sport.[22] The fight to establish the credibility of sports history continued. In 2002, the postgraduate syllabus in history was drastically revised in the North Bengal University,

PERSPECTIVES ON SPORTS HISTORY IN INDIA   165

yet I failed to find sport a place in the social and cultural history of modern India. I was allotted a large portion of social and cultural history and the history of Indian nationalism and the nation-state as teaching assignments. This gave me the long-awaited opportunity to reflect upon the importance of sport as an instrument of nation and national identity in modern India. The students' response was overwhelmingly positive to the lectures and tutorials. In consequence, the moderators now found reason to include a few questions I set on sport in the final question paper. Counting on students' positive response as also on the moral support of a few colleagues, I could convince the Departmental Committee to accept a proposal to introduce Sports History at the MPhil level. The Committee unanimously agreed to 'the introduction of sports history in the M.Phil course with potentiality for external funding' and resolved to 'elevate it to a full-fledged self-financed Diploma Course'.[23] The M.Phil Committee also approved the introduction of sports history as an optional paper in modern Indian history group from the session 2004–5.[24]

I joined the newly founded West Bengal State University in 2009 with the responsibility of framing the syllabus in history for the master's course and making the department a quality one along with my mostly young colleagues. It was a long-desired opportunity for me to introduce sport and other aspects of popular culture into teaching and research. After a battle spanning nearly a decade, sport obtained its worthy place in history in an Indian university. The experience of teaching and supervising research at this place for the last nine years has been really enriching, thanks to the support from the university authority as also from the departmental colleagues. Of course, the positive response from students has been the most significant outcome from this exercise.

With sustained effort, it is possible to introduce the teaching of sports history in India's universities. West Bengal has already taken the lead in this regard, where a number of universities have incorporated sport as part of teaching and research programmes in history.[25] Even secondary educational boards have now included sport in the curriculum in history.[26] Similarly, one undergraduate text book by a senior Indian historian included aspects of popular culture including sport in the history of modern India (Sarkar 2014). However, the scenario with regard to the teaching of sport as part of history and other social sciences does not look healthy at all in other parts of India.

166   REFLECTIONS ON SPORTS STUDIES

The Way Forward

Leopold von Ranke, the architect of 'scientific history', once commented:

> For history is not simply an academic subject: the knowledge of the history
> of mankind should be a common property of humanity and should above
> all benefit our nation, without which our work could not have been accom-
> plished. (Quoted in Marwick 1970: 44)

Although committed to the necessity for specialized research, Ranke was
aware of 'the danger of losing sight of the universal, of the type of *knowledge everyone desires*' (quoted in Marwick 1970: 44; emphasis added). He
acknowledged that 'history is indeed a social necessity, the property of all
humanity' (quoted in Marwick 1970: 44). What Ranke suggested about the
knowledge of history in particular may well be extended to the wider field of
social sciences. Academic research on the central role of sport as an integral
part of popular culture in the everyday life of a community or nation in ancient, medieval, or modern societies requires an eclectic approach that seriously reconsiders the long-lived dichotomy of the *intellectual* and the *popular*
in the study of history and other social sciences. As the greatest Indian poet
Rabindranath Tagore lamented a century ago:

> A careful thought reveals that the difference between the educated and un-
> educated in our country lies in their knowledge of history. Common people
> have no idea of how men have grown strong, got together and achieved
> what they have; they fail to comprehend the flow of the thoughts and ideas
> of the educated and cannot join their activities. It's pathetic on the part
> of humans not to know what man has achieved and has been capable of
> achieving in this world. (Tagore 1992: 453; author's translation)

The sports historian can make an attempt to reflect upon and bridge the intellectual gap that still persists between the two poles. Sport affords a domain
where the social scientist can honestly blend the *intellectual* with the *popular*
without really disturbing their respective sanctities. Works on sports history
in India should make the point that intellectualizing the popular and popularizing the intellectual can go hand in hand and generate a synthesized genre
of scholarship.

PERSPECTIVES ON SPORTS HISTORY IN INDIA   167

While making the above assertion, I share the concern expressed by S.N. Mukherjee in the 1970s, again, with reference to the writing of history as an intellectual discipline:

> We must recognise that historians are made for history and the reverse cannot be true. We should not only concern ourselves with the problems, which the man in the street faced in the past, but make them entertaining and instructive for the man in the street today. . . . [T]he questions we ask about our past must be related to our present day problems. (Mukherjee 1996: 8)

Sports historians have always had the opportunity to translate this concern into action. They can make people aware of the problems, realities and potentials of sport in our country today, and inform and impress the authorities so as to keep them on the right track toward progress and excellence. E.H. Carr (1961: 108) once made a splendid comment: 'Good historians . . . have future in their bones'. Sports history research in India, especially on Indian sport, should not only concern itself with the analytical understanding of specific historical issues, but should offer valuable insights, in the light of past historical experience, to a better future for sport in India.

This chapter has tried to identify a range of realities, problems, and prospects associated with sports history in contemporary India and to offer some thoughts on the teaching of, and research into, the subject with a reflection on editing a journal. J.A. Mangan's much celebrated emphasis on 'a triadic approach' may be recalled here:

> . . . the analytic approach will be multicultural; balance, breadth and depth will be the ambition; completeness of perspective will be the aim. (Mangan 2002: xiii)

A positive start has definitely been made in this direction in India in the last decade and a half, but the teaching and research will have to cast its net across the country to sustain a long-term academic pursuit in sports history. Sports history, it can be justly claimed by now, is peoples' history. I would, therefore, conclude with the suggestion that if Indian historians are to construct an adequate 'Peoples' History of India', they seriously need to consider one of the most integral elements of Indian life, sport.

168   REFLECTIONS ON SPORTS STUDIES

Notes

1. Vast sports fields in central Kolkata with open and enclosed grounds are called *maidans*. It is also here that the enclosed grounds of the three most popular Kolkata clubs—Mohun Bagan, East Bengal, and Mohammedan Sporting—as well as the Eden Gardens, India's famed cricket stadium, are situated.

2. Notable Indian scholars whose works have consistently merited attention on Indian sports in the past two decades include Ramachandra Guha, Boria Majumdar, Nalin Mehta, Souvik Naha, and the author himself, apart from occasional writings by a number of authors.

3. However, this does not imply in any way that there is dearth of popular sports histories written in India. Rather, the number of such amateur writings has been increasing by leaps and bounds in the past two or three decades. These histories, mostly produced by journalists, litterateurs, and sportsmen themselves, deal with general history of particular games, records, and exploits of certain clubs, organizations, and players as well as autobiographical writings. But these works, although important in their own way, more or less remain in the nature of narratives, and are unable to become interpretative that may lead to the formulation of any hypothesis at a more conceptual level.

4. It was followed by his article titled 'Babu at Play: Sporting Nationalism in Bengal: A Study of Football in Bengal, 1880–1911' (Mitra 1991).

5. The most standard text on this interpretation is Mangan (1998), especially Chapters 5 and 7. Also see Holt (1989: 203–18), Guttman (1994), and Mills (2005). For case studies of football, see Mason (1992: 142–53) and Dimeo and Mills (2001).

6. Another other young Indian scholar who has written mostly in journals on a variety of themes on Indian sport is Souvik Naha. There are also a good number of articles published in various journals and edited volumes as well as a few edited works by several scholars on Indian sports, too numerous to mention here.

7. Historical works on ancient and medieval India have occasionally dealt with leisure and amusement activities in those times, where games and sports occupy an important place.

8. Virat Kohli, the batting maestro of present Indian cricket team, is considered to be one of the greatest batsmen in world cricket in the 21st century.

9. P.V. Sindhu, an Indian professional badminton player, became the first Indian woman to win an individual Olympic silver medal at the Rio Olympics in 2016.

10. For more on this instructive perspective, see Fishwick (1989: Introduction).

11. My personal experiences are worth reflecting here. I made two attempts to procure funding for my doctoral research from the University Grants Commission (UGC) and the Indian Council of Historical Research (ICHR), both being rejected, with the ICHR even making the suggestion that I should apply to sports

PERSPECTIVES ON SPORTS HISTORY IN INDIA   169

bodies for financial support. Interestingly, it was the Indian Football Association of Kolkata which partially funded my research.

12. The 'Kolkata Chapter' of the IRCSSS, as the Annex was called, was established in 2003 at the Department of History, University of Calcutta, mostly through the initiative of Boria Majumdar, an ex-student of the Department. Professor J.A. Mangan, director of IRCSSS, and Professor John Coyen, vice-chancellor of De Montfort University, England, came to Kolkata to inaugurate the centre. The Annex was welcomed by the vice-chancellor of University of Calcutta, Professor Ashish Banerjee; pro-vice-chancellor, Professor Suranjan Das; director of the Kolkata Annex, Professor Bhaskar Chakraborty, and the teachers of the Department of History at an official opening. It was followed by an international seminar titled 'Sport, Culture and Society in Modern India' on 18 September, in which Professor Mangan himself was the chief speaker.

13. Interview with Prof. Bhaskar Chakraborty, Director of the Kolkata Chapter of IRCSSS, 8 January 2004.

14. J.A. Mangan and Boria Majumdar on behalf of IRCSSS met Nitasha Devashar, academic publishing manager, and Manzar Khan, editor-in-chief, Oxford University Press; Thomas Sebastian, chief executive officer, and Diya Kar Hazra, associate editor, Penguin India; Arpita Das and Parul Nayar, joint managing directors, Yoda Press; and Theo Braganza, the owner of Marine Sports, Mumbai, during their invitation visits to Delhi from 28–30 September 2003.

15. This was agreed in a meeting between Boria Majumdar, the former deputy director of IRCSSS and Subir Datta, the managing director, and the general manager, Badal Sarkar, of Ananda Publishers.

16. I was a Fellow at the Maulana Abul Kalam Azad Institute of Asian Studies, Kolkata, working on a project titled 'Sport, Culture, National Identity and Regional Cooperation in South Asia' from March 2006 to January 2009. It was during this period that I could generate a lot of interest among students, researchers and scholars from different subjects through presentations and interactions in seminars and workshops in various parts of India and other South Asian countries like Bangladesh, Sri Lanka, and Afghanistan, and publication of books and papers in journals. However, while the interest thus generated has at least encouraged a few young researchers in West Bengal to pursue sports history in India in the last one decade or so, it is yet to receive deserved encouragement elsewhere in India or South Asia.

17. I taught at the North Bengal University from 1999 to 2009 and at the West Bengal State University from 2009 till date.

18. This was because teaching assignments initially allotted to me by the Departmental Committee did not allow me to teach social history.

19. Mention may be made of two papers in this regard: Bijan Das's 'British Sports and Sporting Princes: A Study in Anglicization of Indian Princes', (2001) and

170   REFLECTIONS ON SPORTS STUDIES

Sima Sarcar's, 'Princely light on Cricket: Anglicization of Native Princes through Sport' (2001).

20. Subrata Mallick (2000) and Rasmika Tirwa (2003) both presented their papers on games and sports under the Mughals.

21. Project papers on sport-related themes submitted under my supervision between 2001 and 2004 included: 'The Cricketing Princes: A Study in their Anglicization' by Aref Sheikh (2001) and 'Nationalist Significance of a Sporting Victory: A Survey of Contemporary Newspaper Reports' by Swapan Kumar Pain (2002). Dr Ratna Roy Sanyal, one of my energetic colleagues in the Department, showed keen interest in supervising projects on sports history. Such projects submitted under her supervision included 'The Princes, Public School Sport and the Raj' by Amrita Kumar Shil (2001), 'Nineteen Eleven: Historiography of a Nationalist Sporting Victory' by Suprakash Bhadra (2002), and 'Nineteen Eleven: A Revisionist Perspective' by Seuli Biswas (2004).

22. The onus on the paper-setter alia me was so much that during the moderation of question papers for the M.A. Part-II Annual Examination 2001, I was called by the moderation board to show reasons for setting such *out of syllabus* questions and was asked to revise or substitute such questions by the relevant ones, which I refused to do.

23. *Departmental Committee Resolution*, Department of History, North Bengal University, dated 25 July 2003.

24. *Resolution of the M.Phil Committee*, Department of History, North Bengal University, dated 12 August 2004. It thus becomes the first Indian university to offer such a paper.

25. These include Jadavpur University, Rabindra Bharati University, Vidyasagar University, and Calcutta University.

26. Central Board of Secondary Education (CBSE) and West Bengal Board of Secondary Education (WBBSE) have led in this regard.

References

Alter, J. 1992. *The Wrestler's Body: Identity and Ideology in North India*. Berkeley, CA: University of California Press.

———. 2000. '*Kabaddi*, a National Sport of India: The Internationalism of Nationalism and the Foreignness of Indianness.' In N. Dyck (ed.), *Games, Sports and Cultures*, pp. 83–115. Oxford: Berg.

Appadurai, A. 1995. 'Playing with Modernity: The Decolonization of Indian Cricket'. In C.A. Breckenridge (ed.), *Consuming Modernity: Public Culture in a South Asian World*, pp. 23–48. Minneapolis, MN: University of Minnesota Press.

Bandyopadhyay, Kausik. 2005. 'Sports History in India: Prospects and Problems'. *The International Journal of the History of Sport* 22 (3–4): 708–21.

————. 2011. *Scoring Off the Field: Football Culture in Bengal, 1911–80*. New Delhi: Routledge.

————. 2015. *Sport, Culture and Nation: Perspectives from Indian Football and South Asian Cricket*. New Delhi: SAGE.

————. 2017a. 'Fighting Against Heavy Odds: An Indian Perspective on Sports History'. *The International Journal of the History of Sport* 34 (5–6): 320–5.

————. 2017b. *Mahatma on the Pitch: Gandhi and Cricket in India*. New Delhi: Rupa Publications.

Bose, Mihir. 1990. *A History of Indian Cricket*. London: Andre Deutsch.

Carr, E.H. 1961. *What Is History?* London: Pelican.

Cashman, Richard. 1979. *Patrons, Players and the Crowd: The Phenomenon of Indian Cricket*. Calcutta: Orient Longman.

Dimeo, Paul and James Mill (eds). 2001. *Soccer in South Asia: Empire, Nation, Diaspora*. London: Frank Cass.

Docker, Edward. 1976. *History of Indian Cricket*. Delhi: Macmillan.

Fishwick, Nicholas. 1989. *English Football and Society, 1910–1950*. Manchester: Manchester University Press.

Guha, Ramachandra. 1992. *Wickets in the East*. New Delhi: Oxford University Press.

————. 1994. *Spin and Other Turns: Indian Cricket's Coming of Age*. Delhi: Penguin Books.

————. 1998. 'Cricket and Politics in Colonial India'. *Past and Present* (November): 155–90.

————. 2002. *A Corner of a Foreign Field: The Indian History of a British Sport*. Delhi: Picador.

Guttman, Allen. 1994. *Games and Empires: Modern Sports and Cultural Imperialism*. New York: Columbia University Press.

Holt, Richard. 1989. *Sport and the British: A Modern History*. Oxford: Oxford University Press.

Majumdar, Boria. 2004a. *Once Upon a Furore: Lost Pages of Indian Cricket*. New Delhi: Yoda Press.

————. 2004b. *Twenty Two Yards to Freedom: A Social History of Indian Cricket*. New Delhi: Penguin/Viking.

————. 2018. *Eleven Gods and A Billion Indians: The On and Off the Field Story of Cricket in India and Beyond*. London: Simon & Schuster.

Majumdar, Boria and J.A. Mangan (eds). 2005. *Sport in South Asian Society: Past and Present*. London: Routledge.

Majumdar, Boria and Kausik Bandyopadhyay. 2006. *Goalless! The Story of a Unique Footballing Nation*. New Delhi: Penguin/Viking.

Majumdar, Boria and Nalin Mehta. 2008. *Olympics: The India Story*. Delhi: HarperCollins.

————. 2010. *Sellotape Legacy: Delhi and the Commonwealth Games*. Delhi: HarperCollins.

Mangan, J.A. 1998. *The Games Ethic and Imperialism: Aspects of the Diffusion of an Ideal*. London: Frank Cass.

————. 2002. 'Series Editor's Foreword'. In Paul Dimeo and James Mills (eds), *Soccer in South Asia: Empire, Nation, Diaspora*, pp. xi–xiii. London: Frank Cass.

172　REFLECTIONS ON SPORTS STUDIES

Marwick, Arthur. 1970. *The Nature of History*. London: Macmillan.

Mason, Tony. 1992. 'Football on the Maidan: Cultural Imperialism in Calcutta'. In J.A. Mangan (ed.), *The Cultural Bond: Sport, Empire, Society*, pp. 142–53. London: Frank Cass.

Mills, James, ed. 2005. *Subaltern Sports: Politics and Sport in South Asia*. London: Anthem Press.

Mitra, Soumen. 1988. 'Nationalism, Communalism and Sub-regionalism: A Study of Football in Bengal, 1880–1950'. PhD dissertation. Centre for Historical Studies, Jawaharlal Nehru University, New Delhi, India.

———. 1991. 'Babu at Play: Sporting Nationalism in Bengal: A Study of Football in Bengal, 1880–1911'. In Nisith Roy and Ranjit Roy (eds), *Bengal: Yesterday and Today*, pp. 45–61. Calcutta: Papyrus.

———. 2006. *In Search of an Identity: History of Football in Colonial Calcutta*. Kolkata: Dasgupta & Co.

Mukherjee, S.N. 1996. *Citizen Historian: Explorations in Historiography*. Delhi: Manohar.

Nandy, Ashis. 1989. *The Tao of Cricket: On Games of Destiny and the Destiny of Games*. New York: Viking.

Pearson, M.N. 1984. 'Recreation in Mughal India'. *The International Journal of the History of Sport* 1 (3): 335–50.

Sarkar, Sumit. 2014. *Modern Times: India 1880s–1950s: Environment, Economy, Culture*. Ranikhet: Permanent Black.

Sen, Ronojoy. 2015. *Nation at Play: A History of Indian Sport*. New York, Columbia University Press.

Sen, Satadru. 2004. *Migrant Races: Empire, Identity and K.S. Ranjit Sinhji*. Manchester: Manchester University Press.

Tagore, Rabindranath. 1992. 'Shikhsha'. In *Rabindra Rachanabali*, Volume 10. Calcutta: Government of West Bengal.

Walvin, James. 1984. 'Sport, Social History and the Historian'. *British Journal of Sports History* 1 (1): 5–13.

Zarrilli, P. 2004. *Kalarippayattu, When the Body Becomes All Eyes: Paradigms, Practices and Discourses of Power*. New Delhi: Oxford University Press.

SECTION III
NURTURING SPORTS
Crucibles of Growth

11

A City and a Sport

Hockey in Calcutta

Nikhilesh Bhattacharya

As the twentieth century approached its middle point, Keshav Datt was at a crossroads in life. In this, he was no different from millions of young men and women in the Indian subcontinent—a land of immense diversity recently freed from foreign rule but also severed in two. Like countless families in Bengal and Punjab, the Datts had borne the brunt of Partition.[i] Datt ended up in Bombay, staying with his eldest brother Romesh, who worked in the customs department. In his mid-20s, Datt had no permanent home or a job. There was one thing, though, that set him apart from the unemployed multitudes: He was a top hockey player. A product of Government College, Lahore, he had toured East Africa with an India invitation team led by hockey legend Dhyan Chand in 1947 right after India's independence (Chand 1952: 84–6). He had gone on to represent India in its first Olympic Games as an independent country in London in 1948. Playing as either centre half or right half, he featured in all five of India's matches. The team defeated Great Britain 4–0 in the final to win the gold (Organising Committee for the XIV Olympiad 1951: 406–12). The erstwhile rulers had been humbled and Datt was one of twenty men who were independent India's first Olympic champions (Organising Committee for the XIV Olympiad 1951: 546).

While Datt was in Bombay, he connected with an old friend from college. He stated: 'He was working for Calcutta Port Trust and said, "They are looking for a centre half"'. So Datt went to Calcutta around 1950 and joined Calcutta Port Trust. That was his first permanent job where he stayed for a year. He never left the city, finding employment in the tea sector and continuing with a sporting career that saw him win another Olympic gold medal in Helsinki in 1952. He also played in the domestic circuit for the famous Calcutta club, Mohun Bagan.

Datt's move to Calcutta to join the Port Trust connects him to two other Olympians, Joe Galibardy, a member of the British India team that won

---

Nikhilesh Bhattacharya, *A City and a Sport* In: *Sports Studies in India*. Edited by: Meena Gopal and Padma Prakash, Oxford University Press. © Oxford University Press 2021.
DOI: 10.1093/oso/9780190130640.003.0012

176 NURTURING SPORTS

gold in Berlin in 1936, and Leslie Claudius, who won three Olympic gold medals and one silver for independent India between 1948 and 1960. A third member of the 1948 India Olympic hockey team, Jaswant Singh Rajput, came from Delhi on Claudius's advice to set up a business and settle down in Calcutta.[ii]

Curiously, given the city's current disconnect with the sport, Calcutta was the location of many important firsts in the history of hockey in the subcontinent: the first tournament, the Beighton Cup, started in 1895; the first governing body, the Bengal Hockey Association (BHA), founded in 1908; the first inter-provincial match, Bengal versus Punjab, in 1925; and, the first inter-provincial tournament, in 1928. After Independence, Calcutta continued to attract star hockey players with employment opportunities and a well-organized sporting scene.

This chapter seeks to recreate the days when the city was in love with hockey. It does this, for the period after Independence, through interviews with hockey greats Datt, Rajput, Claudius, and Gurbux Singh, who moved to Calcutta a few years after the other three and won an Olympic gold in Tokyo in 1964, followed by a bronze in Mexico in 1968. Details about Galibardy's life are based on an interview with his son, Neville Galibardy. As for the fifty-odd years before Independence, when hockey was imported to the subcontinent and then evolved into a mass sport, the narrative is built on newspaper reports, magazine articles, and existing literature on hockey.

Sport's emergence as a subject of serious academic study in the past few decades has coincided with another trend prescribed by J.A. Mangan in his role as the general editor of the series, Sport in the Global Society.

> Across the globe, *sport is now too important to be left in the hands of sportsmen and women.* More and more, it is the property of the 'People' in their various manifestations as politicians, entrepreneurs, educationalists, commercialists, publicists and, not least, academics. (Mangan 1998: xiv)

Sportsmen and women might argue that sport was never theirs anyway: They have had to jostle with lawmakers and gamblers, patrons, and promoters for control over what is either their pastime or their profession for ever. Mangan, of course, is concerned with the study of sport and in this there are two clear advantages to adopting his methods. First, it is only by redirecting the gaze at developments off the field, and by observing their connections with events unfolding on the field, that one can examine sport in its true cultural and social context, a task that may well be beyond the person playing the sport.

A CITY AND A SPORT   177

Second, sportsmen and women may find it difficult to achieve the objective distance required to distinguish between 'what is and what is not so', without which, as historian Eric Hobsbawm correctly asserted, 'there can be no history' (Hobsbawm 1998a: ix). Their partial (in both senses of the word) view of events makes the players unreliable sources of information for the historian.

If this is so, why bother with reminiscences of hockey players of yesteryears? To begin with, participants' accounts have been part of historiography from the time of Thucydides (Richie 2015: 20). Also, as Mangan too would probably admit, players are not confined to that single identity: They have lives beyond the field and are part of the ' "People" in their various manifestations' (Mangan 1998: xiv). The career trajectories of the players chosen for this chapter are significant in fleshing out the history of hockey in Calcutta. Moreover, the scarcity of documents and other written sources on hockey, in Calcutta in particular, and the subcontinent in general makes it imperative that other avenues are explored. One must, of course, remember Hobsbawm's warning about 'what can go wrong with memory', especially when 'there is nothing to check it against' (Hobsbawm 1998b: 273). Dhyan Chand mentioned the problem in his memoirs, serialized in the Madras-based magazine, *Sport & Pastime*, between May 1949 and January 1951 before being published as a book in 1952:

I have chosen a game as my most favourite sport which, unlike other games, has no statistician or historian in this country. (Chand 1952: ix)

Lest we forget, Dhyan Chand was writing about the 'national sport' of India: a sport in which the British India teams had won gold in three successive Olympic Games in the inter-War years and the sport in which Independent India had already made its mark.[iii] Dhyan Chand (1952: ix) ended his lament with the assertion: 'Nevertheless I have endeavoured to present as accurate a story as possible.' Maybe it is worthwhile to follow in his footsteps and allow some of his successors to tell their own stories from memory, endeavouring always to ensure that the stories are as accurate as possible.

First Stop, Calcutta

The first hockey clubs in India were established in Calcutta in 1885 (de Mello [1959: 81]; Kapur [1968: 25]). However, no supporting evidence is supplied

178   NURTURING SPORTS

to corroborate the claim. The first reference to hockey in Calcutta in fact dates from February 1864, when a silver tankard was presented to Captain Joseph Ford Sherer, of the 49th Bengal Native Infantry, by the Calcutta Hockey Club.[iv] However, since Captain Sherer is known as the Father of Polo, it is almost certain that hockey in this case meant polo, or 'hockey on ponies' (see Laffaye 2009: 10–11, 303–4).[v] The identity of the first club in India whose members started playing hockey on foot remains a mystery.

More than three decades after Captain Sherer was presented with the silver tankard, an advertisement appeared in *The Statesman*, the leading English language newspaper in Calcutta, on 29 March 1895. It said: 'Beighton Hockey Cup. ENTRIES Rs. 5 Close on April 18th. For conditions apply to Rev. J. L. Peach, St. James School.' This was the beginning of the longest running field hockey tournament in the world.[vi] The cup was named after Thomas Durant Beighton, the remembrancer of legal affairs, Government of Bengal, and member of the Provincial Legislative Council (Great Britain India Office 1905: 437), for a simple reason: He presented the winners' trophy, a silver bowl, to the Indian Football Association (IFA), the tournament organizers. A day after the first appearance of the advertisement, *The Statesman* (1895a) carried a brief report describing the bowl manufactured by Messrs. Hamilton and Co., the well-known British silversmith in India.

The name of the other man who was instrumental in starting the tournament has been lost in the flow of time. Reverend James Legard Peach came to the city as part of the Oxford Mission to Calcutta in November 1888 (Longridge 1900: 39). His links with the city went back further. A member of Trinity College, Cambridge, Peach had visited Calcutta as a layman in 1884 (Longridge 1900: 18).[vii] In 1895, Peach was holding the post of the rector at St. James's, then a school for 'Eurasians' (people of mixed race). Located close to the St. James' Church on Lower Circular Road (both the church and the school still function from the same sites), St. James's had at that time 'fairly good buildings' and 'a good-sized playing field' (Longridge 1900: 64). As rector, Peach oversaw the improvement of both the playground and the buildings, in that order (Longridge 1900: 64–5).

The remit of the Oxford Mission went far beyond education: It had to do with the imperial responsibility of the conversion of India. Is it then a coincidence that Peach was busiest in the fields of education and sport, two strong spheres of English influence in the public domain of a diverse colony?

Peach was certainly busy in the spring of 1895. A report in *The Statesman* on 19 April 1895, a day after entries to the Beighton Cup closed, spoke of Reverend Peach, 'the energetic secretary of the Indian Football Association,

A CITY AND A SPORT   179

who is himself very keen on all outdoor sports' (*Statesman* 1895b). Once
the tournament started, in May, Peach took up additional roles: he refereed
matches,[viii] and when St. James's took on Naval Volunteers in the first round
on 9 May, played as centre forward (*Statesman* 1895d). St. James's lost 2–3 to
the eventual champions.

By then there had been another significant development: the first primarily 'native' Indian team had joined the tournament as a late entrant in end
April. When the Ranchi Mission of Chota Nagpore played against Calcutta
Football Club (CFC) on 14 May 1895, *The Statesman* (1895e) reported that,
except for the captain, the Reverend E.H. Whitley, the team was 'composed
of native Christians, all of whom played without shoes or guards'. The team
lost and was knocked out of the tournament, but in the years to come, (SPG)
Society for the Propagation of the Gospel Mission Ranchi would become a
title contender. It won the trophy in 1897 before repeating the feat five times
in the next ten years. Curiously, Jaipal Singh, the captain of first British India
team to win the Olympic hockey gold in Amsterdam in 1928, had studied at
St. Paul's, SPG Mission's central school in Ranchi.

The Statesman reports on the first Beighton Cup tournament reveal other
aspects of hockey in Calcutta that are of interest. Clearly, hockey had been
played in the city before 1895. 'For some years past hockey . . . has been entirely neglected, or lost sight of', reported *The Statesman* (1895b). The only
exceptions, the newspaper said, were CFC and La Martiniere, and the
Calcutta Naval Club that had 'got together a fairly good team' the previous
season. Did hockey in Calcutta go back as far as 1885? We do not know.

La Martiniere was not the only school where the game was established; the
students of St. James's and the Ranchi Mission appeared thoroughly schooled
in the intricacies of the game. Importantly, the tournament was played under
the rules of the Hockey Association of England, that is, the rules that would
govern international hockey in future. By the time the British India team
went to the Amsterdam Olympics, players in India had been conversant with
those rules for more than three decades.

On the other hand, by instituting a tournament played for a trophy, Indian
hockey took a different route than that followed in the mother country. In
England, the Hockey Association's near-fanatical efforts to preserve hockey's
amateur status meant cup competitions were barred and only leagues were
allowed. In fact, abhorrence of tournaments was one argument put forward by the defenders of the Hockey Association to explain why England
did not take part in Olympic hockey between 1928 and 1936, the period in
which British India won the Olympic hockey gold thrice in succession.[ix]

180   NURTURING SPORTS

It is possible that Indian hockey players, used to competing in high-stake tournaments since the turn of the twentieth century, put that experience to good use in the Olympic Games.

Three other things about the first Beighton Cup need to be remembered. One, it was a civilian tournament. A civil servant, priests, school students, and businessmen and professionals who were members of the civilian clubs of the city constituted Calcutta's hockey circle and this would be the template for the future.[x] Two, Eurasians, or Anglo-Indians, as they would be called later, and 'native' Indians became involved in Calcutta hockey from the beginning. Three, hockey was already a spectator sport. *The Statesman* report on the final of the first Beighton Cup, replayed twice after the first two matches between Naval Volunteers and CFC were tied, said: 'A very large number of spectators, including several ladies, assembled yesterday on the Calcutta ground to witness the final contest in the Beighton Cup competition' (*Statesman* 1895f).

Reverend Peach, like Beighton, left India for England in 1896, probably unaware of his part in a quiet sporting revolution that would eventually lead India to world domination.

A Sporting City

In the years following the first Beighton Cup, hockey spread throughout India rapidly, beginning with the Aga Khan Cup organized at the Bombay Gymkhana from 1896. The development was noted at the home of hockey, England. In 1909, a book published in London contained a chapter, 'Hockey in Other Lands', which included the colony of India. The chapter, written by the then-secretary of the Hockey Association, Phillip Collins, said that India reportedly had 'altogether nearly two thousand hockey teams' and 'a very large number of tournaments are held every year in different part of the country' (Collins 1922: 143).[xi] He added that at the time, there was no Indian Hockey Association, though attempts were being made to form a national body to govern the sport across the country (Collins 1922: 144). While hockey gained popularity across the country, Calcutta continued to lead the way.

The BHA was established in the city on 27 April 1908 (Miller 1988: 3), long before any other provincial body and nearly two decades before the Indian Hockey Federation started functioning properly. The first officer bearers of the BHA reflected the cosmopolitan nature of the city's hockey circle:

A CITY AND A SPORT 181

T. Thornbill as president; N. Banerjee as secretary; and A.B. Rosser as treasurer (Miller 1988: 3). Calcutta also hosted the first inter-provincial match when a strong Punjab team beat Bengal in 1925. An article in *Hockey World*, a London-based weekly, in October 1926, reported that the Bengal-Punjab match was played 'before an enormous crowd at the Eden Gardens' (J.H.B. 1926: 88). Britishers were at the helm of both teams: 'A.A. Ritchie, the old Scottish hockey International, led Punjab while A.L. Hosie, the old Oxonian Blue, captained Bengal' (J.H.B. 1926: 88). The Punjab team then took part in the Beighton Cup and lost to the Calcutta Customs in the final. The result was unexpected because the Punjab XI was considered very strong. In 1926, the Punjab XI beat the Indian Army team 8–4 before the latter sailed for a successful tour of New Zealand and Australia (J.H.B. 1926: 88).

The article in the *Hockey World* went on to make a startling claim: 'The general standard of club hockey in Calcutta is at least 100 per cent. higher than at home' (J.H.B. 1926: 88), despite the fact that the hockey season in Calcutta was comparatively short: held mostly during spring, it began after the cricketers had left the greens and before the football season started.[xii] A common explanation for India's early hockey supremacy was that the game could be played in the country around the year, which meant more opportunities for players to hone their skills. That was not the case in Calcutta. Instead, the *Hockey World* article gave two main reasons for the high standard of hockey in the city: immaculate hockey pitches that were true and fast; and comparatively few teams, which meant only the best players featured in the different XIs (J.H.B. 1926: 88).

Two additional, interconnected reasons can be proffered. First: the position of Calcutta in British India. As historian Sumit Sarkar (1997: 164) writes:

The grandeur of the 'City of Palaces', at times even described as the second city of the British empire, was based in part on its role as headquarters of British Indian administration. . … More fundamental was the twofold economic predominance of Calcutta as the pre-eminent focus of British commerce, shipping, finance, and investments in the East, and as the city where British capital was in command more overwhelmingly than anywhere else in India.

What it meant was that the British influence in India was the strongest in Calcutta and, among other things, their sporting ethos was replicated closely in the Calcutta Maidan. The city patronized all sports. Dhyan Chand (1952: 8) commented on this in his memoirs: 'Calcutta has always perplexed

182   NURTURING SPORTS

me,' he wrote, because it was unlike other cities that take 'special interest in one particular game'.

Calcutta was also a city of opportunities and attracted not only the British but people from different communities. They would form the pool from which hockey, like other spheres of activity, would draw talents. This brings us to the second reason: It helped hockey that one of the communities whose members set up base in Calcutta in large numbers, the Anglo-Indians, took to hockey like ducks to water.

In his book on the history of Indian cricket, Ramachandra Guha (2002: 38) writes: 'In Calcutta, where the low-born preferred football, the gentrified Bengali, or *bhadralok*, took more readily to cricket.' Hockey, Guha forgets to mention, became the adopted sport of the Anglo-Indians, a liminal group caught between the rulers and the ruled. The Anglo-Indians' contribution to Indian hockey has aroused the interest of other academics, though an imprecise understanding of the term 'Anglo-Indian' undermines most of their analysis.[xiii] In a nutshell, the Census of India of 1911 substituted the term Anglo-Indian for Eurasian as the 'designation of the mixed races, descended usually from European fathers and Indian mothers' (Gait 1913: 140); the Government of India Act of 1919, however, modified the definition of Anglo-Indian to include, along with people of mixed descent (European in the male line), any 'pure-blooded' European who did not have close connections to lands other than India, such as British Isles, Canada, Newfoundland, Australia, New Zealand, or the Union of South Africa. Of the forty different hockey players who represented British India in the Olympic Games of 1928, 1932, and 1936, for example, eighteen were Anglo-Indians, but that does not necessarily mean all of them were of mixed descent. It simply meant that unlike, say Beighton and Peach, who could retire to England after serving in India, the fate of the Anglo-Indian players was ultimately tied to the land of their birth, that is, the Empire in India. That is what put them in what the British government often called a 'peculiar' situation: connected to the rulers by blood but still differentiated from Europeans (primarily the British) and also alienated from the native Indians because of their religion (Christianity), lifestyle (Western) and social capital (Anglo-Indians were given special privileges for employment in services such as the railways, post and telegraph, customs, and port trust). Yet, one thing cannot be disputed: they belonged to India.

According to the Census of India of 1911, the Anglo-Indians were the most numerous in the presidencies of Madras (26,000) and Bengal (20,000). A lot of the latter would have been in Calcutta, and also in the important

A CITY AND A SPORT 183

railway town of Kharagpore, the headquarters of Bengal–Nagpur Railway (BNR), where Galibardy and Claudius would play hockey in the 1930s and 1940s. The Calcutta hockey scene in the decades following the first Beighton Cup was ruled by Anglo-Indian institutions like a recreational club (Naval Volunteers, which later amalgamated with the Calcutta Rangers Club), a school (St. James's), and an office team where members of the community predominated (Calcutta Customs). Claudius was right when he said 'The British came and they played soccer, they played cricket, but they couldn't conquer hockey, *na*. So the Anglo-Indians took over. And they mastered hockey.'[xiv]

A City of Opportunities

British India's golden journey in the Olympic Games has been chronicled elsewhere.[xv] Somewhat unexpectedly, Bengal did not provide as many players to the British India teams as Punjab, or even the United Provinces. However, Calcutta was the venue for the first inter-provincial hockey tournament in February 1928, held six-and-a-half years before Indian cricket had a similar competition in the Ranji Trophy. The tournament doubled as a trial to select the first British India team for the Olympics. Calcutta would host what was initially a biennial tournament before the 1932 and 1936 Games as well, because the BHA could promise large gate receipts from the matches that would boost the funds needed for the Olympic tours.

The Second World War meant no Olympics were held in 1940 and 1944. However, hockey continued apace in India. Centres where hockey had deep roots and a robust domestic structure were spread across the subcontinent: Rawalpindi, Lahore, Delhi, and Lucknow in the north; Madras and Bangalore in the south; Pune and Bombay in the west; Allahabad, Jhansi, and Bhopal in central India; and of course, Calcutta in the east. Into this scene stepped Datt.

People in Calcutta today often forget that theirs is a port city. In the late nineteenth and early twentieth centuries, no one could have made that mistake. Although eighty-two miles of precarious navigation through the Hooghly separated Calcutta from the sea, it is through its port that 'Lancashire textiles poured into the country and foodgrains and raw material pumped out, with a favourable balance of trade that paid for Britain's trade deficits with the rest of the world' (Sarkar 1997: 44). The importance of the port led the Government of India to constitute a trust for its improvement

184 NURTURING SPORTS

and the 'first body of 'Port Commissioners'—nine in number—were appointed in October 1870' (Anonymous 1920: 7).

Like the railways and government departments in colonial India, the Calcutta Port Trust patronized sports. From the mid-1920s, Port Commissioners XI—the name reflecting the constitution of the body—had an outstanding talent in the Anglo-Indian goalkeeper Richard Allen, the only player apart from Dhyan Chand to win three Olympic hockey gold in the inter-War years. Later, in 1946, Port Commissioners won the Beighton Cup for the first time, beating the BNR, which boasted former and future Olympians such as Dickie Carr (1932), Carlyle Tapsell (1932, 1936), Galibardy, and Claudius. After the disruption of 1947, Port Commissioners set about reconstituting the team—a process that would ultimately draw Datt from Lahore via Delhi and Bombay to Calcutta.

Right after India's independence, Port Commissioners recruited a precocious right half in the young Claudius and a solid left half in the experienced Galibardy. Both were Anglo-Indians: Galibardy had French ancestry;[xvi] Claudius's father Walter was an Anglo-Indian from Burma.[xvii] Belonging to railway families, both spent their early lives in railway colonies. Joseph Thomas Galibardy was born in Madras on 11 January 1915 and had lived in Chakradharpore before ending up in Kharagpore. He studied at St. Xavier's, Calcutta, before being sent to Goethals Memorial School in the eastern Himalayan hill town of Kurseong in 1930.[xviii] In just over two years there, he ran away from school, not once, but twice. Fed up, his father Emanuel Galibardy got him a job as apprentice boiler-maker in the BNR in April 1934.[xix] Galibardy's status as an Anglo-Indian, and his father's position in the railways (Emanuel was an engine driver on the Bombay Mail), probably helped. What made Joe Galibardy special were his hockey skills, which he employed for BNR and Bengal, helping the latter win the inter-provincial tournament for the first time in 1936. He was one of four Bengal players sent with the British India team to the Berlin Olympics (Chand 1952: 69). Galibardy played all five matches as the team claimed its third successive Olympic gold beating the hosts 8–1 in the final.

At the BNR, Galibardy rose to the position of chargeman boiler maker before resigning in September 1946.[xx] The timing of his resignation raises the interesting possibility that the Galibardys were already contemplating emigrating to another country in the months leading to India's independence (the family would emigrate to the UK in 1956). As it happened, however, Galibardy joined the Calcutta Port Trust in September 1947.[xxi] He was back in the city where he had been a student (at St. Xavier's), a hockey star (for the

A CITY AND A SPORT   185

BNR and Bengal), and a pleasure-seeker (especially while the racing season was on).

Claudius was born in the small railway town of Bilaspur (now in Chhattisgarh) on 25 March 1927. He had had a secluded childhood, using his spare time to pursue his first love, football. Claudius claimed it was football that brought him to Kharagpore after he turned 18: his sporting talent got him work with the Home Department, which protected the important railway town. Later he joined BNR. 'In those pre-Partition (times) there were a lot of battalions in Bilaspur and football was a big craze', Claudius recalled. Kharagpore, on the other hand, was where hockey Olympians graced the fields. The story of Claudius's fortuitous introduction to hockey and his subsequent meteoric rise has been told before.[xxii] It began in Kharagpore and could have ended there, when the BNR team disbanded in 1947. 'Fortunately for me, the Port Commissioners was forming a side in Calcutta and I was taken on by them. I think it happened within a month of Independence', Claudius recalled. If his memory can be trusted, he joined Port Trust around the same time as Galibardy, who had become his mentor in Kharagpore. 'I don't know (why), but he took quite a great interest in me and he used to coach me every day', Claudius said. His performances for the Port Commissioners XI got Claudius into the Bengal side and eventually into the India team for the 1948 Olympics. He joined the Customs circa 1951. Claudius retired from international hockey after India, under his captaincy, lost to Pakistan in the final of the 1960 Rome Olympics, but continued playing for Customs in Calcutta till 1965.

Datt, of course, arrived in Calcutta from farther away than Galibardy and Claudius. For him, the main challenge was managing time, especially after he quit Port Trust. He joined an industry with deep links to Calcutta: Tea grown in the eastern Himalayas and the foothills had always been funnelled through the railhead at Calcutta and eventually the port. 'The tea auctions . . . used to sometimes start at 8 o'clock in the morning and go on till 6.30–7 o'clock in the evening . . . But I could not afford to chuck that job in the hope of getting something equally good. Brooke Bond was a British company and they expected you to work really well to get somewhere', Datt said.

Datt thus moved to a job where hockey was no longer his calling card. He could do so partly because Calcutta was still a city of opportunities, and not just for hockey players. Jaswant Singh Rajput, for example, came to the city after the 1948 Olympics and chose to set up a business in servicing diesel fuel injection equipment in Calcutta instead of his hometown Delhi.[xxiii] Of course, it helped that hockey was 'hot in Calcutta, as popular as football', and big clubs looked for talented players, which is why Claudius advised Rajput to move to Calcutta. Eventually his business ate up most of his time, but Rajput lived in Calcutta till his death on 28 January 2015. Similar is the case of Gurbux Singh. 'I did not come to Calcutta to play hockey', he said.[xxiv] After making a name for himself while representing Agra University in hockey, Gurbux Singh nearly followed his father into the army. But that did not happen. His brother-in-law and sister had a motor spare parts business in Calcutta. 'After my graduation, I came here to join them to learn about the trade. It was in 1956 September. Then some people came to know that I also played hockey', Gurbux Singh recalled. Apart from the India honours, Gurbux Singh had a sterling career in domestic hockey with East Bengal, Calcutta Customs and Mohun Bagan between 1957 and 1969. 'Hockey matches involving the big clubs would draw 25-30,000 people', Gurbux Singh claimed. Rajput said, 'You can say hockey was the opium of our times.'

Explanations abound for the decline of Indian hockey, which is sharply etched in Calcutta's growing apathy towards to the sport. One thing becomes clear from talking to the Olympians from the 1940s and 1950s: Hockey has changed beyond recognition on and, more importantly, off the field. And it is away from the grass-versus-artificial surface debate[xxv] that hockey truly missed the bus. The economics of elite sports has seen a tectonic shift in the past few decades. The failure of the Indian hockey administrators to commercialize the international game meant they could not subsidize domestic hockey in the manner that cricket has done since the early 1990s. The result was a talent drain percolating to all levels of hockey, including in Calcutta. Football in Calcutta, on the other hand, has retained a dedicated following despite a gulf in standard between the game played in the city and the game broadcast on television from across the world. Hockey did not manage that.

If hockey was no longer the same sport, Calcutta was no longer the same city either. From the glory days of the colonial era, the city has steadily lost importance. 'Calcutta is a beautiful place. One of the finest. Those days all activities in India were in Calcutta. It was a wonderful place. There was enjoyment everywhere: dance floors, clubs, everything', Claudius said a few months before his death on 20 December 2012. By then, the city he described existed only in the imagination, along with its love for hockey.

Notes

i. Interview with Keshav Datt, Calcutta, 9 January 2013. All further quotes by Datt are from the same interview. An excerpt of the interview was published in the final report submitted to the IOC Olympic Studies Centre in the framework of the 2015 PhD Students Research Grant Programme. See Bhattacharya (2015).

ii. Interview with Jaswant Singh Rajput, Calcutta, 18 January 2013. All quotes by Rajput are from the same interview.

iii. In comparison, the Indian cricket team defeated England in a test match for the first time in February 1952, three-and-a-half years after the Indian hockey team's triumph against the former rulers in their backyard.

iv. The tankard is part of the collection at the National Army Museum in the UK. It also forms part of the museum's online collection, accession number: NAM. 1998-03-6-1, object URL: http://www.nam.ac.uk/online-collection/detail. php?acc=1998-03-6-1; accessed on 10 April 2018.

v. I am indebted to the following people for bringing to my notice the silver tankard and for offering an explanation to the perplexing reference to the Calcutta Hockey Club: Dr Peter Johnson, collections content team leader at the National Army Museum, UK; Dil Bahra, a trustee at The Hockey Museum, UK; and Mike Smith, Curator, The Hockey Museum, UK.

vi. Since 1895, the Beighton Cup has been held every year, except in 1947, when riots connected to Partition led to the tournament being cancelled.

vii. This page wrongly mentions the year of Peach's first visit to Calcutta as 1894; the correct year is given at the next mention of Peach on p. 39.

viii. See report of the first round of the match between another school team, La Martiniere, and YMCA carried in *The Statesman* (1895c).

ix. The other constituent parts of Great Britain, that is, Scotland, Ireland, and Wales, followed the English and stayed away from those Olympic Games as well.

x. The only army team to win the Beighton Cup in the colonial era was the 1st Royal Irish Rifles, in 1901.

xi. The book was first published in 1909; Collins fell at Flanders on 30 July 1915.

xii. For years, all these games have jostled for space in the *maidan*, the green patch in the centre of the city that is under army control.

xiii. A prime example is Mills (2010).

xiv. Interview with Leslie Claudius, Calcutta, 4 May 2012. All further quotes by Claudius are from the same interview. An excerpt of the interview was published in the final report submitted to the IOC Olympic Studies Centre in the framework of the 2015 PhD Students Research Grant Programme. See Bhattacharya (2015).

xv. See, in chronological order, de Mello (1959); Kapur (1968); Majumdar and Mehta (2012); Bhattacharya (2015).

188   NURTURING SPORTS

xvi. Interview with Neville Galibardy, Chingford, UK, 3 June 2013. Details about Galibardy's life are based on this interview along with documents in the personal collection of the family.

xvii. Interview with Leslie Claudius, Calcutta, 4 May 2012.

xviii. Transfer certificate issued by Goethals Memorial to Joseph T. Galibardy on 19 August 1932, personal collection of the Galibardy family, UK. The school, incidentally, produced another hockey Olympian, Cyril Mitchie, who understudied first-choice goalkeeper Richard Allen in the same 1936 Olympic Games where Galibardy featured.

xix. Service Certificate issued by Bengal Nagpur Railway to J. T. Galibardy on 25 July 1950, personal collection of the Galibardy family, UK.

xx. Service Certificate issued by Bengal Nagpur Railway to J. T. Galibardy on 25 July 1950, personal collection of the Galibardy family, UK.

xxi. Service certificate issued by the Commissioners for the Port of Calcutta to J. Galibardy on 28 June 1956, personal collection of the Galibardy family, UK.

xxii. A good example is the profile by Ezeiel and Arumugam (2012).

xxiii. Interview with Jaswant Singh Rajput, Calcutta, 18 January 2013.

xxiv. Interview with Gurbux Singh, Calcutta, 17 May 2012.

xxv. Most of the Olympians, for example, were in agreement on one thing: the move to Astro-turf was inevitable for the survival and spread of hockey globally.

References

Anonymous. 1920. *The Calcutta Port Trust: A Brief History of Fifty Years' Work 1870–1920*. Calcutta and Simla: Thacker, Spink & Co.

Bhattacharya, Nikhilesh. 2015. 'Where the English Refused to Tread: India's Role in Establishing Hockey as an Olympic Summer Sport'. Olympic Studies Centre Collections. Available at https://library.olympic.org/Default/doc/SYRACUSE/63898/where-the-english-refused-to-tread-india-s-role-in-establishing-hockey-as-an-olympic-summer-sport-ni; accessed on 25 March 2018.

Chand, Dhyan. 1952. *Goal!* Madras: Sport and Pastime.

Collins, Philip. 1922. 'Hockey in Other Lands'. In Eustace E. White (ed.), *The Complete Hockey Player*, 3rd edition, pp. 138–47. London: Methuen & Co.

de Mello, Anthony. 1959. *Portrait of Indian Sport*. Bombay: D.B. Taraporevala Sons & Co.

Ezeiel, Gulu and K. Arumugam. 2012. 'Leslie Claudius: An Enduring Spirit'. In *Great Indian Olympians*, 3rd edition, pp. 39–44. New Delhi: Field Hockey Publications.

Gait, E.A. 1913. *Census of India, 1911*, Volume 1, Part 1. Calcutta: Superintendent of Government Printing.

Great Britain India Office. 1905. *The India List and India Office List for 1905*. London: Harrison & Sons.

Guha, Ramachandra. 2002. *A Corner of a Foreign Field: The Indian History of a British Sport*. London: Picador.

Hobsbawm, Eric. 1998a. 'Preface'. *On History*, pp. viii–xii. London: Abacus.

———.1998b. 'On History from Below'. *On History*, pp. 266–86. London: Abacus.

J.H.B. 1926. 'The Game in Calcutta'. *Hockey World* 5 (5): 88.

Kapur, M.L. 1968. *Romance of Hockey*. Ambala Cantt: M.L. Kapur.

Laffaye, Horace A. 2009. *The Evolution of Polo*. Jefferson, NC; London: McFarland & Co.

Longridge, George 1900. *A History of the Oxford Mission to Calcutta*. London: John Murray.

Majumdar, Boria and Nalin Mehta. 2012. *Olympics: The India Story*. Noida: Harper Sport.

Mangan, J.A. 1998. 'Series Editor's Foreword'. In Mike Cronin and David Mayall (eds), *Sporting Nationalisms: Identity, Ethnicity, Immigration and Assimilation*, pp. xi–xv. London, Portland, ORE: Frank Cass.

Miller, Clary 1988. *Hockey's Grand Slam*. Perth: Clary Miller.

Mills, Megan S. 2010. 'A Most Remarkable Community: Anglo-Indian Contributions to Sport in India'. *Contemporary South Asia* 10 (2). doi: https://doi.org/10.1080/09584930120083828.

Organising Committee for the XIV Olympiad. 1951. *The Official Report of the Organising Committee for the XIV Olympiad*. London: Organising Committee for the XIV Olympiad.

Ritchie, Donald A. 2015. *Doing Oral History*, 3rd edition. Oxford: Oxford University Press.

Sarkar, Sumit 1997. 'The City Imagined: Calcutta of the Nineteenth and Early Twentieth Centuries'. In *Writing Social History*, pp. 159–85. Delhi: Oxford University Press.

Statesman, The. 1895a. 'Calcutta & Suburbs', 30 March.

———. 1895b. 'Hockey', 19 April.

———. 1895c. 'Hockey', 8 May.

———. 1895d. 'Hockey', 10 May.

———. 1895e. 'Hockey', 15 May.

———. 1895f. 'Beighton Challenge Cup', 30 May.

12

Goa's Football Story

A Brief Narrative

Frederick Noronha

Goa's football history is shrouded in some doubt and debate. Contrary to the popular belief, it was not mainly brought here by the Portuguese, Iberian, and early colonial European powers that ruled this region for almost four-and-half centuries from 1510.

An Irish 'priest' who set up one of the earliest English-medium schools in Goa, Father William Robert Lyons, is credited with having 'first brought football to Goa in 1883' (Mills 2002).[i] He started the game in his St Joseph's School, which had been initially set up in the Bardez sub-district village of Siolim, but was then shifted to another nearby village of Arpora. All this happened, incidentally, when Lyons had come to Goa from Udupi, along coastal western India, to recover from 'health problems' (Leitao n.d.).[ii] Other educationists are credited with spreading the sport to villages like Siolim and Assolna, before the end of the nineteenth century, according to Leitao, who also records that seminarians training for the Catholic priesthood also fielded teams, and once ordained priests, they took the sport to the villages.

From there, the world of football in Goa has today grown into having a close nexus with politics and industry (particularly mining), having the ability to stoke emotions and launch the dreams of thousands of young men (and, less often, women). Football has sometimes emphasized Goa's age-old colonial links with the Lusophone (or Portuguese-speaking) world. These links are especially felt during events like the World Cup. If teams like Portugal show a winning streak, their players draw considerable support here. If not, the support could switch to Spain or some Latin American front-rankers team. Football is also what gives tiny Goa, roughly just one-thousandth the population of India, the chance to sometimes shine at the national level. Yet, there has also been some disquiet here as the 'big money' aspect of the game obviously draws more top players from outside the state (or even from foreign shores), and controversial casino groups emerge to take control of popular

Frederick Noronha, *Goa's Football Story* In: *Sports Studies in India*. Edited by: Meena Gopal and Padma Prakash, Oxford University Press. © Oxford University Press 2021.
DOI: 10.1093/oso/9780190130640.003.0013

GOA'S FOOTBALL STORY 191

football clubs, which were once controlled by also questionable mining firms and miscellaneous other organizations. A giant-sized book (Mergulhao 2016), marking the fiftieth anniversary of the Salgaocar Football Club, spends a few pages on the rivalry between Salgaocar's and Dempo's football clubs. Both were, at the time, major players in Goa's private mining sector.

Roots, Church, and *Gaunkaria*[iii]

Mills (2002:11) points out that a number of recent studies point to 'the importance of Christian missionaries in introducing modern games and sporting activities to non-Western societies'. He cites the work of J.A. Mangan in this regard, as well as experiences from the North West Frontier Provinces (today in Pakistan) and Kashmir. Mills, however, suggests that the Church's importance in 'establishing football in Goa was entirely unrelated to the colonial power relations of the period' (Mills 2002: 14). His argument is that existing studies of football (and other sports) in colonial contexts suggest that Christian missionary activity and the colonial government project of encouraging it led colonized populations to 'adopt and adapt' the game (Mills 2002: 11). In Goa, Mills (2002: 11) argues, '[T]he role of indigenous agents in propagating the game at its earliest stages is crucial to understanding how the sport took off and became embedded in local society and culture.'

Mills quotes a description (Pearson 1987: 154, cited in Mills 2002) of the village *gaunkaria* system, the manner in which the local village communities was administered, as being 'ideal [in many ways] for the introduction of football'. Members of the gaunkaria were males of the dominant caste—either Brahmin or Kshatriya (called Chardo among the Goa Catholics, where caste has no ritual sanction, yet maintains its hegemony in social, economic and marital spheres). 'They ran village associations which controlled most village affairs—roads, drainage, irrigation, public security, religion, education and health' (Pearson 1987: 154, cited in Mills 2002: 16).

Goa accounts for just 0.1 per cent of India in terms of population and size, yet it does often take on an impressive role in its footballing achievements, arguably because the real story might just lie elsewhere. The post-Portuguese era (after 1961) of Goa's history throws up repeated hints of such realities. The politics and economic base of Goa's story of football becomes obvious in the light of recent developments. In reality, Goa is a small but amazing case of how these two aspects have intertwined with the sport. These are among the factors, which have also contributed to football's success story here.

192   NURTURING SPORTS

In the 1970s, the then-chief minister, Dayanand Bandodkar, a mineowner-turned-politician, donated the Bandodkar Gold Cup, which later became a rolling trophy for the winning team in the national tournament named after him (A. Fernandes 2018). In parallel, other mining houses patronized the sport and built it up here; so did politicians like the Churchill Alemao. The latter has been an influential player in local Congress politics and at times also supported the Bharatiya Janata Party (BJP) governments in Goa. His team, Churchill Brothers, has often made news, sometimes for the wrong reasons.

In some ways, Goa's links with football cannot be separated from the region's long, 450-year legacy of Portuguese colonial rule. The Goa Football Association (formerly known as the Associação de Futebol de Goa) was founded in 1959, at the fag end of Portuguese rule here. Till date, an international match will draw support in Goa for Portugal, if the team is playing, or for teams like Brazil, in the absence of Portugal.

Of late, the main football club, FC Goa, has been taken over by casino operators who run offshore casinos in Goa, giving a new twist to the potent cocktail of sponsorships, hegemony, and sports that has long dominated this sector. Players are increasingly sourced from diverse parts of the globe, though often ambitious subaltern youth from the underclasses of Goa's stratified society also make it to the teams.

Football has been seen as a route to the Goan heart. After 1993, the Thapar Dupont Limited, a company whose entry into Goa drew protests on environmental grounds (and also due to corporate rivalry, it was believed) sponsored the Goa First Division League (Ribeiro n.d.). It is another matter that continued protests and some violence led to this firm moving out of Goa later, even before it could set up base here.

There are other dimensions too. In the recent often-misunderstood politics of this small state, when the right-wing Hindu supremacist BJP came to power here (Goa has about a quarter of its population Catholic, and a smaller Muslim population), the BJP government was seen as offering sops by declaring football to be the official state sport. It also set up a Goa State Football Development Council (GFDC), while the Goa Football Association (GFA) continues to be the local official administrative body (Noronha 2018). After winning the 2012 elections, the government of Manohar Parrikar, who is seen as having won with some support from Catholics due to many complex reasons including anti-corruption campaigning by the BJP against the Congress, the GFDC was set up. Parrikar's interest in football, a sport that has a significant following among Goa's minority Catholic community, drew him a good press. In 2014, after being in power for two years in that term, Parrikar announced plans for an 'exclusive football stadium' in Goa, besides allotting an annual budget of INR 5 crore to the GFDC, among other steps (Mergulhao 2014). But the results of this initiative have been poor. Noronha points to the fewer Goan players making it to the national team and fewer top clubs getting visibility in 'top-tier football' nationwide. In 2018, Goa was also reported to be facing a lack of teams for its I-League season. D'Souza (2017) commented: 'The questions being asked include: Is Goan football dying? What is wrong with Goan football? Why is Goa, a state that produced a slew of Indian international stars and legends, now producing virtually no outstanding talent?'

Football is facing threats from other directions too, including Goa's burgeoning real estate sector. Marius Fernandes (2017), who co-founded a football academy some years ago, points out that the Baga football ground has vanished and has been converted into a car park. Other paddy fields, once the nursery of this sport, are also coming under real estate pressure.

Politicians and their lackeys have often dominated official sports committees in Goa, including in football. On the other hand, the sport has also helped some of humble origins to gain name, fame, and in some cases, money as well. Gender issues emerge occasionally in retrospectives of the game. For instance, women's football in Goa began as fun as part of a 1973 match during the carnival celebrations, between a women's team and a men's team, called the Eves and the Adams. Anonymous (circa 1999) describes the situation thus: 'The match was played at the Police grounds, Panjim, in a truly festive spirit, with the men in funny Carnival clothes, resorting to all sorts of antics on the field. But the Eves, more determined and serious about the game, walked off with a 3–1 victory'.

There are other aspects of Goan football that emerge along its inadequately-narrated story. Football has been a significant feature among Goa's proportionately large diaspora. In football fields in different pockets of the globe, and also across cyberspace, one can find links to various diaspora football clubs. They carry names such as Football Club de Bardez-Dubai, Vanxim Divar, CAC Cansaulim, SFX Old Goa, Fr Agnel Pilar, among others. Anyone familiar with the home state would recognize names of villages and Catholic patron saints (or local identities) in the above. At Elmers Road in Beckenham, Kent, a GOA (a term which has been sometimes used as an abbreviation for the Goan Overseas Association, which conveniently tallies with the region's name too) five-a-side football tournament has been held in recent years, by The Goan Association (UK).

194 NURTURING SPORTS

Ribeiro (n.d.) argues that football is 'the only game in which Goans have excelled at the National level'. However, depending on one's frame of reference, differing conclusions could be drawn. A recent book, *Stars Next Door* (C. Fernandes 2018) on the expat Goan sportsmen of East Africa, mostly playing during the heyday of British colonialism in the region, reveals a deep involvement in sports like hockey and cricket there.

The Goan diaspora has got involved in football overseas in other ways. Tony Fernandes (of AirAsia, the Malaysian businessman of Goan origin) was co-chairman of Queens Park Rangers, the professional association football club. Tan Sri (Dr) Anthony Francis Fernandes, better known as Tony Fernandes, is the son of a Goan father and Malayali-Asian-Portuguese (Kristang) mother raised in Malacca, and is better known for building the budget no-frills AirAsia airlines.

In Goa, football's story goes beyond sport. It is one of politics, economics, culture, divisions, unity, and hegemony.

Notes

i. William Robert Lyons is often referred to as a 'priest', but he has also been identified by others as a 'Jesuit scholar who was fondly and popularly called as Fr Lyons'. Also, while some credit football as having arrived in Goa in 1883, the St. Joseph High School at Arpora was itself launched only in 1887 (See http://goanchurches.info/institution/st-joseph-high-school-arpora-goa/; accessed on 24 October 2020).

ii. Ironically enough, a political squabble broke out in 2018, with politician and the president of the Churchill Brothers Sports Club, Churchill Almeao alleging that the Bandodkar Gold Trophy 'may not be of pure gold' (A. Fernandes 2018). The then-sports minister, Manohar 'Babu' Azgaonkar, even promised the Goa Assembly that the matter would be looked into. The cup was donated by Goa's first chief minister in 1969 (Mergulhao 2018), after whom it is named and kept in a bank locker since. It was believed to be one of India's most expensive sporting trophies, until the launch of the India Premier League in 2008. News reports speculated that the whereabouts of the cup might not even be known. There were also claims that the trophy had been swapped with a replica between the time the Bandodkar Gold Cup was discontinued in 1994 and restarted as an Under-21 event in 2016 (A. Fernandes 2018).

iii. 'Gaunkari' or 'comunidade' system is the old form of communal ownership and control of land, mainly by the dominant groups or 'early settlers' of a village. It was preserved in Goa, unlike in the rest of India, consequent to the early arrival of Portuguese rule here.

References

Anonymous. circa 1999. 'The Story of Eve'. In *The Grass is Green in Goa: Celebrating 40 Years*. Goa: Goa Football Association.

D'Souza, Stanislaus. 2017. 'Sun, Sand and No Soccer: Why Does Goa Not Have a Single Player in the U-17 India Squad?'. *Scroll*, 2 October. Available at scroll.in/field/851808/sun-sand-and-no-soccer-why-does-goa-not-have-a-single-player-in-the-u-17-; accessed on 20 February 2019.

Fernandes, Andrea. 2018. 'Gold. . . or Gold Plated'. *OHeraldo*, 5 August. Available at http://www.heraldgoa.in/m/details.php?n_id=134358; accessed on 24 October.

Fernandes, Cyprian. 2018. *Stars Next Door*. Saligao: Goa, 1556.

Fernandes, Marius. 2017. 'Is Football Dead in Goa? Let's Check a Few Facts'. *ItsGoa*, 8 November. Available at www.itsgoa.com/is-football-dead-in-goa/; accessed on 20 February 2019.

Leitao, Lima, Noel da. n.d. 'Goan football Has Little Cause to Look Back'. In *The Grass is Green in Goa: Celebrating 40 Years*. Goa: Goa Football Association.

Mergulhao, Marcus. 2014. 'Goa Set to Get an Exclusive Football Stadium' *The Times of India*, 29 January. Available at https://timesofindia.indiatimes.com/city/goa/Goa-set-to-get-an-exclusive-football-stadium/articleshow/29570716.cms; accessed on 20 February 2019.

———. 2016. *Footprints in the Sand: History of Salgaocar Football Club (1956-2016)*. Goa: Salgaocar FC.

———. 2018. 'How Did the Bandodkar Gold Trophy Lose Its Glitter?'. *The Times of India*, 28 July. Available at https://timesofindia.indiatimes.com/city/goa/how-did-the-bandodkar-gold-trophy-lose-its-glitter/articleshow/65181389.cms; accessed on 20 February 2019.

Mills, James. 2002. 'Colonialism, Christians and Sport: The Catholic Church and Football in Goa, 1883–1951'. *Football Studies* 5 (2). Available at https://pureportal.strath.ac.uk/files-asset/63672699/strathprints001611.pdf; accessed on 24 October 2020

Noronha, Anselm. 2018. 'All You Need to Know about the Football League Structure in Goa'. *Goal.com*, 29 June. Available at www.goal.com/en-in/news/goa-football-league-structure-india-gfa/cyy13m81g1r01cvg8auhhwbif; accessed on 20 February 2019.

Pearson, M. 1987. *The New Cambridge History of India I: The Portuguese in India*. Cambridge: Cambridge University Press.

Ribeiro, Francis Xavier Janim. n.d. 'From a Pastime onto An Industry'. In *The Grass is Green in Goa: Celebrating 40 Years*. Goa: Goa Football Association.

13

Local Clubs and Sports Culture in Kerala

Community at the Centre

S. Mohammed Irshad

The promotion of sports through national and international organizations is important in sustaining the institution of sports. Mega events are organized under national or regional banners where participants represent the large public imagination of the nation and the region rather than the sport itself. However, the culture of sports participation does not derive from mega events alone. Local clubs and movements have played a vital role in promoting local sports and civic engagements. These events are close to the community and promote the idea of a civic sports culture. This chapter revolves around the history of a local sport club in Kerala in promoting community sports culture over decades.

Community and neighbourhood sports are active across the world. They create a sense of ownership of sports events and have played a significant role in political mobilization and community movements. This chapter focuses on Udayadhara Samskarika Sangadana, an arts and sports club started in 1988 by a group of local youth in Kavalpura village in Eravipuram Panchayat (later a part of urban municipal corporation) in Kollam district, Kerala. Sports was the only inspiration for starting this club, where caste, religion, and other sectarianisms didn't matter. It did not promote or celebrate religious events, promoting, rather, a civic culture of sports. It had an elected member in-charge and other ordinary members. Local sports practitioners depended on the club with the local community supporting them in promoting civic culture, or 'civic-ness'.

Celebrating sport as a local event through traditional sports such as wrestling and kabaddi is common practice. The village and the community often identify themselves with it and the social life of the community evolves from such sports events. Local community mobilization for particular sports often demonstrates the success of community collectives and organizations. Such community engagements demonstrate the operations of social capital

S. Mohammed Irshad, *Local Clubs and Sports Culture in Kerala* In: *Sports Studies in India*. Edited by: Meena Gopal and Padma Prakash, Oxford University Press. © Oxford University Press 2021.
DOI: 10.1093/oso/9780190130640.003.0014

in building community sports. Putnam (1993: 167) defines social capital as 'features of social organization, such as trust, norms, and networks, that can improve the efficiency of society by facilitating coordinated actions'. Sports and sports events are indeed coordinated actions to promote and sustain the local sports culture. Sports should promote inclusiveness and be free from institutional norms and structures. Bourdieu's (1986: 248–9) definition of social capital endorses this. He explains that

> the aggregate of the actual or potential resources which are linked to pos-
> session of a durable network of more or less institutionalized relationships
> of mutual acquaintance and recognition or in other words, to membership
> in a group which provides each of its members with the backing of the col-
> lectively owned capital, a 'credential' which entitles them to credit, in the
> various senses of the word.

Udayadhara club did not operate on rigid norms in promoting sports but, rather, it promoted local sports as a source of community engagement. The local community saw the club as an informal institution that catered to its desire for sports and developing a civic culture of participation. According to Bjørnskov (2006), 'social capital consists of three orthogonal components corresponding to social trust, social norms and associational activity'. Sports was the most significant associational activity of the area, and it was close to Putnam's (1993: 173) concept of civic-ness that talks about engagement with networks and associations like neighbourhood associations, choral societies, cooperatives, sports clubs, and mass-based parties that promote civic-ness.

Neighbourhood Sports and Community Engagements

A study by Theeboom, Haudenhuyse, and De Knop (2010) finds that non-profit sports clubs and organizations can encourage people to become active and stay in sports. The clubs talk about 'neighbourhood sports' as local sports activities and function differently from the traditional sports organizations. In traditional and mega sports, events revolve around competition and winning culture and not just participation. Moreover, these sports meets cannot ensure inclusiveness and neighbourhood participation. Promoting neighbourhood sports culture is a political activity too, as for instance, Marquand (2000) explains. Western democracies deliberately frame sports policies to engage civil society in activities to ensure the government's direct

198 NURTURING SPORTS

intervention. Civil society associations act as the potential force at a micro level. Civil society is also the terrain of civil associations that are potential forces of civic engagement and mutuality. Hague and Mercer (1998) analysed the importance of football and described the significance of a small football club in a small town in Scotland. The study argued that the local football club provided a sense of local identity and culture and helped to nurture a shared memory about the locality.

For the local community, the club contributes to building a sense of place and identity. The success of local sports movements and organizations is dependent on how they create a sense of belonging with the local community. As Elkington (1982: 75) observed, sport often ensures a sense of belonging to the local community and creates a sense of self-esteem. Burnett (1993: 9) further observed that sport is an opportunity to experience and build self-esteem. This is possible only through a neighbourhood culture in sports and needs the active engagement of clubs in promoting sports, as Persson (2008) attempts to explain. According to him, sports clubs should be responsible and accountable for their actions. They may not possess individual consciousness but still have to take formal decisions to act as legal agents for sports promotion. Misener, Harman, and Doherty (2013) observed that local sports clubs and councils have unique forms of activities, which act as vehicles for community sports development. These clubs are not sports service providers; rather, they work as initiatives that ensure leadership and integration and also act as a collective voice for sports in the community.

Neighbourhood sports and community engagement is a form of social capital that promotes the idea of collective sports and local community mobilization. Coleman (1987, 1988), explaining social capital in a rational choice theory framework, views social capital as the function of action rather than a product of it. Social capital is obligations and expectations underpinned by trust and not just norms followed by sanctions. The very existence of neighbourhood sports culture is dependent on the manifestation of social capital as collective action. So, as Jarvie (2003) observes, the decline of social capital is a process of the gradual decrease in the membership in voluntary organizations, declining level of participation in voluntary organizations, and also less time spent in informal socializing. Neighbourhood sport is collective social mobility and it promotes an inclusive sports movement, unlike traditional sports events and meets. Neighbourhood sports depends on collective memory, openness, and identity of the organizations.

This study using an autoethnographic method and analysis examines Udayadhara Samskarika Sangadana in Eravipuram area of Kollam district in

LOCAL CLUBS AND SPORTS CULTURE IN KERALA   199

Kerala. The sources of data include the author's interaction with the founding members of the club, his close observation of the locality, and his own memories over 30 years. The experience of neighbourhood sports in another coastal village Alappad is also used to analyse critical dimensions of the potential of local sports and how its decline promotes sectarian politics.

Udayadhara Samskarika Sangadana

The history of sports events in this small semi-urban area go back to 1960s and 1970s. The Madhava Vilasam Lower Primary (LP) School's (later Kollorvila LP School) ground was the field for *Gusti* (local name of wrestling competition) and *fayallvans* (wrestlers).[i]

There was community support for Gusti, and, hence, for sports and community gatherings. This was a time in Kerala when these fayallvans were treated as heroes. The origin of sports clubs and sports events in the school ground goes back to this history.

Udayadhara club emerged from the local youth's enthusiasm to promote local sports and arts. The club was started in 1988 by twelve local youth. Shihabuddin Mohammed, known as Kallumoodan, the founding president of the Udayadhara Arts and Sports club, was a member of Chaithnya Arts and Sports Club and Pournami Arts and Sports Club. He took the initiative to revamp the old club Yuvadhara into Udayadhara Arts and Sports Club. It attracted new members, and Ahamed Khan became the club's first secretary and Shihabuddin the president. Ahamed Khan continued his social activism till his last breath through the local citizenship forum that has been demanding better development of local railway stations and social infrastructure. Shihabuddin later started a catering business.

The club, appropriately registered, began an evening volleyball training programme since most members of the club were already active local volleyball players. This daily activity began to attract a crowd of regular spectators. Volleyball was one of the popular sports then and (late) Jimmy George was the icon for the youth at that time. Everybody wanted to be a 'Jimmy George'. Shihabuddin asserts that these daily sessions taught volleyball to many who had no formal sports training. The club converted any available open space into training grounds, with the local LP school ground being the focal coaching ground for years. Those who trained used to participate in the local volleyball competitions and some even played in district level competitions.

200 NURTURING SPORTS

The club taught the local community how to build local sports careers without undue expectations.

The training programme and associated facilitation of sports made the club popular. The second anniversary of the club in 1989 was celebrated with a week-long arts and sports festival, and this annual celebration continued over the next five years. The anniversary celebrations merged with the Onam festival of Kerala. Interestingly, the club did not take part in religious or caste festivals, rituals, or observances, even though the members may have been believers. Anniversary/Onam celebrations of the club cut across the social and religious divides, with people patiently waiting through the night for drama performances. The Onam week was picked for the anniversary celebration, because it was a time when all people of Kerala came together across class, community, and caste divides.

The sports week was the time when the local boys and girls without any formal coaching participated in sports events. Participants themselves collectively selected the sports events for the annual event. The most attractive among the events was the marathon from Kollam town to the club premises. Local sports enthusiasts would celebrate this marathon event, in which everyone participated, not just celebrities. The winner received INR 1,001 as a cash award and a trophy. All the prizes were distributed on the last day of the Onam/Anniversary festival. The club conducted annual local level competitions for school children and young boys and girls: 100-metre run, long jump, high jump, 500-metre run, football, kabaddi, kilithattukali (a local style of kabaddi), cycle slow run, scooter slow run, body building, and so on. Interestingly, although India won the first cricket World Cup in 1983, cricket was not on the list of sports events. There were events such as the cycle slow racing and scooter slow racing, events not formally sports events. The cycle slow racing attracted a huge local participation.

The competitions had the full support of the local community; there were no disputes or disagreements on the decisions of the club. It was fully supported by local financial contributions, with the local community contributing the prize money and trophies. Unlike national or state sports meets, this was open to everyone and there were no pre-selections. This really encouraged the local community to participate in the competitions. Many new local sport icons emerged here, for instance, Ms Geetha K.[ii]

The sports meet lasted a long week and included local events as well. Club members' community engagement was one of the main reasons for the huge participation of the local community. At a time when cricket was not so popular among the local youth, the community allowed the use of local grounds

LOCAL CLUBS AND SPORTS CULTURE IN KERALA 201

for the events. Every bit of public vacant land was converted into sports fields. Landowners allowed the use of their land for free not insisting on formal permissions. The week-long sports meet of the club was advertised with the help of local announcers and printed notices. Young athletes keenly waited for these club-organized sports meets.

Local Sports and Local Clubs

Sport was the only inspiration for these clubs and it was the public sphere that stood for secular values and justice. For instance, Udayadhara Club was formed in Muslim-dominated areas, but it was not influenced by the dominant religion of the area. Shihabuddin pointed out that while the local area and the Muslim community, for instance, actively celebrated Mawlid an-Nabi (the birth day of prophet Mohammed) with illuminations and decorations, the club did not promote or participate in these events, even though the members individually joined the celebrations. Shihabuddin recalls that the club did not want to promote any religious events whatever the religion.

This was the time in Kerala when many sports clubs were named after Netaji, that is, Netaji Subhas Chandra Bose, seeking as they did secular identities, remaining non-aligned with any party or religion. These clubs and the community they mobilized reflected the secular sports culture of the locality. Udayadhara was the centre, and the members of the club wanted to identify themselves mainly as sports promoters. Sports helped them connect with sports enthusiasts and the community.

At that time, there were few mega sports events in a year and there was little opportunity for local sports lovers to participate in competitions. The local clubs thrived with the full support and cooperation from the community. There were no rivalries and no attempts to exclude any club from organizing particular events. In fact, such clubs functioned as information centres to sportspersons on ongoing local competitions and meets in the area.

The spread of organized sports events and the influence of party politics have gradually changed the position and identity of such clubs. This is evident from the transformation of such clubs in the coastal areas of Kollam and Alapuzha districts where the once-secular tendencies have given way to religious politics, with new clubs being named after heroes of epics, such as Pandavas and Kouravas. Sports practices and promotions have also shifted in favour of polarizing politics.

202   NURTURING SPORTS

Hearteningly, however, senior fishermen of this coast have initiated week-long football matches to bring youth together. The success of such meets is yet to be demonstrated, but these matches have certainly drawn youth. According to Sreekumar, a local community member and leader of the local natural resources protection group, they had organized football matches with the intention of attracting youth and recreating the old local sports movements. His inspiration came from the local history of club-based sports movements and their success in mobilizing the community. The larger objective of these local civil society activists is to pull youth away from sectarian associations to community sports events under secular movements.

The rise in stadium-based sports and the loss in importance of collectively owned local sports events have resulted in the demise of the local clubs like Udayadhara. The membership of the clubs has shrunk. This does not mean that the club is closed permanently. It is still running as a local newspaper reading club but is unable to organize sports events as in the past. Interestingly, however, a high-tech multi gymnasium has come up right in front of Udayadhara Club run by a group that has no association with the old club. The founding member of the Club could never have imagined such a gymnasium! The generation born in the mid-1990s that uses the gym has no interest in the history of this club right across the street or its contribution to local sports, nor in the culture of community engagements.

The local sports enthusiasts have moved to stadiums for sports, and traditional and local sports events have completely disappeared from the local sports culture. Organized sports events are for a set of people who have some formal training. While such mega events can promote sports at a national level, they do not necessarily create local sports mobilization and community engagement. Many new associations have formed to promote particular sports rather than generalist local clubs promoting all sports.

One can trace the history of local sports through three time periods: from Gusti to Udayadhara, and to the gymnasium. Gusti represented a tradition of collective participation of the community in the area; Udayadhara came up after a couple of decades to represent a different kind of sports still taking the community along with them, but the gymnasium represents a new individual centric body/style-conscious exercise programme with high (male only) youth activity, where the local community as a collective does not exist.

***

Clubs like Udayadhara represent an identity of community sports mobilization and culture. Such local clubs in rural areas and even in the urban centres of Kerala used to promote a community linked sports culture and a sense of community ownership. These clubs could successfully gather all those interested in sports across a variety of events. Many of the winners of these events might never have been into sports in their lives. While such participation grounded their personal and social life, it did not necessarily lead them to make sports their career choice. They did not play only to gain grace marks for sports participation or obtain access to special quotas in appointments and admissions. These participants were part of the community collective for local sports events, a collective that the local clubs nurtured. The Onam and Sports meet attracted people from neighbouring villages, emphatically defining sports as a community event and to ensure that everyone participated.

Time is not favourable for community-based clubs like Udayadhara today. And local people hardly know the president and secretary of Udayadhara now.[iii] (However, many do remember the founding members and recollect the sports events that the club organized.) How the future will pan out for this tradition of community sports is yet to be determined.

Notes

i. In 1992, Mr Chandran, son of Mr Madhavan on whose name the school was started granted one cent of land (435.6 Sq Ft) to the club to construct a permanent concrete structure. In a gesture of gratitude, Mr Madhavan's portrait still hangs on the walls of the club.

ii. Geetha K was an active participant in sports competitions organized by local clubs. She won prizes in 100-metre run organized by Udayadhara Club. She participated in all these events when she was in school, having no formal training except the school physical training classes. She used to be active in all local sports meets and even participated in the district meet. Her achievements were thus limited to the local events with no avenues for formal training to attain higher achievements in her career. Her sports life ended locally.

iii. I had to ask my brother the names of the current president and secretary of the club. I still know the names of every founding member of the club and their well wishers. I can recollect even the people who participated in the sports events such as bodybuilding, cycle slow run, scooter slow run, marathon run, and so forth.

References

Bjørnskov, Christian. 2006. 'The Multiple Facets of Social Capital'. *European Journal of Political Economy* 22 (1): 22–40.

Bourdieu, P. 1986. 'The Forms of Capital'. In J.G. Richardson (ed), *Handbook of Theory and Research for the Sociology of Education*, pp. 241–58. New York: Greenwood Press.

Burnett, D.J. 1993. *Youth, Sport and Self Esteem: A Guide for Parents.* Indianapolis: Master Press.

Coleman, J.S. 1987. 'Norms as Social Capital'. In G. Radnitzky and P. Bernholz (eds), *Economic Imperialism: The Economic Approach Applied Outside the Field of Economics*, pp. 133–55. New York: Paragon House Publishers.

———. 1988. 'Social Capital in the Creation of Human Capital'. *American Journal of Sociology* 94: 95–120.

Elkington, S. 1982. 'Country Communities: Sport and Recreation'. In *Country Communities: Responding to Change*, pp. 72–83. Wodonga: Clyde Cameron College, Australian Institute of Agricultural Science, Northen Victorian Sub-Branch Australian Farm Management Society, and Department of Planing.

Hague, E. and J. Mercer 1998. 'Geographical Memory and Urban Identity in Scotland: Raith Rovers FC and Kirkcaldy'. *Geography* 83 (2): 105–16.

Jarvie, Grant. 2003. 'Communitarianism, Sports and Social Capital: Neighbourly Insights into Scottish Sport'. *International Review for the Sociology of Sports* 38 (2): 139–53.

Marquand, D. 2000. 'The Fall of Civic Culture'. *New Statesman America* (Nov): 27–30.

Misener, Katie, Alanna Harman, and Alison Doherty. 2013. 'Understanding the Local Sports Council as a Mechanism for Community Sport Development'. *Managing Leisure* 18 (4): 300–15. doi: https://doi.org/10.1080/13606719.2013.809185.

Persson, H.T.R. 2008. 'Social Capital and Social Responsibility in Denmark: More than Gaining Public Trust'. *International Review for the Sociology of Sport* 43 (1): 35–51. doi: https://doi.org/10.1177/1012690208094655.

Putnam, Robert D. 1993. *Making Democracy Work: Civic Traditions in Modern Italy.* Princeton: Princeton University Press.

Theeboom, Marc, Reinhard Haudenhuyse, and Paul De Knop. 2010. 'Community Sports Development for Socially Deprived Groups: A Wider Role for the Commercial Sports Sector? A Look at the Flemish Situation'. *Sport in Society* 13 (9): 1392–410

14

Nurturing Sports Talent

What Role Do Academies Play?[i]

Pulasta Dhar

When you walk into the wrestling academy at Sonepat in north India, you enter a different world. It is remarkably quiet for a place which houses athletes who take part in a sport which involves blood, sweat, and tears. '*Ek sanskaar hai kushti mein. Badde ki, chhote ki. Aur yeh aur kisi game mein nahi hai* [Here is a culture and respect in wrestling—of your seniors and juniors. And this is not there in any other sport],' Yogeshwar Dutt told me in 2016 when I went to Sonepat to write a feature on the Olympic bronze medallist. Then I had written: 'It's surreal to see fully grown men, half naked, stop what they're doing when Yogeshwar walks past, and bow down in respect, like a king is passing through a hallway of ministers' (Dhar 2016). But it is not only the behaviour of the athletes—who are well-grounded despite having Audi SUVs parked outside—that is awe inspiring. Sonepat is home to athletes aspiring to be medallists. It is part of a practice that has yielded India five Olympic medals and fifty-six Asian Games medals.

Are academies like the one in Sonepat the only way to nurture sporting talent in the country? Not really, says footballer Gurpreet Sandhu, the only Indian to have played in a continental European football competition, when his former club Stabæk played in the Europa League.

There can be different perspectives if you have the right people in place—it doesn't matter whether this talent is nurtured at a school or an academy. In China, kids are going to have football mandated in school. . . . Sports education can start as early as in school. That's where it begins—kids go to schools more than they go to academies. It's a development process, not just the sport but also adding human values to those who play.

Gurpreet is India's first-choice goalkeeper and has also led the national side on some occasions. The twenty-six-year-old has never trained at an academy

---

Pulasta Dhar, *Nurturing Sports Talent* In: *Sports Studies in India*. Edited by: Meena Gopal and Padma Prakash, Oxford University Press. © Oxford University Press 2021. DOI: 10.1093/oso/9780190130640.003.0015

206 NURTURING SPORTS

because his school St Stephens in Chandigarh had a strong sporting culture. He retains much of those values even today. He adds:

> The motto of my school is 'semper sursum'—which means always aim high—that has been in my mind ever since and it taught me to be disciplined and to work a way through life. You don't get anything for free and you need to aim higher than you think you do. There are times you think you're not capable of doing much but [they] taught us to keep pushing our limits.

Gurpreet is one of the lucky few to study in a school so steeped in sporting culture that it has an academy of its own. But this is in Punjab, which, according to government data (as of April 2016), had most number of schools with playgrounds.

> The percentage of schools with playground facility in Punjab was 95.38 as on April 2016. The percentage of schools with playground facility in Punjab was higher by 34.91 percentage points as compared to the percentage of schools with playground facility at All India level. (OGD PMU Team 2017)

But here's the thing: A playground could be anything from a patch of rough land to a sand-filled area with slides and see-saws. In the Right of Children to Free and Compulsory Education Act, 2009,[ii] the government does not define what 'playground' means. The Act just uses the word 'playground' as one of the requirements of a school building but there are no minimum requirements for the same. The Central Board of Secondary Education (CBSE) guidelines say schools should provide 'for a 200-metre track and there should be adequate facilities to play games' (*Indian Express* 2015). These rules were later relaxed with this surprising statement:

> The intent of inclusion of playground as an infrastructure requirement of a school is to ensure that children have sufficient open space for sports and other physical activities during school hours. It is not necessary that the school management provides this facility within the school premises.[iii]

For sports talent to be nurtured, schools need facilities that support multiple outdoor sports, such as football, basketball, cricket, and volleyball, and indoor sports, such as table tennis and badminton. It is no secret that these are hard to come by in most schools across India. Talent can be found anywhere, not only among those privileged enough to study in an institution which houses an academy.

Chhatrasal Akhada, New Delhi

Wrestling, for example, is popular in the country but is still mostly practised in the northern parts of India. For the sport to spread, it needs a system that breeds more competitors. Satpal Singh, India's most decorated wrestling coach, says:

> What we need is a system in place to unearth talent—we are at a stage where the *dangals* in villages are also played on mats. But how do we turn this popularity of the sport into medals? . . . We need to do with wrestling what (the late) BCCI [Board of Control for Cricket in India] chief Jagmohan Dalmiya did with cricket. When Sunil Gavaskar was playing a Test for Rs 1500, I was playing wrestling matches for Rs 3 lakh. Now we see Sushil Kumar get auctioned for less than a crore rupees in the wrestling leagues and IPL players go for Rs 15 crore. So it's about turning the success of a sport into popularity and popularity back into success.

Satpal Singh, who has won a bronze, silver, and gold medal at the Asian Games, is the coach of two-time Olympic medallist Sushil Kumar, and has been awarded the Padma Bhushan, Padma Shri, Dronacharya Award, and Arjun Award for his immense contribution to the sport. The sixty-two-year-old has no complaints about how far reaching the sport has become since Sushil won at the Olympics, just like Sakshi Malik. His grievances lie in the culture surrounding the sport. And when it comes to wrestling, it is important to know that even though it is India's best shot at international medals, glory is not always the ultimate goal of those who devote their life to it. He adds:

> The federations are doing school level tournaments. Khelo India was a great initiative to find U17 talent and there are participants from as far out as Pondicherry who are getting into the sport. However, a lot of these players get into it for a secure job - which may follow with brief success at national level as well. . . . *Medal toh humaare jaise pagal hi dekhte hain. Ek nasha tha.* [Only some of us are mad about winning medals. It was an addiction.]

208   NURTURING SPORTS

The champion wrestler Satpal Singh pioneered the modern Chhatrasal Akhada in New Delhi, and continues to make sure that while the facilities may be modern, the approach towards wrestling culture is traditional. There are around 350 wrestlers under Satpal Singh at Chhatrasal, and he says that 180 of them have had international-level experience. That said, he tries to keep the ethos of the academy steeped in what he believes is a unique wrestling culture. 'There is a *guru–shishya* culture in wrestling as in no other sport. It is a sort of reverence among peers and seniors as well. A polite acceptance of people from outside and a need to keep aggression only for the mat. It is imperative that as wrestling is modernised, we keep this alive in the sport,' he says.

Satpal Singh has grown with the times. He refuses to put the blame for its slow growth on the central and state wrestling federations. Instead, he believes in spreading that responsibility among people who know how to run the sport. What is required, he believes, is a change in thinking and a large increment in the number of wrestling coaches. He says:

And these coaches should know the sport very well—how to react, how to behave in last 10 seconds, what to eat and the discipline [required]. India's major cultural block is that if someone loses - they put the wrestler so down - and when he wins - they put him on a pedestal so high that a drop will really hurt. We should treat it as a sport - you win some you lose some.

Bhiwani Boxing Club

If Chhatrasal is Indian wrestling's mecca, then the Bhiwani Boxing Club (BBC) is for India's gloved ring fighters. Four of the five boxers who represented India at the 2008 Olympics were from BBC, as it is known. Also coined as 'Little Cuba', Bhiwani produced Vijender Singh, arguably India's most popular boxer.

The man behind the club's remarkable rise is Jagdish Singh. Singh is categorical that a deeply ingrained mindset in India works against the nurturing of boxing talent. He says:

The Indian government has sports policies, stadiums, and facilities but there is also mismanagement and the lack of resources and corruption. In some up-to-date facilities there are stray animals—no coaches and no system. I am the son of a farmer but I am very sad that at my age - two things - sports policy and agriculture policy never get fully implemented.

Which means we cannot utilise the facilities which we've invested in. *Neeti nahi niyat ki zaroorat hai.* [We do not need good ethics, we need good intensions.]

One of the reasons he kickstarted BBC, he confesses, was to nurture boxers so that they are fit eventually to play for India. He says proudly:

> There are many conditions [to be fulfilled] by athletes if they are to go straight to sports ministry's sponsored academies. For example, [in these academies] I couldn't coach boxers below the age of 14, or those working and above 18. So where will the boxers come from? That made me start BBC, start coaching young children (10-years-old and onwards) and then they can go to the Sports Authority of India's (SAI) academies if they're good enough. I also take in those who are rejected by SAI. I wanted to give these kids a platform. 500 of my students have also found sports-based jobs.

Satpal Singh elaborated on the need for coaches as well, pointing also to the monetary issues: 'We get foreign coaches for a minimum of Rs 5–6 lakh per annum, but have Indian coaches working at Rs 2 lakh per annum. That has to change.'

While Jagdish Singh agrees with this, he also says that one of the vital elements of using academies to nurture sports talent is introducing foreign coaches to the youngest age group. 'There is no point in a foreign coach coming in and trying to change a 28-year-old athlete who is already set in some ways,' he says.

But are academies the only way forward? 'There is no other way to become a boxer, apart from going to an academy, hope to do well when picked by SAI, and then play the nationals and eventually for India,' says Jagdish Singh.

Badminton Academies

Administrators aside, the sports fraternity all seem to agree that academies and infrastructure make up just the tip of the iceberg in developing talent. Badminton star Parupalli Kashyap, who has won bronze, silver, and gold medals at the Commonwealth Games and is also an Arjuna Awardee, points out that academies are worth nothing if there aren't enough coaches in the sport. He says:

210   NURTURING SPORTS

I remember meeting 2004 Olympic silver medallist Shon Seung-mo a few years back in Lucknow during a tournament and realising that he was earning more money as a coach than he was as a player. This is someone from the same generation as] Pullela Gopichand [Kashyap's coach]. This is what's needed for India. . . . Coaches here are unsung, and it's not a very respectable job.

Most badminton players are rewarded with jobs in petroleum companies. How will this help the sport in any way? Instead, he suggests, the government should do everything to keep hold of a crop of players and make them feel wanted and appreciated in a way that they want to give back to society. The thirty-one-year-old says:

There could be good coaches, but there is something different that players with experience at the top level can offer a young badminton player. There has to be a no-matter-what attitude among coaches and that will come through passion and incentives. Technically, one could become a player without joining an academy but badminton is a very expensive sport due to the number of shuttles required. If you decide to train individually, you need shuttles, a court, and a good coach. Rest on the sidelines and gym training as well. Then you're set. But academies offer you good competition to test yourself—they have good facilities, especially if there are national camps happening there. But the person who can make you a champion from an [ordinary] player is the coach—and the quality coaches is poor in India.

India's top badminton players are mostly either from Prakash Padukone's academy in Bangalore or Pullela Gopichand's in Hyderabad. The academies are world class and play a huge role in producing India's champions. Saina Nehwal, who left Gopichand's academy for Prakash Padukone's later in her career, and P.V. Sindhu from Gopichand's academy, both have won Olympic medals for India.

Cricket Academies

The country's most popular sport, cricket, though is slightly different in its approach to nurturing talent, is not dependent on academies to produce players. The stakes are high here, the sport spread out across the country and money even at lower levels significantly more than in any other sport. With the advent of the Indian Premier League (IPL), the focus is on finding raw talent and turning these players into superstars. Scouting, therefore, is far and wide, and local school and Twenty20 tournaments are also ripe with potential. 'In the last 10 years, ever since MS [Mahendra Singh Dhoni] was captain, players have come from small districts and places. . . . Cricket is an expensive sport but still, there are kids coming from small towns and they are getting an opportunity due to the network of scouts,' says Tamil Nadu Ranji team skipper Abhinav Mukund.

Cricket academies are still a great attraction for young cricketers: The badge of an academy can greatly enhance one's experience in competition. But most of these academies are privately run without the support of the Board of Control for Cricket in India (BCCI). 'Only a handful of [cricket] associations have full-fledged all-year academy structures. It's more the private academies that bring in players in India,' Mukund says.

Trials are another great way to spot talent in all these sports. Most private teams also run trials, and these become stepping stones to academies. This is where popular private leagues also play a huge role in nurturing sport, a process which needs lots of opportunities to show and hone talent. 'The moment you finish school you need to be in a position and place where you are working on your skills and basics and in an institution which takes you to the next level. That is where academies come into place,' footballer Gurpreet Singh Sandhu says.

The sports industry is malleable. And while academies are an integral part of this industry and system, it needs an immense effort to support them. Infrastructure, opportunity, and administration are also vital. As Satpal Singh says, 'We have to chase down success.' And that's not something just academies can do. India needs more—much, much more—to nurture sports talent.

Notes

i. All quotes in this chapter are from telephonic interviews conducted between 19–30 March 2018.

ii. See http://mhrd.gov.in/sites/upload_files/mhrd/files/upload_document/rte.pdf; accessed on. 10 November 2020.

iii. http://mhrd.gov.in/sites/upload_files/mhrd/files/upload_document/41_0.pdf; accessed on 10 November 2020.

References

Dhar, Pulasta. 2016. 'Yogeshwar Abhi Baaki Hai: India's Medal Hopes Are Pinned on the Last Legend of Wrestling'. *Scoopwhoop*, 21 August. Available at https://www.scoopwhoop.com/Yogeshwar-Abhi-Baaki-Hai-Indias-Medal-Hopes-Are-Pinned-On-The-Last-Legend-Of-Wrestling/; accessed on 10 November 2020.

Indian Express, The. 2015. 'Outdoor Games Take a Backseat: Most Schools Lack Playgrounds', 15 August. Available at https://indianexpress.com/article/cities/chandigarh/outdoor-games-take-a-backseat-most-schools-lack-playgrounds/; accessed on 23 June 2019.

OGD PMU Team. 2017. 'Schools with Playground Facility as on April 2016'. *Community.data.gov.in.* Available at https://community.data.gov.in/schools-with-playground-facility-as-on-april-2016/; accessed on 10 November 2020.

SECTION IV

STATE, SPORTS, AND DEVELOPMENT

Policy and Regulation

15

The Uneven Development of Sport Policy in India

Need for a Coordinated Governance Structure

Kruthika N.S. and Sarthak Sood

The history of sports governance in India has often been smeared with controversies and disputes. With issues ranging from questionable selection trials by national sports federations (Kamath 2018) and systemic age fraud (Sharma 2020; Shriniwas Rao 2020) to the lack of an efficacious forum for settling disputes plaguing Indian sport, our sporting successes have occurred despite the system, rather than because of it.

The challenges plaguing the Indian sports ecosystem today call for a multi-pronged set of reforms, as posited by the Sports Law and Policy Centre in its 2017 report (henceforth Reforms Report). The Reforms Report identifies ten reforms urgently needed relating to the structure of sports administration in India, integrity and representation in Indian sport, powers of sports federations, and funding of sport. A major structural reform it recommends is transferring 'sport' from the State List of Schedule VII of the Constitution of India to the Concurrent List, a step which would take sport from the exclusive legislative competence of the states to the legislative competence of both the centre and the states. Several shortcomings of the Indian sports ecosystem can be traced to the fact that India does not have a uniform sports policy. Hence, sports policies across Indian states vary widely in terms of comprehensiveness, milestones, and financial commitment.

In this chapter, we take a deep dive into this recommendation of the Reforms Report, and argue that it is crucial for an effective sports policy. Given that the Concurrent List allows for the exercise of both state and central powers, as a first step towards major sports law and policy reform in India, we recommend the inclusion of 'sport' as a Concurrent List subject (*The Sports Law and Policy Centre* 2017). Such a shift would require the states and the centre to work cohesively in developing a sports policy that not only

---

Kruthika N.S. and Sarthak Sood, *The Uneven Development of Sport Policy in India* In: *Sports Studies in India.*
Edited by: Meena Gopal and Padma Prakash, Oxford University Press. © Oxford University Press 2021.
DOI: 10.1093/oso/9780190130640.003.0016

216   STATE, SPORTS, AND DEVELOPMENT

takes into account the differences in each state's needs and resources, but also attempts to maintain a degree of uniformity across states.

The State of Play: India's Many Sports Policies

A comprehensively drafted sports governance policy is a prerequisite for any serious sporting nation. It must set out measurable, attainable goals and the process to achieve them, while providing a vision for sports in the context of the community. Accounting for all stakeholders and institutions involved in sport, from grassroots all the way up, it must provide for smooth collaboration among them (International Olympic Committee [IOC] 2008). Effectively implemented, it can have the potential to benefit the society at large by facilitating a culture where sport is accessible to all citizens, treated as an integral part of health, and perceived as a viable career option (IOC 2008). However, India's sports policy operates in fragments that barely attempts to appear like a functioning whole, as each Indian state has the power to determine its own sports policy. Exercising this power, states have come up with vastly dissimilar approaches to sports administration, and some are barely passable.

At this juncture, one may wonder: Why have so many different policies at all when one good policy would do? Unfortunately, the current legal landscape of sport does not allow this. The Constitution provides a scheme for the federal structure of India where the centre has the exclusive competence to make laws on certain subjects in List I of Schedule VII (Union List), the state legislatures on certain other subjects in List II (State List), and both central and state legislatures on subjects in List III (Concurrent List) (The Constitution of India 1950, Art 246[1] and [3]). As 'sports' is a subject in the State List (in the same entry as 'theatres, entertainments and amusements'), it has become a legislative mandate for individual Indian states. Hence, despite athletes representing the *country* rather than their *state* in global events, India has no central sports regulator.

In the following section, we compare the state sports policies of Karnataka, Kerala, Haryana, and Meghalaya based on four variables considered important determinants of the effectiveness of a sports policy: the policy's framework for funding sports and attracting the identified talent to sport; the process the state should follow to identify young sporting talent; the state's commitment on sports infrastructure; and its framework for pinning

THE UNEVEN DEVELOPMENT OF SPORT POLICY IN INDIA   217

accountability of institutions and officials involved in sport. On analysing
them based on these factors, noticeable differences emerge.

Funding and Incentives

The differences in funding and incentives show perhaps the greatest of
inequalities among the selected states. According to the Karnataka State
Sports Policy, grants made to 'recognised associations' are structured as per
the category of competition (Government of Karnataka 2018: 12). Further,
it specifically provides for cash rewards for successful athletes (Government
of Karnataka 2018: 18). Kerala, like Karnataka, indicates specific amounts
of cash rewards, although the amount differs between the two states
(Government of Kerala 2015). Meghalaya proposes certain amounts to be
given to various sports associations for two years, but has stated that any future funding would be based on performance (Government of Meghalaya
2017). Such a strict condition, and for such a short period of time, could
prove to be detrimental to sport in the state in the long haul. Finally, Haryana
indicates no minimum amount for financing sport, though it assures higher
cash awards than the other three states (Government of Haryana 2015: 42).
It is pertinent to note that the polices of all the selected states focus funds on
cash awards, which forms a reactionary method of fund utilization, rather
than investing in sport at the grassroots level, demonstrating a departure
from a robust sports policy. Further, Indian states favour a reactive incentive
system, where athletes are notably rewarded *after* cementing themselves on
the world stage. There is no policy for quantifying such reactive rewards, providing further scope for disparity in pay.

Talent Identification

Karnataka's sports policy proposes a tiered framework, where fresh talent is
identified at the school level by community coaches, at the district level by
intermediate coaches, at high-performance levels by elite coaches, and at the
final level, coaches are eligible for accreditation, which can result in grants,
performance support, and coaching support (Government of Karnataka
2018: 22). Similarly, Haryana has a robust talent-identification strategy, particularly at the grassroots level. 'Catch them young, catch them right' being
its catchphrase, the Haryana's sports policy requires a mass talent-search

218　STATE, SPORTS, AND DEVELOPMENT

exercise across schools, including standardized tests (Government of Haryana 2015: Clause 24). Kerala's policy intends to have a 'talent-scouting team' to find talent at the school level (Government of Kerala 2015: 32). Meghalaya has no sports policy in place yet, but has come up with a draft policy. While the draft policy has indicated that talent identification will begin at a young age (Government of Meghalaya 2017: 20), it has not set out a definitive selection process or talent-scouting exercises.

Infrastructure

Infrastructure commitments of various states, which perhaps reflect the funding allowance, also show clear disparity among the states. For instance, Karnataka's policy lays much emphasis on the sports ecosystem (Government of Karnataka 2018: 15), with infrastructure development extending from a sporting hub in Bengaluru, to medical facilities for sportspersons, to a website that ensures transparency. It also mandates effective soft infrastructure such as mental health facilities, resource mobilization, and event and calendar management (Government of Karnataka 2018: 6). It places importance on the provision of post-career support, including providing reservation for sportspersons in available governmental posts. Haryana focuses on implementing a public–private partnership (PPP) model and a state sports grid from the district to local levels to ensure maximum exposure to sport (Government of Haryana 2015: 32, 35). It also offers a special focus on rural areas, in collaboration with the Mahatma Gandhi National Rural Employment Guarantee Act, 2005 (MGNREGA) (Government of Haryana 2015: 33). Kerala has a similar plan of setting up a state sports grid (Government of Kerala 2015: 28). Meghalaya's draft policy intends to create international-level sports infrastructure (Government of Meghalaya 2017: 12), but has indicated no funding proposals for the same.

Accountability Framework

With regard to accountability, Karnataka's policy intends to have a three-year monitoring period to oversee the implementation of the policy, headed by the Sports Authority of Karnataka. Further, it intends to create a sports advisory body to aid the Sports Authority of Karnataka to look into auditing, accounts, selection, issues pertaining to fraud, and so on (Government of

THE UNEVEN DEVELOPMENT OF SPORT POLICY IN INDIA   219

Karnataka 2018: 10). Haryana's policy provides for a mechanism ensuring declaration of selection, rankings, and test results to ensure transparency and evaluation of coaches (Government of Haryana 2015: Clause 29), but is silent on holding any other parties which may be accountable. Haryana looks to have a mechanism in place to oversee the implementation of its policy over five years, headed by an implementation and monitoring group (Government of Haryana 2015: 23). However, to the best of our knowledge, no such body has been set up yet. Meghalaya stresses on the accountability of coaches as well (Government of Meghalaya 2017: 35), but does not emphasize on any other party's accountability. Kerala's policy merely states that an implementation and monitoring group shall be set up, with no other details provided (Government of Kerala 2015: 22).

While one cannot claim that a state's performance in sport is solely dependent on its policy, a good policy clearly provides the state's citizens with the *capability* of excelling in sport. Hence, it comes as no surprise that some Indian states contribute disproportionately to India's medal tallies in international multi-sport events and the tallies in the national games' framework. For example, Haryana alone accounted for one-third of the medals in the Commonwealth Games, 2018 (Sharma 2018), and 25 per cent in the Asian Games, 2018 (Indo-Asian News Service [IANS] 2018). It has also dominated the medals tally at Khelo India Youth Games (Singh 2018),[i] surpassing much larger states.

Moreover, our dissimilar sports policies alone cannot explain the uneven development sport across states in India, and the landscape of sports policies cannot change by a mere shift of sports from the State List to the Concurrent List. Various other cultural, socio-economic, and political factors affect the performance of states in various sports and their policies towards improving their sports ecosystem. However, the sports policies of various states are a key to understand the structures in which sport has been allowed to unevenly develop, and a cohesive, enforceable policy can be but a factor that works in India's favour.

Toothless at the Centre

In an attempt to rectify the defects of a fragmented sports governance system, and despite sport falling under the legislative ambit of the states, the centre has made efforts to lay down a uniform set of guidelines for sports governance. The most significant of these are the National Sports Policy, 2001

220   STATE, SPORTS, AND DEVELOPMENT

(henceforth National Sports Policy) and the National Sports Development Code of India, 2011 (NSDCI). These serve as the basis for setting standards for sporting infrastructure and athlete guidelines. However, as the centre is unable to directly legislate on the subject, the National Sports Policy and the NSDCI provide mere guidelines with *largely* no operative provisions; the judiciary has stepped in in certain cases, which is discussed in the following sections. Despite the shortcomings with respect to the enforceability of these guidelines, it is vital to scrutinize their development over time, as they give us a glimpse into what a cohesive framework could resemble and where the current fragmented approach has failed to deliver.

National Sports Policy, 2001

The year 1984 was significant for Indian sport, with a resolution on the National Sports Policy, 1984 (henceforth 1984 Sports Policy), India's first ever central sports policy, being laid in both houses of Parliament (Department of Sports n.d.). Formulated with the objective of raising the standard of sport in India, it stipulated inter alia a five-yearly review system to check the country's sporting progress. However, despite its aspirational text, it soon transpired that its implementation left much to be desired. Consequently, the objectives laid down in the 1984 Sports Policy were not substantially realized, and it was revised several times to set out in more concrete terms the roles of the agencies involved in promoting sport in India. This series of changes led to the current National Sports Policy, whose salient features are as follows:

> (i) broad basing of sports; (ii) development of sporting infrastructure; (iii) supporting National Sports Federations (NSFs) and other sports bodies; (iv) strengthening scientific and coaching support; (v) offering special incentives to promote sports; (vi) enhancing the participation of women, scheduled tribes and rural youth; (vii) involving the corporate sector in sports promotion; and (viii) promoting sports mindedness among the public at large. (Press Information Bureau 2015)

Through the National Sports Policy, the government, the IOA, and the NSFs aimed to achieve excellence in sports at the national and international levels. Notably, it stipulated the inclusion of sports in the Concurrent List as an objective of the National Sports Policy, a goal intended to be a stepping stone for

THE UNEVEN DEVELOPMENT OF SPORT POLICY IN INDIA   221

the introduction of appropriate legislation for guiding all matters involving both the centre and the states.

With the view to effectively implement the previous sports policies and meet the demands of the new century, the Draft Comprehensive Sports Policy, 2007 (henceforth 2007 Draft Policy) was introduced in July 2007 (Press Information Bureau 2007). Its primary objectives were achieving sports for all, excellence in sports, and ensuring the presence of adequate contingent constitutional, legal, and institutional measures to implement its objectives. Most importantly, this draft, on consultation with the Ministry of Law and Justice, specifically suggested that sport be shifted from the State List to the Concurrent List. This suggestion was made with the view to ensure cooperation among the IOA, NSFs, the government, and the Sports Authority of India.

The National Sports Development Code of India, 2011

The NSDCI was framed by the Government of India to promote good governance in sports development. It was primarily drawn up to oversee the working of the NSFs and to ensure cooperation between the government and these independent sporting bodies. The NSDCI compiles all earlier guidelines issued by the government for the NSFs as well as the IOA to adopt good governance practices (Press Information Bureau 2011).It further undertakes other initiatives such as declaring the NSFs as public authorities under the Right to Information Act, 2005 (henceforth RTI Act), due to them availing government grants, holding of fair and transparent elections in the NSFs, and issuing guidelines to prevent vices, age fraud, and sexual harassment in sport.

Primarily dealing with the recognition and responsibility of the NSFs, the NSDCI lays down the role and responsibility of the Ministry of Youth Affairs and Sports (MYAS) and the Sports Authority of India (SAI), and the procedure for the formulation and implementation of Long-Term Development Plans (LTDP) which are to be carried out by the NSFs. As per the NSDCI, its primary objectives are:

(i) defining areas of responsibility of the various agencies involved in the promotion and development of sports; (ii) identifying NSFs that are eligible for coverage under the NSDCI and detailing the procedure required to be followed by the NSFs to avail sponsorship and assistance from the

222   STATE, SPORTS, AND DEVELOPMENT

Government; and (iii) laying down the minimum requirements for NSFs to be eligible for government recognition and grant. (Department of Sports 2011)

In an attempt to bridge the gap between central intent and actual implementation of a robust sports policy, the NSDCI lays emphasis on coaching, talent identification, and conduct of sporting events. It also contains directives and guidelines for the governance of sports bodies, particularly NSFs. However, the explicit power under the NSDCI is the granting of recognition to or derecognizing sports federations operating at a *national* level. Thus, the NSDCI cannot qualify as a comprehensive national policy for two main reasons: First, this power alone does not provide adequate checks and balances, as there is a dearth of accountability for the actions of the NSFs, which has become a bone of contention in the judiciary, discussed in a following section. Second, this leaves the state governments, the State Sports Federations (SSFs), and other state bodies outside the purview of the NSDCI.[ii] Hence, each state in India has been able to treat sport in a different manner leading to vast disparities in development as has been discussed earlier.

Proposed Legislation

The Draft National Sports Development Bill, 2013
In pursuit of an effective sports governance policy, the Draft National Sports Development Bill, 2011, was proposed to incorporate principles of transparency and good governance[iii] to rectify the lack of checks and balances present in the NSDCI. It recommended establishing an independent sports tribunal for inter alia anti-doping matters and espoused the duty to promote Paralympic and Special Olympic Sports. Due to proposals on IOA elections, the Bill was opposed by the IOC and IOA, citing that the central government had no jurisdiction to legislate on the matter, and that the autonomy of sporting organizations would come under threat (Gopalakrishna 2011). Subsequently, the MYAS constituted a working group to prepare a revised draft of this Bill, which was presented in 2013 (Press Information Bureau 2013) as the Draft National Sports Development Bill, 2013 (henceforth 2013 Bill) (Department of Sports 2013).

The 2013 Bill provided for setting up an ethics committee for each sport, an appellate sports tribunal, and a sports election commission to conduct free and fair elections to the National Olympic Committee (NOC), the NSFs, and a then-proposed athletes commission. Further, it imposed duties on the NOC in line with the Olympic Charter, such as the responsibility for bidding for international multi-sport events, having an in-house mechanism in place to address grievances, conducting national games regularly, constituting an athletes commission, and functioning as a public authority under the RTI Act. It also provided that the National Anti-Doping Agency (NADA) would be the apex body to tackle doping in Indian sport and permitted the central government to lay down rules to govern age fraud and sexual harassment. However, the 2013 Bill could not find required consensus in the cabinet of ministers and was finally abandoned (Mishra 2015).

National Sports Ethics Commission Bill, 2016
The underwhelming implementation of the NSDCI, failure of the 2013 Bill, and a series of blows to the integrity of cricket (Kamath 2016) all culminated in the introduction of National Sports Ethics Commission Bill, 2016 (henceforth Ethics Bill). While being built heavily on the 2013 Bill, it also sought to define 'sports fraud', in which sexual harassment, match fixing, doping, and age and gender fraud are included. Further, it created criminal offences, the penalties for which ranged from fines and bans to incarceration. Like the 2013 Bill, it proposed that every sports federation have a code of ethics, which could be enforced through a National Sports Ethics Commission constituted by the central government. However, no headway has been made thus far, and the Ethics Bill remains pending in Parliament.

Although the NSDCI and the proposed legislations highlight the efforts towards an effective and uniform governance structure, these efforts have not been realized. It could be argued that a uniform policy would prove redundant if inadequate and that the issues that plague Indian sport are not *solely* a result of sport being a state subject. However, sports status as a state subject has enabled an avenue for states and the SSFs to function with little accountability.

The Current System:
Teeth That Refuse to Bite

Disparity among State Sports Policies

As the centre does not have the power to directly regulate the sporting space, state governments have the freedom to develop their individual sports

224 STATE, SPORTS, AND DEVELOPMENT

policies. With this power comes a considerable amount of discretion. As discussed earlier, owing to the disparities in state budgets, political will, and resources, there is a vast difference in the commitments of each state to implement the national objectives. We have already highlighted the differences in the sports policies of Karnataka, Haryana, Kerala, and Meghalaya to illustrate this. Hence, a wide disconnect between the aspirations of the unenforceable national framework and those of the present state sports policies has emerged, manifesting as differing standards imposed on stakeholders in sport across the country.

Further, a key takeaway from the earlier comparison of the state policies is not only that the states lack uniformity in their approach, but also that most of them do not specify any accountability mechanism for stakeholders in the state. This gives rise to two problems: one, that certain states are not moving forward in terms of development of sports governance; and two, states lack the power to make SSFs accountable, a power which the centre does not possess. In the status quo, this leaves sport in the lurch, and often, glaring loopholes in its governance. In contrast, shifting sport to Concurrent List would allow the centre to set out the overarching sports policy across all states in India, which each state would be obligated to comply with, ensuring that some states do not lag behind in developing sport. Further, while we do note that several issues arising from lack of accountability of the SSFs can be remedied by affording greater bargaining power to sportspersons and private players vis-à-vis unions and sports clubs, shifting sports to the Concurrent List can also impose some accountability on the SSFs.

Inescapable Consequence of Judicial Intervention

Often, Indian courts have had to step in due to the inadequate safeguards present under current legislation. With little or no legislative control over sports bodies, a major question that has plagued the courts has been whether sports bodies discharge public functions.[iv] Under the Constitution, any challenge to the actions of a body based on a fundamental-rights violation or under writ jurisdiction of a high court can only hold water if that body falls under the ambit of 'State' under Article 12 of the Constitution.[v] And the test has developed largely owing to various constitutional challenges to actions of Indian sports bodies.

In cases such as *Zee Telefilms Ltd.* v. *Union of India*, the Supreme Court of India (SC) has held that the Board of Control for Cricket in India (BCCI)

THE UNEVEN DEVELOPMENT OF SPORT POLICY IN INDIA 225

does not constitute 'State' under Article 12. It reasoned that sports bodies like the BCCI are not a creation of a statute. While they may perform certain functions that have an element of public duty, the mere discharge of such functions is not sufficient to call it 'State'. It is pertinent to note that a primary point noted here was that the BCCI received no financial assistance from the government and generated its own funding. The court in *Zee Telefilms* v. *Union of India* stressed upon the lack of pervasive state control over the BCCI. Similarly, in a case where certain BCCI byelaws that permitted BCCI officials to own IPL franchises were challenged, the court refused to intervene, reasoning that the BCCI was a private body.[vi] However, this reasoning may not hold true for other sports bodies, especially those that depend on government expenditure for their functioning. For example, in *Narinder Batra* v. *Union of India*, the court held that the Indian Hockey Federation was amenable to judicial review.[vii] In another instance, both the IOA and the Organising Committee of the Commonwealth Games, 2010, were held to be public authorities under the RTI Act, considering that they were substantially financed by the central government of India.[viii]

In *Ajay Jadeja* v. *Union of India*[ix] and *Rahul Mehra* v. *Union of India*,[x] the courts shifted from what was laid down in *Zee Telefilms*. Instead, they held that a petition against the BCCI *is* amenable to writ jurisdiction. Soon after came the case that perhaps changed the course of Indian sports jurisprudence: *Board of Control for Cricket in India* v. *Cricket Assn. of Bihar*.[xi] This case arose due to the BCCI's failure to take any action against match-fixing allegations that were made during the 2013 Indian Premier League. In its analysis, the court noted that the functions of the BCCI could not be considered merely private, and that it controls the game of cricket 'to the exclusion of others'.[xii] Further, in its order of January 2015, it mandated the establishment of a committee to look into reforms that Indian cricket required.[xiii] The committee set up was headed by Justice (Retd) R.M. Lodha and presented what is now popularly known as the Lodha Committee Reforms (henceforth Lodha Reforms), which the SC ordered to be followed (Rajagopal 2016). The Lodha Reforms are important not only for their recommendations for Indian cricket but for the Indian sports governance landscape. They extended their ambit to not merely the BCCI but to state bodies as well, which the centre could have previously only done by regulating the BCCI. Whether such a move by the judiciary amounts to judicial overreach is a cause for concern (Bhattacharjee 2015). Further, this instance also demonstrates how the NSDCI and other central rules can only be effective if the centre has a certain degree of power over the NSFs and SSFs (*The Sports Law and Policy Centre*

226 STATE, SPORTS, AND DEVELOPMENT

2017). It also appears as a warning for further judicial interference, if sports governance is not cleaned up by the legislature.

Another area where courts have had to step in is with respect to the implementation of the NSDCI. Despite the NSDCI being a product of the centre, courts have consistently looked to implement the ideas of governance envisaged in it. For instance, in *Indian Olympic Association* v. *Union of India*,[xiv] the Delhi High Court held that the IOA and the NSFs cannot claim complete autonomy in functioning and must adopt democratic principles and good governance practices as elaborated in the NSDCI. Interestingly, the court observed that the legal basis of the NSDCI was under Entry 97 of the *Union List* read with Article 248 of the Constitution, under the centre's residuary powers. It reasoned that the IOA and the NSFs are sui generis entities recognized by the central government, insofar as the matter is international, inter-state or Olympic participation.[xv] Holding that the NSDCI would apply to the petitioner, the court also noted in dismay the state of Indian sports administration.

Further in a 2019 case,[xvi] the SC set aside the constitution of the Archery Association of India (AAI) and ordered a re-election. It also directed the new body that would be elected to amend the constitution of the AAI to make it conform to the NSDCI. These cases demonstrate that judicial intervention merely to order conformity with the NSDCI takes much of the judiciary's valuable time. Instead, an NSDCI with teeth is a much more viable option. Further, as the SSFs do not fall under the ambit of the NSDCI, such judicial intervention does not extend to the SSFs, forming yet another reason to consider a transfer of sport to the Concurrent List.

Benefits of Adding Sport to the Concurrent List

From the discussion thus far, we note two major issues arising from the lack of central power: one, only some states are pulling their respective weights in creating an ecosystem conducive to the development of sports; and two, this grey area on the legislative front, and particularly with regard to accountability, has led to inescapable judicial intervention with regard to NSFs, with no checks and balances on the SSFs. With this background, we argue that it is vital for the development and growth of sports in India that it be transferred from the State List to the Concurrent list for that would pave the way for a uniform comprehensive policy for sports in India.

THE UNEVEN DEVELOPMENT OF SPORT POLICY IN INDIA 227

Before delving into the potential benefits of such a transfer, it is vital to clarify certain things. One, modern sport has outgrown the exclusive mandate of state legislatures, as it involves various aspects which overflow into the domain of the centre. For example, all sports federations and the IOA require the permission of the centre to send Indian players or teams abroad or host foreign players or teams, as pointed out by the Delhi High Court.[xvii] Moreover, this role the centre played was a crucial factor in a case where the ICC Dispute Resolution Committee acknowledged the Indian tradition of requiring the centre's permission before hosting any international cricket in India (ICC Dispute Resolution Committee 2018: 44–9).[xviii] Furthermore, the centre holds a number of other responsibilities for sport in India that fall within the centre's Residuary Powers under Item 97 of the Union List, including organizing coaching camps for national teams, appointing coaches, financially assisting the NSFs in organizing international tournaments in India, and forming the basis of the power of the NSDCI.[xix] Hence, if we proceed with the assumption that Item 33 in the State List covers all aspects of sport, then activities involving inter-state and international sport would fall in a vacuum, and would consequently by subsumed in centre's Residuary Powers.[xx]

Two, there is no clear rationale in the drafting history of the Constitution for sport being in the State List. Sport did not exist as a subject in any of the draft lists till February 1948 when 'sports, entertainment and amusements' were first proposed to be added (Shiva Rao 2004: 321). This suggestion was made to prevent 'sports, entertainment and amusements' from being included in Centre's Residuary Powers (Shiva Rao 2004: 321). However, there was no discussion on *why* an entry such as sports should be in the exclusive domain of the states in the first place. In the Constituent Assembly debates of 2 September 1949, Entry 44 of the State List was debated to be transferred to the Concurrent List,[xxi] though the motion was rejected.[xxii] However, this does not reflect on the position of *sports* because the discussion on the proposal hinged on the opinion that 'theatre, cinema and dramatic performances' should be in the Concurrent List, without sport being discussed. Hence, we posit that transferring sports to the Concurrent List can carry potential benefits in the overall governance of not just sports, but of other things like education, international relations, and trade.

228   STATE, SPORTS, AND DEVELOPMENT

Sports and Education

Sport and physical education are seen as vital components of holistic education.[xxiii] Further, utilizing the education system is seen as the easiest way of creating a broad-based network to nurture future talent in sport. However, sport being a State Subject, the Centre necessarily needs to use indirect ways to promote sport at the grassroots, or school-level. Khelo India, a recent initiative by the MYAS, ostensibly aimed at '[reviving] the sports culture in India at the grass-root level by building a strong framework' (*Khelo India* n.d.). However, an analysis of the past two editions of the Khelo India Games reveals that instead of being a mechanism to nurture young talent, the Games have been 'nothing more than a national-level invitational meet for under-17 and under-21 athletes who have already been making a mark for the last couple of years' (Kulkarni 2019). Khelo India's inability to reach the grassroots has been attributed to states' failure to invest in grassroots sport (Kulkarni 2019). Other initiatives by the centre to integrate sports and physical education with education and for talent identification and training reach just 0.0067 per cent of Indians aged between eight and twenty-five years (Varghese 2018).

This is largely due to the fact that state governments still retain the primary responsibility of investing in sporting infrastructure at the grassroots and such investments vary widely across states. To illustrate, in 2005, the centre transferred a set of schemes for development of sports infrastructure to the states' control (Planning Commission n.d.). These schemes required the states to submit proposals to the centre for infrastructure development to enable the release of required funds. On assessment, the implementation of the schemes was found to be highly uneven as several states never submitted their proposals (Planning Commission n.d.). In this context, the benefits of transferring sports to the Concurrent List are manifold. With both education and sport in the Concurrent List, the centre would be able to better exploit the linkages between the two. As a result, laws framed by the centre, even those on sports in school curricula and sports infrastructure, would then have to be mandatorily implemented by the states.

Sports and International Relations

India's Constitutional framework gives the centre legislative competence over 'foreign affairs' (see Entry 10, List I, 7th Schedule). This competence

THE UNEVEN DEVELOPMENT OF SPORT POLICY IN INDIA   229

is contained in Entries 11 to 21 which provide for specific subjects within the domain of 'foreign affairs'. For example. Entry 11 reads 'Diplomatic, Consular and trade representation' (Basu 2012: 11742) and Entry 10 'confers complete and exclusive authority upon the Union Parliament to deal with all matters which bring the Union into relation with any foreign country' (Basu 2012: 11743). In the sporting context, the centre's permission is essential for hosting any foreign teams or sportspersons in India and sending Indian teams or sportspersons abroad,[xxiv] which is often dependent on the nations' relations.

Fairly often, countries have used sports as a direct tool for diplomacy (Devoss 2002),[xxv] the 'Ping Pong Diplomacy' between USA and China in the 1970s being perhaps the most radical example. Sporting success is viewed as an indicator of progress, often translating into political clout.[xxvi] Thus, transferring sport to the Concurrent List is likely to have the benefit of strengthening India's position in sports diplomacy due to its improved performance in international sporting events. The Indian government already uses India's dominance in cricket as a diplomatic tool. India contributes 80 per cent of cricketing revenues, and a bilateral series with India is highly sought after among cricketing nations for the revenues it brings (Ananth 2014; ICC Dispute Resolution Committee 2018: 35). Recently, the Indian government disallowed the BCCI from holding a bilateral series with Pakistan, bringing heavy financial losses to the Pakistan Cricket Board (ICC Dispute Resolution Committee 2018: 44–9; Press Trust of India 2018).

We do not claim that strong showing in international sports is a panacea to all diplomatic problems of a country, only that it is one of many possible diplomatic tools. And this diplomatic tool is simply not available to India at the moment outside of cricket. For instance, India is not a star performer at the Olympic Games, having won three, six, and two medals in the last three Olympic Games (*India Today* 2016). Therefore, India could not pressurize the IOC to drop Dow Chemicals, a company with links to Union Carbide and the Bhopal Gas Tragedy, as a sponsor for the 2012 London Olympics in spite of correspondences by the IOA, the Union government, and threats to boycott the Games (IANS 2012; Press Trust of India 2012).[xxvii]

Efficient Utilization of Funding

Two major sources of funding for sports in India are both under the control of the central government. First, the Union Budget financial year 2018–19

230   STATE, SPORTS, AND DEVELOPMENT

allocated INR 2,196 crores to the MYAS, which it distributed among Khelo India, SAI, NSFs, and certain other sports-related schemes. A successful venture in this regard has perhaps been the Target Olympic Podium Scheme (TOPS), which identifies and funds professional athletes who seem promising entrants to the upcoming Olympic Games. However, TOPS limits itself to the crème de la crème of athletes in India, without having a direct effect on the grassroots level. Second, funds for sport in India from private bodies amounting to INR 155.57 crores are held in trust in the National Sports Development Fund (NSDF). The NSDF was established[xxviii] in 1998 under the Scheme for the Administration of the National Sports Development Fund.[xxix] From the time of inception of the NSDF to December 2018, individuals and public- and private-sector corporations have collectively contributed INR 155.57 crores, while the Government of India has contributed INR 84.62 crores (Press Information Bureau 2018). However, this sizeable funding has not translated into structural improvement in Indian sport to a desirable extent. The Standing Committee on Human Resource Development (SCHRD) has attributed this to the lack of coordination between the NSFs and the SAI/the ministry, as well as NSFs and SSFs (SCHRD 2014), making a greater case for a shift of sport to the Concurrent List.

Towards a Shift

In 1988, the Constitution (Sixty-First Amendment) Bill was introduced in Parliament proposing the transfer of sports from the State List to the Concurrent List, whose primary objective was to ensure effective implementation of the 1984 Sports Policy. However, no consensus could be obtained for over twenty years since its introduction, and it was withdrawn in 2009 (Press Information Bureau 2009). In 2016, although the then-sports minister indicated that the NSFs were amenable for such a transfer (*Indian Express* 2016), there has been no progress.

However, certain efforts to shift subjects from the State to the Union List outside the realm of sport have proved fruitful, such as in education, wildlife, and administration of justice.[xxx] Presently, the predicament of sports in terms of uneven growth and problems of policy implementation has parallels with circumstances which caused education to be shifted from the State List to the Concurrent List. This occurred after over decade of deliberation and argument,[xxxi] through the forty-second Constitutional Amendment in 1976.

The reason behind the eventual transfer of education is two-fold. First, visible inequality among different states in the standards of education. It was noted that backward states had 'shown neither the will nor the ability to raise the standards of education' and should education remain in the exclusive domain of the states, backward states were likely to recede further.[xxxii] Second, there was much to be desired on the level of policy implementation. National policies, including recommendations and resolutions of conferences of education ministers and the Central Advisory Board of Education, remained unimplemented at the state level, revealing the need for more authority at the centre (National Council of Educational Research and Training 1966: 18.29). Another important aspect of the story of education is that the role of the states in promoting, managing and legislating upon education did not diminish even after the forty-second Amendment (Department of Education n.d.: 3.13). Instead, the centre was given the overarching role of monitoring progress, maintaining standards, and ensuring optimal balance (Department of Education n.d.: 3.13).

The debate on sport also has parallels with the more contemporary debate on transferring water from the State List to the Concurrent List, as states had ignored the National Water Policy, to create their own diverging policies creating a 'multiplicity of principles and rules . . . and the lack of an overall framework' (Committee on Allocation of Natural Resources 2011: 130). Indian sport faces a similar conundrum today, and shifting sport to the Concurrent List can serve as the first step towards a unified as well as *enforceable* set of rules.

***

A comprehensive, cohesive national policy is a key requirement to ensure coordination across all levels of sports administration, from the grassroots to international participation. While various attempts have been made to frame such national sports policy, we have discussed how they have been ineffectual. A key reason for this is that sport is a State List subject, which prevents unenforceable central guidelines from percolating to the SSFs and other units of sports administration at the district and panchayat levels, highlighting the need to shift 'sport' from the State to the Concurrent List.

To produce Olympic medallists, host quality international mega-sporting events, and organize clean and professional sporting leagues, it is vital to establish, fund, and regulate sporting bodies in a coherent, unified manner

232   STATE, SPORTS, AND DEVELOPMENT

while bearing in mind the importance of cultural and geographic diversity. Moreover, with the face of Indian sport rapidly shifting, it is imperative to plan a governance system that can keep up with, sustain, and embrace Indian sport. We believe that a coordinated effort by the centre and the states can offer us, at minimum, the capability to achieve this goal.

Notes

i. See also https://youthgames.kheloindia.gov.in/; accessed on 1 November 2020.

ii. Although, this issue can be remedied in the current legal structure by having states legislate on the issue of accountability of SSFs. Rajasthan has enacted the Rajasthan Sports (Registration, Recognition and Regulation of Associations) Act, 2005, which contains provisions on, inter alia, compulsory registration of sports associations, framing of their constitutions, membership and voting.

iii. https://www.prsindia.org/uploads/media/draft/Revised%20Draft%20of%20 Sports%20Development%20Bill%202011.pdf; accessed on 31 October 2020.

iv. See *Zee Telefilms Ltd.* v. *Union of India,* (2005) 4 SCC 649 and *Board of Control for Cricket in India* v. *Cricket Assn. of Bihar,* (2015) 3 SCC 251.

v. Article 12 reads as: '"[T]he State" includes the Government and Parliament of India and the Government and the Legislature of each of the States and all local or other authorities within the territory of India or under the control of the Government of India.'

vi. *A.C. Muthiah* v. *Board of Control for Cricket in India,* (2011) 6 SCC 617.

vii. *Narinder Batra* v. *Union of India,* ILR (2009) 4 Del 280.

viii. *Indian Olympic Assn.* v. *Veeresh Malik,* ILR (2010) 4 Del 1, 64.

ix. *Ajay Jadeja* v. *Union of India,* (2002) 95 DLT 14.

x. *Rahul Mehra* v. *Union of India,* 2004 SCC OnLine Del 837: (2004) 114 DLT 323.

xi. *Board of Control for Cricket in India* v. *Cricket Assn. of Bihar,* (2015) 3 SCC 251.

xii. *Board of Control for Cricket in India* v. *Cricket Assn. of Bihar,* (2015) 3 SCC 251.

xiii. *Board of Control for Cricket in India* v. *Cricket Assn. of Bihar,* (2015) 3 SCC 251.

xiv. *Indian Olympic Association* v. *Union of India,* (2014) SCC Online Delhi 2967.

xv. *Indian Olympic Association* v. *Union of India,* (2014) SCC Online Delhi 2967, 86.

xvi. *Maharashtra Archery Association* v. *Rahul Mehra,* Arising out of SLP(C) Diary No. 29577/2017, (SC 2019).

xvii. *Indian Olympic Association* v. *Union of India,* (2014) SCC Online Delhi 2967, 46.

xviii. See also Gollapudi (2018).

xix. *Indian Olympic Association* v. *Union of India,* (2014) SCC Online Delhi 2967, 48–9.

THE UNEVEN DEVELOPMENT OF SPORT POLICY IN INDIA   233

xx.   *Indian Olympic Association v. Union of India,* (2014) SCC Online Delhi 2967, 49; Narinder Batra v. Union of India, ILR (2009) 4 Del 280.

xxi.   http://164.100.47.194/loksabha/writereaddata/cadebatefiles/C02091949.pdf

xxii.   http://164.100.47.194/loksabha/writereaddata/cadebatefiles/C02091949.pdf

xxiii.   http://portal.unesco.org/en/ev.php-URL_ID=13150&URL_DO=DO_TOPIC&URL_SECTION=201.html; accessed on 31 October 2020; https://documents-dds-ny.un.org/doc/UNDOC/GEN/N03/453/21/PDF/N0345321.pdf?OpenElement; accessed on 31 October 2020.

xxiv.   *Indian Olympic Association v. Union of India,* (2014) SCC Online Delhi 2967, 46.

xxv.   See also Jha (2017).

xxvi.   For example, in the 1980s, the West Indies, an entity made up of several Caribbean Islands and existing solely for the purpose of cricket, refused to play cricket with an apartheid-era South Africa bringing major consequences for South Africa at the world stage, even though none of the Caribbean nations constituting the West Indies carried great traction in international affairs (Stoddart 2012). See generally, Riley (2010).

xxvii.   Brian Stoddart (2012) remarks, 'The IOC persisted with the sponsorship, but it is interesting to speculate what might have happened had India had greater leverage.'

xxviii.   Gazette Notification S.O. 973 (E), Ministry of Human Resource Development (Department Of Youth Affairs And Sports), 12 November 1998. https://yas.nic.in/sites/default/files/Annexure-X.pdf

xxix.   Charitable Endowments Act, 1890 (Central Act VI of 1890).

xxx.   See the Constitution (Forty-Second Amendment) Act, 1976, 18 December.

xxxi.   See Report of the Education Commission, 1964–6 and P.K. Tripathi, *Submissions Made before the Swaran Singh Committee,* (1976) 2 SCC (Jour) 29.

xxxii.   P.K. Tripathi, *Submissions Made before the Swaran Singh Committee,* (1976) 2 SCC (Jour) 29.

References

Ananth, Venkat. 2014. 'How BCCI Became the 800-Pound Gorilla of Cricket'. *Livemint.* 9 December. Available at https://www.livemint.com/Consumer/pVdCJRSBBid7eVxuCwfqcK/How-India-became-the-800-pound-gorilla-of-cricket.html; accessed on 31 October 2020.

Basu, Durga Das. 2012. *Commentary on the Constitution of India,* Vol. 10, 8th edition. New Delhi: Lexis Nexis.

Bhattacharjee, Saurabh. 2015. 'Private and Yet Public: The Schizophrenia of Modern Sports and Judicial Review'. *NUJS L. Rev.* 8: 153.

Committee on Allocation of Natural Resources. 2011. *Report Of The Committee On Allocation Of Natural Resources (CANR) On Water.* 31 May. Available at http://

234　STATE, SPORTS, AND DEVELOPMENT

www.cuts-ccier.org/pdf/Report_of_the_Committee_on_Allocation_of_Natural_ Resources.pdf; accessed on 31 October 2020.

Department of Education. n.d. 'National Policy Education, 1986'. *Ministry of Human Resource Development*. Available at https://www.mhrd.gov.in/sites/upload_files/ mhrd/files/upload_document/npe.pdf; accessed on 30 October 2020.

Department of Sports. n.d. 'National Policies'. *Ministry of Youth Affairs and Sports (MYAS)*. Available at https://yas.nic.in/sports/national-sports-policy-2001; accessed on 31 October 2020.

———. 2011. 'National Sports Development Code of India, 2011'. *MYAS*. Available at https://yas.nic.in/sites/default/files/File918.compressed.pdf; accessed on 31 October 2020.

———. 2013. 'Draft National Sports Development Bill, 2013'. *MYAS*. Available at https://yas.nic.in/sites/default/files/File921.pdf; accessed on 31 October 2020.

Devoss, David. 2002. 'Ping-Pong Diplomacy'. *Smithsonian Magazine*. Available at https://www.smithsonianmag.com/history/ping-pong-diplomacy-60307544/; accessed on 31 October 2020.

Gollapudi, Nagraj. 2018. 'PCB's Case against BCCI Dismissed by ICC Dispute Panel'. *ESPN Cricinfo*. 20 November. Available at http://www.espncricinfo.com/ci/content/story/1166182.html; accessed on 30 October 2020.

Gopalakrishna, Roshan. 2011. 'A Review Of The Draft National Sports (Development) Bill, 2011'. *The Sports Law and Policy Centre*. Available at https://sportslaw.in/home/ 2011/04/05/a-review-of-the-draft-national-sports-development-bill-2011/; accessed on 31 October 2020.

Government of Haryana. 2015. *Haryana Sports and Physical Fitness Policy*. Available at http://haryanasports.gov.in/pdf/sportspolicyeng.pdf; accessed on 31 October 2020.

Government of Karnataka. 2018. *Karnataka State Sports Policy 2018*. Available at https://www.karnataka.gov.in/dyes/Documents/karnataka_sports_policy_2018_ en.pdf; accessed on 31 October 2020.

Government of Kerala. 2015. *Kerala Sports Policy 2015*. Available at https://kerala. gov.in/documents/10180/46696/KERALA%20SPORTS%20%28DRAFT%29%20 POLICY%202015; accessed on 30 October 2020.

Government of Meghalaya. 2017. *Meghalaya Draft Sports Policy*. Available at http://meghalaya.gov.in/megcms/sites/default/files/documents/Meghalaya%20 Draft%20Sports%20Policy%2027.2.17.pdf; accessed on 31 October 2020.

ICC Dispute Resolution Committee. 2018. *In the Matter of Proceedings before a Dispute Panel of the ICC Dispute Resolution Committee between Pakistan Cricket Board and Board of Control for Cricket in India*, 20 November. Available at https:// icc-static-files.s3.amazonaws.com/ICC/document/2018/11/20/08956740-c9fb- 44f1-89cf-b6d0d97ff0a8/ICC-Disputes-Resolution-Committee-Award-PCB-v- BCCI-20-Nov-2018.pdf; accessed on 30 October 2020.

India Today. 2016. 'India at the Olympics (1900-2016): List of Medallists'. 24 August 24. Available at https://www.indiatoday.in/education-today/gk-current-affairs/ story/india-at-the-olympics-336984-2016-08-24; accessed on 31 October 2020.

Indian Express, The. 2016. 'Resolution Passed to Transfer Sports to Concurrent List: Sports Minister Vijay Goel'. 27 October.

Indo-Asian News Service (IANS). 2012. 'India Asks International Olympic Committee to Drop Dow Chemicals as Olympic Sponsor'. *India Today*. 27 February. Available at https://www.indiatoday.in/india/north/story/india-asks-ioc-to-drop-dow-chemicals-as-olympic-sponsor-94436-2012-02-27; accessed on 31 October 2020.

———. 2018. 'Haryana Sportspersons Won 25 Percent of Medals for Country in Asiad'. *Business Standard*. 6 September. Available at https://www.business-standard.com/article/news-ians/haryana-sportspersons-won-25-per-cent-of-medals-for-country-in-asiad-118090601171_1.html; accessed on 31 October 2020.

International Olympic Committee (IOC) (ed.). 2008. 'Basic Universal Principles of Good Governance of the Olympic and Sports Movement'. in Seminar on Autonomy of Olympic and Sport Movement, Lausanne, Switzerland, 11–12 February.

Jha, Martand 2017. 'India and Pakistan's Cricket Diplomacy'. *The Diplomat*. 15 March. Available at https://thediplomat.com/2017/03/india-and-pakistans-cricket-diplomacy/; accessed on 31 October 2020.

Kamath, Amit. 2018. 'The Stories behind India's Historic 69 Medals at the 2018 Asian Games at Indonesia in Graphics'. *Firstpost*. 5 September. Available at https://www.firstpost.com/sports/the-stories-behind-indias-69-medals-at-the-2018-asian-games-in-graphics-5112651.html; accessed on 31 October 2020.

Kamath, Nandan. 2016. 'Fighting Sports Corruption in India: A Review of the National Sports Ethics Commission Bill 2016'. *Law in Sport*. 1 July.

Khelo India. n.d. 'About Khelo India'. Available at https://kheloindia.gov.in/about; accessed on 31 October 2020.

Kulkarni, Abhijeet. 2019. 'Khelo India Initiative Is Meant to Discover Raw Diamonds So Why Is It Celebrating Established Stars?'. *Scroll*. 23 January. Available at https://scroll.in/field/910474/khelo-india-initiative-is-meant-to-discover-raw-diamonds-so-why-is-it-celebrating-established-stars; accessed on 31 October 2020.

Mishra, Abhinandan. 2015. 'National Sports Development Bill Abandoned by NDA'. *Sunday Guardian*. 4 July. Available at https://www.sunday-guardian.com/news/national-sports-development-bill-abandoned-by-nda; accessed on 31 October 2020.

National Council of Educational Research and Training. 1966. *Report of the Education Commission, 1964–66*. Ministry of Education.

Planning Commission. n.d. *Report of Working Group on Sports and Physical Education for the 11th Five Year Plan, 2007–12*. New Delhi: Government of India.

Press Information Bureau. 2007. 'Comprehensive National Sports Policy 2007 (Draft): Highlights'. *MYAS*. 26 July. Available at http://pib.nic.in/newsite/erelcontent.aspx?relid=29424

———. 2009. 'Withdrawal of the Constitution (Sixty First Amendment) Bill, 1988 Proposing Transfer of the Subject "Sports" from the State List to the Concurrent List of the Constitution of India'. *MYAS*. 2 July.

———. 2011. 'Sports Ministry Compiles National Sports Development Code of India, 2011'. *MYAS*. 1 February. Available at http://pib.nic.in/newsite/PrintRelease.aspx?relid=69503.

236 STATE, SPORTS, AND DEVELOPMENT

———. 2013. 'Draft National Sports Development Bill, 2013'. *MYAS*. 10 July. Available at http://pib.nic.in/newsite/PrintRelease.aspx?relid=97118; accessed on 31 October 2020.

———. 2015. 'Sports/Youth Policy'. *MYAS*. 10 March. Available at http://pib.nic.in/newsite/PrintRelease.aspx?relid=116699; accessed on 31 October 2020.

———. 2018. 'Sports Funding in the Country'. *MYAS*. 20 December.

Press Trust of India. 2012. 'IOC Not to Drop Dow Chemicals as London Games Sponsor'. *Times of India*. 7 March. Available at https://timesofindia.indiatimes.com/news/ioc-not-to-drop-dow-chemicals-as-london-games-sponsor/articleshow/12176933.cms; accessed on 30 October 2019.

———. 2018. 'Near-Bankrupt Pakistan Had the Need for Bilateral Ties, India Didn't: ICC's Reason to Dismiss Appeal'. *Scroll*. 30 November. Available at https://scroll.in/field/902869/near-bankrupt-pakistan-had-the-need-for-bilateral-ties-india-didnt-iccs-reason-to-dismiss-appeal; accessed on 31 October 2020.

Rajagopal, Krishna Das. 2016. 'Accept Lodha Report: Fall in Line, Supreme Court Tells BCCI'. *The Hindu*. 4 February.

Rao, Shriniwas K. 2020. 'Age Fraud: Different Yardsticks for Different Players'. *Times of India*. 9 January. Available at https://timesofindia.indiatimes.com/sports/cricket/news/age-fraud-different-yardsticks-for-different-players/articleshow/73165653.cms; accessed on 31 October 2020.

Riley, Stevan. 2010. *Fire in Babylon*. Cowboy Films/Passion Pictures.

Sharma, Akarsh. 2020. 'Risk of Exposure: Systemic Age Fraud Threatens the Future of Indian Football'. *The Caravan*. 1 April. Available at https://caravanmagazine.in/sports/systematic-age-fraud-threatens-future-indian-football; accessed on 31 October 2020.

Sharma, Nitin. 2018. 'CWG 2018: With 22 Medals, Haryana Basks in Commonwealth Games Glory'. *Indian Express*. 16 April. Available at https://indianexpress.com/article/sports/commonwealth-games/with-22-medals-haryana-basks-in-cwg-glory-5138929/; accessed on 31 October 2020.

Shiva Rao, B. 2004. *The Framing of India's Constitution*, Vol. 4. New Delhi: N.M. Tripathi Private Limited.

Singh, Navneet. 2018. 'Haryana Crowned Champions of Khelo India School Games with 38 Gold Medals'. *Hindustan Times*. 8 February. Available at https://www.hindustantimes.com/other-sports/haryana-crowned-champions-of-khelo-india-school-games-with-38-gold-medals/story-PNmMSpei1Ev1xzcZF8DrSI.html; accessed on 31 October 2020.

Standing Committee on Human Resource Development (SCHRD). 2014. *Report 262: The Functioning of National Sports Federations*. 20 February. Rajya Sabha.

Stoddart, Brian. 2012. 'Changing Perspectives on Global Sport, International Relations and World Politics'. *Global Policy*. 16 July. Available at https://www.globalpolicyjournal.com/blog/16/07/2012/changing-perspectives-global-sport-international-relations-and-world-politics-0; accessed on 30 October 2019.

The Sports Law and Policy Centre. 2017. 'Ten Reforms Indian Sports Administration Need'. Bengaluru: The Sports Law and Policy Centre and GoSports Foundation.

Varghese, Peter. 2018. 'An Indian Economic Strategy to 2035: Navigating from Potential to Delivery: A Report to the Australian Government'. *Department of Foreign Affairs and Trade, Australia*, p 257. https://dfat.gov.au/geo/india/ies/chapter-11.html.

16

Mega Sport Events, Development, and Tourism

Case Study of the Commonwealth Games 2010[*]

EQUATIONS[i]

Sport has little to do with the playground these days. Sport events, particularly mega sport events, are being used by nations in interesting and often contestable ways: as political statements; for image building and branding; as a nation-building exercise; as a means to urban renewal, creating top-class cities by investing heavily in city infrastructure and state-of-the-art sporting facilities, economic growth, and employment; to promote tourism; and as a money-spinning exercise for individuals involved as well as the organizers.

India's tryst with international sport events started in 1951, with Delhi hosting the Asian Games. Subsequent to this were the Asian Games hosted in 1982, the Afro-Asian Games in 2003, and the World Military Games in 2007. The Commonwealth Youth Games were held in 2008, but the nature and scale of sporting events changed when India was awarded the bid to host the Commonwealth Games (CWG) in Delhi in 2010. Soon after it won this bid, the government signalled their intent to bid for the 2020 Olympics, indicating India falling victim to the growing 'mega-events addiction' (Black 2007).

Post the CWG 2010, there has been a growing trend within the country of hosting international sport events, with thirty-four events organized until 2017. Earlier, it was mainly the Asian and South Asian Games as well as cricket and hockey tournaments that India hosted. However, post the CWG 2010, the range has expanded to also include motor sports, golf, football, basketball, badminton, and wrestling, among others (Anushka Academy 2018). Many of these events are used as an impetus to prioritize and fast-track urban

---

[*] This chapter draws key findings from EQUATIONS' report titled *Humanity-Equality-Destiny? Implicating Tourism in the Commonwealth Games 2010.* The full text of the report may be accessed at http://www.equitabletourism.org.

Equations, *Mega Sport Events, Development, and Tourism* In: *Sports Studies in India.* Edited by: Meena Gopal and Padma Prakash, Oxford University Press. © Oxford University Press 2021.
DOI: 10.1093/oso/9780190130640.003.0017

238   STATE, SPORTS AND DEVELOPMENT

regeneration and upgradation/renovation of stadiums, significantly costing the exchequer.

While there is a strong connection between mega sport events and urban regeneration (Essex and Chalkley n.d.), the hosting of some of the earlier events had broader political agendas. The Asian Games of 1951 were hosted with the political intent of building solidarity in the Group of 77 (G77).[ii] The 1982 Asian Games came at a juncture when India was interested in liberalizing, projecting itself as a leader within and outside the country, and signalling the end of Nehruvian socialism. The agenda of the CWG 2010 must be understood in the context of India positioning itself as a key player in the BRICS (Brazil, Russia, India, China, South Africa) group, distancing itself from the G77 so as to be seen closer to the Group of 20 (G20),[iii] and the aspiration for a permanent seat in the UN Security Council. There was a strong strain of wanting to shed its developing country image and announcing its arrival as a global super power to be reckoned with economically and, therefore, politically. However, what was the cost it was willing to pay for this transformation?

Literature on the links between mega sport events, tourism, and development from across nations, based on empirical evidence, indicates that the benefits claimed by an event are exaggerated, even detrimental to the nation and its people in many ways (Higham 1999). The pressure to deliver infrastructure and sporting facilities does not address issues of social displacement, land acquisition, environmental degradation, violation of worker's rights, disruption of residents' lifestyles, and area issues, and overrides traditional participatory planning processes. Of equal concern is that these large projects are susceptible to cost overruns. Oftentimes, money spent by tourists does not remain within the local economy and the 'crowding out' effect results in interested domestic and international tourists staying away from the destination to avoid the congestion associated with the mega sport event.

In rare instances, countries such as Canada, Trinidad and Tobago, and New Zealand have withdrawn from the bidding process in the recent past. This is mainly on the account of high economic costs and, at times, in the light of the criticism on various fronts raised by inhabitants. Nevertheless, the mythical benefits often outweigh the reality costs.

This chapter focuses on the developments associated with CWG 2010 in Delhi. It attempts to understand India's hopes by staging the CWG and looks at India's bid, the exponentially growing budgets, and the assumptions about tourism's potential linked to the mega sport event. The case study explores the economic, environmental, and social impacts, some being labelled as unintended consequences and others simply as collateral damage. It concludes by highlighting that the trend of mega sport events, city beautification, and evictions is not a story of the CWG alone but has continued even during the FIFA U17 World Cup that took place in Kolkata as well as at other venues across the country in October 2017.

India's Bid for the CWG

India bid for the CWG in 1990 and 1994 and failed both times. Therefore, winning the bid for 2010 was a matter of prestige, and the Games were hosted without even a discussion in the cabinet, let alone any form of public consultation on its implication. Thus, approval was granted by the cabinet ex-post-facto, thereby sacrificing basic democratic processes. At the very least, as per the Government of India (Transaction of Business) Rules, 1961 (Cabinet Secretariat 2016), a proposal for the staging of the CWG should have been made and put before the cabinet for deliberations before any decision was taken. However, Rule 12 on the Departure from Rules, which states that 'The Prime Minister may, in any case or classes of cases permit or condone a departure from these rules, to the extent he deems necessary', was invoked, as the result of which a process that was initiated by the NDA (National Democratic Alliance) government was continued by the UPA (United Progressive Alliance) government, fait accompli.

Use of Public Funds

The concept of 'legacy of the games' is often used to justify the mammoth investments and expenditure required to host a mega sport event, arguing that better roads, better infrastructure, and world-class facilities will go beyond the Games.

The Comptroller and Auditor General of India (CAG), in its Audit Report of the XIX Commonwealth Games, 2010, indicated in a note submitted by the Ministry of Youth Affairs and Sports to the cabinet that Indian Olympic Association's (IOA) assessment of the total cost estimate was INR 297 crore in May 2003. However, it is interesting that IOA, in its bid document submitted to the Commonwealth Games Federation (CGF) in May 2003, projected expenditure at INR 1,199.92 crore, a document that was not submitted to the government. From April 2007 to September 2010, there were seven upward

240   STATE, SPORTS AND DEVELOPMENT

revisions at short intervals from INR 3,566 crore to INR 11,687.25 crore, which reached INR 18,532 crore by October 2010, indicating a fifteen-fold increase from the original estimate (CAG 2011).

The Government of India and Delhi government had to sign an over-riding undertaking to say that they would meet the costs of the Games to be conducted in accordance with the requirements of the CGF and under-write any operating or capital budget shortfall. In short, it was the taxpayers' money being unconditionally pledged in order for the Games to take place.

According to CAG Audit report of 2011, the Organising Committee (OC) consistently presented the staging the Games as revenue neutral. This argument was used to justify the independence and financial autonomy of the OC. However, the projections were seriously flawed, as they were not supported by robust and appropriately validated evidence. In July 2008, the projection stood at INR 1,780 crore. In reality, the total committed revenues amounted to just INR 682.06 crore, and the net revenue actually realized by the OC (after deducting revenue generation costs) was INR 173.96 crore (CAG 2011).

The CWG 2010 was an expensive affair and saw obscenely escalating costs. Delhi's state budget also found novel ways of increasing taxes and removing subsidies that would go toward recovering the costs of the infrastructure and other expenditure commitments for the Commonwealth Games, an unin-vited burden on its citizens.

Legacy for Whom?

With respect to the legacy of the Games, the CAG Report (2009) is partic-ularly indicting on the lack of legacy planning for the sports infrastructure. It noted that the OC had not developed a comprehensive legacy plan for the overall legacy and long-term impact of the Games. There was a risk that the sporting infrastructure created through substantial investments may not be fully exploited after the Games.

A significant part of the expenses were on sporting facilities. However, who would these sporting facilities benefit? World-class facilities are beyond the need of the majority. Besides it can be expected that high membership/ entry fees required for the upkeep of facilities would make it an unviable option for low income groups. Thus, while a privileged few might use these facilities beyond the Games, the cost for its upkeep would be the responsi-bility of the state.

MEGA SPORT EVENTS, DEVELOPMENT, AND TOURISM   241

Degeneration of sport facilities after a mega sport event is not uncommon. Stadium Australia, the centrepiece of the sports park constructed for the Sydney 2000 Olympics, has not found a sustainable use, as four years later, the stadium incurred operating losses of AUD\$ 11.1 million (INR 55.5 crore). The infrastructure developed for the Asian Games held in Delhi in 1982 has seen shoddy maintenance. Stadiums of the University of Delhi, which were renovated and used during the CWG, remained out of bounds to varsity students even four years after the Games. Not a single sporting event has been hosted in these stadiums, unlike earlier when the public had access to the sporting arenas (*Down to Earth* 2015).

Game of Tourism Numbers

Bolstering the tourism industry formed a large part of the government's agenda in hosting the CWG. Post the Mumbai attacks and the global economic slump, the recovery phase in tourism had only just begun (*Thaindian News* 2009).

Predictions of tourist arrivals had been of utmost importance to the government as it was required to estimate the accommodation needs generated by the Games. The Ministry of Tourism (MoT) (2009) commissioned a study on tourist arrivals and room requirement for the CWG, which was prepared by the Indian Institute of Tourism and Travel Management in 2009. The MoT study projected the number of tourists to be 100,000, which translated to a requirement of 40,000 rooms. After considering the already available 11,000 hotel rooms in Delhi and National Capital Region, an additional requirement of about 30,000 rooms for tourists and visitors was projected. This in turn spiralled the allotment of land for 39 hotels in 2007. In April 2010, in response to a Parliament Question,[iv] the minister of state for urban development confirmed that out of thirty-nine hotels, where land was allotted by Delhi Development Authority, only four had completed construction; there was substantial progress in twelve, some progress in ten, and no progress at all in thirteen.

A cause for alarm was non-hoteliers buying land. It became increasingly clear that the 'opportunity' that the CWG provided had been used by real estate developers and builders to enter the hotel industry, catering to higher-end clientele. On the other hand, under the Incredible India Bed and Breakfast (B&B) scheme, there were many middle- and lower-middle class people who took loans to meet several guidelines but did not receive the approval of the classification committee to get listed as a B&B[v] on various grounds related to facilities and possibly shabby approach roads.

Post the Games, the MoT, in a press release on 19 October 2010, stated that 75,606 foreign tourists arrived from 1 October to 14 October 2010 to Delhi and that there was no shortage of rooms for visitors during the CWG (MoT 2010). This was the extent of their assessment. Because of their obsession with foreign tourists, what they failed to highlight was that in 2009 and 2010, domestic tourists to Delhi saw a sharp increase by 314 per cent and 53 per cent, respectively (see Figure 16.1), and have been steadily increasing. On the other hand, the pattern of foreign tourist arrivals has been erratic, with 2009 and 2010 actually registering a negative growth rate of −16 per cent and −3.3 per cent, respectively (see Figure 16.1). It was the hospitality industry that was most vociferous in its disappointment and the hoteliers acknowledged that their assumptions and predictions about the CWG were misguided. While the writing on the wall was pretty clear, many chose to ignore it because of the hype about the arrival of 100,000 tourists. Also, the hope of showcasing the arrival of Delhi as a world-class city to the tourists of the world does not seem to have resulted in the desirable impact, as two years after the Games, the growth of foreign tourist arrival to the city had stagnated.

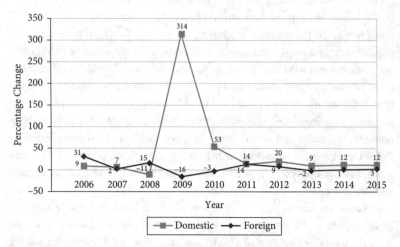

Figure 16.1 Percentage Change in Tourist Arrivals to Delhi

Source: The graph has been created by author based on the data from the India Tourism Statistics that is published every year by the Ministry of Tourism, Government of India. See http://tourism.gov.in/market-research-and-statistics; accessed on 14 September 2020.

MEGA SPORT EVENTS, DEVELOPMENT, AND TOURISM 243

This trend is not surprising, as even earlier, occasions like the Asian Games held in Delhi in 1982 brought only 200 foreign tourists. India saw only a 0.69 per cent growth in 1982. It subsequently grew to 1.30 and then dropped to –8.52 in 1983 and 1984, respectively, which does not indicate that the Asian Games could have done much about improving the tourist potential in the country. In fact, the high point of that decade came only in 1989, with a growth rate of 9.14 per cent, which was first surpassed only as recently as 2005, with a 13.33 per cent growth.

Economic Impact

Employment generation was hailed as an important boon of the Games, in addition to the economic and infrastructural benefits claimed. The trump card that was played by the OC was that the CWG would create 2.5 million jobs, an impact of approximately INR 20,940 crore for India over a period from 2008 to 2012 (*The Sports Campus* 2009). According to Uppal (2009), the effects of employment and economic activity were likely to be transitory, taking into account previously held games.

Historically, with the exception of the Games in Los Angeles (LA) in 1984, no similar event has made money, and the success of LA has not been replicated till date. The debt of US$ 1.5 billion (INR 6,750 crore) over the Summer Olympics held in 1976 in Montreal was cleared three decades later. The Asian Games saw little success on the revenue front, as expenditure on the Games was approximately INR 700 crore to INR 1000 crore, and revenue through ticket sales, donations, and franchising revenue cost yielded hardly INR 6 crore (Uppal 2009).

The 'economic benefits' of hosting a mega sport event are being found to be increasingly doubtful, from the limited post-game research that takes place. Even as the cost of hosting the Olympics touched a dizzying $40 billion in Beijing in 2008, more than the entire Gross Domestic Product (GDP) of Sri Lanka, the literature on the economic effects of such games has grown. Most scholars see only negative economic benefits to hosting these events (Subramanian and Raghav 2009).

During a verbal discussion with the Appellate Authority in an appeal process for a Right to Information (RTI) application filed by an EQUATIONS representative, seeking information on pre- and post-economic impact analysis studies related to the Games, it was found that the OC did not know if an economic impact study was done post Games. Whether the Games delivered

244 STATE, SPORTS AND DEVELOPMENT

on its economic promises was nobody's particular concern, in spite of the
spending of INR 18,532 crore from public funds.

Ducking the Environmental Impact Assessment Process

An attempt to bypass democratic process and public consultation was the
request by the Delhi government to exempt all constructions related to the
CWG from having to procure the Environmental Impact Assessment (EIA)
certificate, and by extension, the entire EIA process, on the grounds that it
would cause delays in meeting infrastructure deadlines. If exemptions were
not possible, the Ministry of Environment and Forest (MoEF) was requested
to 'rationalise guidelines' as a special case.

The MoEF confirmed that the CWG projects were prioritized but claimed
that no concessions were made with respect to exemptions from procedure.[vi]
However, a Public Interest Litigation (PIL)[vii] gives a detailed documenta-
tion (EQUATIONS 2010) of the process by which the environmental clearance letter for the CWG Village issued by the MoEF was modified to allow
permanent constructions instead of the original temporary structures on
the riverbed without the approval of the Expert Appraisal Committee,
thus disregarding the procedure laid down in the Environment Impact
Assessment Notification, 2006. Despite alternative sites being available,
and in the face of vociferous public opposition on ecological and environmental grounds, the MoEF's actions disregarded both public and ecological
concerns.

Tourism in a World-Class City

There is a significant link between the idea of tourism development and
beautification of cities. Akhil Katyal and Shalini Sharma (2010) commented
that 'the Delhi Government's ideal viewer of the city is the figure of the tourist
who should have an uninterrupted passage through the city's streets and
sidewalks, malls and monuments. A city amenable to perfect holidays but
not to democratic dissent'. However, making Delhi world class and 'tourism
ready' resulted in the heartless eviction of lakhs of people. According to the
Centre on Housing Rights and Evictions, 300,000 people were evicted till
2007 in Delhi in developments linked to the CWG.

MEGA SPORT EVENTS, DEVELOPMENT, AND TOURISM   245

A significant portion of the evictions were from the banks of the Yamuna, an area that was central to the 'developments' linked to the Games, whether it was the location of stadiums, the construction or upgradation of many link roads and flyovers, or the Games Village itself. This area was witness to some of the early tourism induced displacement that took place in 2004. Jagmohan, the (then) union minister for Culture and Tourism (2001–4) was at the forefront of evicting people. His motive for such large-scale evictions was the development of the Yamuna River Front (Gopalakrishnan 2004). Within a span of two months (March–April 2004), backed by court orders, an estimated 40,000 homes housing 150,000 people in the Yamuna Pushta settlements were demolished in an unprecedented and inhuman drive to clear the floodplains, leaving people to fend for themselves with no arrangements made for their resettlement (People's Union for Democratic Rights [PUDR] 2004). The Pushta population was mostly from Bihar, Bengal, and Uttar Pradesh, and about 70 per cent were Muslim (Menon-Sen and Bhan 2008). The tragic irony is that most of them came into the city as construction labour for the 1982 Asian Games and stayed on to make a living in the big city.

Fast forward to 2009–10, where the land was now with the Delhi government, but the eviction continued in the same vein. It took on the master planning of the entire area of Yamuna bed upto the Yamuna Pushta, which covered development of an additional 1,000 acres of land. The plan proposed development of both banks of the river, comprising 48 kilometres of land from Palla to Jaitpur in a span of five years (Banerjee 2010). This fitted well as with the road and rail network in place, the super luxury apartments built in the Games Village would have been sold at premium prices. In an ironic twist, the first stretch that was taken up for development was the site from where the 'encroachers' were evicted and supposedly given a new lease of life to live in 'dignity'. The site was to have a flower garden, nursery, parking, and playground.

Large-scale slum evictions took place, with several families being relocated to Bawana. Slums that could not be evicted in time were hidden behind bamboo screens. In the process of the evictions, many lost their livelihoods and/or were forced to spend far more on transportation to their workplace, one of the factors that resulted in them slipping below the poverty line. Additionally, they had inadequate access to basic necessities, including electricity, water, health services, and education.

246   STATE, SPORTS AND DEVELOPMENT

Purging the Poor

The social consequences of staging a mega sport event are many. While transport, hospitality, power supply, airport modernization, metro project, and street lighting were addressed with zeal to create the myth of the 'world-class city', equal concerted efforts were made to conceal and in fact get rid of Delhi's poor. The link between mega events and increased sex work has been established in earlier games (Dhawan 2010). With the onset of the Games and arrival of a large number of tourists, media reports indicated the growing possibility of increased demand for sex work. Sex workers continued to be regarded as a problem of law and order with no access to health services or security, and continued to be subjected to harassment and brutality from the police as well as from pimps and clients.

Employment generation, particularly in construction and unskilled labour, is certainly an outcome of hosting a mega sport event. (Estimates of number of hawkers range from 25,000 to 55,000, both skilled and unskilled.) Much of the employment generated, however, was short term and exploitative, and violated basic rights. The PUDR Report (2009) highlighted their plight. Irregular payment; lack of proof of employment; amount pending with the contractor, resulting in a final settlement that depended upon the contractor; no weekly offs; no wage slips; and women being routinely paid less were realities the workers faced. Workers from Games sites were rotated once in two months, making it difficult to monitor the application of labour laws and making unionization difficult.

The Delhi government set up mobile courts under the Bombay Prevention of Begging Act, 1959, and beggars were rounded up and treated as criminals in an effort at making the streets appear cleaner and poverty less visible. In March 2010, the Delhi government informed the High Court that it had written letters to ten states, including Uttar Pradesh, Bihar, and West Bengal, asking the states to take back their beggars from Delhi: a move that is 'completely unconstitutional'.[viii]

Street vendors were the target of street-cleaning operations. Delhi had an estimated 300,000 street vendors, with a sales turnover of INR 3,500 crore contributing to the city economy. Yet, only 14,000 out of 131,000 street vendors who applied received a licence from the Municipal Corporation of Delhi.

The FIFA U-17 World Cup took place in India across six venues (Mumbai, Guwahati, Kochi, New Delhi, Goa, and Kolkata) from 8 October 2017 to 28 October 2017. The media was all praise for India for being a brilliant host and having shattered the 'highest attendance' record. However, in order to 'beautify' areas for the World Cup tournament, the Kolkata Municipal Corporation and Bidhannagar Municipal Corporation (BMC) demolished eighty-eight low-income homes and evicted 5,000 street vendors and 18,000 rickshaw pullers in Kolkata and Salt Lake City, resulting in loss of incomes and livelihoods.[ix]

City beautification and economic reasons are two key causes sighted for this mass eviction. The earlier plan was to evict vendors within a 100-metre radius of the stadium, but in reality, the radius has extended to 3 kilometres. The Joint Forum Against Evictions, the National Hawkers Federation, and the Association for Protection of Democratic Rights have been fighting for the rights of the slum dwellers and the vendors.

The Story Continues

'Humanity, equality, destiny' were the three core values endorsed by the CWG movement. Inspiring as this was intended to be, the CWG 2010 impacts that are visible have not reflected any of these values. Construction workers, street vendors, beggars, the evicted and displaced, the Yamuna, the environment, the taxpayer, the street children, the homeless, trees and birds, the government exchequer, all emerge as casualties of the Commonwealth Games.

It seems that India is unwilling to learn from its past experience and the addiction of mega sport events continues. The IOA has asked the government for permission to bid for the 2032 Olympics and 2030 Asian Games as part of a drive to put the country at the heart of the international sporting community. Dismissing concerns about whether India can afford to stage such large-scale sport spectacles, the IOA president said, 'India is one of the emerging economies. Even assuming we spend $12 billion on an Olympic event, $6 billion will be given to us by the IOC. What is $6 billion over a period of eight years for a country?' (Ganguly 2017)

Can the country justify splurging on national pride amidst rampant hunger and malnutrition, ever-increasing food-prices, farmer's suicides, child labour, inadequate access to clean water, health facilities, lack of housing and sanitation, and induced displacement?

248 STATE, SPORTS AND DEVELOPMENT

Notes

i. Equitable Tourism Options (EQUATIONS) is a research, campaign and advocacy organization that studies the social, cultural, economic, and environmental impacts of tourism from the perspective of local communities. The research team for this study comprised Aditi Chanchani, Ananya Dasgupta, Divya Badami Rao and Rosemary Vishwanath. This case study has been compiled by Aditi Chanchani, who has her master's degree in tourism and leisure from Lancaster University, UK. Ms Chanchani was with EQUATIONS until April 2019 and is currently involved in ideating and implementing alternative models of community-based tourism.

ii. The G77 was established on 15 June 1964 by seventy-seven developing countries signatories of the Joint Declaration of the Seventy-Seven Countries issued at the end of the first session of the United Nations Conference on Trade and Development in Geneva. The G 77 is the largest intergovernmental organization of developing states, which provides the means for the countries of the Global South to articulate and promote their collective economic interests and enhance their joint negotiating capacity on all major international economic issues within the UN system and promote South–South cooperation for development. See http://www.g77.org/doc/; accessed on 14 September 2020.

iii. The Group of Twenty (G20) comprising Finance Ministers and Central Bank Governors was established in 1999 to bring together systemically important industrialized and developing economies to discuss key issues in the global economy. See http://www.g20.org/about_what_is_g20.aspx; accessed on 3 April 2018.

iv. Lok Sabha Q. No. 4588. The Ministry of Urban Development responded on 23 April 2010.

v. Interview with Kalyani Menon-Sen, 13 March 2010.

vi. Interview with Bharat Bhushan, director (Scientific), MoEF, on 4 March 2010.

vii. *Rajendra Singh & Others* vs. *Govt. Of Delhi and Others*, Constitution Filing No. 134027/2007.

viii. Interview with Usha Ramanathan on 6 March 2010.

ix. Interview with Pratim, National Hawkers Federation, on 6 November 2017.

References

Anushka Academy. 2018. 'List of International Sports Events Hosted by India'. *GK India Today*. 13 April. Available at https://gkindiatoday.com/list-of-international-sports-events-hosted-by-india/; accessed on 14 September 2020.

Banerjee, R. 2010. 'Revitalizing the Yamuna Riverfront'. *Times News Network*, 3 May. Available at http://epaper.timesofindia.com/Repository/ml.asp?Ref=Q0FQLzIw MTAvMDUvMDMjQXIwMDIwMA==; accessed on 3 April 2018.

MEGA SPORT EVENTS, DEVELOPMENT, AND TOURISM   249

Black, D. 2007. 'The Symbolic Politics of Sport Mega-Events: 2010 in Comparative Perspective'. *Politikon* 34 (3): 261–76.

Cabinet Secretariat, Government of India. 2016. 'Complete ToB upto Amendment Series No. 69'. Available at https://cabsec.gov.in/writereaddata/transactionofbusi nessrulescomplete/completeaobrules/english/1_Upload_30.pdf; accessed on 14 September 2020.

Comptroller and Auditor General of India (CAG). 2009. *A Report on the Preparedness for the XIX Commonwealth Games, 2010.* Available at http://www.cag.gov.in/html/commonwealth.pdf; accessed in January 2010.

———. 2011. *Audit Report on XIXth Commonwealth Games 2010.* Available at https://cag.gov.in/uploads/download_audit_report/2011/Union_Performance_Civil_XIXth_Commonwealth_Games_6_2011.pdf; accessed on 14 September 2020.

Dhawan, H. 2010. 'Global Sports Events a Trafficking Hazard?'. *Times of India*, 3 July. Retrieved from http://timesofindia.indiatimes.com/India/Global-sports-events-a-trafficking-hazard/articleshow/6122532.cms; accessed in July 2010.

Down to Earth. 2015. 'What Impact?'. 4 July. Available at https://www.downtoearth.org.in/news/what-impact-7733; accessed on 3 April 2018.

EQUATIONS. 2010. *Humanity-Equality-Destiny? Implicating Tourism in the Commonwealth Games 2010*, p. 104. Available at http://equitabletourism.org/documentation/humanity-equality-destiny; accessed on 14 September 2020.

Essex, S. and B. Chalkley. 2004. 'Mega-Events as a Strategy for Urban Regeneration'. *Dialoghi Internazionali–Città Nel Mondo* 5: 18–29.

Ganguly, S. 2017. 'India Wants to Host 2032 Olympics, 2030 Asian Games: IOA Chief'. *Reuters*, 21 June. Retrieved from https://www.reuters.com/article/us-olympics-india/india-wants-to-host-2032-olympics-2030-asian-games-ioa-chief-idUSKBN19C0QJ; accessed on 14 September 2020.

Gopalakrishnan, A. 2004. 'A Tussle on the Yamuna's Banks'. *Frontline* 21 (5): 12 March 2004.

Higham, J. 1999. 'Commentary—Sport As an Avenue of Tourism Development: An Analysis of the Positive and Negative Impacts of Sport Tourism'. *Current Issues in Tourism* 2 (1): 82–90. doi: https://doi.org/10.1080/13683509908667845.

Katyal, A. and S. Sharma. 2010, 'What Does A Beautiful Delhi Look Like?'. *Countercurrents.* 22 March. Available at http://www.countercurrents.org/katyal220310.htm; accessed on 14 September 2020.

Menon-Sen K. and G. Bhan. 2008. *Swept off the Map: Surviving Eviction and Resettlement in Delhi.* New Delhi: Yoda Press.

Ministry of Tourism (MoT). 2009. *Report of the Ministry of Tourism: Assessment of Number of Tourists Expected to Visit Delhi during Commonwealth Games 2010 and Requirement of Rooms for Them.* New Delhi.

———. 2010. 'More than 75 Thousand Foreign Tourist Arrivals at Delhi Airport During 1st to 14th October, 2010'. *Press Information Bureau*, 19 October. Available at http://pib.nic.in/newsite/pmreleases.aspx?mincode=36; accessed on 3 April 2018.

People's Union for Democratic Rights (PUDR). 2004. *'India Shining': A Report on Demolition and Resettlement of Yamuna Pushta Bastis.* Available at https://pudr.

org/sites/default/files/2019-02/yamuna_pushta_india_shining.pdf; accessed on 14 September 2020.

———. 2009. *In the Name of National Pride—Blatant Violation of Workers Rights in the Commonwealth Games Construction Sites.* Available at https://pudr.org/sites/default/files/2019-02/In%20the%20name%20of%20national%20pride-common%20wealth%20games.pdf; accessed on 14 September 2020.

Subramanian, S. and K. Raghav. 2009. 'The Economics of the Games'. *Livemint.* 26 October. Available at https://www.livemint.com/Companies/F9kz5Q3WjsTEpe5mqJkCKK/The-economics-of-the-Games.html; accessed on 14 September 2020.

Thaindian News. 2009. 'Tourism in India Has Grown Steadily Despite Economic Meltdown: Selja'. 18 August. Available at http://www.thaindian.com/newsportal/business/tourism-in-india-has-grown-steadily-despite-meltdown-selja_100234441.html; accessed in June 2010.

The Sports Campus. 2009. 'Commonwealth Games to Have $4500 Million Impact: Kalmadi'. 28 November. Available at http://www.thesportscampus. com/200911282877/news-bytes/cwg-economic-impact; accessed on 14 September 2020.

Uppal, V. 2009. 'The Impact of the Commonwealth Games 2010 on Urban Development of Delhi'. *Theoretical and Empirical Researches in Urban Management* 4 (10): 7–29.

17

Doping in Sports

Ramifications for India

K.P. Mohan

More than half a century has passed since anti-doping measures were introduced in the Olympic Games. If anything, doping has flourished through the years. The fact that more than 100 positive results have so far been reported from retesting of samples alone since the 2004 Athens Olympics shows how far ahead the dope cheats are. Doping, the practice of enhancing performance through the aid of drugs and prohibited methods, is prevalent in almost all sports across the world. Athletics (295 adverse analytical findings), cycling (280), football (167), and weightlifting (155) took the top spots among Olympic sports in the 2017 World Anti-Doping Agency (WADA) testing figures.

In India, doping in sports has flourished since the late 1990s despite the claims of 'zero tolerance' by the authorities. From the early days, when weightlifters were caught doping at the international level, to the present, Indian doping has gained in sophistication but not enough to comprehensively beat the system. At a time when doping is threatening to isolate nations from the mainstream of Olympic sports, and Russia is struggling to shed its 'state-sponsored' doping image to retain its place in the world of sports, India seems unperturbed by its status as one of the leading countries in the world of doping. For three successive years from 2013, India has had the dubious distinction of being number three in the world doping charts but the attempts to curb the menace have not met with desired results. The routine statistical data that the National Anti-Doping Agency (NADA) releases every year represents more of the 'also-rans' rather than the 'achievers' among the elite athletes.

The birth of the WADA in 1999 brought about a transformation in how countries and sports bodies dealt with doping in sports. The anti-doping rules were codified and the responsibilities of various organizations spelt out.

K.P. Mohan, *Doping in Sports* In: *Sports Studies in India*. Edited by: Meena Gopal and Padma Prakash, Oxford University Press. © Oxford University Press 2021. DOI: 10.1093/oso/9780190130640.003.0018

252   STATE, SPORTS AND DEVELOPMENT

Today, most sports organizations of the world are signatories to the WADA (also known simply as the 'Code') implemented from 2004.

The Russian doping saga, brought out in 2015–16 with telling impact through reports of the WADA's commissions and media reports, has shaken the world as never before. Russia topped the dopers' list for three consecutive years from 2013. In 2013, Russia had 184 cases of anti-doping rule violations (ADRVs), followed by Turkey (144) and India (90). The figures for 2014 were: Russia (148), Italy (123), India (96). For 2015 they were: Russia (176), Italy (129), India (117). India shared the sixth place for the violations with Russia, with 69 each, in 2016 when the latter's anti-doping agency was under suspension.

Athletics and weightlifting, among Olympic sports, saw the most frequent doping defaulters in India since 2009, when the NADA became functional, though its formation was announced in 2005. Among non-Olympic sports, powerlifting, kabaddi, and bodybuilding figured prominently. Before the NADA's birth, the first batch of Indian sportspersons caught using drugs was from the Seoul Asian Games in 1986. Weightlifters N.G. Naidu, Balwinder Singh, and Tara Singh, along with boxer Daljit Singh, were caught and suspended. In subsequent years, weightlifter Subrata Kumar Paul (1990), Satish Rai and Krishnan Madasamy (2002), and Jitender Singh and Edwin Raju (2006) were charged with anti-doping rule violations in the Commonwealth Games.

It was not until the 2004 Athens Olympics when weightlifters Pratima Kumari and Sanamacha Chanu tested positive and were ejected from the Games that the Indian Olympic Association (IOA) and the Government of India felt the need to make more vigorous efforts to arrest the trend. The IOA's attempts tended to be rhetorical rather than result-oriented.

NADA: Fuzzy Definitions, Poor Organization

The NADA's organizational structure has suffered from problems since inception. The government and IOA representatives monopolized its governing body so that it was almost a government department. Today, the IOA still retains its representation while sportspersons are conspicuous by their absence. The NADA General Body had two sportspersons in 2018, female cricketer Anjum Chopra and former kho-kho player Suresh Sharma, although doping is not a problem in either sport. The IOA and federations are represented in the governing body of the National Dope Testing Laboratory

DOPING IN SPORTS 253

(NDTL), which should have rightly comprised scientists, pharmacologists, and so on.

Not surprisingly, given its structure, the NADA became vulnerable to government and political interference. The decision of the Court of Arbitration for Sport (CAS) on wrestler Narsingh Yadav (CAS Ad hoc Division: Olympic Games Rio 2016), on the eve of his Olympic Games competition in Rio in 2016, was an indictment of a system which apparently succumbed to political pressure. The CAS upheld the WADA appeal and suspended the Indian wrestler for four years, ruling that there was nothing to substantiate the 'sabotage' theory put forward by Yadav, but, on the contrary, scientific evidence pointed towards deliberate doping. Yadav filed a court case to get the Central Bureau of Investigation inquiry into his sabotage charge speeded up (see *Indian Express* 2019).

Though the NADA has not remained totally independent, it did stick to the WADA guidelines in appointing members of the hearing panels, nominating independent persons. The problem was, it did very little in subsequent years to educate them about rules and procedures. The tardy disposal of cases became such a feature that even an amended set of procedural rules in 2015 could not help eliminate the bottlenecks.[1] The revised rules stipulated a single hearing at both disciplinary panel and appeal panel hearings unless the panel granted adjournments. In practice, cases dragged on for months, and in some cases years, instead of the stipulated three months. Adjournments, so routine in civil and criminal courts in our country, became part of the system.

The hearing panels were prone to accept prescriptions in place of therapeutic use exemption (TUE) that enables an athlete to use prohibited drugs through an exemption based on medical history and approval. Though complete exoneration based on a prescription was still difficult, many managed to gain reduced sanctions for the use of steroids like nandrolone, stanozolol, and methandienone ostensibly prescribed for the treatment of back ache, knee pain, foot and thumb injury, low blood pressure, and even typhoid.

Nothing looked impossible in the world of doping in India. Athletes were mostly unaware of TUE (or so they argued) and were not familiar with the Internet. Their 'village background' and 'poor English' often proved beneficial in their defence. Athletes generally 'forgot' to mention the names of the supplements and medicines they were taking on the doping control form. The NADA often argued that the drugs and supplements that they mentioned in time for the hearing were, in most of the cases, 'afterthoughts' to

254   STATE, SPORTS AND DEVELOPMENT

suit a particular line of defence. A panel or two would accept the NADA's contentions, while a few others would be inclined to side with the athletes.

Functioning of Hearing Panels

Some insight into the functioning of the hearing panels may be drawn from some of the decisions handed down by the Anti-Doping Disciplinary Panel (ADDP) over the years.

Jagdish Patel, a cross-country runner from Uttar Pradesh, tested positive for 19-norandrosterone (metabolite of nandrolone, a steroid produced within the body) in January 2012.[2] He argued before a hearing panel that he was prescribed Decabolin 50 mg (nandrolone) for the treatment of typhoid in November 2011 by a doctor at a health centre in Kerakat, Jaunpur, Uttar Pradesh. He produced a prescription. The panel accepted his contention and decided it was a fit case for reduced sanction of one year, especially considering his age (sixteen years) and his village background. It was explained that nandrolone was given for treatment of typhoid at these health centres, though this could not be confirmed (see *The Hindu* 2012). Patel tested positive again twenty months after his first sample collection! They caught him again for nandrolone when he had gone to the NADA for a reinstatement test. He was suspended again, this time for six years. Could it be that even after twenty months, his system was yet to wash out the steroid he had originally taken or else was it a fresh dose? We may never know. Deca injections are known to leave traces beyond ten months.

In another instance, Sombir, a Haryana wrestler produced a prescription for Methylhexaneamine (MHA) tablet. The MHA was banned in 2010 and this was a case that came up in March 2012. The ADDP rejected his contention and termed the prescription 'fake'. The so-called medicine, it noted, was not government-approved and was unavailable in the market. The panel imposed a two-year ban on the wrestler (see *The Hindu* 2014).

At that time there were no medicines with MHA as an ingredient. The only company that used it as a component in a nasal decongestant, in inhaler form, had discontinued its production in the 1980s. Yet, here we were with a claim that a doctor at a community health centre had prescribed such a medicine, along with the injection mephentermine for low blood pressure, cough, and cold.

The athlete went into appeal. Shockingly, the appeal panel accepted his contention that the MHA tablet had caused his positive test for the substance.

DOPING IN SPORTS   255

It noted that the prescription was given by the medical superintendent of a government dispensary at Baraut in Baghpat, Uttar Pradesh. The appeal panel said that the wrestler used the medicine, methylhexaneamine, as a nasal decongestant. The appeal panel's decision meant that the Haryana wrestler could gain a little over two months. The period gained was irrelevant in this case; what was glaring and of consequence was the acceptance of a prescription that contained a medicine that the world had not seen for decades.

In a country where getting a medical prescription is as easy as buying a packet of cigarettes, panels, especially the doctor-members on them, should have been extra vigilant in spotting the fake one from the genuine. A prescription could be a useful piece of evidence to have in an anti-doping rule violation case, depending on the circumstances that forced the athlete to use the banned drug. In India, hearing panels invariably take a lenient view if an athlete produces a prescription. A reduced sanction often becomes a possibility when the doctor member in the panel is prepared to accept that steroids were prescribed as first choice for back ache, knee pain, or enteric fever.

Punjab shot putter Ketki Sethi tested positive for 19-norandrosterone (metabolite of nandrolone) in the Central Board of Secondary Education (CBSE) National Championship in December 2012. She argued before the ADDP that she was prescribed Duraboline (nandrolone) for the treatment of low blood pressure and low back pain by a physician who had been her doctor for several years. The NADA's argument that Duraboline was not the first choice of medicine for back pain was rejected by the panel, which agreed with its contention but pointed out that in India, such steroids were routinely given by the doctors for pain management. Sethi was given a reduced suspension of one year, keeping in mind her age and her unfamiliarity with anti-doping requirements. Seven months into her return to competition in 2014, the Punjab athlete tested positive again for nandrolone. This time she copped eight years.[3]

Akshay Shinde, a junior weightlifter from Maharashtra, was not so lucky. He was prescribed Metadec (nandrolone) injection for enteric fever in a doping case that came up in July 2013. He submitted a prescription, but the panel wrote in its order: 'Since there was no proper diagnosis before prescribing such banned drug to athlete, the panel is not satisfied with the plea of the athlete. Moreover, the athlete should have applied (for) Therapeutic Use Exemption (TUE) to NADA before taking any prohibited medicines' (Anti Doping Disciplinary Panel 2013). Shinde was suspended for two years.

256 STATE, SPORTS AND DEVELOPMENT

So, here we have two different approaches, one in which the requirement of a TUE is ignored and the other in which it is asserted. This pattern has remained through the years.

The prescription versus TUE debate has continued in India. While there may be some truth in the general assumption that Indian athletes get caught for anti-doping violations because they are unfamiliar with banned drugs and have no access to sports medicine experts, it is largely exaggerated. The village background and the 'no-English-no-internet' image may fit in nicely for a feature for a foreign publication, but those who know of the extent of doping that goes on in India—coaches, former athletes, doctors, administrators, and journalists—and who still believe in 'clean sports' will easily see through this smokescreen, even if they do not openly acknowledge it.

Of the 867 positive cases listed on the NADA website till 1 April 2019, more than 650 (74.9 per cent) were for steroid offences.[4] Steroids are the most unlikely substances to get into the system inadvertently. In this list of 867, athletics led with 212 positive cases, followed by weightlifting with 194, wrestling 64, and boxing 56 among Olympic sports. Among non-Olympic disciplines, powerlifting headed the charts with 101 positive cases.

The Issue of Food Supplements

Federations invariably went soft on dope offenders till the NADA came into being and took over control of testing and 'results management' in 2009. Athletes, coaches, support staff, federation officials, and bureaucrats assert that athletes take contaminated supplements and test positive. There is even an occasional suggestion that 'banned supplements' find an easy way into the hands of our athletes and there is a need to make available 'WADA-approved supplements'. However, there are no WADA-approved supplements; only a published list of drugs prohibited by the WADA. The WADA and anti-doping authorities around the world have been warning athletes that dietary supplements pose a serious risk to them through contamination.

The keenness of the government to make available drug-free supplements to our sportspersons has resulted in the Food Safety and Standards Authority of India (FSSAI) formulating guidelines for the production and sale of supplements in India. The government apparently thinks it can bring down the number of doping cases in the country if athletes are supplied dope-free supplements. The FSSAI expects to regulate online and offline sale of supplements.

Will this solve the problem of supplements contamination? It may depend on what the athletes are looking for and whether they have been victims of contaminated supplements until now, as the government, the NADA, and many observers seem to have concluded.

The truth is that for cases where details of sanctions are available, majority of the athletes charged during 2015–16 did not fall back on the 'supplements defence'. In a batch of 86 cases that the author managed to check for 2015–16, there were only 18 (20.9 per cent) that sought to use the supplements defence and none of them offered credible, scientific evidence to pinpoint a 'contaminated' supplement as having caused the positive result, let alone get even a partial reprieve. Many who did not take the 'prescription route' mentioned the type of supplements they had consumed in their submissions. No supplements were, however, tested, no test was sought, and no panel ordered one to be tested.

The 2015 NADA Code introduced a clause for contaminated products that, if established, could help an athlete get as little as a mere 'reprimand' as a sanction.[5] One would have expected the Indian athletes, if not athletes around the world, to benefit from this clause. But that did not happen, at least in the immediate aftermath, perhaps exposing the myth that contaminated supplements were ruining careers of Indian sportspersons.

Regulating supply of supplements is a welcome move, even though it may not bring down the number of dope positive results in India. But there appears to be no move to strictly monitor the sale of prescription drugs. Steroids such as Winstrol (stanozolol), Deca-Duraboline (nandrolone), and Dianobol (methandienone) are among the drugs easily available in our country without prescription. Athletes freely talk of such drugs being sold at chemists near the National Institute of Sports (NIS), Patiala. But barring sporadic attempts to punish the culprits, the malaise remains unchecked.

Indian authorities have also shifted focus to an old favourite, performance enhancement through ayurvedic medicines. This had been tried out in India in the late 1990s with little success. The latest attempt promises to deliver, though why any government organization should attempt to provide substances for enhancement of performance at all is baffling. The All India Institute of Ayurveda (AIIA) is expected to take up the challenge to provide injury management, rehabilitation, and recovery support to sportspersons. The idea is to help enhance performance through permissible routes rather than resort to banned substances.

In this context, at a meeting of the All India Council of Sports (AICS) in New Delhi in January 2018, the director-general of the NADA made the

258 STATE, SPORTS AND DEVELOPMENT

startling claim that Ginseng, a herbal supplement which had been earlier banned, had been reinstated in the exempt list by the WADA under pressure from China and South Korea. He suggested that the AIIA should submit its research to the NADA that could then seek to have the WADA include them as 'traditional medicine'. Oddly enough, the WADA does not have a list of certified as exempt; there is just that one banned list. The WADA has a prohibited list of substances and methods that it publishes every year, but no approved substances list. To a query from the author, the WADA clarified that Ginseng had never been on its prohibited list. It also said that though plant extracts were not banned, if an extract contained a prohibited substance, athletes could get into trouble. Here is the reason to be careful in opting for ayurvedic enhancement. Kuchla, for example, is an ayurvedic medicine derived from strychnos nux-vomica or the poison nut tree, which is nothing but strychnine, a stimulant that is in the WADA's prohibited list.

Opportunity for Reform

In 2011, Indian athletics plunged into turmoil on the eve of the Asian championships in Kobe, Japan, when six of the country's top female 400-metre runners—Mandeep Kaur, Jauna Murmu, Ashwini Akkunji, Priyanka Panwar, Sini Jose, and Tiana Mary Thomas—were caught for steroid offences. A possible qualification in the 4 x 400 metres relay for the London Olympics was ruined as Indian panels went through an elaborate exercise, under intense media glare, to eventually order a reduced suspension of one year each for all the six women. The IAAF appealed to the CAS and got two-year sanctions imposed on all the athletes. Panwar has since been caught for a second offence and slapped with an eight-year ban, which she has appealed.

The 2011 incident provided the authorities with a great opportunity to clean up the system. An inquiry ordered by the government could have brought out the bitter truth of doping aided by coaches, had Justice Mukul Mudgal, the one-man inquiry committee, pursued the strips of papers reportedly recovered from the Ukrainian coach Yuriy Ogorodnik's room at the NIS, Patiala, suggesting banned drug use or recommended a fresh probe by an official investigation agency. The handwriting on the strips of papers could have been matched with the dope charts of 2002–4, which listed a variety of banned drugs purportedly prescribed for use by Indian athletes in camps, to establish whether the Ukrainian coach had long been engaged in facilitating a doping programme among Indian athletes.

DOPING IN SPORTS   259

Packed off surreptitiously following the 2011 scandal, Ogorodnik was brought back despite initial objections by the government and media criticism, for preparing the relay teams for the Rio Olympics. The waste of public funds in having a long camp in Spala, Poland, under Ogorodnik was realized only after a disastrous Olympic experience for the Indian relay teams. After the Rio debacle, a ministry official confided that they were misled. A hasty return from Spala had followed the surprise visit of a WADA testing team to the Polish training base. It was reminiscent of a similar hasty departure from Potchefstroom, South Africa, in 2006, when a batch of thirty-nine athletes cut short training and rushed back home with an international testing team literally on its tail.

A second chance at a possible clean-up of Indian athletics came about when the AFI president, Adille Sumariwalla, alleged on Republic TV in July 2017 that urine samples could be switched for a price.[6] This was confirmation of an allegation that former national hammer throw champion Sukanya Mishra made during her dope case hearings in 2011. She told panels that chaperons at the NIS, Patiala, were ready to provide substitute urine samples for a price. No one pursued Mishra's allegations, although the NADA did an in-house inquiry into Sumariwalla's charges. However, nothing materialized.

Success at the international level through apparent doping (judged from sudden improvement) has been very rare in Indian athletics. Such a phenomenon has possibly led to the impression that there has been no systematic doping in India. However, interestingly, the advent of the 'Russian coaches' (euphemistically termed so for Ukrainians, Georgians, and Belarusians) in the late 1990s somehow coincided with a spurt in doping cases in Indian athletics. Former Asian marathon champion Sunita Godara alleged that from the late 1990s, the authorities had hushed up hundreds of 'positive' cases in a systematic doping programme. She filed a petition in the Delhi High Court and fought the case for more than a decade before her plea to institute an inquiry commission was dismissed by the ADDP, to which the court had transferred the relevant files (see News18 2011).

On the plea that the New Delhi laboratory was not accredited during those days, the IOA and various national sporting federations took no action against dope offenders in more than 100 cases. This included a batch of eighteen violations at the National Games in Punjab in 2001. Athletics and weightlifting contributed five each to this list.

Ideally, the NADA should be engaged more in catching the dope cheats and conducting more athlete awareness programmes than in giving expert opinion on performance-enhancing substances or in the exercise of

260   STATE, SPORTS AND DEVELOPMENT

'how-to-bring-down-the-positive-numbers'. Since 2016, its total sample collections have come down drastically. In 2017, it missed most of the major athletics competitions or only managed to collect a token number of samples (See Table 17.1). Athletics happens to be one of the two Olympic sports (the other being weightlifting) that contribute the maximum positive results to the Indian doping numbers annually.

The AFI has argued that athletes training outside national camps are more prone to doping, since the NADA's frequent visits to camps dissuades athletes from resorting to doping. This is fallacious. The truth is, testing is not as frequent even in camps as the AFI has made it out to be, and testing teams have found athletes difficult to trace in camps. For instance, an IAAF team had to go in search of two female quarter-milers at a camp in 2015 on two different occasions. Both attempts failed. International testing teams failed to trace dozens of athletes at Patiala in 2006 when they went after them following the Potchefstroom escapade of a large batch of Indian athletes. Insiders say athletes often get tipped off about the arrival of testing teams (see Vasavda 2018).

In its lopsided test-distribution plan (TDP), the NADA placed hockey (seven violations since 2009 against 212 in athletics) on top of all sports, recording 92 tests in the sport up to July end in 2018, while athletics, one of the perennial 'doping sport', had 90, and weightlifting 63. The NADA's illogical

Table 17.1 NADA Testing Statistics

Year	Number or urine samples	Adverse Analytical Findings	Percentage of positive results
2009	2,331	67	2.9
2010	2,794	107	3.8
2011	3,206	116	3.6
2012	3,813	138	3.6
2013	4,073	93	2.2
2014	4,045	99	2.4
2015	4,734	110	2.3
2016	2,699	73	2.7
2017	2,964	71	2.3

Source: Compiled by author from data drawn from WADA (n.d.) and NADA (n.d.).

DOPING IN SPORTS 261

TDP resulted in some of the track and field medal winners in the Asian Games, held in Indonesia in August–September 2018, not being tested till July end and some others in the Asiad squad being tested just once during domestic competition, well away from the games schedule. Testing too far ahead of Asian Games would have served little purpose. A test in February, with the games scheduled August, makes little sense if that is the only test prior to the major competition. Athletes need about four to six weeks to wash out traces of steroids and other drugs from their system. Testing for drugs too close to a competition may also prove futile since athletes taper off drug consumption closer to the event, particularly as far as steroids are concerned.

The NADA's Registered Testing Pool (RTP) also came under scrutiny, since it tended to include many inactive athletes while ignoring some of the top-ranked ones in athletics. For example, right up to November 2018, it did not have a single female athlete among the top-sixteen 400-metre runners in the country, while it was no secret that the AFI, SAI, and the government had been pinning hopes of the women's 4 x 400 metres relay team securing a medal in the Tokyo Olympics. In November, Hima Das, the World U-20 Athletics champion and Asian Games silver medallist in the 400 metres, was included in the NADA RTP.

From an athlete's perspective, the NADA has not offered the athletes any concession for 'admitting guilt', an expression that keeps coming up in various orders of the ADDP. The NADA Code provides for a reduced sanction even without a hearing if an athlete promptly admits his or her offence. Many Indian athletes admit their guilt but are probably unaware that under the 'prompt admission' clause, they could forgo a hearing and get a much milder punishment. The NADA must take the initiative to rectify this anomaly.

While wrong interpretation of rules by hearing panels might have allowed quite a few dopers to escape or to get lenient punishment, limited understanding of the rules by the panels has also led to harsher sanctions being imposed on the athletes. Tamil Nadu quarter miler Binu Aquito was one such athlete who suffered after testing positive for betamethasone, a glucocorticosteroid. He was given a four-year suspension on the argument that he failed to prove that his violation was unintentional. Haryana weightlifter Harjeet Kaur tested positive for stimulant strychnine and was penalized by a four-year suspension on the same argument as that given in the Aquito case. Both cases involved 'specified' substances (those that are categorized as such because of the possibility of these drugs getting into the system inadvertently due to their presence in common medications) that required the anti-doping authority to prove 'intentional' use, as against an athlete proving

262 STATE, SPORTS AND DEVELOPMENT

'unintentional' ingestion that would attract a milder sanction than four years for a steroid offence. Luckily for both, the appeal panel spotted the mistake and reduced their suspensions to two years.

Mantu Roy, a Bengali kabaddi player, was not as fortunate as Aquito and Harjeet. He tested positive in the All-India Police meet in March 2016 for betamethasone, normally found in corticosteroid ointments. A panel found him guilty since the prescription he produced did not contain any prohibited medicine. 'In the present case the anti-doping rule violation involved a specified substance and the athlete was not able to prove that the anti-doping rule violation was not intentional', wrote the Anti-Doping Disciplinary Panel (2016). Getting four years for a corticosteroid is the worst an athlete can suffer in the anti-doping proceedings. Roy could have sat silently and expressed his ignorance and yet got just two years since the onus, as per rules, was on the NADA to prove that the athlete had intentionally attempted to enhance performance. He did not appeal.

This should not mean that athletes often fall prey to banned substances through medications for common cold, fever, and back ache, an impression that has gained ground through the years by the claims of athletes, coaches and others. Four out of twelve cases (recorded up till September 2017) of terbutaline (often found in cold and cough medications) were let off with a reprimand; three attracted six-month suspensions; two got three months; one, a year; and another, two years. One athlete was exonerated. Ephedrine and pseudoephedrine, substances found in cold and cough medications that are commonly used, have threshold levels prescribed by the WADA. Only if an athlete crosses this threshold is he/she reported for doping. Only one athlete, a discus thrower, had showed an ephedrine positive in India, back in 2010, and received a two-year sanction. There had been none for pseudoephedrine.

The NADA website should have been the ideal platform to help athletes with information related to commonly-used medicines apart from propagating the dangers of supplements use, new supplements and drugs in the market and general news about anti-doping. Unfortunately, the website (as of the beginning of 2019) offers little to the athletes and support staff and is of little use to lawyers and the media, other than displaying the Code, the NADA anti-doping rules, and some do's and don't's. The NADA, however, did step up its education programme in 2018, though it could have offered more awareness about the menace of doping among young athletes.

To its credit, the NADA, even with a limited number of staff, has managed to catch hundreds of dope cheats. The real task is to weed out the dopers from the elite bunch of athletes, especially in track and field. The level-playing field for the clean athletes remains a mirage. Athletes quite often turn in dope-induced world-class performances at home but flop in major championships abroad. The odd success should not mean they have shed the practice of doping. There is a need to target athletes in the Target Olympic Podium (TOP) scheme and those in the RTP.

Only a few of the national federations have met the WADA Code-compliance requirements till 2017, despite shortcomings in several areas, but with stricter compliance stipulations coming in, there is a rough ride ahead. Few national federations have also incorporated NADA rules into their constitution or regulations, thus providing a legal loophole. Without the federations delegating authority, the NADA does not have the right to test or impose sanctions in any sport, although its authority has never been challenged. The Board of Control for Cricket in India (BCCI) has managed to stay away from the jurisdiction of the NADA, arguing that it is not a national sports federation. Neither the International Cricket Council nor the WADA has been able to set right this ludicrous stand-off though last reports indicated a softening of the BCCI's stance in agreeing to allow the NADA to be its agency to transport a few samples to the New Delhi lab. Such a laughable proposal, and still, the NADA seemed to be willing to consider it!

Many a junior talent in India has been wasted because of doping. People express surprise over junior athletes testing positive, forgetting that for the past fifteen years, if not more, the juniors have embraced the practice whole-heartedly. Between March 2001 and March 2005, as many as sixty juniors, including twenty-three weightlifters from a single edition of the Junior National Championships in Chennai in 2003, were caught for doping. Reports of washrooms strewn with syringes and vials after a junior meet or schools meet have been routine during the past decade and more. The National School Games came under the NADA testing in 2011–12. Of eighty samples collected from competitions in boxing, wrestling, and weightlifting, eleven were positive, indicating a high incidence of doping among students. The fact that the inaugural Khelo India School Games and Khelo India Youth Games returned substantial numbers of positive dope results shows how deep-rooted the problem is. We should not eventually replace the slogan 'catch them young' with the motto 'dope them young'.

In such a context, the draft legislation submitted by the Justice Mukul Mudgal Committee offers only a knuckle rap rather than stringent measures to deter dopers and their abettors. In a country where steroids and other banned drugs are easily available, it is difficult to see the proposed legislation

264 STATE, SPORTS AND DEVELOPMENT

deterring suppliers or athletes. A sincerer effort on the part of the NADA could be the answer to the mounting problem of doping in Indian sports.

Notes

1. See https://www.nadaindia.org/upload_file/document/1493557039.pdf; accessed on 15 March 2019.
2. See https://www.nadaindia.org/upload_file/document/1545833154.pdf; accessed on 15 March 2019.
3. See the list of appeals disposed of by the Anti-Doping Appeal Panel at https://www.nadaindia.org/upload_file/document/1545827657.pdf; accessed 15 March 2019.
4. See https://www.nadaindia.org/upload_file/document/1554120316.pdf; accessed on 15 March 2019.
5. See https://www.nadaindia.org/upload_file/document/1493557039.pdf; accessed on 15 March 2019.
6. See https://www.youtube.com/watch?v=f3jnRMObeMk; accessed on 15 March 2019.

References

Anti Doping Disciplinary Panel. 2013. 'Decision of the Anti Doping Disciplinary Panel-Case No.11.ADDP.02.2013'. *National Anti Doping Agency.* Available at https://www.nadaindia.org/en/anti-doping-disciplinary-panel-candidate-list; accessed on 15 March 2019.
———. 2016. 'Decision of the Anti Doping Disciplinary Panel-Case No.17. ADDP.01.2016'. *National Anti Doping Agency.* Available at https://www.nadaindia.org/en/anti-doping-disciplinary-panel-candidate-list; accessed on 15 March 2019.
Hindu, The. 2012. 'Five Athletes Suspended in Doping Cases', 30 May. Available at https://www.thehindu.com/sport/athletics/five-athletes-suspended-in-doping-cases/article3469588.ece; accessed on 15 March 2019.
———. 2014. 'NADA Fails to Establish There Is No Methylhexaneamine Tablet', 14 March. Available at https://www.thehindu.com/sport/nada-fails-to-establish-there-is-no-methylhexaneamine-tablet/article5802057.ece; accessed on 15 March 2019.
Indian Express. 2019. 'Wrestler Claimed Dal Was Spiked, CBI Finds No Evidence', 4 March. Available at https://indianexpress.com/article/india/wrestler-claimed-dal-was-spiked-cbi-finds-no-evidence-5609402/; accessed on 15 March 2019.
National Anti Doping Agency (NADA). n.d. 'Anti Doping Disciplinary Panel'. Available at https://www.nadaindia.org/en/anti-doping-disciplinary-panel-candidate-list; accessed on 15 March 2019.

News18. 2011. 'NADA Doping List Shows Athletes Not Penalised', 18 November. Available at https://www.news18.com/news/india/nada-doping-list-shows-athletes-not-penalised-420074.html; accessed on 15 March.

Vasavda, Mihir. 2018. 'How NADA Rested As Athletes Trained'. *Indian Express*, 4 November. Available at https://indianexpress.com/article/sports/sport-others/how-nada-rested-as-athletes-trained-5433098/; accessed on 15 March 2019.

World Anti-Doping Agency (WADA). n.d. 'Anti-doping Testing Figures Report'. Available at https://www.wada-ama.org/en/resources/laboratories/anti-doping-testing-figures-report; accessed on 15 March 2019.

18

Performance-Enhancing Substances in Sports

Towards Country-Specific Harm Reduction Strategies[1]

Kaveri Prakash

Modern-day sports is all about competition. Competition is what drives neighbourhood children to play cricket, race one another down the road, or adopt chest-thumping demeanours in international arenas. Winning a race or a game is an integral philosophy of modern-day sports. It is gainsaying the truth that improving performance and bettering the rival by all means is the driving factor. The use of performance-enhancing drugs sits on this fundamental character of modern-day sports.

In consequence, a major thread in attempts to control the use of performance-enhancing substances (PES) (also referred to as performance-enhancing drugs, PED) in sports is the necessity of ensuring a level playing field. This is the oldest and single most important consideration in anti-doping policies.

The movement against doping led the International Olympic Committee to form the World Anti-Doping Agency (WADA) in 1999. The WADA was meant to harmonize anti-doping policies, rules, and regulations, and it has achieved this largely through detection-deterrence and punitive measures. The WADA's policies and programmes have come in for criticism with calls for reform based on a more nuanced and truly global perspective on doping. This chapter explores the growing discourse on alternate approaches to controlling the use of PES in sports and reflects on the fact that social and cultural behaviour patterns, plus a lack of ethics in the practice of medicine, are the issues that need to be tackled urgently in this eagerness to ensure a level playing field in sports.

---

[1] I thank the editors for inviting me to write this chapter. I am grateful to Padma Prakash for her suggestions and encouragement.

Kaveri Prakash, *Performance-Enhancing Substance in Sports* In: *Sports Studies in India*. Edited by: Meena Gopal and Padma Prakash, Oxford University Press. © Oxford University Press 2021. DOI: 10.1093/oso/9780190130640.003.0019

In 2005, the United Nations Educational, Scientific and Cultural Organization (UNESCO) adopted a convention against doping for signatures from member states (UNESCO 2005). The WADA policy and the UNESCO convention are based on several postulates. In 2008, a number of scholars put out a document strongly seeking a debate on these international policies. They argued:

Current anti-doping policy is inherently contradictory, as it fails to achieve its stated aims of detecting and eradicating drug use, protecting the integrity of sporting competition, and preserving parity on the field. We suggest that its prohibition approach may be deleterious to public health, and that it fails to take into account the complex network of values and behaviours in which drug use in contemporary sport and society is embedded. In the absence of reliable empirical evidence on the impact of doping technology on health and performance, and given the limited data about the effective-ness of the current anti-doping policy based on deterrence, rigorous clinical and policy studies are imperative. (Kayser and Smith 2008)

The document challenged the current policies on a number of grounds: The reasons advanced for anti-doping policies are false and do not warrant the costly practices they prescribe; that prohibition as a means of regulating doping behaviour is a questionable practice and yields no insight into the harm done by doping; testing for doping as it is done will never ensure clean competition; rules in place violate athletes personal freedom; war on doping and war on drugs tend to merge, creating much confusion; and well-designed harm reduction policies need to be formulated and are likely to be more effective in democratic societies. Given that a variety of enhancement technologies flourish and are accepted in society outside sports, the zero tolerance of performance enhancement in sports appears in contradiction to existing social norms and practices (Kayser and Smith 2008: 85).

Challenging the fundamental premises of anti-doping policy, that of creating a level playing field, the author contends that merely eliminating the use of PEDs will not create a level playing field in societies and cultures and across the globe that have so many other disparities. Since 2008, with the long economic downturn, this is even more obvious both across nations and within countries.

Throwing a different light on PES use in sports, Dennis Hemphill (2009) looks at the issue from a philosophical perspective. He examines the usually cited reasons for controlling PES use in sports, namely, that drugs should

268   STATE, SPORTS AND DEVELOPMENT

be banned because they introduce artificial substances in an environment where natural abilities are being tested, that the use of drugs gives an unfair advantage to some, that the use of certain drugs poses dangers to health, and the slightly more remote reason that the athlete using the drug may coerce other athletes posing a danger to all athletes. He finds none of them supportable or even consistent. However, since despite this the disapproval of drugs in sports persists, Hemphill proceeds to examine what he calls the ethical perspective and the moral angle.

Without going into his engaging review, it is pertinent that he points out:

> Drug prevention and control programmes in sport focus largely on the individual athlete as the problem and as the target of education, surveillance and control. As a result sport authorities may overlook other contributing factors. An alternative way of looking at drug use and control is to examine the role that the institution of sports has for rewarding high performance and promoting a high-tech scientific culture of performance enhancement. (Hemphill 2009: 320)

As the commercial value of sporting success increases so too do the temptations for players, coaches and mangers and sponsors to employ dubious means.

Others (see Kirkwood 2009) too point to the resistance—subliminal, unspelt—from sporting organization to anti-doping programmes because they see drug-enhanced performances as 'good for business'. Assuming that athletes take a rational decision when taking a PES, the battle for drug-free sports becomes one for changing the rationale of the athletes, which is influenced by this 'business-led' need to improve performance.

Notwithstanding several such voices, a 2013 WADA-sponsored study (Overbye, Knuddsen, and Pfister 2013) to investigate if there was a need for more diversified prevention strategies reported that, indeed, these measures were successful. The fact that the study's entire data came from Danish athletes has been largely overlooked and not without reason. For, there are hardly any studies, small or large that have explored the issue of PES use in non-European countries or USA, many of which, like India, are just making their name in the international sporting arena.

This, we believe, is where part of the problem of ineffective doping control lies: the imposition of international policies across countries without effectively generating national data and understanding that would enable a customization of policy to country needs.

PERFORMANCE-ENHANCING SUBSTANCE IN SPORTS   269

Internationally standardized anti-doping policies have long since been enforced on all countries as a means to even the playing field for all. As countries with established sporting cultures continue to adapt to technological progress and enforce strategies to minimize these behaviours, the situation is somewhat different in those regions with a different perception of sports, and where competitive sports may primarily be not a leisure activity or even a competitive enterprise but rather a means of livelihood for entire families. Competitive sports are an expensive career alternative in a socio-economic landscape where taking a person out of a steady-income job (or family profession) can severely impact their means. And yet, in recent decades, sports is becoming a sought-after choice of livelihood for several reasons. Chiefly, there are high returns on investment. Plus, the publicity, exposure, and fame so garnered may themselves be a pathway to other earning possibilities. However, these critical differences in the social location of sports in poorer countries have not been well recognized. This has had consequences in many areas, but especially in the realm of management and control of doping in sports.

Recognizing the need for a social science approach, the WADA has been commissioning several studies. Among these was a major review by a team from the Research Institute of Sport, Physical Activity and Leisure, Leeds Beckett University, UK, headed by Susan Backhouse. The review focused on: '(i) psychosocial correlates and predictors of doping in sport, (ii) knowledge, attitudes, beliefs and behaviours towards (anti-) doping, (iii) efficacy and effectiveness of anti-doping education programmes, and (iv) doping specific models and theories' (Institute for Sport, Physical Activity and Leisure 2015). The review, examining 212 peer-reviewed papers, showed that while there has been increased activity in this area, only a few studies have ventured to examine the outcomes of anti-doping education programmes and even fewer have attempted to develop specific anti-doping theory/models. However, they support in varying degrees, the understanding that

(a) sport doping exists in a complex web of socio- demographic and psychosocial correlates and predictors, (b) critical incidents, both within sport and beyond, increase doping vulnerability, (c) social context and the role of reference groups – such as the coach, family, or peers – can facilitate and/ or inhibit doping, (d) there is a perception that the likelihood of doping detection is low; often this is combined with deep doubts about the legitimacy of the current detection-deterrence system, (e) athletes' and athlete support personnels' exposure to formal anti-doping education appears insufficient

270   STATE, SPORTS AND DEVELOPMENT

and knowledge of anti-doping is moderate at best. (Institute for Sport, Physical Activity and Leisure 2015)

The study underlines the fact that human behaviour is strongly influenced not only by knowledge and attitudes but may also be prompted by the environmental stimuli that may be institutional (sporting rules and policies), social (social norms, social support), or physical (infrastructure, facilities).

The WADA's claim, that over a period, the culture of a drug-free sport will develop, does not seem to have materialized. Instead, the WADA's policies in this regard have become more rigid and more intrusive. Today elite athletes not only have to submit to urine testing (in the presence of an official) at any time that officials require, they also have to undertake to inform the WADA of their entire year-long schedules. The mere failure to keep the WADA informed of athletes' schedules may be regarded as reason for being barred, (as happened in the case of Christine Ohuruogu, a very successful British sprinter who was suspended from competition in 2006— not because of drug-use, but because she missed three unannounced out-of-competition drug tests), or at the least being pulled up (see Kayser and Broers 2012).

The Tour de France is often cited to show the genuine difficulties of imposing anti-doping measures and of some unintended consequences. Either the winner or the runners-up have tested positive or have been suspected of use consistently. Reportedly while doping practices may have changed, the culture of doping in professional cycling continues to prevail (Lentillon-Kaestner 2013). In 2007, an editorial in *Nature* (2007: 512) provocatively pointed out that the Tour de France perhaps ought to be the first competition to allow 'pharmacological performance enhancement'.

What have been the outcomes and consequences of the WADA's current anti-doping policy? For one, while its two-pronged repression and surveillance has gotten ever more rigid, the jury is still out on its success in controlling doping in sports. But more seriously, perhaps this has led to several countries enacting repressive laws that also impact on non-elite recreational sports. More countries under pressure from the WADA are likely to enact repressive anti-doping laws affecting all sports at all levels, even as the Global Commission on Drug Policy has acknowledged the failure of its 'war on drugs' campaign, which was the model for the WADA's anti-doping initiative. Many countries are today moving towards strategies other than 'war', and introducing harm reduction approaches to drug control.

PERFORMANCE-ENHANCING SUBSTANCE IN SPORTS   271

Towards a New Approach

An increasingly popular argument for a different strategy for doping control points to a successful strategy being adopted for control of drug abuse, namely, harm reduction strategy. The objective of such a strategy is to ensure that athletes come to the least harm in taking PES. As Kirkwood (2009: 181) an emphatic advocate points out, '[I]n light of the failure of prohibition to eliminate drug use in sport, and thereby protect athletes from the harms of doping, alternative measures, such as harm reduction, must be considered.' He draws attention to three factors that suggest a move towards a harm-reduction policy in place of the prohibitions:

- A drug problem poses the greatest potential harm to the user.
- Drug use has been undeterred by prohibitive policies.
- The risk to the user is enhanced by the prohibitive policies.

With little progress in changing the athletes' rationale for drug use or developing convincing moral justification arguments for refusing PES, there is need for a different approach. Many commentators have pointed to the fact that given the ever more stringent and lengthening list of prohibited substances, athletes are being driven to experimental and inadequately tested drugs, where the major criteria for use is that they do not show up in testing, making them ever more dangerous.

Why exactly is harm reduction a better approach to address doping in sports? For one, there is no such entity as an 'independent' athlete today in the international arena, nor is there an 'independent will' that the athlete possesses. The driving force of international competition embodied in the Olympic credo 'higher, faster and stronger' demolishes any notion of competing to the best of one's abilities. In other words, the structural, social, and economic context of modern sports will only push sportspersons into a high pitch of doped performance that aims at enhancing the marketability of the athlete as well as of the sporting institution. If, on the other hand, there was a way to use PES under ethical medical supervision, might not the athlete and the sport benefit?

The situation is even more dire in countries like India, which are just emerging into the international limelight in sports, offering untold possibilities. And it is especially urgent that India advocate and espouse harm reduction as an alternative approach. There are obvious and complex problems in introducing this approach. Undoubtedly, the idea of doping under supervision

272   STATE, SPORTS AND DEVELOPMENT

would seem unacceptable at first thought. Kirkwood (2009) points out that from the 1950s to the late twentieth century, Canada, Soviet Union (Russia), and East European countries allowed doctors' support to athletes in the use of PED, and were duly criticized and penalized. On the other hand, these measures were indeed safer than the athlete- or coach-led (and surreptitious, undetected) PED use that was ongoing at that time in other countries.

In recent years, a harm reduction approach has been found to be demonstrably successful in controlling drug abuse in some European countries and in Canada. Moreover, it also affords a more positive opportunity for education, which is not obtainable in a deterrence-based programme. Today, the entire WADA strategy is to turn a blind eye to the fact that PES use exists and is flourishing, notwithstanding the testing, restrictions, and bans. The first step is to acknowledge that the use of PES is a part of elite sports and, indeed, all forms of competitive sports.

Larger Dimensions in India

The use of PES is likely to see a sharp increase in countries newly making a mark in international sports. Rising Indian athletes, for instance, are likely to come across more sophisticated drugs and, indeed, ostensibly undetectable, experimental drugs without sufficient clinical data on their safety. The push from state, market, family, and institutions to constantly improve performance may well be persuasive forces manoeuvring the athlete towards dicey performance-enhancing drugs. Detection, punishment, and 'fear of god' may not be sufficient deterrents. The National Anti-Doping Agency (NADA) has yet to recognize the wider social, economic, and market ramifications impacting young athletes today. It is still struggling to internalize and cope with the stringent WADA regulations.

The journey of the emerging Indian athlete from town to national and global arenas leads to the fraying of the safe and secure social fabric. Without going into the larger aspects of this, a particular outcome is to be seen in the reconstruction that occurs in terms of the jettisoning of the 'familiar' and the tried-and-tested methods of training, food regimes, nutritional intakes, and so on. Typically, small-town athletes have to rapidly learn to cope with their own urban transformation that includes, but is not limited to, what they eat, how they play a sport, and what rules and regulations they follow. This struggle of small-town athletes to 'globalize' is well depicted in several recent

PERFORMANCE-ENHANCING SUBSTANCE IN SPORTS 273

Bollywood movies such as *Dangal* (2016), where a small-town trained wrestler struggles to adapt to the new rules of the game that are so alien to her.

On the one hand, it may be that ignorance of doping regulations leads to the inadvertent breaking of rules. But even more importantly, and not easily detected, is the fact of the wide range of products the newly minted athlete confronts and is subtly led to use by his/her sponsor, coach, and/or team physician. While the NADA website may give a list of substances to be avoided in the supplements that the athlete may take, it may be unrealistic to assume that the athlete will independently make an informed choice given that relevant information is poorly disseminated. Pertinently, a study that systematically examined and clinically assessed sevety-five nutritional supplements that could be bought over the internet in Europe (six from Switzerland and the rest from USA) found that most of them would lead to athletes testing positive for drugs (Kamber et al. 2001).

We have no similar study in India on the use of nutritional supplements although these are heavily advocated, widely sold and used, and athletes have repeatedly claimed their use as a reason for testing positive for banned substances (See K P Mohan in this volume for instances of Indian athletes' ignorance of of banned substances.). The author's own enquiry, albeit preliminary, showed that nutritional supplements to enhance performance were freely available not only in 'health shops' that are proliferating even in small cities, but even in small general stores (Prakash 2013). And these cater not only to an adolescent, upwardly mobile fitness- and beauty-conscious population, but also to a younger generation among which are competitive athletes.

It is here that the role of the medical community, not just sports medicine practitioners but paediatricians as well, must come into ugly light. First, it is in fact paediatricians and small-town physicians who would prescribe the first of performance-enhancing supplements. The range of over-the-counter supplements is phenomenal and ever increasing, all of it quite legal, starting with something as innocuous as protein-enhanced malt drinks to a variety of capsules and tablets one may take only during busy or stressful times or if feeling poorly just before a competition (or an exam). From here on, it is a slippery slope to PES, with neither the young athlete, nor the guardians quite recognizing the transition. It is here that the medical practitioner and/or the sports medicine specialist must advocate caution and point to the deleterious effects of such supplements, even if undetected or quite legal. But this does not happen.

On the other hand, sports medicine practitioners are also actively prescribing supplements often at the behest of coaches. There appears to be no regulatory body to oversee or monitor their practice. The Indian Association

274   STATE, SPORTS AND DEVELOPMENT

of Sports Medicine was set up in 1971, but there appears to be no code of ethics available on its website. Its Constitution (see Indian Association of Sports Medicine n.d.) declares:

- To guide and assist in the promotion of physical fitness among people.
- To provide scientific guidance and assistance to the sports fraternity, regarding the medical and health aspects of training in sports.
- To conduct research in the field of sports medicine, sports sciences and allied sciences.

That there are difficult ethical issues that sports medicine confronts is well documented. The athlete–physician relationship is ethically different from the norm of patient–physician. In the latter, both parties are striving towards the same goal of wellness. In the former, however, the athlete's focus is on return to play that may go against the physician's focus of ensuring the athlete's wellness. This often encompasses areas such as the use of PES that will fulfil the athlete's objectives but not necessarily be ethically correct from the perspective of the physician. There are also any number of situations where ethical considerations must come into play, as whether an injury is deemed too serious to allow active play to the detriment of the player, or when a team's advantages and disadvantages need to be weighed against those of the player. Given this apparent worrying lack of concern for ethics among sports medicine practitioners, would a harm reduction approach turn out to be even more dangerous?

On the contrary, allowing for the use of PES under medical supervision will charge sports physicians with a sharper responsibility towards the health of the athlete and enable them to resist the pressures from sponsors or coaches. A stricter surveillance also becomes possible, especially with a reduced list of really harmful and therefore banned drugs.

There is little indication that in India ethics in sports medicine has received much attention. Surely, medical ethics even among those not directly practising sports medicine but are dealing with those playing sports, must come up for discussion and debate? It is only then that issues like prescription of PES to young athletes will be questioned.

Ultimately, any strategy for controlling the use of PES in sports hinges on how well we know and can predict the behaviour of athletes to any set of regulations. This means having a better grasp of emerging sporting population. There is a huge scope for the study of sports in this wider context. This must prompt a rethinking of whether single-fit international doping policies should really give way to one that allows country-specific strategies within broad parameters which would be especially critical if a harm reduction approach were to be adopted.

References

Hemphill, Dennis. 2009. 'Performance Enhancement and Drug Control in Sport: Ethical Considerations'. *Sport in Society* 12 (3): 313–326.

Indian Association of Sports Medicine. n.d. *Constitution of IASM*. Available at http://www.iasm.co.in/constitution.html; accessed on 12 September 2020.

Institute for Sport, Physical Activity and Leisure. 2015. *Social psychology of doping in sport: a mixed-studies narrative synthesis.* Commissioned by World Anti-Doping Agency. Institute for Sport, Physical Activity and Leisure Leeds Beckett University. Available at https://www.wada-ama.org/sites/default/files/resources/files/literature_review_update_-_final_2016.pdf

Kamber, Matthias, Norbert Baume, Martial Saugy, and Laurent Rivier. 2001. 'Nutritional Supplements As a Source for Positive Doping Cases?'. *International Journal of Sport Nutrition and Exercise Metabolism* 11 (2): 258–63.

Kayser, Bengt and Barbara Broers. 2012. 'The Olympics and Harm Reduction?'. *Harm Reduction Journal* 9: 33. doi: https://doi.org/10.1186/1477-7517-9-33

Kayser, Bengt and Aaron C.T. Smith 2008. 'Globalisation of Anti-doping: The Reverse Side of the Medal—Current Anti-doping Policy Is Sufficiently Problematic to Call for Debate and Change'. *BMJ* 337 (7661): 85–7.

Kirkwood, K. 2009. 'Considering Harm Reduction as the Future of Doping Control Policy in International Sport'. *Quest.* 61 (2): 180–90.

Lentillon-Kaestner, V. 2013. 'The Development of Doping Use in High-Level Cycling: From Team-Organized Doping to Advances in the Fight against Doping'. *Scandinavian Journal of Medicine & Science in Sports* 23 (2):189–97. doi: https://doi.org/10.1111/j.1600-0838.2011.01370.x

Nature. 2007. 'Editorial'. 448: 512.

Overbye, Marie, Mette Lykke Knudsen, and Gerrud Pfister 2013. *Anti-doping Policies and Reasons (Not) to Dope. A Need for Diversified Prevention Strategies?* Final Report, WADA.

Prakash, Kaveri 2013. 'Performance-Enhancing Drugs in Sports and the Role of Doctor: Are There Guidelines?'. *Indian Journal of Medical Ethics* 10 (2). doi: https://doi.org/10.20529/IJME.2013.034.

UNESCO. 2005. International Convention against Doping, UNESCO. Available at: https://unesdoc.unesco.org/ark:/48223/pf0000142594; accessed on 8 April 2021.

19

Sport for Development and Peace

From Global to the Local

S. Ananthakrishnan

The United Nations Office on Sports for Development and Peace (UNOSDP) promotes the view that sports play a significant role in social integration and economic development irrespective of geographical, cultural, and political contexts. The United Nations (UN) General Assembly in its declaration, *Transforming Our World: The 2030 Agenda for Sustainable Development* (2015), affirms in this regard:

> Sport is also an important enabler of sustainable development. We recognize the growing contribution of sport to the realization of development and peace in its promotion of tolerance and respect and the contributions it makes to the empowerment of women and of young people, individuals and communities as well as to health, education and social inclusion.

India has been slow in linking sports and SDGs in policy documents, even though there is ample reason to do so. However, there is a realization that sport for development can produce a wide range of positive outcomes at the individual, community, national, and international levels (*sportanddev.org* n.d.). The full potential of harnessing sport for development and peace is yet to be realized in many countries, especially in the developing world.

Contribution of Sports to Achieving SDGs

In September 2015, 193 member states of the UN, including India, adopted the 2030 Agenda for Sustainable Development, which aims to raise the world's development and raise the quality of life for all people, hence the

---

S. Ananthakrishnan, *Sport for Development and Peace* In: *Sports Studies in India*. Edited by: Meena Gopal and Padma Prakash, Oxford University Press. © Oxford University Press 2021.
DOI: 10.1093/oso/9780190130640.003.0020

motto 'do not leave anyone behind'.[1] On 1 January 2016, the seventeen SDGs of the 2030 Agenda for Sustainable Development were adopted and came into force.

Sports can play a role in achieving several of the SDGs. These are: to ensure healthy lives and promote well-being; to ensure inclusive and equitable quality education where sports can teach transferable life skills and key values such as tolerance and inclusion; and to reduce inequality within and among countries where sports can be used as a tool to advocate these values (Commonwealth 2015).

Regional groupings such as Commonwealth and the Caribbean Community (CARICOM) have also stressed the importance of sports in development. Ambassador Irwin LaRocque, secretary general of CARICOM, and Giovanni Infantino, president of the Fédération Internationale de Football Association (FIFA), agree on the importance of sports to develop young people and the society as a whole.[2] This follows the historic commitment made by more than thirty governments at the Commonwealth Sports Ministers Meeting in August 2015 to ensure that national sports policies are aligned to deliver the SDGs. This international policy impetus provided by the UN to use sports as a tool for development has been followed up by individual countries through focused interventions at different levels of government. They have facilitated and adopted the implementation of sport-based approaches to development. (The Commonwealth 2015).

There is also a recognition of limitations with regard to the scale and quality of these approaches in the developing regions (Lindsey et al. 2016), as further effort is required to ensure that context-relevant knowledge is effectively administered towards the practices of sports to development.

Catalytic Potential of Sports

Combating Discrimination

Tomorrow's Foundation (TF), an NGO in India has increasingly incorporated the use of sports in various projects to enrich the learning experience for students, in addition to promoting unity and teamwork among the beneficiaries (Tomorrow's Foundation Annual Reports n.d.). The Uttaran Bastar, launched in 2010, comprises two hostels for children who

278   STATE, SPORTS AND DEVELOPMENT

have lost their homes and families to insurgency in the area in Dantewada and Bijapur, is run by TF in collaboration with district authorities. As a form of rehabilitation and mainstreaming, the children are trained to excel in sport activities to ensure their all-round development (TF n.d.). Another organisation doing similar work is the Sukma Football Academy (SFA) established in January 2017. Sukma is an under-developed and conflicted (due to the Naxalite movement) district in India. The SFA provides children modern infrastructure and training, giving them an opportunity to play football and get an education to get out of poverty and insecurity.

Countries in Latin America have been seen to produce many commendable football athletes, mostly from the deprived communities who live in the *favela* (a Brazilian shack or a shanty town; a slum) (Perlman 2011). These communities have produced some of the biggest names in football such as Pelé. Football camps in Brazil have become places for young people of all races to/ have a common ground to unite. An example is the Corinthians Football Club, founded in the favela by low-income railway workers in 1910. As a club from a poor region, despite being excluded from the elite echelons, it has become common space for all races and classes, creating employment for many.[3] This is an example of how sports have transcended structural discrimination and depravation (see Sutton 2015).

Through competitions like the Paralympic Games, which focus on the skills of these individuals, the communities' centre of attention becomes the person rather than his or her ability.[4]

Improvement of Public Policies: An Example

In many countries, the practice of sports is continuously used as a mechanism of recovery, social insertion, and transformation, and many times, is the only exit of the youths prone to crime and abandoned in the society. Brazil invested enormously in the training of young people in the run-off to the Olympics in 2016. Established in 2012, 'the Brazil Medals' Plan' (Santos Neto et al. 2017) was aimed at ensuring that the country was ranked among the top ten in the 2016 Olympic Games and top five in the Rio 2016 Paralympic Games. This plan included an overall investment of hiring technicians, sportsmen, and professional coaches to allow for participation of the youths in games outside of the country as well as the discovery of new talents. It also aimed to provide quality infrastructure for amateur teams

SPORT FOR DEVELOPMENT AND PEACE   279

during trainings and maintenance expenses to allow for the commitment of the youths, relieving them of other responsibilities to earn a living. A beneficiary of some of these programmes is the gymnast Flavia Saraiva, three-time Youth Olympic medallist. Also, this was the case of the majority that participated from the Brazilian favelas in the Rio 2016 Olympics, as they were all beneficiaries of this plan. It remains to be seen if, after the mega events, the momentum will continue.

On the same lines is India's plan of action 'Development of Talent in Olympic Sports' (Government of India 2013) that proposes massive investment in developing talent, especially among those who cannot afford to pursue sports.

Youth, Sports, and Governance

For statistical purposes the UN defines 'youth' as persons between the ages of fifteen and twenty-four. In India, youth is anyone between the ages of fifteen and twenty-nine in the National Youth Policy. This population of 1.8 billion youth according to UN statistics is most concentrated in the developing countries. These young people, therefore, are a decisive factor in the social, economic, political, and cultural development of the developing world. Youth's role as peace builders is widely recognized. However, a survey carried out by the UN-Habitat for the research report on urban youth and sport for development (UN-Habitat 2012) shows that the potential of sports as a tool for development is yet to be fully realized.

Sports as a vehicle of social inclusion have shown their capacity to help prevent crime and violence. Sports also have a transformational capacity, in that they help create a healthy lifestyle for the young people who engage in it.[5] Even if the role of the young people is visible, recognized, and lauded in sports, this is not translated into receiving their contributions in other areas of society such as in governance and influencing public policies. It is also ironic that their leadership role in sports or in matters of sports governance are hardly visible. Thus, young people are often alienated due to the lack of trust in them to lead the society.

The United Nations Office on Sport for Development and Peace (UNOSDP) was established by the former UN secretary general Kofi Annan in 2001. Its mandate is to coordinate the efforts undertaken by the UN in promoting sports in a systematic and coherent way as a means to contribute to the achievement of development and peace. In the UNOSDP Youth

280 STATE, SPORTS AND DEVELOPMENT

Leadership programme, most of the young people have only basic education levels, limited resources with which to carry out their projects, and most do not have a proper forum where they can learn practices or develop their leadership skills; they need access to theoretical and practical training to improve their projects and professional progress (UNOSDP 2017).

Women, Sports, and Development

Sports can be used as a tool to transcend gender discrimination and has become one of the enablers of the agents for equality. Women are making their mark in football, rugby, swimming, as well as in many sports considered traditionally masculine. At present, there are many female presidents of sports clubs, female referees, and even female soccer players. India has several examples of successful initiatives in using sports as a means of empowering women, one case study of which is included in this volume (see Sabah Khan's chapter in this volume).

However, there is a realization that sports and gender inequality have a much more complex relationship, and though sports serve to ritually support the aura of male competence and superiority, there still exists an inferior perspective of women and their skills. In the face of social pressures and gender stereotypes, more than half of the girls who begin to practice a new sport quit as they reach puberty, a rate six times higher than the number of boys who quit, as studies have consistently proved that these girls lose their self-esteem as they reach adolescence (see *Agência Brasil* 2016). Research from UN Women claims that at puberty, a girl's confidence drops at twice the rate of a boy's. However, Laura Trott, one of the UK's most successful female Olympic medallist, disagrees with this by arguing that even though there are various hindrances to being a sportswoman, such as the problems of playing during her menstruation, the love of the sport keeps her on the track (Harvey-Jenner 2016).[6]

The role of women in development is universally accepted. Development policies and projects have more emphasis in the past decade in gender equity and equality. However, the role of sports and development adds another dimension in the empowerment of women. Women are far more visible in various sports today than at any previous point in history, and in the words of Lakshmi Puri (2016), former UN assistant secretary general and UN Women's deputy executive director (2011), 'Women in sport defy the misperception that they are weak or incapable, and every time they clear a hurdle or kick a ball, they demonstrate not only physical strength, but also leadership and strategic thinking, they take a step towards gender equality."

Sports as a Diffuser of Conflicts?

Sports has the capability to resolve conflicts, even if temporarily, as seen in the recent alliance of the North Korea and South Korea to be represented by a single team in the 2020 Tokyo Olympics. UNESCO International Charter for Physical Education and Sports (UN Educational, Scientific and Cultural Organization [UNESCO 1978]) says,

> Through co-operation and the pursuit of mutual interests in the universal language of physical education and sport, all peoples will contribute to the preservation of lasting peace, mutual respect and friendship and will thus create a propitious climate for solving international problems. (Article 11.3, p. 7)

Also, the Olympic charter[7] that touches on the core value of sports in people's lives does not simply regard sport as recreation or games played individually. Instead, the charter placed sports 'at the service of the harmonious development of humankind, with a view to promoting a (peaceful) society concerned with the preservation of human dignity' (IOC 2020). The UN resolution titled *Sports as a Means to Promote Education, Health, Development and Peace* (UN General Assembly 2003) was adopted, advocating the active roles that sports can play in the field of cooperation. The resolution paved the way for conceptualizing cooperation through sports as well as the recognition of the effects of sports toward solving development issues and conflicts that may arise.

Though sports celebrate healthy competition between opponents and the input of their efforts, in many cases, it also can provoke conflicts among both individuals and communities. There have been innumerable occasions that show sports bringing down barriers between individuals and communities and, at the same time, engagement in sports can exacerbate social tensions and divide communities (Medcalf and Biscomb 2016). Bertoli (2017) argues that international sporting events could cause problems as they increase the feelings of nationalism and antipathy towards other countries that participate in the same events as in the FIFA World Cup. He cites examples of the Football War between El Salvador and Honduras in 1969, the Egypt–Algeria World Cup dispute in 2009, and the Serbia–Albania Drone Conflict in 2014 as cases where nationalism from sporting events have triggered military or

282 STATE, SPORTS AND DEVELOPMENT

political conflicts. The result from this analysis shows an increased aggression among countries that barely qualified for the World Cup during the year of the competition, as participation in the competition elevates state hostility by about two-fifths as much as a revolution does.

The practice of using sports in peace and development is rapidly expanding as the numerous ways it positively impacts communities is being recognized. The UNOSDP uses sports to reintegrate youths and to promote reconciliation in various countries in Africa, the Middle East, Central America, as well as in other regions.

Various UN agencies have also integrated sports as part of their activities to promote their mandate. For example, the UN-Habitat is developing an urban sports programme with the purpose of using sports as a tool to advocate for greater access to safe public spaces for young people and to promote sustainable and adequate sports infrastructure. The UNODC has launched a global youth crime prevention initiative that builds on the power of sports as a tool for peace. This initiative aims to promote sports and related activities to prevent crime. United Nations Women, in partnership with Women Win (founded in 2007) has impacted the lives of many adolescent girls and young women in over 100 countries by collaborating with variety of grassroots women's organizations, sports bodies, and government agencies. This is also to ensure that girls and young women have access to their rights, develop confidence, and become leaders. There is a lot of potential in India for such initiatives. There are already several initiatives in this direction, and even if they have been short-lived so far, they are good illustrations of the potential for sports for women.

Since 2007, the UN Development Programme (UNDP) has been applying the concept of peace fairs and sports to the peace and reconciliation process of Papua New Guinea among other developing regions. The UN High Commissioner for Refugees (UNHCR) and the International Olympic Committee (IOC) reaffirmed their long-standing cooperation and agreed to work together to engage young men and women in sports projects. This cooperation addresses sexual- and gender-based violence (SGBV). Initial projects were implemented in Panama, as well as in Venezuela, Uganda, and Kenya.

Since 1994, UN Environment Programme has partnered with premier international sports associations, federations, manufacturers, and athletes, harnessing its expertise to influence fans and reduce the ecological footprint of major sporting events. The UN Children's Fund (UNICEF), for example, has been actively empowering children and young people through sports in

SPORT FOR DEVELOPMENT AND PEACE 283

various communities across the world.[8] The UNESCO is another UN agency that has used sports as a catalyst for peace and social development.

By its very nature, sports have the power to divide by way of parochial ethnic, national, or regional identities. But it also has a greater ability to unify. President Nelson Mandela, a statesman who truly believed in the power of sports for good, rightly affirmed:

> Sports have the power to change the world . . . it has the power to inspire, it has the power to unite people in a way that little else does. It speaks to youths in a language they understand, and can create hope where there was once only despair. It is more powerful than government in breaking down barriers. (Mandela 2011: 378)

As much as sports and sporting events have the potential to promote harmony and development, nations have also boycotted these events to express political animosity. During the Cold War and apartheid times, boycott was a common 'non-political' tool used for political purposes.

Sports as a Tool for Development and Peace

The international movement around sports as a tool for development is often connected with other efforts to use sports for the purposes of social and environmental interventions, crime prevention, and risk reduction as measures used by UN agencies in achieving the SDGs.

Hartmann and Kwauk (2011) attest that sport-based development programmes are often targeted specifically towards 'at-risk' communities and populations, where sports are used as an attraction to get marginalized young people actively involved team building and engagedin activities of sports programmes. Initiatives such as the Street Child World Cup are providing opportunities for children in difficult and dangerous circumstances and giving them a sense of self-confidence and pride. Street children in Brazil, India, Tanzania, and Sierra Leone get hope through sports activities such as the aforementioned one (*The Guardian* 2012).

The UN-Habitat report, *Urban Youth and Sport for Development* (2012), indicates that tournaments and 'sports for development' programmes act as arenas for education and awareness, advocacy, cultural understanding and exchange, empowerment, community development, and poverty alleviation. Another example is the Grassroot Soccer programme, where soccer

284 STATE, SPORTS AND DEVELOPMENT

is used to educate, inspire, and mobilize at-risk young people in developing countries to overcome health challenges, live healthier and more productive lives.[9] The UNOSDP promotes sports as a powerful tool to strengthen social ties and networks, ideals of peace, fraternity, solidarity, non-violence, tolerance, and justice.

Initially, the Sport for Development and Peace (SDP) 'movement' was presumed to be an effective way of contributing to peace building and social development. However, critical scholarship has challenged the 'messianic claims' that sport is a universally beneficial way to usher in First World aid and development (Coalter 2007; 2009; 2010; Kidd 2011a). An increasingly robust SDP research agenda has been extended beyond monitoring and evaluation of project outcomes and has examined the power relations and structural inequalities that underpin both sport and international development. Indeed, a growing body of literature examines the social and political implications of tying sport to development as well as the manner in which sport too frequently perpetuates and sustains contemporary neocolonial aid relationships. In addition, a wealth of empirical literature and case studies outline the potential, pitfalls, and limits of SDP initiatives, and highlight the challenge of SDP's disengagement with broader trends within international development.

An analysis of global sporting events, however, point towards a Western approach to sports with the ideas of popular sports either resisting or furthering neocolonialism. Either way, the locality and possibility of southern regional alliances are compromised.

There is no utopian design to the structure of sports as a tool for peace and development. The sustainable impact, however, can only be arrived at by building regional cooperation and a global South–South collaboration that reflects and responds to common problems that can be highlighted using regional sporting meets and consciously furthering an engagement with young people.

Enabling the Environment

According to the UNDP (2015), development is about creating an environment in which individuals can strive to reach their full potential, lead productive and creative lives in accordance with their needs and interests, and expand the choices they have that may lead to them living the lives they value.

In the Global North, richer countries have more means to invest in sports, with significant national or corporate funding. The need for an enabling environment to facilitate growth, resource mobilization mechanisms to provide assistance to the least developed countries in particular, and the construction or reconstruction of infrastructure can build and restore confidence so that all can commit themselves to engaging in sports.

Brazil, for example, with planning through investment in structures and the popularization process, sees a high potential in the development of volleyball. According to coach Giovane Gavio, two-time champion in the Olympic Games of 1992 and 2004,

> Brazil did not become a force in volleyball by chance, there was a process of planning the modality and popularization through television broadcast which were fundamental to the growth of the sport in the country, and with the success of the teams, it created idols with profusion. . . I think that the whole system works well and meets the demands.[10]

Corporate- and private-sector promotions like Nike endorsements in basketball in USA have also helped to promote iconic figures, making for the product's market appeal in the country, while private corporations in Argentina have promoted polo, making it the greatest polo-playing nation on the planet.

Egypt is an example of a place where the involvement of state policies and investments have helped to build squash as a competitive sport. The South Korean government invests roughly three times more than any other country in archery, providing the inspiration for generations and further reasons for more funding and state interventions (see Bradshaw 2017).

China is another example of state intervention. There has been a transformation of the sports system in the country. The sports governance system has gradually reformed over the last two decades, especially in conjunction with the Beijing 2008 Olympics. Today, the governments at all levels have the extensive control of sports operations and functions; they create a national sports framework and promote, organize, and implement sports activities with foreign associations and teams. Recent reports show that China's sports industry is growing faster than that of the nation's economy. The continued investment and policy actions taken are reasons for this growth because most of the sports industry's growth is directly tied to government interventions (see Rick 2018). Many corporate organizations and private investors are also taking advantage of these policies, as companies such as Kaisa and Alibaba already have established sports industries.[11] Needless to say, the multinational companies producing sports goods do have large scale production

286   STATE, SPORTS AND DEVELOPMENT

facilities. This can also be seen in the context of economic and employment potential of sports industry.

India is at a stage when there is a tremendous potential for state and private investment in sports. Some corporates, such as Reliance, have been involved in cricket for some time now. Earlier, it was indeed the public-sector entities, Indian Railways, for instance, that promoted sports. While they continue to do so, efforts to develop and nurture talent or finance sports facilities are not that evident.

Possibilities and Pitfalls

Almost a decade ago, Levermore (2008) asked if sports were becoming the 'new engine of development'. He argued that the traditional field of development was taking longer to warm up to the idea that sports might be an engine that drives development initiatives forward. Meanwhile, Kidd (2011b) observed that while development studies scholars have largely overlooked sports for the development of peace, it has become a recognized strategy for social intervention in disadvantaged communities throughout the world.

The 2012 London Olympics is an example of a sporting mega event that prioritized the inspiration of young people (Anyangwe 2015). As a result of this event, corporate organizations, such as Barclays, Standard Chartered, and Nike, have sponsored social projects, joining many existing independent grassroots initiatives. Brazil is an example of a country where sports connects with the most marginalized people, to whom government policies may never reach.

Though this is true in many developing countries, cases of exploitation, extortion, unfair competition, insider trading, money laundering, and violence against women among others still mar the complete advancement of sports. In football, for example, a sport widely acknowledged as lucrative and boosted by television rights, global transfers of young football players is known to attract human traffickers (as massive amounts of money flows in and out of tax havens), irrational transfer payments, and inflated agent fees, and betting networks are known to help criminals to try to pass off their illicit gains as legal. Sports image also plays a role as big clubs are less likely to report money laundering for fear of losing sponsors, while certain individuals may use ownership of a smaller club to forge legal business ties and win huge construction contracts (see *The Guardian* 2009). While the appeal of football is universal, it has crept into millions of peoples' everyday lives. For example, many people in

Nigeria would be more preoccupied with the English Premier League players of the UK than players of their own local league. This is the case of attracting global attention than promoting local development.

Discussions of sexual abuse of women in sports have also generated interactive public hearings in Brazil, where a case became known and is divulged by the victim herself, for example, that of swimmer Joanna Maranhao's sexual abused by her coach of nine years.

Sporting activities are becoming increasingly important aspects of infrastructural development. In particular, participation and attendance of sports events have become an big part of the recreational lifestyle of people, from sports marketing events to small local initiatives, sports training camps, and matches of professional sports teams that are large scale (Roach 2000). Many governments and city-marketers worldwide have encouraged these engagements to boost urban regeneration and renovation, and also improved quality of life for visitors and citizens. However, post the original use of these structures, activities that are not directly linked to the sport are evident as stadiums become shopping malls and become run down and desolate due to their abandonment.

Even if mega sport events cannot represent a long-lasting solution to social and economic problems, they can prove to be a useful instrument in facilitating development (Andreff and Szymanski 2006).

Sport has been used as a core component of programming and in building inclusive social spaces long before it was finally recognized and mainstreamed as a part of the Millennium Development Goals (MDGs) and later in the Sustainable Development Goals (SDGs).

Sport, until recognized by the world as a significant missing link in developmental practices, will find it difficult to become a part of mainstream dialogue around development and humanitarian assistance. A large advocacy is therefore needed to build systematic capacities and understanding of the entire portfolio of sports and its larger impact on people living on the margins of the society. This chapter calls for a specific focus on indigenous, ancient, traditional, and non-elitist games across the world. A recognition of these would further the identities and cohesion within the social framework.

Sport is a wonderful equalizer and a very efficient tool to ensure inclusion. It can certainly place everyone on a level playing field' Wilfried Lemke Quoted in a Facebook post. https://www.facebook.com/thinkpacific/ photos/sport-is-a-wonderful-equalizer-and-a-very-efficient-tool-to-ensure-inclusion-it-/10156592558136241/; accessed 8 April 2021.

288   STATE, SPORTS AND DEVELOPMENT

Notes

1. See https://sustainabledevelopment.un.org/content/documents/2754713_July_
   PM_2._Leaving_no_one_behind_Summary_from_UN_Committee_for_
   Development_Policy.pdf; accessed on 9 November 2020.
2. See more: Meeting of the Secretary General of CARICOM and FIFA at
   CARICOM Secretariat, Georgetown.
3. See https://www.corinthians.com.br/clube/historia; accessed on 8 April 2021.
4. See https://www.un.org/development/desa/disabilities/issues/disability-and-
   sports.html; accessed on 8 April 2021.
5. See more https://www.sportanddev.org/en/learn-more/health/health-benefits-
   sport-and-physical-activity; accessed on 7 April 2021.
6. See also UN Women and IOC Project in Rio de Janeiro boosts gender equality
   in sports practice. 2016, Available in https://www.unwomen.org/en/news/
   stories/2017/11/announcement-un-women-and-the-international-olympic-
   committee-renew-partnership; accessed 9 April 2021.
7. Enacted by the International Olympic Committee (IOC) in 1925. Revisions have
   been made as needed. The latest version is in force as of 17 July 2020.
8. See www.righttoplay.com; accessed on 11 December 2020.
9. See grassrootsoccer.com; accessed on. See also www.yedi.ng/our-story/sport-
   for-development/; accessed on.
10. See more: Brazil becomes a force in volleyball (2013). Available in https://
    esportes.estadao.com.br/brasil-vira-potencia-no-volei-com-planejamento-
    imp/. See also Barone and Marinho (2016).
11. See more: Corporate investment flooding into China's sports sector. 2016,
    Available in https://www.scmp.com/business/article/2017193/investment-
    flooding-chinas-sports-sector; accessed 8 April 2021.

References

Agência Brasil. 2016. 'Esporte é ferramenta na luta por igualdade de gênero, diz
ONU Mulheres', 6 August. Available at https://agenciabrasil.ebc.com.br/rio-2016/
noticia/2016-08/esporte-e-ferramenta-na-luta-por-igualdade-de-genero-diz-
onu-mulheres; accessed on 7 April 2021.

Andreff, W. and S. Szymanski. 2006. *Handbook on the Economics of Sport*. Edward
Elgar Publishing, Chetenham, UK.

Anyangwe, Eliza. 2015. 'Sports for Development: More Than Just Fun and Games?'.
The Guardian, 10 August. Available at https://www.theguardian.com/global-
development-professionals-network/2015/aug/10/sport-for-development-
charity-ngo-effective-change; accessed on 6 April 2021.

Barone, Marcelo and Raphael Marinho. 2016. 'Potência no masculino, mas
proibido para mulheres: o boxe em Cuba'. *Globo*.com, 28 July. Available at http://

globoesporte.globo.com/olimpiadas/boxe/noticia/2016/07/potencia-no-masculino-mas-proibido-para-mulheres-o-boxe-em-cuba.html; accessed on 8 April 2021.

Bertoli, Andrew D. 2017. 'Nationalism and Conflict: Lessons from International Sports'. *International Studies Quarterly* 61 (4): 835–49.

Bracht, V. 2005. *Critical Sociology of Sport: An Introduction*, 3rd edition. Ijui: Unijui. Physical Education Collection.

Bradshaw, Luke. 2017. 'Why Do Certain Countries Excel at Certain Sports?'. *Culture Trip*, 25 October.

Coalter, F. 2007. *A Wider Social Role for Sport: Who Is Keeping the Score?* London: Routledge.

———. 2009. 'Sport-in-Development: Accountability or Development?'. In R. Levermore and A. Beacom (eds), *Sport and International Development*, pp. 55–75. New York: Palgrave Macmillan.

———. 2010. 'The Politics of Sport-for-Development: Limited Focus Programmes and Broad Gauge Problems?'. *International Review for the Sociology of Sports*, 45 (3): 295–314. https://journals.sagepub.com/doi/10.1177/1012690210366791.

Commonwealth, The. 2015. *Sport for Development and Peace and the 2030 Agenda for Sustainable Development*. London: Commonwealth Secretariat.

Government of India. 2013. 'Concept Note of Development of Talent in Olympic Sport', Ministry of Youth Affairs & Sports, Department of Sports, 18 pp.

Guardian, The. 2009. '"Football Clubs Are the Perfect Vehicles for Laundering Money"', 1 July. Available at https://www.theguardian.com/football/2009/jul/01/money-laundering-football-anti-corruption; accessed on 11 December 2020.

———. 2012. 'Street Child World Cup More Than Just a Game for the Street Kids of São Paulo', 16 April. Available at https://www.theguardian.com/global-development/poverty-matters/2012/apr/16/street-child-world-cup-sao-paolo; accessed on 11 December 2020.

Hartmann, D. and C. Kwauk. 2011. 'Sport and Development: An Overview, Critique and Reconstruction'. *Journal of Sport and Social Issues* 35 (3): 284–305.

Harvey-Jenner, Catorina. 2016. 'This Is How Female Olympic Athletes Deal with Their Periods: Because They Bleed Once a Month Too'. *Cosmopolitan*. 21 August. Available at https://www.cosmopolitan.com/uk/body/health/news/a45448/how-olympic-athletes-deal-with-periods/; accessed on 9 November 2020.

Kidd, B. 2011a. *A New Social Movement: Sport for Development and Peace.* Toronto: Routledge.

———. 2011b. 'Cautions, Questions and Opportunities in Sport for Development and Peace'. *Third World Quarterly* 32 (3): 603–9.

Levermore, R. 2008. 'Sport: A New Engine of Development?'. *Progress for Development Studies* 8 (2): 183–90.

Lindsey, I., T. Kay, R. Jeanes, and D. Banda. 2016. *Localizing Global Sport for Development.* Manchester: Manchester University Press.

Medcalf, R. and K. Biscomb. 2016. 'Opportunity through Sports'. In Kay Biscomb, Richard Medcalf, and Gerald Griggs (eds)., *Current Issues in Contemporary Sport Development*, pp. 1–8. Cambridge Scholars Publishing.

290 STATE, SPORTS AND DEVELOPMENT

Mandela, Nelson 2011. 'Nelson Mandela by Himself'. In *The Authorised Book of Quotations*. Pan Macmillan.

Niti Aayog. 2016. *Let's Play!: Target 50 Olympic Medals—Action Plan for Revitalising Sports in India*. Available at http://niti.gov.in/writereaddata/files/document_publication/Olympics%20Action%20Plan%20Booklet%20FInal.pdf; accessed on 9 November 2020.

Oloyede, R., T.Akinsanmi, and N. Fajembola. 2012. 'The Role of Sports in National Development'. *Journal of Science and Science Education* 3 (1): 1–6.

International Olympic Committee (IOC). 2020. Olympic Charter. p. 11. 103 pp. Switzerland. https://stillmedab.olympic.org/media/Document%20Library/OlympicOrg/General/EN-Olympic-Charter.pdf#_ga=2.104950851.1785499532.1618147782-587842528.1618147782; accessed 9 April 2021.

Perlman, Janice. 2011. *Favela: Four Decades of Living on the Edge in Rio de Janeiro*, reprint edition. Oxford University Press.

Puri, Lakshmi. 2016. 'The Value of Hosting Mega Sports Events as a Social, Economic and Environmental Sustainable Development Tool'. *UN Women*. Available at https://www.unwomen.org/en/news/stories/2016/2/lakshmi-puri-speech-at-value-of-hosting-mega-sport-event; accessed on 9 November 2020.

Rehabilitation International. 2012. 'September 2012'. *Rehabilitation International: Monthly Newsletter*. Available at https://www.dvfr.de/fileadmin/user_upload/DVfR/Downloads/Internationales/RI-Newsletter_September_2012.pdf; accessed on 9 November 2020.

Rick, August. 2018. 'China's Sports Industry Is Allegedly Growing Faster Than the National Economy'. *Forbes*, 17 January. Available at https://www.forbes.com/sites/augustrick/2018/01/17/chinas-sports-industry-is-allegedly-growing-faster-than-the-national-economy/#3ebb8d82a4d3; accessed on 7 April 2021.

Roach, M. 2000. *Mega-Events and Modernity: Olympics and Expos in the Growth of Global Culture*. London: Routledge.

Ronday, M. 2012. *Elite National Sports Systems: A Comparison of Australia and the Netherlands*. Newcastle: University of Newcastle.

Santos Neto, Silvestre Cirilo dos, Virgílio Franceschi Neto, Flávia da Cunha Bastos, Marcelo de Castro Haiachi, Leonardo Mataruna-Dos-Santos, and Lamartine Pereira da Costa. 2017. 'Brazilian Medals' Plan: Strategic or Emergency Plan?'. *Rev Bras Educ Fís Esporte* 31 (3): 709–20.

sportanddev.org. n.d. 'What Is Sport and Development?' Available at https://www.sportanddev.org/en/learn-more/what-sport-and-development; accessed on 9 November 2020.

Sutton, Brett. 2015. 'Addis Ababa Training Camps'. *Trisutto*. Available at http://blog.trisutto.com/Ethiopia-training-camps/; accessed on 8 April 2021.

Thibault, L. 2009. 'Globalisation of Sport: An Inconvenient Truth'. *Journal of Sport Management* 23: 1–20.

Tomorrow's Foundation (TF). n.d. *Annual Report: 2016–2017*. Available at https://www.tomorrowsfoundation.org/pdf/TF-Annual-Report-2016-2017.pdf; accessed on 9 November 2011.

United Nations (UN). 2003. *Sport for Development and Peace: Towards Achieving the Millennium Development Goals*. New York.

United Nations Development Programme (UNDP). 2015. 'What Is Human Development?' Available at http://hdr.undp.org/en/content/what-human-development; accessed on 9 November 2020.

UN General Assembly. 2003. *Sports as a Means to Promote Education, Health, Development and Peace.* United Nations Resolution 58/5. Available at https://www.sportanddev.org/sites/default/files/downloads/36__un_general_assembly_reso-lution_59_10___sport_as_a_means_to_promote_education_heal.pdf; accessed on 11 December 2020.

———. 2015. *Transforming Our World: The 2030 Agenda for Sustainable Development* (2015). Available at https://www.unfpa.org/sites/default/files/resource-pdf/Resolution_A_RES_70_1_EN.pdf; accessed on 11 December 2020.

UN-Habitat. 2012. *Urban Youth and Sport for Development.* Nairobi.

UNESCO. 1978. International Charter of Physical Education and Sport, November. 7 pp. https://unesdoc.unesco.org/ark:/48223/pf0000216489?posInSet=1&queryId=ae61703c-524f-4e46-a065-2093fe3c579c; accessed 9 April 2021.

United Nations Office on Sport for Development and Peace (UNOSDP). 2017. 'How does sport contribute to the Sustainable Development Goals? UNOSDP has been working on achieving the #SDGs through several initiatives'. *Facebook.* 26 January. Available at https://www.facebook.com/watch/?v=1210291229055181; accessed on 9 November 2020.

20

Reimagining Play

Football, Muslim Women, and Empowerment

Sabah Khan

'Free Free Free! Football Training for Girls in Mumbra!' Armed with xerox copies of a handwritten flier, we stood outside schools and colleges identifying young girls in the age range of thirteen to eighteen years, asking them if they were interested in joining a football team. Short of money, we had a miserly 100 copies with which we hoped to attract forty girls to play football. Thus began the journey of Parcham's football initiative in Mumbra in 2012.

Mumbra is a Muslim ghetto close to Bombay (now Mumbai). Nearly 80 per cent of its 800,000 population is Muslim. Mumbra witnessed an exponential increase in its population following the 1984 riots in Bhiwandi and then again in 1992–3, as Muslims who had lost family members, homes, and livelihoods to the communal violence fled to Mumbra. When you have experienced persecution on account of your identity, the response is to either hide the identity to save yourself from further persecution and discrimination or to consolidate and assert the identity. In a ghetto like Mumbra, the Muslim identity is asserted through various markers such as the many mosques and madrasas, Islamic schools, women in veil, and school uniforms requiring the scarf for the girls and skull caps for boys.

The characteristics of a ghetto, namely, lack of infrastructure, poor planning, and state neglect in provisioning basic services stare you in the face in Mumbra. While the state falters in providing basic services, it outdoes itself in surveillance. Any incident of terror in the country is followed by 'successful' combing operations in Mumbra. During these operations, youth are randomly picked up by the police on the suspicion of their allegiance to terrorist organizations like Islamic State in Iraq and Syria (ISIS), Lashkar-e-Taiba (LeT), or Students Islamic Movement of India (SIMI), whichever is in focus at the home ministry at that point in time. Media images of Mumbra speak of a fundamentalist haven, oppressed Muslim women, regressiveness, and criminal activity. Being a Muslim from Mumbra adds an additional layer

Sabah Khan, *Reimagining Play* In: *Sports Studies in India*. Edited by: Meena Gopal and Padma Prakash, Oxford University Press. © Oxford University Press 2021. DOI: 10.1093/oso/9780190130640.003.0021

of stigma to an already stigmatized identity. This has generated a sense of disrepute and mistrust of those residing here that has resulted in youth from Mumbra facing discrimination in finding jobs and admissions in educational institutions outside the area.

Spatially, Mumbra town is a linear strip of land sandwiched between the Sahyadri Range on one side and the mangroves on the other. A status report on Mumbra commissioned by the Ministry of Minority Affairs (Jain with support from Sinha 2014) notes Mumbra accommodating Muslims on account of the secular Nana Bhagat, the then-sarpanch (elected head) of Mumbra *gaon* (village), unlike the neighbouring suburb of Diva, which did not allow Muslims to buy property. Older residents of Mumbra speak nostalgically of Nana Bhagat, who owned much of the land on which chawls were built and sold at affordable rates to the poor Muslims who had fled Bombay. The relationship between Hindus and Muslims in Mumbra has changed since then. Even in the small area of Mumbra, there exists an established Muslim area and Hindu area with the Hindus never stepping into the Muslim side of the suburb and the Muslims transiting the Hindu part only to get to the train station. A number of Hindus living in Mumbra fear the people from the Muslim side, a fear instilled especially in young girls whose 'honour' might be compromised by the aggressive Muslim men on 'that' side. With no opportunity to interact with the 'other', hate thrives on misconceptions.

It is in this context that Parcham, a feminist collective, began a football initiative for young girls in 2012, which was aimed at bringing about interaction between Hindu and Muslim girls. The objective was also to challenge the stereotypes of the Muslim and the Muslim from Mumbra.

Struggle to Play

Magic Bus, a non-governmental organization (NGO) known for its sports-for-development programme, sought to collaborate with local activists to start a football programme in Mumbra. It would provide coaches, while the activist group had to mobilize a team of forty adolescents and secure the use of grounds where they could play. The group of forty had to have boys and girls to ensure diversity. The girls were sure they would not be allowed to play with boys. Most of them wore a hijab, and seeking permission from their families to play football was in itself a challenge. But the idea of play had taken root in the girls' imagination and there was no looking back. To realize their dream, the girls called for a meeting with Magic Bus to discuss possible alternatives.

They proposed an all-girls team in which diversity would be reflected in the inclusion of Muslims and non-Muslims in the group. Fortunately, Magic Bus agreed.

The next task was securing the grounds. Some activists who had worked with Muslim girls in the past approached schools asking to use the playgrounds, assuming that an enclosed ground was necessary to ensure the participation of the girls. Without finances, we could only barter labour for the use of the ground. In one school, the girls offered to clean the ground of debris and make it ready for play in return for permission to use it for their Sunday football training. The offer was rejected. In yet another school, the trustees flung the letter seeking permission at us, letting us know we were wasting their time. Help came from members of Maharashtra Mahila Parishad (MMP), a women's group promoting women's leadership in political spaces. The MMP was enthusiastic about girls playing football in Mumbra and persuaded a trustee of a temple trust that had an open ground to allow the group to play. So, the Muslim girls entered a predominantly Hindu area and the training commenced. Not only did the MMP help us get access to the ground, they also offered us the use of their office as a changing room and a space for discussions after the game.

On the first day, forty girls reached the ground where the game was to start. To everyone's shock, the ground was completely occupied with multiple teams of boys playing cricket. We had thought that the permission meant that we would have exclusive right to use the ground during the two hours on Sunday. So, we spoke to the boys, informed them that we had the permission to use the ground, then asked them to allow us to play in a small part of the ground. After an hour of negotiations, the boys benevolently informed the girls that they would wrap up their game shortly and the girls would have the ground. The girls, mostly wearing hijab, took them off, dutifully put on bibs, wrapped their dupatta around it and started chasing the ball. No sooner did the game begin than we were surrounded by male onlookers who had never before witnessed young girls playing in Mumbra.

In the second week, the benevolence of the boys had disappeared. They had thought that this was a one-off activity of an NGO to get girls to play. They were unwilling to give the girls space week after week. We learnt to make space for ourselves, the way the boys did; by simply being there and taking over. The boys complained that they only had a Sunday when they could play and if the girls took over, where would they go? It helped that the temple trust had given us permission to use the ground, but the trustees also let us know that it was a public ground, so the boys would also use the grounds.

So, the girls played football and the boys played cricket. Often, the batting was directed to hit one of the girls, but the girls responded by kicking the ball at them in retaliation. Eventually, mutual respect for the right to space was established.

The crowd of onlookers took some time to get over the novelty of girls at play. They gawked, hooted, leered. And we responded with threats of police complaints. Over time, the novelty wore off and we lost our audience. We also lost a few players whose family were aghast at the tales carried home by the girls' brothers and brothers' friends, the male folk who felt responsible for keeping the women (their reputation) in check.

Women's Bodies and Sports

Girls have been raised to be ashamed of their bodies. Being a girl means oozing femininity, being admired for one's looks, while making sure that it is not the 'wrong' kind of attention. While the 'perfect' figure is important, she must also haunch her shoulders and/or wear a dupatta to conceal her breasts. Running, laughing, making one's presence felt, getting noticed, and attracting attention to one's body are signs of a 'bad' woman. A good Muslim woman requires one more layer of external clothing than the other girls to be considered virtuous; hence the hijab.

It was no wonder, then, that when the girls started to play, they held their bodies rigidly. They tried hard to ensure that the running did not make their breasts jiggle or the exercise make their nipples stand out. Their kick lacked strength and the football barely moved. It took a few weeks for them to forget about their bodies and concentrate on the game. Soon enough, the girls discarded the dupatta when playing. Some even started wearing T-shirts and track pants.

However, some parents feared that an injury would mar their daughter's chances of a marriage, while some others felt that their daughter were becoming muscular and losing their femininity. Everything that came in the way of the girls' marriage prospects was used as an excuse to prohibit them from playing. Then there were girls who had not yet told their parents they were playing football but instead that they were attending English-speaking classes every Sunday. They feared injury because then they would have to explain how they sustained it and would be forced to confess to participating in the game. So, in order to avoid injury, these girls tended to dodge the ball

296 STATE, SPORTS AND DEVELOPMENT

rather than take charge of it. Within a few months, the group shrank from forty to twenty girls.

Claiming Public Space

Cities seem to be designed by men whose imagination does not factor women outside the home or inhabiting public spaces. They reflect an apathy to the needs of women, evident in many ways: the lack of public toilets for women, lack of pedestrian friendly streets, absence of street lighting and other safety measures, and closing of parks in the afternoons just when women are able to find time to use these resources.

Given these constraints, the act of women occupying public space becomes an act of rebellion, of defiance. Women playing in an open public ground is unusual even in a cosmopolitan city like Bombay. This is not a space that is easily granted to them. Women are meant to be indoors as caregivers, or if outdoors, serve a domestic purpose such as shopping for the family, picking up children from school, paying the bills, and so on. Play in public spaces is for boys and men. Women in a public ground threaten the uncontested right of men to the space. If you are a man, you 'own' the public space. Women? Why do they need to take up such a space? What will happen to their homes in their absence? To their families? If women play, will it not compromise their femininity? Who would want to marry a muscular woman or a woman with a competitive spirit? Since marriage is the end goal of a girl's life, disregard for the institution is read as a feminist conspiracy that girls have to be saved from.

Women playing football is an act of making the self visible. It is an assertion of one's being and a claiming of a right to the streets and public spaces, which has long been denied to them. Parcham's experience of almost losing the opportunity to play for lack of a ground brought about the realization of the lack of spaces for women to play. The shrinking numbers in the team for no reason except the brothers' objections to sisters playing in an open ground added to the anger. A discussion ensued, and it was felt that the ones who had continued to play despite all this were able to do so because they had been exposed to feminist thought. In the absence of a feminist perspective, it was difficult to counter the community pressure or stand up to the double standards of brothers and of their family. It was felt that either we should invest in building perspective and then start playing or we need to simultaneously build a safe space for the girls to play even as we develop and promote a pro-feminist perspective within the community. We decided to do the latter.

We looked up the development plan[1] of Mumbra, which had quite a few plots reserved for 'Recreation Grounds' and 'Play Grounds' that were yet to be developed. We chose one that was centrally located and safe for girls. A letter was drafted explaining the need for a sports ground for girls and women in Mumbra and a signature campaign initiated. Yet again, the girls stood outside colleges, schools, and markets and began to talk to women and girls of the need for a ground exclusively for girls and women, the need for such a space in Mumbra and a demand for reserving it for women. The signature drive resulted in 900 odd signatures. Armed with the letter containing these signatures, a delegation of girls went to meet the member of Legislative Assembly (MLA) of Mumbra-Kalwa. He was completely taken aback by the demand, shocked that Muslim girls wanted a playground. But soon, after some discussion, he was as enthusiastic as the girls and decided we should meet the commissioner the very next day. This meeting created history with the first ever sports ground being declared, reserved exclusively for girls in the entire state of Maharashtra.

In the meantime, while waiting for this reservation to take effect, the deputy municipal commissioner in charge of education offered us the use of grounds of the newly-constructed Municipal School. Not only were we given space but we were asked to train the girls from the Municipal School as well. For this, one of the volunteers of Parcham was to be paid an honorarium by the Municipal Corporation. A new innings had begun for Parcham.

What Changes When Women Play Sports?

The acceptance of sports as a tool/means for development rests on the premise that young people, which includes girls, participate in sports or have access to play. This assumption is not grounded in reality. For many young girls, especially those who cannot afford the privacy of gymkhana grounds or private coaches, this is not the case. Parcham's work is in a constituency where training in sports is a luxury for boys and is not just unnecessary but sinful for girls, who have no right to be visible in public spaces. The repression is so great that any challenge to it has corresponding implications and benefits.

Even with the limited agenda of most sports-for-development programmes (behaviour change on health, drug abuse, education), women engaging in sports on account of such programmes push the boundaries of organizing and debate beyond the confines of the home. This influences the narrative about women to include issues beyond matrimonial rights: civic issues around availability and access to public space and the right to play and leisure. It challenges the patriarchal exclusion of women from public space. Muslim women engaging in sports shatters the stereotype of the repressed, veiled Muslim woman who is devoid of agency.

Play as an intervention is a lot more fun and, hence, has more willing participants than other initiatives. Play has the potential of being a political tool to bring together diverse identities and initiate dialogue on intersectionality. For the context that Parcham has chosen to work in, which are ghettos, the sport needed to be one that brought together communities that had had no reason to interact with each other, communities that have been at odds with each other because of the misconceptions they have each been fed about the other by those promoting a politics of hate.

Competitive games such as football can provoke discussions on responses to a set of very difficult emotions such as frustration, fear, and anxiety under pressure on the field. What happens on-field could very well be the response to situations off-field. We were able to have discussions off the field on how the girls played against each other. Did they follow the ethics of sports? We were also able to discuss power resulting from competence, the meaning of competence, the meaning of power, the sources of power, and if one's power was dependent on another less powerful. Play provides an opportunity for such discussions as participants experience these situations and, so, generating empathy becomes possible.

Choosing which sport to use as an intervention is an important decision. The sport that we chose needed to be a team sport where communication among the players was necessary. While cricket is a team sport, not everyone plays together at the same time. We needed a sport where the entire team was on the field, interacting with each other, and football seemed to suit our needs. We ensured that the team had Muslims and non-Muslims. This helped them bond together, talk to each other, start a dialogue on stereotypes, and understand each other and the commonalities of their experience as young girls.

Fun versus Excellence

When the group was first formed, the purpose was to organize girls through an activity they would enjoy. Training was an integral part of the intervention just as much as perspective building. Having learnt football, an opportunity had to be created to test their skills through participation in tournaments. Tournaments are competitive, and everyone wants to win. In a team game, the self's competitive spirit requires that everyone on the team be equally competent and aspiring for victory. What, then, of those who do not play well enough to win but want to be part of the team? How does one explain choosing collaboration and growing together over winning to individuals who are competitive and who have sports as the only opportunity to show their worth and competence?

To popularize sports, one needs role models that young girls can look up to and aspire to be. A Muslim girl from Mumbra playing and winning at the national level will ensure girls' participation in the sport without much mobilizing. It is a limitation that legitimacy of an activity is derived from demonstration of success and usefulness in life. The dilemma, hence, was: Should the sports-for-development agenda limit itself to creating access to play through which to discuss social concerns and build perspective or create successful sportswomen? Parcham chose a middle ground in continuing with a sports programme that would engage girls from across communities, selecting from among them those who have the potential to play in competitions and training them for the same. The specialized training, however, cost a lot more money that could be used to reach a larger number of girls.

Influencing Mainstream Narratives

Muslim women's issues are often understood to be restricted to unilateral talaq, polygamy, and halal. This understanding results in interventions of education, livelihoods (unfortunately often limited to mehendi and tailoring), and life skills to empower young girls. These interventions are possible in closed spaces where taking off the hijab is easy and yet not made mandatory.

Sports requires that young Muslim girls, who are meant to be invisible, occupy a public space. Do the girls want to continue to be invisible or would it be too much of a risk to write up such a proposal for funders and fail? It is likely that the lack of money or the need to be abide by the rules of an external entity enabled Parcham to risk such an intervention. For, if we did fail, it would probably have no implications for a non-funded group like ours. When we tried fundraising for the football initiative, many asked us if we did anything to promote education. While they were willing to offer support to some students, they considered promoting football for girls a waste of time. However, now that the legitimacy of the intervention has been established, organizations working with Muslim women and girls have also begun football initiatives.

Patriarchy works in insidious ways, making one's own oppression seem respectable and useful to society. The good woman is one who follows the diktats of patriarchal imposition without question. Almost all the Muslim girls in Mumbra wear a hijab, which was cast aside when playing, that too in an open ground. This requires immense courage.

However, we also found young girls informing us that the hijab was their choice, an assertion of their identity. The hijab has become a very tricky issue for us as feminists. The external pressure to conform coupled with the anti-Muslim sentiment makes it difficult to have discussions around the hijab without one's secular credentials being questioned. The right-wing demonization of Muslims includes a sharp critique of the hijab as evidence of regressiveness of Muslims. Such positions seem to compel feminists, liberals, and progressives to defend the hijab rather than call it what it is: a symbol of religion marking you as good woman, much like the bindi and the *mangalsutra*.[2] Accepting and defending the right of a hijab among Muslims girls is a condescension and needs to be overlooked because it makes possible girls' mobility in a public space.

A hijab-wearing Muslim girl playing football makes for a much stronger media image than that of one who has had the courage to defy the imposition of the hijab and play the sport. In the absence of the hijab or the bindi, how would an onlooker guess the religion of the girl? Therefore, photographers accompanying journalists often ask the girls to wear the scarf while playing to get the 'sensational' photograph.

Then again, as we grow, girls with whom we have not interacted before, who have had no experience of feminist politics, insist on the hijab/scarf, arguing that it does not interfere with their ability to kick the ball. But when one girl wears a scarf while playing, others feel compelled to wear it too for fear of being branded as not Muslim enough. The founding members of Parcham have a Muslim identity, which makes it possible for them to question diktats of religion without their secular credentials being doubted. Our experience is that girls love to wear T shirts and track pants, some even love to wear shorts. It is for us to create a non-judgemental space where girls will be able to wear what they like rather than what is expected of them.

Towards a Conclusion

The perception of sports as frivolous and a waste of time has changed over a period. Bollywood films like *Chak De! India* (2007) and *Dangal* (2016) have played a role in raising consciousness of women in sports. Parcham has come a long way since it began with adolescent girls negotiating with their families to let them play football. Once the girls started winning local tournaments, parents—who are rickshaw drivers, tea sellers—have started coming to practice sessions and matches, and they share with us their dream of their daughters playing at the district and national levels.

How do we create an enabling environment for girls to be able to realize the simple joy of play? Open grounds for play are being taken over for residential buildings and parking lots and the few grounds that survive are occupied by men. Even in a cosmopolitan city like Bombay, it is rare if not impossible to have girls playing in a public ground in the absence of a tournament or sports event. Men find it difficult to accept girls playing. Their hooting, leering, and unwanted attention is aimed at scaring them away. For girls, access to sports grounds with clean public toilets, changing spaces, and a sense of safety are imperative.

One needs all-girls teams to encourage girls to play. Organizations that have tried mixed teams find that girls inevitably drop out. Boys do not feel inhibited while playing and are generally stronger. This advantage makes them better players who get the attention of the coach. The importance of having an all-girls team cannot be stressed enough. The insistence on parental permission to play means a number of girls will be kept out of the training. One of our best football player played an entire year before she told her mother that she had been playing football. She was responsible for the team winning a number of tournaments and went on to become a coach for young girls.

Finally, sports in development needs be a strategy rather than an end goal. As a strategy, it can aid collectivizing, bringing people together, and helping to realize an intersectional politics. Such an intervention requires tremendous facilitation. To conclude, play and sports is a game changer in activism, especially Muslim women's activism. It effectively shatters the stereotype of the Muslim woman. The one reminder we need for ourselves is that football is not an end; it is a means towards so much more.

Notes

1. The Maharashtra Regional and Town Planning Act, 1996, of Maharashtra State has the provision for spatial planning of a city every twenty years. The plans for each city are available with the local municipal corporation. These plans have reservations for all kind of land use including play and recreation.
2. A necklace of black beads worn by married Maharashtrian Hindu women (a custom which now finds favour among some Maharashtrian Muslims too), signifying their marital status.

Reference

Jain, Ranu with support from Ruchi Sinha. 2014. *Mumbra: A Status Report*. Available on https://mdd.maharashtra.gov.in/Site/Upload/Pdf/Mumbra.pdf; accessed on.

SECTION V
MOVIES, MEDIA, AND TECHNOLOGY

21

The Nationalist Imaginary in the Bollywood Sports Film

Nissim Mannathukkaren

Nationalism has overcome the hegemonic narrative of modernity. Thus, it plays a dominant role in popular culture as well. In India, sports was one of the fields where the idea of India as a nation took shape in the pre-colonial era emphasizing the intricate links between culture and politics. In the post-colonial era, nationalism in the cultural domain, especially in visual media like cinema, solidified itself. This is not surprising in a society where the number of literate people is low. This tendency was most pronounced in the commercial Hindi or Bombay (now Mumbai) cinema. Hindi, by having the largest numbers of speakers, assumed the role of the 'national' language, although this was not officially prescribed in the Indian Constitution.[i] The nationalist imaginary was one which was built in opposition to the global and the foreign, and which found its extreme manifestation in jingoistic films. The sports genre must be analysed in the context of the narrative of nationalism that has been a hegemonic feature of post-Independence Hindi film. The sports film, given the nature of international sporting competition based on national identities, is obviously skewed further in its structuring as a nationalist narrative.

Important changes began with the opening up or liberalizing of the Indian economy in the early 1990s and the consequent linking of the nation with the global. However, the nationalist narrative, which has taken new forms in the post-liberalization era, has endured. The post-liberalization period has led some scholars to argue that the post-national trope—the imaginations that go beyond nation or nationalism—has been inaugurated in the Hindi film. By looking at a few popular sports films of the last two decades, this chapter will interrogate this contention. It will argue that the post-national is not yet realized in the sports film genre. If nationalism has been a majoritarian and hegemonic construct in all phases, in the post-liberalization era, the most important transformation has been the fusing of the idea of the market and the

Nissim Mannathukkaren, *The Nationalist Imaginary in the Bollywood Sports Film* In: *Sports Studies in India.*
Edited by: Meena Gopal and Padma Prakash, Oxford University Press. © Oxford University Press 2021.
DOI: 10.1093/oso/9780190130640.003.0022

306 MOVIES, MEDIA, AND TECHNOLOGY

idea of the nation. Instead of the linking of the national and global leading to a truly syncretic and post-national culture, what emerges is a nationalism in sync with the logic of the market, leading to further exclusions. The chapter argues that the sports film is not immune to this tendency.

The Nationalist Narrative

Talking about the early phase of post-independent Hindi film, Sumita Chakravarty (2008: 84) argues: 'The distinct tendency within the Bombay film to identify and nullify marks of (intercultural) difference in a wide variety of textual situations allows national identity to surface as so many styles of the flesh.' What it means to be an Indian is also not fixed, but has seen shifts. Thus, in Nehruvian India, 'being national also meant, in some sense, to declare oneself to be international' (Chakravarty 2008: 87). The Indian identity was a composite one, which accommodated other cultures yet acquired primacy over other national identities (Chakravarty 2008: 87). Thus, 'all extranational identities are ultimately collapsible into a hypostatized Indianness, left suitably vague and no longer expressly articulated either through iconography or patriotic dialogue' (Chakravarty 2008: 93). This idea of nationalism, although hegemonic, was not jingoistic.[ii] But with changing social and economic changes, the idea of nationalism also changes. The emergence of the right wing as an electoral force in Indian politics since the 1980s gave a ballast to the narrow versions of nationalism.

With the liberalization of the Indian economy, the Hindi film itself changed character drastically, and this has important implications for the sports film. Therefore, this new genre of Hindi films (from the mid-1990s) must be distinguished from the old one, and the former should be termed as Bollywood, as Ashish Rajadhyaksha argues. He also points out correctly that Bollywood must be separated from the larger Indian cinema which is often reduced to it in the West (Rajadhyaksha 2003: 28). Similarly, Ajay Gehlawat distinguishes between Bollywood as 'a nationally (and globally) dominant cinema' and 'the national, i.e. "Indian" cinema'. Gehlawat employs the term 'Bollywood' to 'define it as popular Hindi rather than Indian cinema, so as to avoid a nationalizing discourse' (quoted in Gooptu 2011: 770). The fundamental shift in Bollywood was towards creating a new central audience for the film: the non-resident and mainly affluent Indian. Thus, diasporic nationalism became the underlying basis of the Bollywood film. This itself was

THE BOLLYWOOD SPORTS FILM 307

connected to globalization and to the changed nature of film production and financing which sought international capital (Rajadhyaksha 2003: 31). As Brahmachari (2012: 6) argues,

In adapting to the opportunities provided by a globalized market the industry was undergoing substantial shifts in terms of patterns and modes production, and in ideological and formal realignments necessitated by its changing audience base and sites of exhibition and circulation.

Here, the rise of the multiplex is an important feature because it saw the return of the affluent audiences to cinema theatres. The revenue structure is radically overhauled with the biggest percentage of returns now coming from multiplexes and foreign territories (Brahmachari 2012: 10, 36). This is what leads to the urban turn and the gentrification of Hindi cinema (Ganti 2012: 17). There is also a severing of the concept of being an Indian from any territorial connotation under the right-wing imagination. Thus, the non-resident Indian (NRI) may be a foreign citizen without political rights in India but can still be an 'Indian' (D'Souza and Mannathukkaren 2015). I argue that, thus, there is a simultaneous expansion as well as contraction of the idea of an Indian. Yet, the expansion is not broad enough to accommodate anything 'foreign' except in its most instrumental sense.

This is what Rajadhyaksha (2003: 30) calls 'techno-nostalgia': Bollywood exemplifying 'the insatiable taste for nostalgia with the felt need to keep "our (national) culture alive"'. At the same time, the class base shifted to the middle and elite classes anchoring the new ideological content:

Hindi cinema's social transformation or path to "coolness" [which] began in the mid-1990s with the erasure of the signs and symbols of poverty, labour, and rural life from films, and with the decline in plots that focused on class conflict, social injustice, and youthful rebellion (Ganti 2012: 79).

There is a shift from the Nehruvian socialist imaginaries which had farmers and workers as the heroes to contemporary 'mainstream national political discourses that increasingly portray urban middle-class consumers as the representative citizens of liberalizing India' (Fernandes 2006: xv). The Bombay film in the 1970s, which was targeted at the masses, was termed by Ashis Nandy (1999: 2) as 'the slum's point of view of Indian politics and society'. In the Bollywood film, the poor classes are not only *not* the audience,

308 MOVIES, MEDIA, AND TECHNOLOGY

but also banished from being seen—they simply do not exist. It is important to understand these drastic changes in the nature of the Hindi film
from the mid-1990s in order to understand the sports film and the nationalist narrative. My arguments here are not to emphasize that the Hindi film
can only be studied within the nationalist narrative or as 'national' cinema
as has been a dominant tendency. The changes from the 1990s that I have
outlined above negate such a reading. In the present, the trans-nationalized
'production, distribution and consumption' of South Asian films would
mean that 'cross-border movements', 'diasporic flows and contra flows', 'sub-
national disjunctures that are frequently and increasingly transnational', and
'movements to the West and non-West' cannot be ignored (Roy and Huat
2012: xiii). Yet, what I am arguing is that despite these changes, the consecra-
tion of the nationalist framework, especially in the sports genre, is dominant.
Let us examine a few films of the last two decades.

The Films

Lagaan (2001)

Lagaan is probably the most iconic sporting film in Hindi. It is not a conventional sporting film in which sport is the central focus, but sport becomes
an instrument to push forward the narrative of anti-colonial struggle. It is
a simple tale of peasants in a village in a nineteenth-century colonial India
being challenged by a British officer to a game of cricket and the former's triumph leading to the revocation of the tax imposed by the colonial state (as
was agreed upon) as well as the disbandment of the British cantonment from
the village. The film is not couched in any explicit or jingoist nationalist mes-
saging as are many other commercial films, but the imaginary of the nation is
brought back into the narrative by locating the other in the white colonizer.[iii]
Absolving local oppressors of any part in the oppression of the peasants by
attributing their position to the compulsions of the colonial power is a reduction of the multifaceted (class, caste, race, gender) nature of exploitation
of the colonized to only a single factor—the external oppressor in the form of
the colonial state—and the struggle against exploitation to only the struggle
for the 'nation'. Thus, a later-day, full-fledged nationalism is transposed onto
a period when nationalism was in its nascence. The associations of the game
of cricket, in any case, in the present, are mostly with a deeply jingoistic cultural nationalism.

THE BOLLYWOOD SPORTS FILM   309

Lagaan is ostensibly based on subaltern peasant protagonists. Yet, it seeks to appropriate the critical impulses of the subaltern to the cause of a nationalism, which simultaneously silences the question of 'national liberation' in the Fanonian sense. Therefore, the nationalism that emerges is a hegemonic elite nationalism which is sync with the ideological framework of Bollywood. Ashis Nandy's (1995: 235) statement, 'However much we may bemoan the entry of mass culture through the commercial cinema, the fact remains that it is commercial cinema which, if only by default, has been . . . more protective towards non-modern categories', does not throw light on how the critical potential of popular culture is appropriated by the middle classes and elites to serve as a means for imagining homogenized exclusivist nationalisms.

Patiala House (2011)

The entire narrative is built around a Sikh family in Southall, England, and the strong anti-white and anti-British sentiments of the family's patriarch. The context of his visceral hatred is the violent racism from the dominant white society that he faced as a young immigrant (and this draws on actual history of Southall). As a result, his entire world view is governed by protecting his (national) culture and his extended family from the baneful influences of white English culture.[iv] All the younger family members, despite having been born and brought up in England, are shown to be thoroughly Indian (there are breaks like a daughter having a white British boyfriend, but she is not able to get her father's consent for a marriage until the film's end).

The biggest casualty of the 'tyrannical' hold of the patriarch on the family is that the eldest son Gattu (and the hero of the film) had to sacrifice his cricketing career at a young age and a potential spot on the English cricket team. The father had threatened suicide if Gattu even contemplated playing for England. The film's plot is taken forward when Gattu gets a second chance to play for England at the age of thirty-four, and he finally rebels against his father, goaded by other family members and supported by the Southall Indian community. The film ends happily with father finally accepting his son who becomes a national star, helping England win the cricket World Cup. The resolution is aided by the younger members turning against the patriarch to pursue their own dreams, which are tied to embracing some aspect of the English culture, but, more importantly, by the patriarch's wife convincing him that Gattu playing for England does not mean an insult to their own culture but is in fact an honour, for, the English themselves cannot do without

310 MOVIES, MEDIA, AND TECHNOLOGY

an Indian helping them. The acceptance of English culture is not from an understanding that overcomes racial animosities and proposes a broader understanding of what it means to be an Indian. Rather, it is an instrumental one in which adjustments are made to the changed reality, where the younger generation is inextricably enmeshed in the social and economic structures of the no-longer foreign land. Thus, the expansion of the horizons of the NRI in the age of globalization is not necessarily tied to a loosening of the national identity. The film also cleverly avoids the difficult choice of pitting the British-Indian Gattu playing for England against the Indian cricket team.

Kai Po Che (2013)

Of all the Bollywood sports films, this one is different, for it is attempting to question the nationalist narrative and exploring its fractures. It is a story of three young Hindu men and a poor Muslim cricketing prodigy, set in the backdrop of the Gujarat riots of 2002. The story focuses on personal friendships and how they are affected by the larger politics of communalism. While one of the friends is dedicated to making the young Muslim boy a national cricketer, another is drawn to anti-Muslim radical Hindu politics which culminated in one of the worst riots of Independent India, in which over 1,000 people were killed. For a Bollywood film to even touch upon the topic is considered out of the ordinary, as avoidance of thorny political questions and reality is a hallmark of Bollywood films. Despite this, the film reinforces the nationalist narrative. That is because by focusing on the personal, the politics of riots gets a superficial treatment. While a Hindu party is shown as the aggressor, the machinations are shown to be localized and the responsibility is placed on a local leader. Thus, it occludes the fact the riots could have been state-sponsored with the participation of the highest echelons of the administration. Nor does it make any mention of the then-chief minister, Narendra Modi, and his controversial role in the riots, which has been the subject of national and international discussion and criticism. Further, the moral culpability of the perpetrators is deflected by showing the riots as a result of the burning of a train with Hindu pilgrims allegedly by a group of Muslims. Thus, a certain justifiability is ascribed to the actions of one of the protagonists who loses his parents in the train fire, and then participates in the riots. Rather than stress on the state-conspiracy angle, the film portrays the riots more to be a result of spontaneous Hindu anger to the burning of the train. Here, it has to be noted, the film also substantially

THE BOLLYWOOD SPORTS FILM   311

dilutes the political content of the original novel that it is based on. Chetan Bhagat, the author of the novel, defended the decision to make the film less political by arguing that 'it's a Bollywood film' (Poonam 2013). The enormity and severity of the riots is also reduced: 'There are no shots of the relief camps built for the survivors of 2002 riots (there were 85,000 displaced in Ahmedabad alone), nor are there shots of entire rows of homes burned down' (Janmohamed 2013).

The film, like other commercial films, constructs a stereotypical image of the Muslims in attire and comportment as religious and unmodern, thus reinforcing the negative perception among the majority community. Critically, the success of the Muslim boy is dependent on the goodwill and benevolence of the Hindu protagonist. The boy does not speak at all; neither do other Muslim characters. They are devoid of agency. As a commentator puts it:

> This way of imagining and depicting Hindu-Muslim co-existence is of course not new. Most famously, Mahatma Gandhi, in his philosophy of *mitrata* or friendship, states that ultimately Hindu-Muslim unity would only be possible if the Hindu was willing to unconditionally sacrifice himself for this cause. This is exactly what happens in the film (Mahmudabad 2013).

Mary Kom (2014)

Hegemonic and majoritarian nationalism is something that is reinforced in films like *Mary Kom* about India's first female boxing star and an Olympic medal winner. Kom hailed from a poor family in Manipur, a northeastern state of India. Geographically and politically, India's northeast is on the margins. These regions have seen substantial and ongoing violent ethnic insurgencies against the Indian state. Numbering less than 4 per cent of India's population, the eight northeastern states do not have the demographic clout that mainland Indian states have. Besides, racially belonging to the Mongoloid race and mostly speaking Sino-Tibetan languages, the people of the Northeast are the racial and linguistic 'other'. In major Indian cities, they are subject to significant racism. And in the commercial Hindi film, they do not have any presence.

Therefore, a biopic of Mary Kom, a national sporting star, would have been an ideal opportunity for a person from the Northeast to make a mark on the Hindi film as well as on mainstream Indian popular culture. But the

312 MOVIES, MEDIA, AND TECHNOLOGY

constraints of Bollywood, both in terms of the ideological framework of a homogenized nationalism and the economic framework of global finance capitalism, prevented it from casting an actor from the Northeast in the title role. Instead, Bollywood star Priyanka Chopra played the role of Mary Kom, using prosthetics and make up to acquire some of the racial features of the latter. In ideological terms, it is as offensive as the blackface tradition of American theatre and television, which lasted until the Civil Rights Movement. None of the problems of the Northeast or that of sportspersons hailing from the region are depicted in the film (except for a stray and superficial reference by the protagonist to discrimination faced by Manipuri sportspersons). It is almost as if the nationalist teleology of a sportsperson winning the medal for the nation and the national anthem playing at the end is all that matters.

Sultan (2016)

In this wrestling drama, which became one of the biggest blockbusters in Hindi film, again, the goal of winning a medal for the country is the overriding problem that pushes the narrative forward. But unlike other male superstar films, this Salman Khan starrer tries to make some politically correct noises about women's empowerment. (It is another matter that these mirror the present government's campaigns and thus are overly deferential to the statist narrative. This statism is another aspect of the nationalist framework.) Yet, the heroine, who is as capable as the hero as a wrestler and poised for a national medal, has to sacrifice her career for her child. As Joshi (2016a) points out: 'There is Aarfa, a woman wrestler for a heroine. But for every step forward in breaking the stereotypes there is the curiously disconcerting comfort of the status quo.' Like *Lagaan*, the film sacrifices gender liberation at the altar of a patriarchal nationalism.

Dangal (2016)

The Aamir Khan film *Dangal*, which became the highest grossing Indian film ever, is much celebrated. It is the story of a former national-level wrestler who had to give up the sport before he could win a medal for the nation. He vows to make his sons achieve his dream. But he is shattered when his wife delivers four daughters consecutively. He, nevertheless, decides, against

THE BOLLYWOOD SPORTS FILM 313

great opposition from a patriarchal village, to make the eldest two wrestlers. The two daughters grow up, under the father's authoritarian methods and against their own will initially, to be wrestlers representing the nation. And the crowning glory of the film is one of the daughters winning the first gold medal for the nation in an international competition. The film has attracted a lot of debate, mainly revolving around women, sports, and empowerment. In a state such as Haryana, where the most egregious forms of patriarchy operate, it is indeed exhilarating to see women in *Dangal* beat men in/at their own game. And in a nation such as India, where women's bodies are subject to perpetual surveillance and shaming, it is definitely liberating for women to vicariously participate in the sporting triumph of *Dangal*. Yet the nationalist framework is overpowering. As Joshi (2016b) puts it:

> The tagline of the film might be about asserting that women are no less than men but ultimately, like every other sports film, it's all about winning a gold medal for India. *Dangal* also carries the burden of patriotism right down to the fictional twist in the tale, the ultra-jingoistic finale, complete with the national anthem (remember Mary Kom?) and Bharat Mata Ki Jai sloganeering.

The film[v] throws up several interesting questions around women's empowerment, which, obviously, cannot be resolved in the context of the film or a single film. Besides, it is illogical to expect a commercial film backed by Walt Disney Studios, the world's largest film studio, to deal with the complexities of women's liberation. Yet, it is important to understand what a nationalist framework and its dominance in the narrative occludes as well as deflects in terms of possibilities. Here, questions like women's unpaid care work, public–private binary mirroring the man–woman binary, the efficacy of bringing a few women on board to the male side of the division of labour, and the commodification of global sport through corporate control are aspects which cannot be explored by *Dangal* circumscribed by a nationalist trope and a commercial format. It questions patriarchy and affords the daughters some agency (even when they are coaxed by the father into wrestling, which was not their own choice) like when one of them takes on the father with respect to coaching technique and challenges him to a bout. Given that choice does not occur in a vacuum and that the other option for the daughters would have been an early marriage and relegation to the household, wrestling offers some kind of liberation. Some gender stereotypes are broken (like women's place is in the home, or that wrestling is a men's sport),

314   MOVIES, MEDIA, AND TECHNOLOGY

but the patriarchy of the father is not questioned enough, not just from an extended feminist critique but also from a simpler premise that the gender empowerment portrayed is an instrumental one—instrumental to the ultimate cause of a medal for the country. It is the father's nationalist dream that the daughters are forced to enact.

Nationalism as a Hindi Film Preoccupation

Nation is one of the central pre-occupations of the Hindi film. This is exaggerated further in the sports film. One of the central problems of Indian modernity is the predominant weightage of Hindi and Hindi-speaking regions in it. Thus, the Hindi film stands in for the nation. As Virdi (2003: 2) asserts:

> Though Hindi is a regional northern language, Hindi cinema's audience transcends lingual-regional boundaries within the nation, making it fit the national cinema billing like no other.

This is how the Bombay Hindi cinema, as Gooptu (2011) argues, assumes the role of the national-popular. As Gooptu (2011: 771) points out, this denotes an

> underlying tendency in Indian cinema studies, wherein the 'regional' (non-Bombay) is 'simply' a subsidiary of the normative 'Indian (Bombay) cinema'. The prevalence of the trope of 'the nation' has, on the whole, diverted attention from other centres of film production and other language cinemas, and most studies have tended to subsume the complex structure of filmgoers' preferences within the rubric of a 'national' popular/public culture.

The Hindi film nationalism, as I have argued, is thus exclusionary and homogenous. Non-Hindi cultures are completely absent or caricatured in it. In contrast, in the 1930s and the 1940s, internationalism was a hallmark of the Hindi film which saw 'unusual collaborations between producers, directors, actors and screenwriters from diverse socioeconomic and linguistic groups that produced the eclectic, autotelic space of Hindi cinema' (Roy and Huat 2012: xiv). The resistance to homogeneous nationalism has more potential to be visible in the non-dominant, 'regional' languages. For example, 'Tamil cinema has always maintained an ambivalent relationship with the idea of the "Indian" nation' and has even articulated the idea of Tamils themselves

THE BOLLYWOOD SPORTS FILM 315

as a nation (Gooptu 2011: 771). Trans-nationalization has further, ironically, led to the strengthening of regional and sub-national identity in films (Roy and Huat 2012: xx).

This does not mean that non-Hindi films do not have nationalist tropes or that they are not influenced by the pervasive ideology of nationalism.[vi] It is only that the scope for a critique is more possible in them. The bilingual sporting film *Sala Khadoos* (*Irudhi Suttru* in Tamil) is a boxing film about a talented but failed boxer who becomes the coach of the women's team. But the same machinations of the Boxing Association which ended his career are now threatening his coaching stint as well. Yet, he manages to find talent in a young woman, who is actually a fish seller from a poor family, and transforms her, by overcoming the conspiracies of the Association, into a champion boxer. As the film is mostly set in Tamil Nadu and directed by a Tamil director, one can immediately see the different emphasis in the sporting drama. Even though the film traverses the familiar terrain of the sporting genre of the underdog turning triumphant at the end, it is not marked by a nationalist teleology. Sure, the boxer wins a medal for the nation at the end, but the film focuses more on the individual triumph as well as the boxer–coach relationship, which culminates in a romantic relationship. Nationalism does not overwhelm the narrative showing that the other possibilities of plot development exist in sporting films, which have been discarded for the sake of an all-encompassing nationalism the Hindi sporting film.

Post-nationalism?

After the above discussion, it is very difficult to conclude that there is a post-national trend in Bollywood as argued by Gooptu. This is especially so when it comes to the sporting film. According to Gooptu (2006), 'For current Bollywood, national is a fluid essence, that which finds its comfort zone through negotiations between local and global.' She calls this the 'post-national' in Hindi cinema, overcoming the nationalist framework and the flurry of jingoistic anti-Pakistan films of the 1990s. The post-national is something in which 'Indianness is much more than some kind of innate spirit . . . it is a special sense of being that transcends nationalities and cultures.' Nationalism is 'to be participated in and constituted by entities that, strictly speaking, lie beyond the sphere of the Indian nation' (Gooptu 2006). Gooptu attributes these changes to the ones that I have outlined above, in terms of the changing nature of the finances of Hindi film production of the

1990s and 2000s. Yet, she comes to opposite conclusion to the one reached here: 'For the current target audience, upwardly mobile urban middle classes, nationalism has been redefined as compatible with their location in a globalised economy' (Gooptu 2006).

But I argue that this expansion of economic horizons has not necessarily seen an expansion in terms of cultural horizons or a loosening of the idea of nationalism. Instead, global capitalism can go hand in hand with cultural revivalism and illiberal nationalism. India, since 2014, when a right-wing Hindu nationalist government was elected, is a good example of this. The years since 2014 have seen fractious debates on nationalism, which have had a deleterious effect on the cultural sphere. There have been attempts to re-write the nation's history, foster nationalism by playing national anthems in cinema theatres and flying the national flag in universities, and so on. All this has happened in the backdrop of violent attacks on religious minorities and cultural practices like eating beef, which go against the majoritarian Hindu nationalist project. Any opposition to the government is now countered with the tag of 'anti-national'. The biggest stars of Hindi film like Aamir Khan were subject to such attacks and patriotism tests. There was a huge row when Pakistani artistes were banned from Bollywood and even films that had already been shot with Pakistani actors faced censure. A slew of Hindi films, that reflect the Hindu nationalist ideology, have been made since 2014, and very controversially, some of these commercial entertainers with very little artistic value have been awarded the highest prizes in the prestigious government-sponsored National Awards competition (Kumar 2016). This is a very dangerous trend.

Thus, the expansion of global capitalist networks and the integration of the nation into these can provoke reactionary cultural movements precisely because there is no automatic relationship between capitalism, and cultural and political freedoms, a point that Gooptu ignores. Instead, what is more prevalent is capitalism instrumentally using global cultures rather than fostering an authentic inter-cultural communication. The pastiche of global locations that we relentlessly see in Bollywood is an example of this, which participates in global consumerism without necessarily taking on board the vibrant global conversations on democracy and human rights. Here 'tradition' and capitalism go together, unlike the Hindi films of the early post-Independence era, in which the values of capitalism and the 'modern' were the 'other' (Basu 2010: 84). Religious myths are reassembled here with 'touristic and consumerist trappings' (Basu 2010: 87). And as a result, because of this insularity and instrumentality, Bollywood has not necessarily become more attractive

THE BOLLYWOOD SPORTS FILM   317

to the Western audiences as Gooptu (2006) had imagined: 'With the concept of Bollywood catching on among mainstream western audiences, depiction of India as syncretic is certainly a more selling proposition.' It is still overwhelmingly consumed by the diasporic Indian audiences in the Western city (Roy and Huat, xi).

Thus, unlike Gooptu's 'post-nationalism', there is another kind of post-nationalism that characterizes Bollywood as well as its sport genre. And that is the post-nationalism identified by Sanjay Srivastava in his research on urban middle-class religiosity. According to Srivastava, post-nationalism is different from classical nationalism with its vocabularies of personal and collective sacrifice, duty and valour. According to him, post-nationalism is 'the articulation of nationalist emotion with the robust desires engendered through new practices of consumerism and their associated cultures of privatization and individuation' unlike in the early years of independence when nationalism was 'anti-consumerist and pro-industrialization' (Srivastava 2017: 97, 110). As Mazzarella (quoted in Brahmachari 2012: 23) argues, 'globalized consumerism' was an 'opportunity for a comprehensive revitalization of "Indianness"' and one that emphasized 'a new vision of citizenship based on aspirational consumption'.

This is what marks Bollywood and other cultural productions in the present. There is a 'confident cosmopolitanism' that is not marked by the earlier angst about (Western) 'cultural imperialism' (Srivastava 2017: 103). Local cultures are suffused with transnational and market symbols. Market is fundamental here. Rather than tradition and modernity being opposed to each other, here, they go together.[vii] Just as in Bollywood, 'suburban religiosities [arise] in tandem with consolidation of the suburban (middle-class) family as the focus of post-national consumerist modernity' (Srivastava 2017: 104). Thus, here, 'a contemporary Hindu identity whose religiosity is in tune with the cadence of neoliberal capitalism and whose neoliberalism is informed by the requirements of religious belief' (Srivastava 2017: 111) is shaped. This 'moral consumption' has to be central to understand Bollywood too.

Despite the urban elite-/middle-class-centric focus of Bollywood, the sports genre has to focus on the rural areas as many of the stories are actually set there. The irony is that in this makeover of Hindi film as Bollywood, the sports genre is the only one that allows a foray into the non-urban and non-middle-class India, the margins of the Indian nation. Otherwise, even urban India is missing, replaced by the inevitable Western city. Thus, sports films like *Lagaan, Mary Kom, Sultan, Dangal, Saala Khadoos* all deal with rural or non-metropolitan India. But this verisimilitude is coerced and not borne out

318 MOVIES, MEDIA, AND TECHNOLOGY

of an attempt at genuine understanding. Therefore, it appears as an idyllic and mythical place, shorn of all social conflicts.

Further, a running thread through all the sports films is the narrative that all the ills plaguing the sports persons are caused by the government sporting bodies. While the public sector/government in the form of officials, coaches, and infrastructure are the villains, the private sector and corporations are the saviours of sport.[viii] Or films like *Mary Kom* are filled with advertisements for goods and product placements (Pal 2014). As Brahmachari (2012: 18) argues, this 'tendency of rendering the screen as a repository of commodities was thus also symptomatic of the nature of funding that Bollywood had increasingly depended upon from the 1990s onwards'.

***

The sports genre in Hindi film virtually recreates the nationalist paradigm prevalent in the dominant society.[ix] This is the same when it comes to sports nationalism as well which papers over fractures and breaks. Nationalism is homogeneous and essentialized. Hindi cinema, by and large, elided 'regional cultural expressions' and normalization of the 'Hindi/Hindu subject' (Roy and Huat 2012: xvii). This is the 'Hindi film's textual, discursive, and economic hegemony over the rest of the Indian languages', which has also been mirrored in the academic discourse (Roy and Huat 2012: xvii). In reality, sports nationalism, like nationalism, is a contested terrain with subnationalisms being a prominent history of India's sporting culture. Mani and Krishnamurthy outline literature dealing with the communal and subnational turns of Indian sports. Thus,

It seems that the football grounds in Bengal deeply reflected the anxieties, uncertainties, and aspirations of various communal identities in the process of nation-state formation. In addition to that, the history of football in Bengal speaks specifically of a certain mode of Bengali/East Bengali nationalism and/or Hindu/Muslim nationalism, given its tense, and communal, colonial and post-colonial history (Mani and Krishnamurthy 2016: 46).

These are the fissures that do not get portrayed in the Bollywood sporting film as the nationalist teleology predominates:

THE BOLLYWOOD SPORTS FILM 319

The biopic is in danger of becoming the new fantasy movie—a fantasy of individual achievement against a hostile and corrupt system that is designed to hold back Indians. If this system did not exist, films as varied as *Bhaag Milkha Bhaag* and *Dangal* argue, Indians would have been sitting at the top of gold medal charts (Ramnath 2017).

This is the fundamental problem that animates Bollywood stemming from its structure. It limits the narratives of the sports biopic to stories of nationalist triumph. This is disappointing considering that only in the last two decades or so has the sports genre in Hindi cinema finally become a viable proposition (Chintamani 2017). And this is seen even in films like *Kai Po Che* or *Dangal*, which make some attempts at complicating the nationalist narrative, absent from films like *Saala Khadoos*, emerging as it does from a non-Hindi milieu. As Ramnath (2017) correctly argues:

The emphasis on achieving glory for the sake of national pride robs the sports biopic of one of its fundamental qualities: an individual's struggle to overcome doubt and personal adversity. . . They reduce the grit of the lone athlete to an act of patriotism.

Notes

i. While the linguistic question was relatively considered settled after the 1960s, the election of the Bharatiya Janata Party (BJP) government in 2014 has again led attempts to impose Hindi on non-Hindi-speaking states.

ii. This Nehruvian internationalism also reflected in features like bilateral trade with the socialist bloc, which saw a success of Hindi films there (Rajadhyaksha 2003: 29).

iii. For an elaborate treatment, see Mannathukkaren (2001) from which the argument following this is drawn.

iv. Boria Majumdar (quoted in Mani and Krishnamurthy 2016: 43) has argued that cricket 'became a site of cultural nationalism even outside the geographical boundaries of the nation' in the diaspora.

v. The following is drawn from Pandey and Mannathukkaren (2017).

vi. For example, the war films of Malayalam starring superstar Mohanlal.

vii. Hindi blockbusters like *Kuch Kuch Hota Hai* (1998) are examples of this.

viii. In *Saala Khadoos*, the Boxing Association official sexually exploits women boxers; in *Dangal*, the coach of the Indian team goes as far as locking up the protagonist while his daughter was fighting in the final match.

ix. It is important to note that the domination of Hindi also marginalizes languages and cultures within the so-called 'Hindi heartland'. There are many languages spoken here and they have been reduced to the status of being a dialect of Hindi; Bhojpuri is one example.

References

Basu, Anustup. 2010. *Bollywood in the Age of New Media: The Geo-televisual Aesthetic.* Edinburgh: Edinburgh University Press.

Brahmachari, Paramita. 2012. 'Othering Spaces, Forging Selves: Contemporary Cinema, Globalization and The New Indian Middle Class'. PhD Dissertation, Jadavpur University, Kolkata, India.

Chakravarty, Sumita 2008. 'The National-Heroic Image: Masculinity and Masquerade'. In Rajinder Dudrah and Jigna Desai (eds), *The Bollywood Reader*, pp. 84–95. Maidenhead, Berkshire, England; New York: McGraw-Hill; Open University Press.

Chintamani, Gautam. 2017. 'How the Sports Film Genre in Hindi Cinema Has Finally Come of Age'. *Swarajya*, 20 January. Available at https://swarajyamag.com/culture/how-the-sports-film-genre-in-hindi-cinema-has-finally-come-of-age; accessed on 10 October 2020.

D'Souza, Rohan and Nissim Mannathukkaren. 2015. 'The Nationalist in the NRI'. *The Hindu*, 11 December.

Fernandes, Leela. 2006. *India's New Middle Class: Democratic Politics in an Era of Economic Reform.* Minneapolis, MN: University of Minnesota Press.

Ganti, Tejaswini. 2012. *Producing Bollywood: Inside the Contemporary Hindi Film Industry.* Durham, London: Duke University Press.

Gooptu, Sharmistha. 2006. 'Transcending Nationalism'. *Times of India*, 10 February. Available at https://timesofindia.indiatimes.com/edit-page/Transcending-Nationalism/articleshow/1408595.cms; accessed on 10 October 2020.

———. 2011. 'The "Nation" in Indian Cinema'. *History Compass* 9 (10): 767–75.

Janmohamed, Zahir. 2013. 'Kai Po Che and the Reduction Of 2002'. *Outlook*, 4 March. Available at https://www.outlookindia.com/website/story/kai-po-che-and-the-reduction-of-2002/284177; accessed on 10 October 2020.

Joshi, Namrata. 2016a. 'Sultan Review: Salman, Not Quite on Top of This Game'. *The Hindu*, July 6.

———. 2016b. 'Dangal: Nationalism Over Feminism'. *The Hindu*, Available at http://www.thehindu.com/entertainment/movies/Dangal-nationalism-over-feminism/article16924087.ece1; accessed on 10 October 2020.

Kumar, Anuj. 2016. 'The Right Turn?'. *The Hindu*, 12 August. Available at http://www.thehindu.com/todays-paper/tp-features/tp-metroplus/The-Right-turn/article14566655.ece; accessed on 10 October 2020.

Mahmudabad, Ali Khan. 2013. 'The Kai Po Che Question'. *Outlook*, 8 March. Available at http://test.outlookindia.com/website/story/the-kai-po-che-question/284287; accessed on 10 October 2020.

Mani, Veena and Mathangi Krishnamurthy. 2016. 'Sociology of Sport: India'. In Kevin Young (ed.), *Sociology of Sport: A Global Subdiscipline in Review (Research in the Sociology of Sport, Volume 9)*, pp. 37–57. Bingley, UK: Emerald Group Publishing Limited.

Mannathukkaren, Nissim. 2001. 'Subalterns, Cricket and the Nation: The Silences of "Lagaan"'. *Economic and Political Weekly* 36 (49): 4580–8.

Nandy, Ashis. 1995. *The Savage Freud and Other Essays on Possible and Retrievable Selves*. Princeton: Princeton University Press.

———. 1999. 'Popular Cinema and the Slum's Eye View of Indian Politics'. In Ashis Nandy (ed.), *The Secret Politics of our Desires*, pp. 1–18, London: Zed Books.

Pal, Deepanjana. 2014. 'Mary Kom Review: This Priyanka Chopra Film Is a Disservice to the Boxer'. *First Post*, 6 September. Available at https://www.firstpost.com/entertainment/mary-kom-review-this-priyanka-chopra-film-is-a-disservice-to-the-boxer-1696517.html; accessed on 10 October 2020.

Pande, Rohini and Charity Troyer Moore. 2015. 'Why Aren't India's Women Working?'. *New York Times*, 23 August. Available at https://www.nytimes.com/2015/08/24/opinion/why-arent-indias-women-working.html; accessed on 10 October 2020.

Pandey, Anu and Nissim Mannathukkaren. 2017. 'Women and Invisible Work'. *The Hindu*, 28 January.

Poonam, Snigdha. 2013. '"Kai Po Che" and the Strange Case of the Vanishing Villain'. *India Ink*, 27 February. Available at https://india.blogs.nytimes.com/2013/02/27/did-chetan-bhagat-scrub-whitewash-the-godhra-riots-in-kai-po-che/; accessed on.

Rajadhyaksha, Ashish. 2003. 'The "Bollywoodization" of The Indian Cinema: Cultural Nationalism in a Global Arena'. *Inter-Asia Cultural Studies* 4 (1): 25–39.

Ramnath, Nandini. 2017. 'Three Things Dangal's Mind-Boggling Success Taught Us'. *Scroll*, 5 January. Available at https://scroll.in/reel/825909/three-things-dangals-mind-boggling-success-taught us; accessed on 10 October 2020.

Roy, Anjali Gera and Chua Beng Huat. 2012. 'The Bollywood Turn in South Asian Cinema'. In Anjali Gera Roy and Chua Beng Huat (eds), *Travels of Bollywood Cinema: From Bombay to LA*, pp. ix–xxxi. New Delhi: Oxford University Press.

Srivastava, Sanjay. 2017. 'Divine Markets: Ethnographic Notes on Postnationalism and Moral Consumption in India'. In Daromir Rudnyckyj and Filippo Osella (eds), *Religion and the Morality of the Market*, pp. 94–115. Cambridge: Cambridge University Press.

Virdi, Jyotika. 2003. *The Cinematic Imagination: Indian Popular Films as Social History*. New Brunswick, NJ: Rutgers University Press.

22

Sports, Celebrity, and the Sports Biopic[i]

Pramod K. Nayar

This chapter merges two domains of analysis: the sports celebrity and the biopic. The key texts for the essay are three recent biopics, *M.S. Dhoni: The Untold Story* (Pandey 2016), *Sachin: A Billion Dreams* (Erskine 2017), and the older *Bhaag Milkha Bhaag* (Mehra 2013), all based on the lives and careers of India's most celebrated sports figures. The chapter assumes that these are already established as celebrity figures at the time of the biopic and this chapter. They are more than sports persons: they are sports *personae*. In what follows, I shall unpack the constituents of the celebrity power: the factors that make them 'notable subjects' worthy of the biopics and our adulation/emulation.

Further, the argument presents itself that a nation as obsessed with film culture—and film celebrities—would enable the rise and popularity of the biopic as well. The sports biopic, especially in the case of cricket stars, brings together India's favourite cultural practices: cricket and cinema. The same appeal may not accrue to athletes or badminton sportspeople as biopic stars. It would be interesting to see how the nature of 'appeal' of these sports stars differs from the appeal of screen stars.[ii]

This chapter does not examine the textual and technical features of the documentary or biopic as a genre, except in so far as they are relevant to the understanding of the celebrity culture around the sports star.

Notable Subjects, Biopower, and the Conjunctural Economy

If the 'Angry Young Man' of yesteryear Bollywood iconized a specific kind of social hero whose merits included incorruptibility, patriotism, and personal courage, among others, the 'Talented Young Man' of the sports biopic is also a social hero today. Like the Angry Young Man, the Talented Young Man, who evolves into a sports star in the biopic, has a specific life plot. His ascent to sport stardom is attributed, or reduced, to individual qualities such as talent,

Pramod K. Nayar, *Sports, Celebrity, and the Sports Biopic* In: *Sports Studies in India*. Edited by: Meena Gopal and Padma Prakash, Oxford University Press. © Oxford University Press 2021.
DOI: 10.1093/oso/9780190130640.003.0023

SPORTS, CELEBRITY, AND THE SPORTS BIOPIC   323

commitment, and some luck.[iii] The biopic generates a particular meritocratic popular imaginary with this reductive life plot because it positions the sports star as a deserved recipient of his/her dedication to success.

The hagiographic biopic bestows a certain immortality upon the 'character' of the story. In addition, this immortality is also bestowed through the concentrated attention audiences bring to bear upon the figure. Murray Pomerance (2016: 30) writes:

> We participate to some degree in the experiences and events by virtue of which some other person has apparently become notable. We explore the notability that lingers in the story as a kind of shadow trace that follows the subject. The biopic subject is at once notable in objective terms, having become what he is; and notable dramaturgically, since the adoration of crowds is an ostensible component of the subject's story as recounted on the screen.

The notability of the subject is the effect of a dual discourse in the biopic. First, the sporting biopics, appropriating the public discourse around figures like Sachin Tendulkar, highlight their grandest achievements, which are presented as being nearly miraculous. 'Sachin's magic' was a commonly heard comment in connection with his batting, and M.S. Dhoni's great powers in finishing off a match to India's advantage was also often deemed miraculous in public discourse. When India won despite all odds, mainly due to Tendulkar's batting, it was described as a 'miracle'. Second, the biopic shows us what exactly—action, behaviour, achievement—has made the subject notable: Tendulkar practising in the rain on a squelching wicket is one of the more unforgettable scenes from his biopic. The biopic moves from the miraculous-magical to the *marvellous*, where the former is associated with the domain of the supernatural and the divine, and the latter with human wonders, or wondrous humans. If the first discourse renders the stars supernatural beings (Tendulkar, Dhoni, Milkha Singh), the second casts them as mortals endowed with extraordinarily amplified but decidedly human virtues: grit, endurance, determination, ambition. The biopic's rhetoric works at the level of both process and product, oscillating between the two, so that the sporting magic of a Tendulkar or a Dhoni is explained as the product of a strenuous but very *human* process. Further, in this shift from the miraculous to the marvellous, the biopic offers up an aspirational model for the rest of the nation, and *reframes* the marvellous as a success story that could serve as such a model.

This model success story explicitly instantiates a biopolitics when it focuses on the physical-corporeal dimension of this success, whether in terms of

324   MOVIES, MEDIA AND TECHNOLOGY

Singh's strict regimen of training or Tendulkar's commitment to practice sessions or their physical courage: injuries, stresses and strains, and crowd adulation (and rejections). Expectedly, images of sweaty bodies abound in these texts. We see Singh's muscles corded into tension as he jogs and Tendulkar practising in the rain, all suggesting *embodied* will power and determination. We see anxious and downcast expressions when they fail. The biopic, by focusing on embodiment, emphasizes that we are viewing *real* individuals. Tears, sweat, and blood are integral to the sports biopic as a means of underscoring what may be thought of as the corporeality of sporting success. As David Andrews and Steven Jackson (2001: 8) put it in their introduction to a volume on sport celebrities, 'Sport celebrity then becomes the assumed corollary of performative excellence.'

I suggest that the emphasis on biopower achieves two spectacular results. First, it makes the statement that the star's achievements are born of real physical effort that talent may be inhered in the body, but it has to be honed through rigorous training. Second, in sharp contrast to screen stars whose bodies acquire a magical aura in the Hindi film, the sports body is caught in uncertain situations and unpredictable sporting events and whose subsequent triumph is then attributable solely to their individual efforts. In other words, it is biopower rather than magic that defines the sports celebrity in the biopic.

Central to this rhetoric of biopower is the suggestion that the star's body is *transformative* and adaptable. The young boy fleeing Partition (Mehra 2013) or the scrawny curly-haired adolescent (Erskine 2017) growing up to conquer the world's track fields (Mehra 2013) and the cricket grounds (Erskine 2017). It is a perfectible body and hence implies that there is agency inhering in the body that has to be drawn out as power, skill, and endurance. I propose that the sports biopics, in mapping the transformation of Singh, Dhoni, and Tendulkar, participate in the public discourses of fashion, makeover, and celebrity TV by suggesting a form of self-fashioning. Ouellette and Hay (2008: 103) write about makeover TV shows:

[they] convey the idea that the quickest way to success is "strategic" self-fashioning, a practice that includes remaking one's body, personality and image in calculated ways to bring about personal advantage in a competitive marketplace.

SPORTS, CELEBRITY, AND THE SPORTS BIOPIC   325

I have elsewhere forwarded the argument about such programmes:

> Reality makeover TV is the drama of a transformation where real bodies
> become something else, where this 'something' is on the lines of what has
> become valued in that culture. Transformation TV reflects the cultural
> values of the time: what kind of looks are desirable and 'in', what clothing
> and accessories are current, places where these looks and clothes can be ac-
> quired, which experts to consult. (Nayar 2012: 169)

These biopics, made in retrospect, *after* the sterling careers of at least Singh
and Tendulkar, valorise hard work, training, and endurance, and thereby
might be read as the endorsement of a set of cultural values for the youth, and
perhaps their families, in India.

The result of this participation and endorsement of public discourses
around specific values is that the sports *person* becomes a sports *star*,
embodying in his (our 'heroes' are male in most of the biopics that have
appeared at the time of writing) self the qualities that the nation aspires to for
its youth. Thus, the sports star becomes a 'notable subject' as he demonstrates
his transformed, trained body out in the field, in full public view, and we see
in the biopics (with metaleptically inserted video, news, and other clips from
the original sporting event) the crowds surging to their feet, the chants (notably in Pandey [2016] and Erskine [2017]), and the adulation.

This is not the desirable body of the film star, although it is desirable in
another sense. Tendulkar's fitness seen in the merging of offscreen real with
onscreen representations, like that of Dhoni's powerful pulls and brilliant
running, do embody the ideal body but for a different set of reasons. Their
bodies are triumphal bodies, not in the same way as Shahrukh Khan's or
Ranveer Singh's—they are triumphal because they have conquered injuries,
defeats, and inimical conditions to attain victory on the battlefield of sports.
The body here represents power, skill, and training, and that is a different
order of beauty.

If a certain biopolitics of the sporting body plays out on the fields, the
same body is employed to generate a different order of meaning and cultural values. Tendulkar and then Dhoni promoted brands like Boost, Dabur
Chyawanprash, among others, and the entire cricket team supported a campaign from the National Egg Coordination Committee. These endorsements,
often portraying children, family, and the home, present the sports star as
a 'sign value . . . frequently attached to that of children and members of his
family . . . suggesting a kinder, gentler masculinity', as a commentator noted

326 MOVIES, MEDIA AND TECHNOLOGY

once of Michael Jordan in the American context (McDonald and Andrews 2001: 29). The sports star's body moves in signification from endorsing training, hard work, and commitment within the field of sports to endorsing health, energy, and growth within the field of the family. The sporting body remaining in sporting costume implies a recognizable continuity: It is the same sports star who can function effectively within a competitive arena and a familial space.

The biopics then ease into a discourse of social and economic mobility, again via the embodied sign of the sporting hero. The initial costs of equipment, travel, and training having been already emphasized in the case of Singh (who is shown running barefoot in the film because he does not possess appropriate footwear), Tendulkar, and Dhoni, the biopics show their upward social mobility. We are taken around their new homes, the camera pans across their fashionably turned out bodies now, their vehicles, and branded accessories—all gesturing at the sporting body as a commodity–consumer sign. (Ellis Cashmore [2004:196], in his study of David Beckham, has argued that stars like Beckham 'exist in a kind of parallel universe populated only by celebrities, all of whom are different from us'.) The social scene has also shifted, and the sports star is at the centre of a lot of adulatory attention at gatherings. Implicitly revealed in these representations of the freshly transformed, fashionable sporting body are the (desirable) qualities of the middle-class Indian (male) whose investment in work, training, and commitment has enabled social and economic mobility, and not just sporting success.

In short, the celebrity body of the sports star embodies fitness, health, training, suffering, skills, fashion, and success. It is the aspirational body of millions of Indian youth. But it also serves as a marker of the brand culture of the postmodern era. Therefore, the star body of a Dhoni or Tendulkar—Singh's career predates the era of heavy postmodern signage—literally serves as a cultural *and* commodity–consumer sign.[iv] The cultural sign, as argued above, embodies and signifies cultural values. The commodity sign, festooned in trademarks and logos but also endorsing various products, ensures their acceptance as embodiments of contemporary consumer culture. The acquisition of one (cultural value) cannot but lead to, the biopics imply, the acquisition of the other (commodity–consumer sign value). It is this conjunctural economy of the sports body that the biopic implicitly and explicitly emphasizes.[v]

SPORTS, CELEBRITY, AND THE SPORTS BIOPIC 327

The Biopic, the National Imaginary, and the Global

The sports biopic constructs a national identity. The genre, argues William Epstein (2016: 12), takes recourse to specific strategies of repetition and of the spectator's knowledge of the biographical subject's fate: We *all* know Tendulkar's career graph and Singh's unfortunate failure. This means the biopic entails a 'remythologizing' of the already well-known, heroic national figure (Epstein 2016:12).

Let us begin with Milkha Singh. The biopic clearly—perhaps even jingoistically—links his sporting success with national identity, especially highlighting his success against the Pakistani athlete Iqbal Khaliq (following which Pakistani general Ayub Khan gave Singh the epithet that still stands: 'the Flying Sikh'). His triumphs at the Asian Games and fourth-place finish at the Rome Olympics (1960) are all highlighted on screen in conjunction with three clear markers: Partition (in which Singh lost half his family); the tricolour flag; and the Indian Army (Singh's employer). Onscreen montages of Singh's (recreated and fictionalized) memories of Partition and its violence with the (real) newspaper clips of his triumphs, awards, and such do not for a minute allow us to see Singh as anything other than a national asset and a national icon. This same mode may be seen in Erskine (2017) and Pandey (2016). Even when the biopic turns the attention towards their families, friends, and social settings, we are not allowed to forget that these are primarily national heroes. Thus, the fictionalizing of Dhoni's family in the biopic shows them watching Dhoni play for India, implying that even his immediate family is invested in Dhoni not as their son but as a national hero and national hope. The neat anastomosis between Dhoni's or Tendulkar's family and the Indian nation in these biopics re-inscribes one into the other. The star's individual family is metonymic of the Indian nation *as* 'family', and the nation-as-family cheers Dhoni or Tendulkar as its scion. It becomes, therefore, difficult to determine where one family ends and the other begins, hence anastomosis .

The sports biopic generates, through strategies of memorializing and mythologizing, a certain *communitas* among the film's viewers. It appropriates and generates a 'strategic patriotic memory' (Epstein 2016). In this, the sports *biopic* is a civic ritual on par with sporting *events* that generates not necessarily a permanent community but a temporary communitas (Ingham and McDonald 2003: 28). Ingham and McDonald suggest that 'only the exceptional can provoke spontaneous *communitas*. But spontaneous *communitas* is fleeting and cannot form the basis for community per se.' While one

328 MOVIES, MEDIA AND TECHNOLOGY

concedes that such a communitas spontaneously flowers into existence during, say, an Indo-Pak cricket match, or the World Cup victories in T20, or any other format (the standard news report the next day would speak of crowds standing outside television [TV] showrooms to watch the match and thinner traffic as people left work early to watch it in their homes), such an explanation does not suffice. Spontaneously forming communitas do not necessarily lead to a more permanent, reliable, sense of a 'national community'.

Instead, perhaps, we can see a communitas built up around the sports celebrity as *potentiality*. In the 'coming community' (as Giorgio Agamben terms it), it is neither the singularity of identity nor universalism that constitutes being. That is, one cannot think of a community built around an essence, or essential identity, but neither can we build it around a homogenizing, universal commonality. It is 'neither particular nor universal' (Agamben 1993: 10). Instead, Agamben focuses on the 'communication of singularities' which 'does not unite them in essence, but scatters them in existence'. This might well be an 'inessential commonality'. While Agamben's self-conscious refusal to name a political project that would enable such a 'coming community' can, and is, frustrating to say the least, it gestures at something slightly different. The communitas and the coming community share this in common: an inessential commonality that could, for our purposes, well be sports and the sports celebrity. This star is not central to the quest for modernity or development or democracy. Scattered and singular instances of what Ingham and McDonald (2003), following Victor Turner, deem 'civic rituals' are instantiations of a communitas within which we can discern, even temporarily, the coming community. It could then be proposed that spontaneous celebrations across the geopolitical space, around the figure of the sports star, brings together people notionally under the sign of the nation. *Each* tournament victory, *each* Tendulkar century, *each* Dhoni rescue-mission at the wicket, is a celebratory singularity (one could perhaps make a similar case around high-order frauds and scams in India, from Bofors to Nirav Modi). Inessential to the idea of our polity but unavoidable as an instantiation of a commonality, sports stars are singularities that we wear as badges of national identity in an increasingly globalized world.

The sports star is, then, a part of the national imaginary, the national idiom and therefore of India's public culture. If Bollywood is a key constituent of the 'national symbolic' (as Lauren Berlant terms it), the Bollywood's sports biopic is an emergent subgenre within this symbolic. Dhoni, Singh, Tendulkar, Virat Kohli, P.V. Sindhu, Dhanraj Pillay, Viswanathan Anand, Narain Karthikeyan, Leander Paes constitute this national symbolic. They

SPORTS, CELEBRITY, AND THE SPORTS BIOPIC   329

accrue national sentiment, and with their ability to trigger the communitas among a diverse population (even when Sindhu loses to the world champion, the nation erupts in sorrow but also in admiration).

But to claim that Tendulkar and Dhoni are primarily national icons is to detract from their participation in the global corporate sports cultures. Their appearance in the World Cup, the Olympics, and other globally organized and televised events means that 'transnational events are populated—and indeed popularized—by a coterie of sport celebrity figures, acting as representative subjectivities of the national collective configurations with whom they are affiliated' (Silk, Andrews, and Cole 2005: 7). They are co-opted into the comity of the *world* sports regimes, as recognizable stars *and* as representatives of specific national cultures. Silk, Andrews, and Cole (2005: 7) write:

> [T]ransnational capital's encroachment into the symbolic orchestration of national cultures has usurped the productive role of modern political institutions. . . . The nation is thus corporatized, and reduced to a branded expression of global capitalism's commandeering of collective identity and memory.

India's insertion into the global community, driven by global branding, franchisee culture, and televised events, then, requires the presence of *branded* players as well, and Sindhu, Dhoni, and Tendulkar fit this bill. National identity at the global level is literally and figuratively embodied in the celebrity sports star. Even as India corporatizes its sports and sports stars (the premier leagues for cricket, football, and *kabbadi*; the sponsorships by Pepsi, Coca Cola; among others), the global brands appropriate the game for the world stage, once again proposing a communitas.[vi]

The biopics draw our attention to the Indian sportsperson performing at the global levels through various means. Footage from original matches and events and news clippings are a part of the biopics, as noted earlier. They are internal paratexts because, like extratextual elements (statistics, tables, or figures), they designate *additional* information. They 'extend, ramif[y], and modulate rather than comment on' the main text (Genette 1997: 321, 328). The paratexts constitute the documentary dimension of the biopic, a historical record of the sport star's life and social contexts. The clips and footage comment on and supplement the main text: the story being told of Tendulkar's or Dhoni's life. The documentary realism from the footage, then, merges with the aesthetic or artifactual (Michael Chaney [2007: 180–1] has argued that artifice and artefact in graphic biographies merge to produce an 'artifactuality'). The aesthetic is my equivalent of Chaney's 'artifice', and refers to the biographies of the sportsmen that need to be read alongside and into the documentary history of their country (India), of the sport itself, and the global packaging of that sport. If the aesthetic is the dramatization of an individual life, the documentary is the presentation of a socio-cultural condition. The documentary–aesthetic merger in the biopic is a metaleptic one: It forces us to move between and across narrative and temporal levels—the historical narrative (documentary) and the biographical narrative (the fictionalized, dramatized *story* of Tendulkar, Singh and Dhoni), and the autobiographical reminiscences (from the same characters, or their families, acquaintances, and so on).[vii] The global sporting event—the Rome Olympics with Singh, the World Cup victory with Tendulkar—delivered as documentary literally serves as the stage for the unfolding of India's star contribution to the event in the form of these bodies, and India's star sportspersons generate the world's interest in the global event.

The attention that Tendulkar, Dhoni, and now Sindhu obtain when travelling and playing abroad—at Lord's, Sharjah, Perth, Durban—imply what Aihwa Ong (1999) termed 'flexible citizenship' and what Michael Giardina (2001) appropriates in order to examine a transnational sports celebrity such as Martina Hingis. Giardina argues that such stars, through their global appearances; endorsements of global brands like Adidas, Reebok, and more recently Mars chocolate (Dhoni); and ambassadorships for global organizations such as the World Health Organization (WHO) position them within global circuits of wealth *and* social capital.[viii] This positioning then enables a flexible citizenship in relation to 'markets, governments and cultural regimes' (Ong, cited in Giardina 2001: 206).

Clearly, then, the biopics generate and draw upon a congeries of distinct yet conflationary processes of local stardom, biopolitical regimes, cultural regimes of meaning-making, the national symbolic and global corporatized sporting events. The local sportsperson is not a *celebrity* sportsperson until a global brand endorsement is visible in the form of apparel logos, participation in the global event/process (sporting events as well as cultural ambassadorships), and global visibility. Disentangling the local from the global becomes a messy but also unprofitable business because each feeds off the other. Sports culture may have once been local, and even national. The fact remains that the generating of a *national* pride demands cooperation in the form of telecasts by ESPN and *multinational* companies, events that are commented upon by a host of prominent *transnational* sports personalities (cricket commentators now include Mike Brearley, Wasim Raja, Ian Bishop,

SPORTS, CELEBRITY, AND THE SPORTS BIOPIC 331

the Waughs, and Michael Vaughan) from outside the national/geopolitical borders. Tendulkar, Dhoni, Singh, P.V. Sindhu, and other star sportspeople are at once the subject of national biopics, but the making of the biopics is a validation, ironically, of their global status as recognizable celebrities.

Biopics are integral to the sports culture industry and to celebrity cultures. They document lives but, in the doing so, draw attention to the processes through which lives become spectacles and aspirational models for a country. The transnationalization of local/regional/national celebrities enhances their local values and implies a two-way process between the national and the global.

Notes

i. Parts of this essay first appeared in the form of a review essay: Nayar, Pramod K. 2017. 'Biopics: The Year in India'. *Biography* 40 (4): 604–10.

ii. I am grateful to Padma Prakash for drawing my attention to this anomaly within sports stardom.

iii. There are fewer films about sports *women*, with a film on the celebrity boxer Mary Kom (Kumar 2014), being an exception, indicating a Bollywood bias towards the sports men.

iv. Prashant Kidambi (2011: 187) proposes that 'Tendulkar's image within Indian society makes him more than a frothy confection of the sport–media nexus'.

v. It should be noted that while the cultural sign value might be read as 'national', the commodity–consumer sign value is *global*, given the endorsements of global brands like Pepsi or Coca Cola. One could argue that the conjunctural economy embodied in the sports star's body is the conjunction of two economies: the national and the global. That figures like Tendulkar and Dhoni are global icons is of course a truism.

vi. Ellis Cashmore, in his study of David Beckham, has argued that English football itself becomes 'cosmopolitan' from the late 1980s and 1990s with the arrival of Ruud Gullit and Jürgen Klinsmann on the English league scene (2004: 17).

vii. I adapt here the arguments I made in Nayar (2016a).

viii. I have elsewhere examined the links between such ambassadorships, charity work, activism, and Bollywood stars' global celebrityhood and 'vernacular cosmopolitanism' that draw upon their local embeddedness but aligns these with global works (Nayar 2016b).

References

Agamben, G. 1993 [1990]. *The Coming Community*. Translated by M. Hardt. Minneapolis: University of Minnesota Press.

Andrews, David L. and Stephen L. Jackson. 2001. 'Introduction: Sport Celebrities, Public Culture, and Private Experience'. In David L. Andrews and Stephen L. Jackson (eds), *Sport Stars: The Cultural Politics of Sporting Celebrity*, pp. 1–19. London: Routledge.

Cashmore, Ellis. 2004. *Beckham*. Cambridge: Polity.

Chaney, Michael. 2007. 'Drawing on History in Recent African American Graphic Novels', *MELUS* 32 (3): 175–200.

Epstein, William H. 2016. 'Introduction: Strategic Patriotic Memories'. In William H. Epstein and R. Barton Palmer (eds), *Invented Lives, Imagined Communities: The Biopic and American National Identity*, pp. 1–21. Albany: State University of New York Press.

Erskine, James. 2017. *Sachin: A Billion Dreams*. 200 NotOut Productions.

Genette, Gerard. 1997. *Paratexts: Thresholds of Interpretation*, translated by Jane E. Lewin. Cambridge: Cambridge University Press.

Giardina, Michael D. 2001. 'Global Hingis: Flexible Citizenship and the Transnational Celebrity'. In David L. Andrews and Steven J. Jackson (eds), *Sport Stars: The Cultural Politics of Sporting Celebrity*, pp. 201–17. London and New York: Routledge.

Ingham, Alan G. and Mary G. McDonald. 2003. 'Sport and Community/*Communitas*'. In Ralph C. Wilcox, David L. Andrews, Robert Pitter, and Richard L. Irwin (eds), *Sporting Dystopias: The Making and Meaning of Urban Sport Cultures*, pp. 17–34. Albany: State University of New York Press.

Kidambi, Prashant. 2011. 'Hero, Celebrity and Icon: Sachin Tendulkar and Indian Public Culture'. In Anthony Bateman and Jeffrey Hill (eds), *The Cambridge Companion to Cricket*, pp. 187–202. Cambridge: Cambridge University Press.

Kumar, Omung (dir). 2014. *Mary Kom*. Viacom18 Motion Pictures.

McDonald, Mary G. and David L. Andrews. 2001. 'Michael Jordan: Corporate Sport and Postmodern Celebrityhood'. In David L. Andrews and Steven J. Jackson (eds), *Sport Stars: The Cultural Politics of Sporting Celebrity*, pp. 20–35. London and New York: Routledge.

Mehra, Rakeysh Omprakash (dir). 2013. *Bhaag Milkha Bhaag*. 2013. ROMP.

Nayar, Pramod K. 2012. *Digital Cool: Life in the Age of New Media*. Hyderabad: Orient Black Swan.

———. 2016a. 'Radical Graphics: Martin Luther King., Jr, B.R. Ambedkar and Comics Auto/Biography', *Biography* 39 (2): 146–71.

———. 2016b. 'Brand Bollywood Care: Celebrity, Charity, and Vernacular Cosmopolitanism', in P. David Marshall and Sean Redmond (eds), *The Blackwell Companion to Celebrity*, pp. 273–87. Malden, MA: Wiley.

———. 2017. 'Biopics: The Year in India'. *Biography* 40 (4): 604–10.

Ong, Aihwa. 1999. *Flexible Citizenship: The Cultural Logics of Transnationality*. Durham: Duke University Press.

Ouellette, Laurie and James Hay. 2008. *Better Living Through Reality TV: Television and Post-Welfare Citizenship*. Malden, MA: Wiley-Blackwell.

Pandey, Neeraj (dir). 2016. *M.S. Dhoni: The Untold Story*. Fox Star Studios.

Pomerance, Murray. 2016. 'Empty Words: Houdini and Houdini'. In William H. Epstein and R. Barton Palmer (eds), *Invented Lives, Imagined Communities: The Biopic and American National Identity*, pp. 25–48. Albany: State University of New York Press.

Silk, Michael L., David L. Andrews, and C.L. Cole. 2005. 'Corporate Nationalism(s)?: The Spatial Dimensions of Sporting Capital'. In Michael L. Silk, David L. Andrews, and C.L. Cole (eds), *Sport and Corporate Nationalisms*, pp. 1–12. Oxford: Berg.

23

Breaking into the Press Box and After

A First-Person Account[*]

Sharda Ugra

In the rolling, roiling news universe, the sports beat is considered low down the food chain. Its journalism has always been, for the most part, emotional, celebratory, and uplifting. The significance of its words and pictures are more symbolic than far-reaching. Sport is the stuff of fun and games, the impact of athletic victories and defeats ephemeral to humankind. Orwell's (1945) metaphor of 'war minus the shooting' is accurate—usually, while fostering tribalism, sport does not destroy lives in its wake. As proof of the nobility of sports and its journalism, every jock will cite the words of the US Supreme Court chief justice Earl Warren (quoted in *SportsMediaGuy* 2015), 'I always turn to the sports section first. The sports page records people's accomplishments; the front page has nothing but man's failures.' More prosaically, in some Australian newspapers, for example, I have been told the sport desk is casually referred to as the establishment's 'toy department'.

Yet it is in the lightness of leisure that peoples and societies find the masks that accompany their studied selves slipping away. Often sport is where they, in fact, we, inadvertently hold a mirror to ourselves.

In the three decades I have spent as a sports journalist, Indian sport has revealed itself in slow layers. Its drive and its hierarchies, its generosities and its insularities, its quirks and its limitations, its purpose and its striving. The stories around Indian sport, however, rarely follow the happy arc of the sports movie with perfect endings tied in. It takes a lifetime of work to understand the fractures and failings in Indian sport and then make peace with that fact itself. Industry veterans with years on the job are commonly described as being 'hardened', 'jaded', and 'cynical'. What is less known is that it is possible, thirty years on, to go into a working day anticipating a regular miracle. To

---

[*] I would like to express my gratitude for and thanks to Priyanka Shankar for recording and transcribing a conversation that framed the broad outlines and content of this chapter.

Sharda Ugra, *Breaking into the Press Box and After* In: *Sports Studies in India*. Edited by: Meena Gopal and Padma Prakash, Oxford University Press. © Oxford University Press 2021.
DOI: 10.1093/oso/9780190130640.003.0024

BREAKING INTO THE PRESS BOX AND AFTER   335

know that you will still be uplifted by sport, Indian sport - around an unexpected corner, by a split second act of athletic brilliance or the studied,
tread towards a destination which while never yours, once reached, is going
to be owned by a multitude. Like the Abhinav Bindra gold medal at the 2008
Beijing Olympics, for example. For an Indian sports journalist embedded in
the ecosystem, the longer their career, the more this will happen—fitfully,
yes, but always gratifying.

Early Years

As the first woman to be hired full-time on the sports desk of an Indian newspaper (*Mid-Day*, in Bombay [now Mumbai] in November 1989), work life
began being an oddity along with learning on the job. As time passed, it became, without deliberate purpose, an opportunity to become an anthropologist observing my tribe: a vantage point to observe 'patrons, players, and the
crowd' (in tribute to the title of Richard Cashman's book [1980]).

In retrospect, I realized that sports had been perhaps the last male bar-
ricade in journalism. Decades ago, women journalists had fought hard and
bitter battles and stood their ground: for the right to do night shifts on copy
desks and for reporting duties in beats like politics, business, strategic affairs,
science, and crime—beats considered 'serious' and, therefore, only capable
of being comprehended and handled by men. The rights of women, tribals,
and Dalits; environment; wildlife; and development were considered 'soft' issues, where women appeared to find themselves 'better suited'. Only now is it
acknowledged that more is understood about politics and business in these
'development' beats than in their specialized, often blinkered domains.

In the 1990s, sport journalism remained the final frontier for women. It
was a male preserve, its ethos was tied in with history, heritage, inaccessi-
bility, a complex web of rules, and the science—and art—of every sport's
internal architecture, the constant reassurance in a changing world of the sacred space of boys' toys. The complex relationship of women and sport began
to play itself out only in the post-Victorian age in the Western world, but the
journalism around it also remained 'Boy's Own'.[i]

The presence of women as participants and fans was far from common in
Indian sport. As I grew up in the 1970s, India sent only one female athlete to
two Olympic Games (1972, 1976) in that decade, the redoubtable Kamaljit
Sandhu (Munich 1972). Prior to that, in seventy years of India's Olympic participation (1900–70), a total of seven women participated in the Games and

only three between the years 1952 and 1980.[ii] The first time India's Olympic contingent had women athletes in double digits was in 1980. There were sixteen: two athletes and fourteen players on the hockey team. (The next time the number of women reached double digits was twenty years later, in 2000). As I went through high school and college, the career of the greatest female athlete in Indian sport was playing itself out in the background: P.T. Usha, athletic trailblazer.

Female fans were hard to spot in events in India as well. The sight of a stand full of Pakistani women during India's 1979 cricket tour across the border, was a visual of wonder. We consumed our sport mostly on television (TV), devoured in print through newspapers and magazines, (three weeklies in English at the time) and only very sporadically actually watched it live at a venue. But if you loved sport and words, what could you do other than be drawn obsessively to both and remain there, knowing that you could not abandon either? For me, that meant being 'realistic', that is, setting the sport aside in order to make a career in words and doing something, I had hoped in the business of journalism and writing.

Sport is not a beat that people fall into after dabbling in others; its entrants usually are hard-core sports fans. I grew up in a Bombay suburb, in a housing complex of flats inhabited by the employees of an engineering company, which had open spaces, two fields, a badminton court and swimming pool, and a company of children of varied ages to play with and against. It gave me an appetite for sport, the pre-requisite condition needed for being drawn towards sports journalism. The writing and reporting skills are acquired in the trenches.

I entered sports journalism due to a fortituous set of circumstances, thanks to an advertisement for a sports reporter in Bombay's then popular afternoon tabloid *Mid-Day*. It was a job vacancy advertised, as it rarely is, in the business. My theory is that at the time, *Mid-Day's* editor Anil Dharker offered me the job out of curiosity and the fact that my curriculum vitae (CV) also contained a set of interviews with some of the biggest names in cricket in the 1980s. The pieces had been published by *Mid-Day's* rival, the *Afternoon Despatch & Courier* (ADC), after a friend Ramola Talwar (now a journalist at *The National* in Dubai) had this hare-brained idea: trying to interview the charismatic Imran Khan passing through Bombay in 1987. A third cricket fan among us friends, Shaziya Khan (now a high-ranking advertising professional at J. Walter Thompson [JWT, now Wunderman Thompson]), completed the team. Imran had obliged three college students; ADC had published the interview. With the Reliance World Cup being held in India that year, we went on an interview rampage of sorts over the next two years: seven cricket stars from around the world had found their way into the tabloid.

The absurd novelty of this enterprise and the timing of the advertisement may have been reason I was given a chance, a foot through the door. At the time, sports journalism was a tight-knit brotherhood, and not just on the fields of play or in press boxes. Vacancies were usually known word of mouth; people moved around jobs through this grapevine. Who knew how else people were otherwise hired without advertisements other than inside-track knowhow or personal recommendation. This is why the *Mid-Day* advertisement stood out. I wish I had kept the clipping.

It was November 1989, and I have made it a personal boast that Sachin Tendulkar and I made our professional debuts at the same time. The Internet had not arrived in India yet, and sports journalism was fairly formulaic: the morning papers did reports, resembling bald wire-service facts, with a little colour and flourish. Mumbai's afternoon papers were an oddity and my task was to look for an 'angle' that would not be found in the morning papers. This meant seeking out athletes, the 'performer of the day', to find out their point of view on the day's performance or finding an official to comment on goof-ups, controversies, or a sign of progress made with longer features for the Sunday paper.

Many years down the line, I began to be asked what it was like being the first woman into the mancave and what the obstacles were that I faced. What I remember most clearly was the divided response to my presence: officials and athletes were perplexed but polite, helpful, curious. One section of older journalists treated my presence with cold silence and ignored it completely, not for weeks or months, but years. Young men in their first jobs who were in my own age group were my comrades in story-anxiety: We were anxious, eager, and wanted to make a mark. A smaller handful of senior pros were amused, courteous, and helpful. The biggest strength was the support from my employers and colleagues: *Mid-Day* was a small city paper known for its irreverent approach, and its young and irreverent staff.

This does not mean that there was no disparagement of my gender in a largely male business, but it came through only in a series of 'Chinese whispers', never directly communicated to me. Usually, it was doubt over my 'genuine' interest in sport and knowledge about the 'technicalities', far too-unfathomable for the feminine gender. Think of it as a further dumbing down of an already dumbed-down lazy trope about why there are fewer women in maths, science, and technology.

338   MOVIES, MEDIA AND TECHNOLOGY

When *Mid-Day* hired two more women sports reporters, a media columnist in a weekly newsmagazine chose to write about the novelty and then produce a head-patting misquote. When asked whether I understood cricket intricacies like the leg-before-wicket (LBW) rule and the techniques of batting, I said that while I did understand the LBW rule, I was not about to give Dilip Vengsarkar tips about his batting. In the article, I was quoted as saying I did *not* understand the LBW rule and was not going to give Vengsarkar tips about batting!

There lay the proof of what was meant to settle the ultimate male argument—that women were not really cut out for the sports beat. We did not understand the finer points of sports technique; we were drawn to it by the glamour and its glamour boys. Women sports journalists were, as the general drift went, groupies in disguise. What helped me at the time was putting on a set of blinkers and staying tone deaf, seeking neither validation nor approval from my colleagues. If there were teams to be picked in my early innings as sports reporter, I picked my employers. The folk who paid the salary sent me on exciting assignments around the country and the world (to a cricket event in Sharjah within two years of the job; Wimbledon in three) and provided both praise and criticism. My employers, to use a trendy colloquialism, had my back.

A Champion

In the early 1990s, for reasons that remain unknown, more women began to come into sports journalism in India. There were soon four of us in Bombay and we saw female bylines on the sports pages of English newspapers in Delhi, Calcutta (now Kolkata), Bangalore (now Bengauru), and Chennai. This was a decade before the Internet and two before mobile phones and social media. So we could not speak to each other, read each others' writing frequently, or meet often. But we knew we were not alone and that we were not oddities but a minority that changed the composition of press boxes. It caused some degree of alarm in the sports universe: 'Can you let the girl in if someone wants to give a post-game interview in a dressing room with males clad only in towels? Suppose it made the men uncomfortable?'; 'Where is closest toilet for women? Is there one at all?'. Around the early 2000, an article appeared in an obscure magazine seeking to bust the 'myth' of women sports reporters stating that they were being hired as tokens, were far from serious beat reporters, could only produce 'soft' features, and were doing well professionally only because of their way with words and not because of a deep knowledge of sports and/or analytical ability. The byline at the top of the article read 'Anonymous', surely a man who did not have the courage to write his name!

There is a very good chance that many women were drawn to cricket as players and fans, like the men, due to the euphoria following the India's 1983 World Cup victory. In June 1983, I was fourteen, a way-below-average recreational competitor, and most of the first wave of Indian women sports journalists was two to five years younger than me. As much as 1983 may have made a ripple in our lives, I think of us as P.T. Usha's generation: the woman who broke the boundaries of what Indian women could do on the track. Usha, who caused a ruckus due to her speed and her no-fuss consistency of performance. P.T. Usha showed what she was made of in the times she clocked and the medals she won. People remember her fourth-place finish at the Los Angeles 1984. But what is not celebrated enough is the number of medals she won in international races of many kinds all over the world: 102! No one has done it before or since.

We could not have had a greater champion.

Today, sports journalism in India is not widely represented by women, but our presence, in the English-language media particularly, is a given: either in the news industry, be it print or digital, or on television as reporters, broadcasters, analysts, commentators. The numbers grew slowly and the younger generation of women reporters for television were far less retiring than I had been in my early years, willing to put themselves on the frontlines of the judgementalism.

The biggest growth of women sports journalists in print and digital has taken place in the English-language media. While there is certainly a bigger and more visible language spread across TV, women sports journalists writing in regional languages tend to be smaller in number. It is language itself that separate them from their larger sisterhood. It can be recorded, though, that on a rough reckoning, there is a certainly a presence of women sports journalists writing in Bengali, Hindi, and Marathi, albeit in very small numbers. The response of regional language newsrooms to the presence of women writing on sport will require greater investigation. I have heard stray cases of opposition to women in sports reporting from their senior peers in Marathi publications, which came with a familiar soundtrack, 'What does she know about sport?', with its silent subtext, 'Who does she think she is?'.

The world around us, though, has changed from the time I began. This is not only related to an increase in the number of women entering Indian sports journalism. I attempted to calculate a ball-park figure of Indian women sports journalists in the written media and the best number I could guess across the country would only be between thirty and forty, including freelancers and bloggers. The presence of women in television, however, is much larger.

There are cases of women sports journalists leaving the beat after being blackballed by their older male colleagues or due to family responsibilities. What I hear from younger women now is sobering. Whatever lines of formal conduct may have been established by the mores of the time when I entered the profession, they are now blurred. Regardless of their own professional conduct, Indian women sports journalists find themselves more of a target of unwanted attention or dismissive commentary both from athletes themselves and others in the sports industry.

In the first ten seasons of the highly popular Indian Premier League (2008–17), cricket TV institutionalized the 'women as eye candy' phenomenon in its programming. The signing of four women commentators in 2016 marked a shift in the production philosophy of the IPL (see Ugra 2016), but the sports television industry and social media that it spawns continues to normalize sexism and misogyny. An anonymous #MeToo survey about harassment or discrimination starting with Indian sports television and moving across wider sports media would perhaps reveal more maltreatment than can be imagined.

Sports Non-profits and Media

Young entrants into Indian sports journalism will always find themselves craving a beloved 'beat' of a sport they love. In India, that happens to be cricket. Naturally, there is a glut in the cricket media, and the newcomer, if given the opportunity at the start, must find a niche for themselves and make their presence felt amidst the large volume of noise that India's favourite sport generates. Should they be told that cricket is a full house, the newcomer then must adapt themselves to a vast choice of the sport available. In the 1990s, the pecking order of sports-beat choices available to young reporters apart from cricket was: tennis or hockey, other Olympic sports, football, and golf.

Outside of the general, wider boundaries of covering a sport—reportage of events and athletic interviews—hindsight shows two trends.

Cricket flexed the power of the market and the force of personality of its biggest stars. Other disciplines appeared to demonstrate, the power of the use of power, both institutional and governmental. A journalist will find that the people controlling the levers of the power—sports officials and government bureaucrats—also control the narrative and, in many cases, the career of its best practitioners too. Earlier, the reasons for India's failure to make their mark in Olympic disciplines or at other international events were squarely placed on the Indian athlete. The sports' administration hid behind a firewall of clichés—lack of talent, limited ambition, no 'killer instinct', even vegetarianism, and a recalcitrant ministry in Delhi. The athletes themselves put it down to official apathy, lack of funding, opportunity, and/or expertise.

The story repeated itself every four years between Olympics. Working in Mumbai, it may have been hard for a young idealist to accept but it was the only 'truth' that was being 'told'. Moving to Delhi in 2000 to work for *India Today* magazine took me closer to the undercarriage of Indian sport and gave me a chance to examine its working parts. I found that Indian sports administrators, like those around the world, used 'autonomy' as a fig leaf to cover up demands for transparency or good governance. Political patronage across party lines had fed off Indian sport. Amongst Olympic disciplines, those patrons rode for decades the gravy train that spent public money with no questions asked. For the patrons, sport was not core activity; it was a means of holding on to power.

The situation has changed considerably as is reflected in the narrative that is now in play around Indian sport. In the past, Olympic sports administrators could control the access of Indian journalists to global multidiscipline events like the Olympic Games or Asian Games by controlling access to media accreditation for these events. The chances of getting to those Games could be made difficult for those outside the circle of favour. Access to say football World Cup accreditation, with India's negligible presence at the event, could be cut off for a small publication that exposed the functioning of footballing bodies in their state. Alternatively, journalists in the circle of favour of administrators were rewarded by free trips that are part of the global gravy train of Olympic sports.

Cricket happened to be a lot more lenient with its critics, except column inches of newspaper and space on websites were used and are still being used to fight internal political battles between individuals. It has led to the creation of what is colloquially called the 'Board of Control for Cricket in India (BCCI) beat' in cricket, where journalists must choose between objectively judging opposing views or taking dictation from one side. The demand through legal intervention for the professionalization of cricket administration, spread evenly until now between politicians, businessmen, and bureaucrats, is proving hard for the conventional powerbrokers to accept.

Over the last decade, an overall administrative failure in Indian Olympic sport witnessed the creation of an intermediary of the kind not found elsewhere in the world. Sporting non-profits today work with elite Indian athletes as a bridge between the establishment, their national federations, and the fund-providing sports ministry. To sports journalists, their emergence became a crash course on how athletic excellence can be achieved. The sports non-profits—Olympic Gold Quest (formed 2001), Mittal's Champions Trust (2003, now defunct), Go Sports Foundation (2008), Anglian Medal Hunt (2012), and JSW Sport (2013)—began to do what the national federations should have always done: Place the athlete at the centre of attention and provide support in finance, training, competitions, medical attention, and rehabilitation. Their arrival has spelt a shift in the route through which athletes and their sport could be accessed. It has meant more sport, more success, more champions, more stories. For a sports journalist, it is gold dust!

Sports journalism in India is undergoing a quiet but distinct evolution. Online media has created room for a variety of journalism free of the shackles of the entrenched voices and rules of engagement of conventional sources of information. A wider range of sport and a deeper range of subjects are now being covered by a new generation of journalists. They are operating outside the constricted borderlines of 'focus on the game' trope. They could be the foot soldiers of beat reporting, looking for a new storyline, gutsy freelancers willing to challenge accepted notions, or editors looking out for a nuanced understanding of the dynamics of Indian sport. Even as social media increases the volume and spread of what is seen or heard about India's athletes, drawing the market towards them, the growing breed of younger Indian sports journalists are willing to go deeper into examining the diverse knots—gender, region, class, caste, power, and patronage—that Indian sport is entangled in. A website called Nation of Sport (https://www.nationofsport.com/) was set up in July 2016, self-funded by two thirty-somethings, one a sport professional and one an ad film director, with the purpose of encouraging long-form writing focused on Indian sport.

Why Cover Sports?

I will return to the question put to me by the editors of this volume: whether sports journalism is the last resort for new entrants into the profession. For the majority of Indian sports journalists, male or female, it is safe to say that sports journalism is not the last but often the first resort, our first choice. It is, for many of us, the dream job. When we land that dream job, it is as if the heavens have tossed a magic morsel our way. How we consume it, how we digest everything we are made to taste, and how long it fills us is up to us.

This is because no matter how successful or unsuccessful our careers may go onto be or how satisfied we are about them, majority of sports journalists in India, maybe even everywhere in the world, enter the profession as fans. Over the years, when the stardust begins to fade away and the gilt begins to chip, it is then that our love for sport at large is tested. What was that 'love of sport' about: the individual athlete who drew us into the sport, who retired, walked away from the centre stage, and gave us flashes of their feet of clay? Or the sport itself, one sport, another sport or all sport, the unique singularity of competition that they presented us with – against an opponent, against the elements, against one's self? For some, it is through our profession, our vocation, our calling, that we find ourselves. As our heroes come and go, it is through our jobs that we come to discover what is that which gets us going. It is through our work that we come of age.

Notes

i. This is a reference to a UK publication that was known to young readers through the 1970s and 1980s, even though its last date of publication was 1964. It was called *The Boy's Own Paper*.
ii. http://www.olympedia.org/countries/IND; accessed on 25 May 2018.

References

Cashman, Richard. 1980. *Patrons, Players, and the Crowd: The Phenomenon of Indian Cricket*. New Delhi: Orient Longman.

Orwell, George. 1945. 'The Sporting Spirit'. *Orwell.ru*. Available at http://www.orwell.ru/library/articles/spirit/english/e_spirit; accessed on 10 June 2018.

SportsMediaGuy. 2015. 'https://www.sportsmediaguy.com/blog/2015/7/15/earl-warrens-view-of-the-sports-page', 15 July. Available at https://www.sportsmediaguy.com/blog/2015/7/15/earl-warrens-view-of-the-sports-page; accessed on 10 June 2018.

Ugra, Sharda. 2016. 'Girls Aloud: Or How the IPL Is Redefining Television Commentary'. *Cricket Monthly*, June. Available at http://www.thecricketmonthly.com/story/1013165/girls-aloud; accessed on 10 May 2018.

24

State, Market, and Media in Indian Cricket

Avipsu Halder

India's economic liberalization redefined the contours of state functioning and state–market interplay. In the domain of global cricket, state and market forces operate both independently and interdependently. The ramifications of India's integration with the world economy can be effectively examined in the game of cricket. This chapter examines how the logic of economic liberalization in India has influenced the trajectory of broadcasting of international cricket and how governance of cricket has been affected by the state- and national-level political dynamics.

Broadcasting Cricket: The Tug of War

Prior to the opening up of the Indian economy and the entry of foreign interests, public broadcasters (Doordarshan [DD] and All India Radio [AIR]) were entirely responsible for taking cricket to the public (Wagg 2018: 95). As the public broadcasting agency enjoyed monopoly in the realm of sports broadcasting, the Board of Control for Cricket in India (BCCI) had no other options. However, post liberalization, the scenario changed with the emergence of private broadcasters.

The Hero Cup was a five-nation international cricket tournament, in which, apart from the host nation, India, teams from South Africa, West Indies, Sri Lanka, and Zimbabwe featured. It was organized to mark the diamond jubilee of the Cricket Association of Bengal (CAB). In 1993, DD demanded payment from the CAB for telecasting the matches (Majumdar 2018: 105). However, the organizing authority sold the broadcasting rights to Trans World International (TWI), a private broadcaster. This meant that DD did not have absolute rights to telecast cricket within the country any longer. Doordarshan was forced to consider a collaborative venture with an

Avipsu Halder, *State, Market, and Media in Indian Cricket* In: *Sports Studies in India*. Edited by: Meena Gopal and Padma Prakash, Oxford University Press. © Oxford University Press 2021.
DOI: 10.1093/oso/9780190130640.003.0025

346 MOVIES, MEDIA AND TECHNOLOGY

alien firm (Majumdar 2018: 103). It responded by citing the Indian Telegraph Act of 1885, arguing that televising cricket by a foreign broadcaster violated the law (Mehta 2010: 159). Doordarshan even boycotted the broadcasting of the matches of the Hero Cup. However, the standpoint of the CAB cannot be completely repudiated. Having a private broadcaster definitely bolstered the chances of commercialization of cricket. Moreover, it helped in generating revenues for the organization. As the Indian government had already invited private players in other domains of the economy, why should cricket be an exception?

Interestingly enough, DD did not conform with the broader logic of the Indian state. The public broadcaster was aware that it did not possess the necessary equipment and know-how to compete with private sporting channels. However, the CAB was eager to break the deadlock and proposed certain options for negotiation. It suggested that DD become the host creator, so that it would have the right to broadcast all the matches. However, the television (TV) right to telecast the Hero Cup worldwide would remain with the foreign broadcasting entity. In other words, the CAB was trying to maintain its autonomy pertaining to media rights of the tournament. Moreover, the CAB was not pleased with the fee offered by DD. It was suggested that TWI and DD should carry out the responsibility for televising the matches of the competition in their respective capacities. Both parties were to exchange signals with one another (Majumdar 2004: 371–2). However, with little positive response from DD, the CAB finalized its deal with TWI. Doordarshan, on the other hand, was in no mood to accept the situation.

Trans World International remained unaffected by this controversy. It was looking forward to entering the realm of sport broadcasting in the subcontinent. It approached the Videsh Sanchar Nigam Limited (VSNL) for requisite administrative clearances. The VSNL readily agreed to cooperate with TWI (Mehta 2010: 160). In addition, the Ministry of Finance approved TWI's plea to import its own equipment and gadgets required for covering the cricket matches (Majumdar 2004: 374). The Ministry of Home Affairs was also supportive. Not only did it give official clearance for the coverage of the matches but also approved the use of walkie-talkies inside the stadium (Majumdar 2018: 105). In sum, it was only the broadcasting department that opposed these moves that brought in a foreign player in broadcasting. The dispute had wider ramifications in cricket. The National Cricket Board of South Africa was sceptical about the telecasting possibility of the Hero Cup matches. It was apprehensive about supporting the subcontinent's bid for the hosting the 1996 Cricket World Cup (Majumdar 2018: 109).

In the global realm, it is difficult to carve out any compartmentalization between the domestic and the international. Both are enmeshed with one another (Risse-Kappen 1995: 29). Changes in one stimulates a spill-over effect on the other. In order to respond to the exigencies of globalization, it becomes imperative for states to revisit their functional dynamics. The essence of these arguments gets reflected in the verdict of the Indian judiciary on cricket broadcasting.

Eventually, the broadcasting dispute between the CAB and DD was referred to the Calcutta (now Kolkata) High Court and to the Supreme Court of India. The judicial authorities adjudicated that the government should provide assistance to the CAB and TWI so that the matches of the Hero Cup could be conducted smoothly. The Calcutta High Court also formally appealed to the Department of Telecommunication to issue a license to TWI. Importantly, the Court enunciated that both Doordarshan and Star TV (which bought the rights from TWI) could telecast the Hero Cup matches (Mascarhenas 1997: 22).

In this case, the judicial arm of the state played a balancing role in resolving the rift between the private and the public domain. By acting as a facilitator of the private players, it underlined the spirit of liberalization. On the other hand, it did not repudiate the significance of DD. This brings out an interesting understanding of the Indian state. Even though market forces have become more influential than ever before (Harvey 2005: 65), the state continues to wield considerable influence. It acts both as a catalyst for and a regulator of market forces (Weiss 2003: 8, 17). The decision of the apex judicial authority of the country ensured that neither TWI nor DD would create hindrances for one another. The private broadcaster must operate in conformity with the national law of the country (Majumdar 2004: 384). By allowing the private and public entities to televise cricket matches, the interest of both the people from the affluent middle class and those belonging to the lower rungs of the social hierarchy had been addressed. The judiciary's decision extrapolates a degree of inclusiveness.

There have been three similar such occasions where the contentious issue of cricket broadcasting has resurfaced: the India–West Indies bilateral cricket series of 1994; the Cricket World Cup of 1996; and the India–Pakistan friendship series of 2004. Economic liberalization has been pivotal in championing the case of interdependence between the state and the market forces (Sen Narayan 2014: 209). The BCCI entered into a contract with ESPN (a foreign sport broadcasting agency) empowering it to provide unhindered coverage of all matches to be played in India. However, the Ministry of Information

348 MOVIES, MEDIA AND TECHNOLOGY

and Broadcasting opposed the growing pre-eminence of private entities. This served to worsen its relations with the VSNL as the latter was inclined to assist the private broadcasters. On the other hand, ESPN was also unhappy with its public counterparts. Once again, the intervention of the judiciary became inevitable. Adjudicating on the broadcasting of India–West Indies cricket series, the Indian Supreme Court enunciated that it was unfair on the part of public broadcasters to claim absolute right over satellite links. Once again, the decision revealed the indispensability of the market forces (Mehta 2010: 162). As a process, economic liberalization in India was becoming irreversible.

The BCCI's drive towards commercialization of cricket was the prime cause of concern for DD. The 2004 India–Pakistan 'friendship series' is a case that illustrates this. In this case, Ten Sports owned the telecasting rights. Doordarshan argued that the significance of 'Indo-Pak' cricketing ties stretched beyond the sporting domain. It underlined the deeper political and diplomatic relationship between the two countries (Bandyopadhyay 2008: 1661). Thus, DD appealed to Ten Sports to share the satellite feeds, citing noble ideals of national interest. The real objective underlying the proposal was to obtain commercial benefits by attracting more advertising. Doordarshan was aware of the economic potential of the series. Ten Sports approached the Supreme Court complaining against DD's move. The Court adjudicated in favour of the private channel. Its decisions directed DD to make necessary arrangements to ensure that Ten Sport did not suffer commercial losses. Moreover, the judiciary ordered DD to carry the symbol of the private sports channel while televising the matches (Mehta 2010: 162).

However, the fate of cricketing ties between India and Pakistan is determined more by political factors than economic ones. A favourable political climate and satisfactory security arrangements are mandatory for the conduct of cricket matches between these two nations. The politico-administrative wing of the state assumes great importance. Despite the growing importance of the economic domain, the relevance of security has not waned. This highlights the fact that the conventional functions of the state continue to persist even in the globalized context of a sport. In a similar vein, providing internal security remains the sole prerogative of its administrative apparatus (Beland 2010: 176).

The story of the 1996 Cricket World Cup is even more fascinating. Political hostility in Sri Lanka posed a security problem for the organizers. Matters became complex when national teams of Australia and West Indies cited security reasons for not playing in Sri Lanka (Wagg 2018: 147). Besides, disputes

STATE, MARKET, AND MEDIA IN INDIAN CRICKET   349

arose over ownership of media rights. The Indian Ministry of Information and Broadcasting was not willing to cooperate with an alien broadcaster as it might jeopardize the country's national security. Doordarshan wanted to be the sole broadcaster for the tournament, but it was hard to rule out the claims of the private sports telecasting units like WorldTel. The ice was broken when DD and WorldTel together agreed to televise the 1996 Cricket World Cup (Mascarhenas 1997: 22–3).

These cases depict India's experience in the globalized economy. As a measure to promote economic openness, the Indian state has revoked the legislations, such as the Monopolistic and Restrictive Trade Practice (MRTP) Act and the Foreign Exchange Regulation Act (FERA), which were meant to regulate private industry (Chandrasekhar and Ghosh 2000: 122). These norms were regressive in character. The state has subsequently eagerly promoted public–private partnership and cumbersome bureaucratic processes have been done away with. The post-liberalization era regards unnecessary administrative formalism as an impediment to effective governance. The Indian state has viewed privatization in a positive light. Private and the public domains have acted simultaneously (Mathur 2013: 167–8). However, the attitude of DD and the Ministry of Information and Broadcasting underlines the case of unhealthy competition. They have viewed the private sports broadcasters with suspicion. The idea of a win-win situation seems to have skipped their vision. The public broadcasters have visualized the commercial gains and losses in relative terms. Thus, their line of action has considerably deviated from the larger ideals of the government. The political economy of cricket broadcasting in India shows that different arms of the government bear somewhat contradictory opinions on economic liberalization.

From the outset, cricket shared a close link with the corridors of power. In the post colonial era, similar trends may be observed. The political and the economic elites have shown interest in managing the game. The involvement of central ministers, such as Sharad Pawar and Lalu Prasad Yadav, lends weight to this argument (Astill 2013: 89; Gemmell 2018: 203). On the other hand, eminent business personalities, such as Jagmohan Dalmiya, Lalit Modi, and N. Srinivasan, have emerged as cricket administrators at the national level (Astill 2013: 91–2).

Although the BCCI is a non-public organization, the configuration of national politics in the functioning of the organization is undeniable. The story of state-level cricket organizations is somewhat similar. It may not be incorrect to regard them as 'quasi-state' organizations. Despite having autonomy in their respective domains, these organizations reflect the broader interests

350 MOVIES, MEDIA AND TECHNOLOGY

of the existing political regime. The intervention of the state apparatus in the realm of cricket governance is not explicit. It is done selectively and tacitly. Cricket has become a new theatre for national and state level politics. The rivalry between Pawar and Dalmiya substantiates this point. It intensified over the control of the BCCI. The former possessed considerable political clout, while Dalmiya's contribution in commercializing cricket in India cannot be ignored (Srinivas 2014: 55).

Eventually, this translated into proxy political rivalry. The CAB elections of 2005 provided an ideal platform. The chief minister of West Bengal, Buddhadeb Bhattacharya, openly campaigned against Dalmiya. Bhattacharya backed his own candidate Prasun Mukherjee for the post of the CAB president. The West Bengal chief minister drew wide support from many of his Communist Part of India (Marxist) (CPI [M]) party members (Majumdar 2009: 131). Both camps took recourse to political muscle flexing for achieving their desired ends. The state government issued a directive according to which the district sports associations were to be represented either by the district magistrate or police superintendent of their respective jurisdiction. The actual motive was to acquire the votes of the district level sporting units. Since individuals occupying these slots formed the integral cog of state administration, they were likely to vote in favour of the candidate backed by the ruling regime. However, Dalmiya ably responded to this situation. He struck an alliance with the then Union Railway Minister Lalu Prasad Yadav to ensure that the votes of the Railway Association went in his favour (Majumdar 2009:134). This illustration hinges on the importance of the relationship between political and economic elites which is punctuated by both cooperation and conflict.

The Indian Premier League and India's Tryst with Globalization

The Indian Premier League (IPL) took the commercialization of Indian cricket to a higher level. The BCCI was well aware of the benefits accruing from global capital. The IPL was initiated in response to the Indian Cricket League (ICL). The root of the IPL lay in competition over ownership of television rights by leading media house. A brief discussion of its background is essential.

Zee Television Network (Zee TV) vied for television rights from the BCCI in 2004. However, it was unsuccessful in its endeavour (Agur 2013: 542). The

STATE, MARKET, AND MEDIA IN INDIAN CRICKET   351

Zee TV group responded by initiating the ICL. Cricketers from different parts of the world participated in it. The Essel Group provided the main financial base for the ICL (Sekhri 2016: 12). The ICL emerged as a challenge to the cricketing and financial prowess of the BCCI. With a view to suppressing the ICL, the BCCI threatened to take disciplinary actions against players participating in the rebel league (Sekhri 2016: 22). The conflict of business interests was being extrapolated through cricket.

An understanding of the political economy of the IPL would remain incomplete without examining the role of two eminent cricket administrators, N. Srinivasan and Lalit Modi. There is one similarity between these two (Srinivas 2014: 44–5, 79): Both are influential business personalities and possess political connections. As business houses have been an important source of funding for the political parties, a confluence of political and economic interest is obvious (Kochaneck 2007: 416). The existence of identical interest among business entities brightens the chances of smooth governance of cricket associations. Lalit Modi's contribution in providing momentum to the commercializing trend of Indian cricket must be acknowledged. First, he essayed a deal with ESPN pertaining to the broadcasting of Indian cricket. Second, he aligned with several multinational companies (MNCs), such as Nike, Sahara, and Viacom, in order to boost the financial position of the BCCI. Third, he developed cordial ties with the cricket boards of the major test-playing countries (Srinivas 2014: 79, 95).

The flourishing of the IPL owes much to the contributions of the transnational capitalist class (TCC) (Sklair 2010: 188), which comprises four major groups of individuals: heads of TNCs and their various regional affiliates of the world; international bureaucrats; global technocrats and media houses; and leading international business personalities. All of them act in synchrony to promote the values of global capitalism. The owners of the IPL franchises bear semblance with the spirit of the TCC. The franchises primarily consist of international businessmen, media giants, and executives of leading MNCs. The IPL has indeed expanded the genre of Indian business and a new brand of the Indian capitalist class (Damodaran 2008: 3, 28). United Brewery, GMR group, Sahara India Parivar, Kochi Private Limited, Deccan Chronicle, Indian Cements, and Reliance Industries variously own the IPL teams Royal Challengers Bangalore (RCB), Delhi Daredevils, Pune Warriors, Kochi Tuskers, Deccan Chargers, Chennai Super Kings, and Mumbai Indians, respectively (Holton 2010: 22; Rasul and Proffitt 2011: 378). IPL has provided a platform for Indian business to market their products on a worldwide scale.

352 MOVIES, MEDIA AND TECHNOLOGY

The fusion between Bollywood and cricket has also taken place through this transnational cricket league. Eminent silver screen personalities have stakes in franchises such as Kolkata Knight Riders (Sharukh Khan), Kings XI Punjab (Preity Zinta), and Rajasthan Royals (Shilpa Shetty) (Rasul and Profitt 2013: 378, 382). Moreover, the franchises have acquired the status of a global brand by virtue of their inherent transnational character. Rajasthan Royals can be cited as an example. This Indian franchise has entered into collaborative ventures with Trinidad and Tobago (West Indies), Cape Cobras (South Africa), Hampshire (England), and Victoria Cricket Club (Australia) (Rumford and Wagg 2010: 4, 7). The commercial success of the IPL is beyond doubt. Leading players from other parts of the world try to negotiate with their respective cricket boards so that their schedules do not overlap with the IPL (English 2011: 1373–4).

There was little controversy over the broadcasting of the IPL matches. The BCCI sold the telecasting rights to Sony Entertainment Television (SET) MAX, a Japan-based media house. World Sports Group acquired the rights for broadcasting the matches internationally (Sekhri 2016: 31). However, the second edition of the IPL in 2009 opened up new horizons for exploring the interaction between state and market forces.

The role of the Indian government assumed importance on both economic and political grounds. The government indicated that as the country would face general elections that year, it may not be in a position to provide adequate security arrangement for the players and organizers (Gupta 2011: 1320). The BCCI decided to shift the tournament to South Africa. The BCCI was supposed to pay a substantial amount of money to Cricket South Africa (CSA), South Africa's apex cricket governing body. However, the BCCI did not take prior permission either from the government or from the Reserve Bank of India (RBI). The BCCI was pulled up for violating the FERA. The South African Reserve Bank refused to permit the BCCI to open an account as it was an alien entity. Therefore, it was decided that the CSA would meet all the expenditure of 2009 IPL and the BCCI would reimburse it (Srinivas 2014: 59–60). This incident indicates the role of national financial institutions in the era of global finance. A structural framework exists, at both national and international levels, that defines the functioning of global capital. In the context of global cricket, national cricket boards can be conceived as firms or commercial organizations. They prioritize activities that involve financial gains. In this endeavour, they normally enter into a network of transnational firms across the globe. Yet, they cannot override certain domestic norms of the state.

STATE, MARKET, AND MEDIA IN INDIAN CRICKET   353

Nevertheless, the commercial aspect of the IPL had not been compromised. There was a sound rationale for choosing South Africa over England. In the UK, Sky Sports broadcasted international cricket. Its rival sports channel, Setanta, possessed the television right for the IPL. For the BCCI, the existing competition between these broadcasters posed a threat to revenues. Moreover, match timings had to be arranged in a manner which would suit the television audiences of the South Asian region (Srinivas and Vivek 2009: 2, 8). Hence, television-friendly time zones (Gupta 2004: 257) became an important factor for the commercial success of the IPL. Market forces and communication technology are the cornerstones of contemporary globalization. The Internet has emerged as another means through which matches can be viewed. The example of Cricinfo, a leading cricketing website, drives home this argument (Joshi 2007: 1227). In a similar vein, mobile phones and YouTube have supplemented television as a medium for millions of IPL viewers across time and space (Axford and Huggins 2010: 126, 133).

***

The dominant socio-economic groups that play a vital role in state functioning also form the nucleus for governing cricket in the country. The BCCI and state-level cricket organizations can be regarded as 'quasi-state' entities as they are not only being controlled by political elites of the country in an indirect manner but also reveal the dynamics of the national politics to a considerable extent. The elites of economic and political domain influence the governing of cricket. Moreover, globalizing trends in cricket were not welcomed by certain institutions of the Indian state. The dispute between DD and the CAB regarding the broadcasting of Hero Cup sheds light on this point. This case contradicts the logic of 'public–private' partnership as propagated by economic liberalization. Finally, the discussion of the IPL has pointed out the congruity of the domestic and transnational capitalist class in the globalized era. Nevertheless, the IPL also exemplifies that national economic institutions of the state still retain considerable bargaining power despite the growing predominance of market fundamentalism. In addition, provision of security, internal and external, remains the function of the state. Hence, globalization of cricket shows that on numerous occasions, the political realm facilitates as well as restrains its economic counterpart.

References

Agur, Colin. 2013. 'A Foreign Field No Longer: India, the IPL, and the Global Business of Cricket'. *Journal of Asian and African Studies* 48 (5): 541–56.

Astill, James. 2013. *The Great Tamasha: Cricket, Corruption and the Turbulent Rise of Modern India.* London: Bloomsbury.

Axford, B. and Richard Higgins. 2010. 'The Telemediazation of Cricket: Commerce, Connectivity and Culture in a Post-television age'. In Chris Rumford and Stephen Wagg (eds), *Cricket and Globalization,* pp. 122–49. Newcastle, United Kingdom: Cambridge Scholars Publishing.

Bandyopadhay, Kausik. 2008. 'Feel Good, Goodwill and India's Friendship Tour of Pakistan, 2004: Cricket, Politics and Diplomacy in Twenty-First-Century India'. *The International Journal of the History of Sport* 25 (12): 1654–70.

Beland, Daniel. 2010. 'Globalization and the Resilience of State Power'. In George Ritzer and Zeynep Atalay (eds), *Readings in Globalization: Key Concepts and Major Debates,* pp. 175–9. UK: Wiley-Blackwell.

Chandrasekhar, C.P. and Jayati Ghosh. 2000. *The Market That Failed: Neoliberal Economic Reforms in India.* New Delhi, India: LeftWord Books.

Damodaran, Harish. 2008. *India's New Capitalists: Caste, Business and Industry in a Modern.* India: Permanent Black.

English, Peter. 2011. 'Twenty20 and the Changing Face of Australian Cricket'. *Sport in Society: Cultures, Commerce, Media, Politics* 14 (10): 1369–82.

Gemmell, Jon. 2018. *Cricket's Changing Ethos: Nobles, Nationalists and IPL.* London: Palgrave Macmillan.

Gupta, Amit. 2004. 'The Globalization of Cricket: The Rise of the Non-West'. *The International Journal of the History of Sport* 21(2): 257–76.

———. 2011. 'The IPL and the Indian Domination of Global Cricket'. *Sport in Society, Cultures, Commerce, Media, Politics* 14 (10): 1316–25.

Harvey, David. 2005. *A Brief History of Neoliberalism.* New York: Oxford University Press.

Holton, Robert. 2010. 'Globalization and Cricket'. in Chris Rumford and Stephen Wagg (eds), *Cricket and Globalization,* pp. 18–40. UK: Cambridge Scholars Publishing.

Joshi, Sanjay. 2007. 'Virtually There: Cricket, Community and Commerce on the Internet'. *The International Journal of the History of Sport* 24 (8): 1226–41.

Kochanek, Stanley A. 2007. 'Liberalization and Business Lobbying in India'. In Rahul Mukherji (ed), *India's Economic Transition: The Politics of Reforms,* pp. 412–31. New Delhi: Oxford University Press.

Majumdar, Boria. 2004. *Twenty-Two Yards to Freedom: A Social History of Indian Cricket.* New Delhi, India: Viking Publications.

———. 2009. 'Soaps, Serials and the CPI(M), Cricket Beats Them All: Cricket and Television in Contemporary India'. In Nalin Mehta (ed.), *Television in India: Satellites, Politics and Cultural Changes,* pp. 124–39. London and New York: Routledge.

————. 2018. *Eleven Gods and a Billion Dream: The On and Off the field Story of Cricket in India and Beyond.* New Delhi: Simon and Schuster.

Mascarenhas, Mark. 1997. *My World Cup.* Middletown, USA: Grantha Corporations.

Mathur, Kuldeep. 2013. *Public Policy and Politics in India.* New Delhi: Oxford University Press.

Mehta, Nalin. 2010. 'Batting for the Flag: Cricket, Television and Globalization in India'. In Dominic Malcolm, Jon Gemmell, and Nalin Mehta (eds), *The Changing face of Cricket: From Imperial to Global Game*, pp. 149–69. London and New York: Routledge.

Rasul, Azmat and Jenniffer M. Proffitt. 2011. 'Bollywood and the Indian Premier League (IPL): The Political Economy of Bollywood's New Blockbuster'. *Asian Journal of Communication* 21 (4): 373–88.

Risse-Kappen, Thomas. 1995. *Bringing Transnational Relations Back in: Non-state Actors, Domestic Structures and International institutions.* Cambridge, UK: Cambridge University Press.

Rumford, Chris and Stephen Wagg. 2010. *Cricket and Globalization.* Newcastle, UK: Cambridge Scholars Publishing.

Sekhri, Gaurav Desh. 2016. *Not Out: The Incredible Story of the Indian Premier League.* India: Penguin Viking Books.

Rasul, Azmat and Jenniffer M. Proffitt. 2011. 'Bollywood and the Indian Premier League (IPL): The Political Economy of Bollywood's New Blockbuster'. *Asian Journal of Communication* 21 (4): 373–88.

Sassen, Saskia. 1998. *Globalization and Its Discontents*, USA: New York Press.

Sen Narayan, Sunetra. 2014. *Globalization and Television: A Study of the Indian Experience, 1990-2010.* New Delhi: Oxford University Press.

Sklair, Leslie. 2010. 'Transnational Practices'. In George Ritzer and Zeynep Atalay (eds), *Readings in Globalization: Key Concepts and Major Debates*, pp. 184–94. West Sussex, UK: Wiley-Blackwell.

Srinivas, Alam. 2014. *Cricket Czars: Two Men Who Changed the Gentlemen's Game.* New Delhi: Har Anand Publications.

Srinivas, Alam and T.R Vivek. 2009. *IPL—An Inside Story: Cricket and Commerce.* New Delhi, India: Roli Books.

Wagg, Stephen. 2018. *Cricket: A Political History of the Global Game, 1945–2017.* London and New York: Routldege.

Weiss, Linda. 2003. *States in the Global Economy: Bringing the Domestic Institutions Back In.* Cambridge, UK: Cambridge University Press.

25

Who Watches Cricket?

The New Spectator in the Sporting-Entertainment Complex[*]

Vidya Subramanian

The spectacle of sport—be it an individual sport like tennis, team sports like football, or even endurance sports like the Tour de France—exists in service of, and in order to entertain and enrich, the lives of those who watch it. That has not changed from the time of the ancient Olympic Games to the present televised spectacle. A glaring difference, however, is in the nature of the 'crowd' in the present day. While in ancient Greece the audience was physically present at the site of the spectacle, the primary audience for televised sport is, curiously enough, absent from the stadium.

The manner in which an event, sporting or otherwise, is broadcast 'live' to millions of people around the world changes the notion of the 'crowd' that exists at the heart of a spectacle. The 'crowd' now is all of those people watching the show on television, on the internet, and in public spaces, all put together. This fragmented, non-unified 'crowd' belongs to what French theorist Paul Virilio (quoted in Redhead 2007) has called the 'city of the instant'. This 'city' is a virtual space in which almost everyone, everywhere in the world can be watching an event 'live' on screens, even if in individual isolation. 'Those absent from the stadium are always right', posits Virilio (quoted in Redhead 2007), since it is those that watch the spectacle of the event on television and the internet for who the event is, he argues, 'produced'.

Cricket, a sport played by the British elite, taking five days to play out a single game, often a draw with no winners or losers, was a unique and leisurely sport. Today, cricket in India is as much entertainment as it is sport. When our team is winning, the players are gods, but when they are not, their homes and family may be pelted with stones (see NDTVSports 2013). Many fans I spoke to seem to believe that even though cricket may have originated in Britain, its spiritual home is now in India.[i] Played everywhere from

---

Vidya Subramanian, *Who Watches Cricket?* In: *Sports Studies in India.* Edited by: Meena Gopal and Padma Prakash, Oxford University Press. © Oxford University Press 2021.
DOI: 10.1093/oso/9780190130640.003.0026

WHO WATCHES CRICKET? 357

maidans[ii] to narrow streets, cricket is as ubiquitous in India as that other national pastime—Bollywood.

Alongside this seemingly passionate adoration of the sport and its practitioners, however, there exist many observers who feel that typical Indian sports fans are not exactly connoisseurs of good cricket. A senior member of a television crew who has extensively covered cricket told me that he believed that Indian fans are simply chasing the idea of a 'win' for their team and do not really care about or understand the nuance and technique that makes cricket such a unique sport in the world. He went as far as to call the hoopla surrounding the Indian Premier League (IPL) a *tamasha*.[iii]

Satadru Sen (2005) attempts to explain this proclivity of modern day Indian fans of cricket. The word 'tamasha' pops up in his work too, and he suggests that more of cricket than just the playing 'field' has begun to come into focus since Kerry Packer revolutionized the game with his World Series Cricket (WSC).[iv] Sen seems to be implying that the off-field happenings in the cricket world, such as the birth of the 'celebrity cricketer' and the treatment of cricketing heroes like those of the movies, made it easier for the non-connoisseur to engage with cricket. This 'gossipy, personality-driven' and glamorous mode of engagement with cricket, Sen (2005: 101) suggests, led to a 'democratisation of the culture of sport in India—that is, its emergence from the confines of the field and the world of male experts'. Together with economic liberalization, increasing spending power and the emergence of cable TV in India, 'a flush new market' (Sen 2005: 102) was made available for cricket.

Spectators, Crowd, and the 'Post Fandom'

The expert connoisseur gave way to the boisterous fan—a spectator-consumer—who solely watched matches in which India played, hoping for victory and enjoyed the carnival that cricket became precisely in order to attract audience like him/her. This new fan—one that seeks to merely enjoy the moment of the match—is perhaps what Steve Redhead (1997) refers to as a 'post-fandom' where fans as consumers are influenced by advertising, globalization, and the mediatization of sports culture.

According to Richard Giulianotti (2002), the 'hypercommodification' of football has led to a change in the manner of engagement of the spectator with the sport and the club. He categorizes the football spectator (a sport that is primarily played by small, local clubs) into four types: supporters, followers, fans, and flâneurs (Giulianotti 2002). Giulianotti's analysis posits that there are four 'ideal-type categories', into which spectators can be classified. Since the analysis is based on spectators of football in Europe, which is dominated by a deeply entrenched club culture and in which local club affiliations are potent cultural identifiers, the categories cannot be adapted directly to fit cricket and the IPL. However, the categorization merits analysis and provides a useful lens through which to view the fandom of cricket in general and the IPL in particular.

Giulianotti charts four categories as being underpinned by two basic binary oppositions: 'hot–cool' and 'traditional–consumer' (Figure 25.1). The horizontal axis has been set up to measure 'the basis of the individual's investment in a specific club: Traditional spectators will have a longer, more local... cultural identification with the club, whereas consumer fans will have a more market-centred relationship' (Giulianotti 2002: 31). The vertical axis reflects 'the different degrees to which the club is central to the individual's project of self-formation' (Giulianotti 2002: 31). Hot forms of loyalty emphasize intense kinds of identification and solidarity with the club; cool forms denote the reverse (Giulianotti 2002).

The traditional-hot spectator here is defined as a 'supporter', who has a 'topophillic'[v] relationship with the club. For such supporters, 'subcultural capital' cannot be acquired by simply purchasing club commodities. They have an intimate relationship with the club and consider themselves

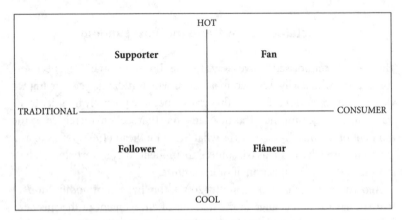

Figure 25.1 Richard Giulianotti's Classification of Spectators
Source: Richard Giulianotti (2002: 31).

WHO WATCHES CRICKET? 359

'members' having a stake (of 'thick personal solidarity') in it (Giulianotti 2002: 33).

The traditional-cool spectator is classified as a 'follower'—not just of the club but also of 'other football people'. The follower keeps up with the club, and 'arrives at such identification through a vicarious form of communion, most obviously via the cool medium of the electronic media' (Giulianotti 2002: 35).

The consumer-hot spectator is described as a 'modern fan of a club or its players, particularly its celebrities'. This fan is described as 'hot' in terms of identification—'the sense of intimacy is strong and is a key element of the individual's self'—but is still distant compared to that of a supporter. This sort of relationship is also 'inordinately unidirectional in its affections (Giulianotti 2002: 36).

Since the fan primarily engages with the club through market-centred relationships, this makes these fans of football rather similar to fans of leading musicians or actors. All of these relationships are 'largely unidirectional' in terms of identification. Giulianotti (2002: 38) posits that, 'these ... mediated forms of acting help to preserve the highly profitable, parallel football universe that has been constructed to supply the fan market'.

The last category of consumer-cool—of a flâneur—is of the 'unreconstructed cool consumer'. A category more carefully understood by Walter Benjamin, a flâneur is typically described as usually male, adult, bourgeois, 'an idler and a traveller', 'an urban stroller ... (who) would promenade through boulevards and markets' (Giulianotti 2002: 39). Drawing on that, Giulianotti (2002: 39) writes,

The flaneur ... consumes these signifiers in a disposable and cliché-like fashion, as if adopting a temporary tattoo. Moreover, the football flâneur's natural habitat is increasingly the virtual arena, seeking the sensations of football as represented through television, (or the) internet.

Flâneurs are expected to be able to switch connections with teams or players, and even relinquish the game in favour of other forms of entertainment. They have no topophilic identification with the club, and are 'emptied of any sense of home, but house instead the cool and ungrounded circulation of football's commodity ephemera' (Giulianotti 2002: 40).

While club cricket is (and indeed, has always been) a thriving sport, it is not the most popular form of the game. Corporate tournaments and other city- and club-level tournaments exist, and have their share of fans and

360 MOVIES, MEDIA AND TECHNOLOGY

following. But in cricket, the larger and most popular forms have always been state- or country-level competitions. Giulianotti's analysis and classification provides a useful taxonomy through which to view the spectators of cricket. I argue that the 'supporter' category cannot be directly transposed to cricket because it does not apply to either the national form of the game or even to the IPL form of the game. While club loyalty at a local level exists, it cannot be compared to the football fandom in which 'members' buy season tickets and a reciprocal relationship of membership drives an emotional investment in it.

The categories of 'follower' and 'fan' could perhaps be collapsed into one single category in terms of fans of cricket, particularly in India, since the fandom is largely unidirectional, without the teams actually considering fans 'members' of the administrative or emotional core of the team. The topophilia of the 'member', the engagement with the sport and teams through the 'cool medium of electronic media' of the 'follower', and the strong sense of intimacy that the 'fan' feels for his or her team are all markers of the traditional Indian cricket fan (Giulianotti 2002: 35). There has been, largely, only one team that most traditional Indian cricket fans have rooted for—the national team—and their loyalty is both passionate and topophilic, and also primarily engaged with through various 'cool forms' of media.

The identity of the 'flâneur', though, is one that is easily identifiable as that of the target demographic of the IPL. Subject to what Giulianotti (2002: 39) calls 'the growing commodification of social relationships and objects', the IPL fan's social practices are oriented more towards consumption than a deeper engagement with the sport. The television presentation of football, maintains Giulianotti (2002: 39), is 'tailored toward a flâneur type experience'. This is true for the IPL as well. The description of flâneurs as 'window shoppers' too can be easily transposed to fans of the IPL, who are also 'motivated to seek sensation, excitement, and thus to switch their gaze across clubs, players, and nations' (Giulianotti 2002: 41). The IPL, then, as Giulianotti (2002: 40) suggests, 'encourages the germination of a proxy form of narcissistic self-identity for the cool consumers'.

New Roles for Spectators

In 2009, Brian Lara, the West Indian batting legend, identified the importance of the flâneur for the sport of cricket. Believing cricket (in its then-dominant one-day form) to be a 'dying sport', he was enthusiastic about the new Twenty20 format, and suggested that the format would bring new kinds of spectators to the sport, 'ones that just want to go to the game and don't even know what happens' (Cricinfo Staff 2009). He appears to suggest that the draw of cricket, and indeed the IPL, is not the game of cricket itself but all the razzmatazz attached to the televised version of the sport. The lack of knowledge about the longer version of the game or the nuances and intensity of the sport does not seem to bother the fans of this new-age spectacle.

In contrast to that position, some viewers of cricket maintain (the topic came up in more than one focus group discussion) that television was creating a more engaged audience. Add-ons such as ultra-motion cameras, HawkEye, and so on allow this generation of viewers to be more knowledgeable than any before, they argued. The argument is a viable one. The great number of available technologies within broadcast that are seen to be making television viewing 'better than ever before' are a great way of learning and engaging more deeply with the sport. With analysis of games with experts that go on for hours (and not just in English) before and after the match, it would be unsurprising to find better informed viewers and more engaged fans. But is it really making the viewer experience 'better'? If television ratings, the amount of cricket programming on air at any given time, and the almost unbelievable amounts of money spent on acquiring television rights are any indication, then the answer must be in the affirmative, some respondents stated.

On the contrary, I believe that these very markers may denote a different phenomenon. While it may be true that the number of people watching cricket on television has gone up, there is no way to gauge whether those watching are indeed more knowledgeable than ever before. The increase in the number of people with access to technologies such as smartphones and streaming devices may also be a reason for the rise in viewership numbers. The increasing emphasis on the 'entertainment quotient' of sports broadcasts indicates attempts to attract audiences that are not always only interested in the sport. A clear indication of this is the dwindling television ratings of cricket before the launch of the IPL. According to Rohit Gupta, president of Sony Entertainment Television, television ratings[vi] for one-day matches had tapered off from over ten in 2003 to almost three in 2008 (Srinivas and Vivek 2009: 44–6). 'It meant that youngsters were moving away from cricket, forget about adding new consumers', he said (Srinivas and Vivek 2009).

It was at this time that the IPL came to be. Importing the idea of privately owned franchises from a combination of soccer's English Premier League (EPL) and the US National Football League (NFL), Lalit Modi created a television-centric, cash-rich, celebrity-driven, non-national, cricket-based product that he went on to sell to the world. With a format borrowed from English football, a power centre in India, television programming structured on the lines of USA's NFL, and with players from cricket playing countries all over the world, the IPL was a truly globalized event. With corporate owners, player auctions, cheerleaders, and night matches to ensure maximum viewership, this was a version of cricket that had its centre in business acumen and free market philosophies than in the game of cricket. Liquor barons, movie stars, large real estate developers, media management firms—everyone was invited.

The IPL was targeted not at the traditional cricket fan, but at everyone who had an interest in television, cinema, and celebrities, particularly the young, upwardly mobile city dwellers. Television commentator Harsha Bhogle attributes the birth of the IPL to the need for cricket to keep the attention of youngsters who were now more inclined to watch football. The attempt, once again, seems to be to lure the spectator in the periphery (Memon 1992: 68). Bhogle (quoted in Srinivas and Vivek 2009: 56) said, 'Cricket was desperately in need of fresh ideas because at least in the big metros it was losing kids to EPL. Children had begun to think of cricket as the dad's game.'

David Rowe and Callum Gilmour (2009: 172) describe the IPL as a 'strange hybrid of the English village green, "Bollywood", and the Super Bowl'. They speak of modern sport as a 'mediated "live" cultural form in which the in-stadium crowd is a key part of the spectacle' (Rowe and Gilmour 2009: 172). They quote Andrew Wildblood, a senior employee of the global sports marketing and management firm IMG that helped prepare a blueprint for the league, to have said that the IPL was intended to cater to the expanding leisure and entertainment economy.

Cricket writer Ivo Tennant (2011) speaks of the modern 'instant everything' age and the viewer's need for the 'gratification of the ball flying over the boundary rather than studying the immaculate Boycottesque defence of the craftsman'. He bemoans the loss of 'Messrs Craft and Guile' in the Twenty20 framework, calling it a game for 'the modern, fidgety, fast-evolving society in which concentration levels are miniscule' (Tennant 2011). The trappings and the suits, as it were, of this televised spectacle are but attempts to keep this 'fidgety' viewer from reaching for the remote.

WHO WATCHES CRICKET? 363

Transcending Boundaries

Unlike other club-based sports, cricket was always primarily a game played by nations, or, in domestic games, states and counties. Fans picked allegiances based on the happy accidents of geography, and tournaments were organized around geographic boundaries. On the surface, the IPL is a fundamental reworking of that notion. With city-based clubs competing for the top spot, the fan-base could have been expected to be localized around the cities and stadiums used as 'home grounds', perhaps envisioning in the long run spectators who will become 'members', as Giulianotti (2002) defines them. But since the IPL is primarily a televised spectacle, the fans of the tournament do not end up coalescing around the local cricket ground or cities.

During field work conducted in several public places in Delhi, it was found that most respondents did not name the local team, Delhi Daredevils, among their favourite teams. On further questioning, several respondents answered that it was because the team was one of the most unsuccessful ones in the League. Several others named their favourite players as reasons for picking other teams (such as M.S. Dhoni for Chennai Super Kings, Yuvraj Singh and Chris Gayle for the Royal Challengers Bangalore in 2014, and so on). This was somewhat different for IPL fans in Chennai, many of whom seemed to revel in the fact that the team named for their city was so successful, and it appeared to have come together into a sort of brand identity of their city that is different from the 'madrasi' descriptor that they are usually assigned.

Another criterion for fans picking 'favourite' teams seemed to be the fame of actor Shah Rukh Khan. Several fans picked the Kolkata Knight Riders because of its association with the movie star, in spite of them (or him) having no association with the city of Kolkata. Several respondents (mostly women, who admitted to not being interested in cricket at all) knew not only which team the superstar owned but were able to correctly identify almost all teams in which movie stars held a stake, such as Preity Zinta's Kings XI Punjab and Shilpa Shetty's Rajasthan Royals.

However, it was also clear that the main loyalty of the fans surveyed was first to the national team. The World Cup is considered the most important cricketing event and beating Pakistan the most 'satisfying victory'. Patriotic identity associated with the national cricket team provides a sense of pride in its victories and collective shame in its losses. It is not a large leap to conjecture that it is this deep emotional investment in the fortunes of the national team that emerges as the public outpouring of joy at India's victories

364   MOVIES, MEDIA AND TECHNOLOGY

and a violent backlash against the players after losses. It is not just the team of eleven men who win or lose. It is 'we won' or 'we lost'.

The IPL is attempting to harness that same emotional appeal of India's winning by creating a league in which no matter which teams played, India never lost. To put it in the words of Gideon Haigh,[vii] 'India always wins.' Haigh's theory is that it was the aftermath of the 2007 World Cup that gave a fillip to the setting up of the IPL. This World Cup, held in West Indies, in which both India and Pakistan had been knocked out in the league stages, has been widely reported to have been a financial disaster (J.A. 2015). This was because there was a major drop in interest in the subcontinent once the two teams were knocked out, and most of the advertising revenue for cricket matches comes from the subcontinent, especially when India is playing. This led to the reworking of the World Cup format to ensure that the 'best' teams stayed in the fray as long as possible.

Recovering from India's humiliating exit from the 2007 World Cup, Lalit Modi and the BCCI pitched the IPL. In the words of Gideon Haigh,

> So, Lalit Modi went around in the wake of the 2007 World Cup and said, 'Okay Indian corporate and Indian broadcasters, that was really bad, but I'll tell you what I've got. I've got a tournament in which India always wins. And Indian participation is guaranteed all the way through.' That's the essence of the IPL

Set up to lure disappointed Indian broadcasters, corporate advertisers, and Indian spectators back to cricket, the IPL brought the best international talent from around the world to play for local teams and created a spectacle that was to be played and contested within India but looked and felt every bit as international as the World Cup. And the underlying theme of the entire enterprise would be that no matter who won and who lost, the famously mercurial Indian spectators would always have an Indian victory to celebrate.

Much of sports sociological theory is in agreement that sport is able to whip up national frenzy just like war, and events like the Olympics serve to consolidate the feeling of 'playing for one's country' or 'doing it for the motherland'. Scholars such as Chris Schilling and Philip Mellor (2014) have even written on reconceptualizing sport as a religious phenomenon in the modern era. They argue that the old tropes of focusing on sport as a religious or quasi-religious phenomenon does not adequately explain the sentiment attached to sport. It requires, rather, an understanding that embraces both secular and religious phenomenon.

WHO WATCHES CRICKET? 365

Comparing sport with war, Amarnath Amarasingam (2011) has noted that, 'international sporting events like cricket serve not only as a form of national recreation, but also national re-creation'. He quotes Rob Nixon as having said that sporting events are 'exhibitionist events imbued with the authority to recreate or simulate the nation, offering a vigorous display of a proxy body politic' (Amarasingam 2011). The IPL too, I argue, is a part of this project.

In an online survey conducted as part of my field work, several respondents, when talking of the IPL, expressed a positive sentiment regarding the manner in which the League allowed Indian players to closely interact with the best international talent. The IPL was, they seemed to suggest, an excellent place for Indian players to better their skills and learn from the international players participating in the league. In spite of the corruption scandals, over-the-top frenzy, cheerleaders, and famous IPL parties that seemed to draw forth a negative response, there appeared to be a wide positive reaction to the Indian players playing alongside and learning from international talent and making India look good in international competitions.[viii]

That nationalism is one of the IPL's important central themes is also made evident in the highlighting of the country in the advertising campaigns for the league. The 2015 edition of the IPL that came hot on the heels of the World Cup, was advertised as '*yeh hai India ka tyohar*' ['This is the festival of India'], making it abundantly clear that the emphasis was still on the country as an emotional resonating point with the target audience. Fan identity in the IPL, after nearly a decade of existence, has not organically developed around the geography of the teams in the League. This is in spite of the vigorous social media campaigns that IPL teams set up. Taglines that obviously aim to imbue a local flavour in fan engagement, such as the use of a Tamil slogan in the hashtag '#WhistlePodu' on Twitter and Facebook for the Chennai Super Kings or the extensive ad campaign worded in simple Punjabi for the Delhi Daredevils—'*Dilli ke apne munde*' ['Delhi's own boys'], have failed to elicit the kind of local fervour that the marketing teams had perhaps hoped for.

That is not to say that there is no following at all, given the several internet forums, Facebook pages, and blogs that seem to overflow with fan loyalty to one or another IPL team or player, but this outpouring of sentiment does not appear to be either widespread or in any way city or region based. An interesting point to flag here would be that large parts of India remain unrepresented in the yearly gala that is the IPL.

In some editions of the IPL, several teams switched or added an extra 'home ground' on which to play. Kings XI Punjab played no matches at the picturesque Dharamsala ground in 2015 and moved instead to Pune, while the Delhi Daredevils added Ranchi as a second 'home ground'. In 2013, Ranchi was the second 'home ground' to the Kolkata Knight Riders. In 2018, Chennai Super Kings moved to Pune and Kings XI Punjab added Indore. Some of this has been attributed to financial concerns regarding gate money and other revenue sources (Kanthwal 2015) or, as in the case of the Chennai Super Kings, Pune was picked due to protests in Chennai on the Cauvery issue (Pansare 2018). It seems like a tall order, then, to expect the people of Pune, Maharashtra—be they follower-fans or flâneurs—to embrace a team called 'Kings XI Punjab' or 'Chennai Super Kings' as their home team and to identify with the team simply based on the venue of their new home ground. The Delhi Daredevils and Kolkata Knight Riders may have brought the IPL to Ranchi (home of Indian captain M.S. Dhoni and site of one of the BCCI's new stadia), but to expect any sort of fan loyalty for either team from the people of the city might perhaps be asking for too much.

It is thus my contention that the main motivation for spectators who follow the IPL is still the consideration of country above all else. To be able to watch current and future stars of the Indian team play explosive cricket and to be able to see international fan favourites play alongside Indian superstar cricketers is still the thrill of the IPL, eleven years after the idea was first executed.

With the advent of this 'city-based cricket' (Rowe and Gilmour 2009: 172) in which loyalties are divided among cities, players, and even owners of franchises (as has been seen in the IPL), the identity of the cricket fan has become almost indefinable. I engaged in an informal conversation with a set of former cricket enthusiasts, all professionals between the ages of twenty-five and thirty-five who watched cricket with undiluted enthusiasm through their school years and now follow football with much of the same zeal. During the course of this conversation, it emerged that their interest in cricket had begun to dwindle around the time that the match fixing scandal of 2000 (ESPNcricinfo Staff 2013) broke and football (in the form of the EPL) began to be televised in India in 2001 (*Times of India* 2001). Having switched allegiances almost entirely to football now (so much so that while speaking about football, they refer to the team they support as 'we'), these city-bred professionals are cynical about cricket as a sport and the team (the Indian team) that they once loved.

The number and manner of advertisements in cricket was mentioned as another common irritant that made them feel 'put off' by televised cricket. One respondent compared it to coverage of the EPL, in which there were not

WHO WATCHES CRICKET? 367

too many intrusive ads till half time. A few respondents declared that they had nothing against the Twenty20 game, and in fact lauded administrators for coming up with a cricket format to rival football, and that one could go to with friends after work and enjoy a riveting game with players of an international standing. But watching cricket on television, they maintained, was 'irritating'. The over breaks, the repeated advertisements, the length of the one-day game, and the suspicion of corruption in every match all contributed to their irritation. When the group did however discuss the game of cricket, it was with more than a superficial understanding. They commented on the abilities of certain batsmen to combat spin, made comments on field placements for specific batsmen, and the amount of swing specific bowlers could get on certain pitches, among others, and often ended up comparing present players with those they remembered as heroes from their childhood.

Emergence of a Sporting-Entertainment Complex

The sporting-entertainment complex as it exists today is a peculiar beast, put together by several allied industries, including sports, marketing, broadcast, and business. It has managed to transform the once sedately-paced game of cricket into a platform for adrenaline-pumping action sequences like the IPL, in which cricket is but one of several treats on offer to the spectator. The IPL has been structured, deliberately and carefully, as a platform, not just for advertisers seeking more eyeballs but also for businesses that need more brand recognition, business people who need to pad their public image, and film stars who seek publicity, no matter which team wins. No longer just a game, the IPL has become the kind of platform that can provide more 'eyeballs' than any other marketing gimmick (Subramanian 2012).

While it has been argued that the vast amount of technology that creates and brings us the sport of cricket has enhanced the viewing experience, what with HawkEye and spider-cams and Umpire-vision cameras, the main draw of the spectacle remains the carnivalesque atmosphere of the event driven by celebrity and non-stop action. The tamasha that so many observers of the game have commented on is the main draw of the IPL. Set up particularly to appeal to the non-traditional cricket fan and to attract more and newer members to the cricket carnival, the IPL has been richly peppered with controversy (such as the much-publicized slapping incident involving S. Sreesanth and Harbhajan Singh in 2008 [Press Trust of India 2008]), gossip (such as Virat Kohli's encounters with his then-girlfriend and now-wife,

368   MOVIES, MEDIA AND TECHNOLOGY

movie star Anushka Sharma in 2015 [*Zee News* 2015]), and scandal (Shah Rukh Khan's altercation with a security guard at Wankhede stadium, and his consequent banning in 2012 [ESPNcricinfo Staff 2012]).

The centre of attention of all 'eyeball' seekers is the spectator who watches the spectacle being produced upon this platform. Created on a substrate of the information and communication tecnnologies, such as the internet and broadcast media, the platform brings to the spectator—the fan, the consumer, the flâneur alike—a version of the sport of cricket that is profitable to those organizing it. Giulianotti's categories of fans and flâneurs place in perspective those for whom the platform is assembled. The IPL is especially designed to catch the attention of the roving entertainment seeker, whether idly channel surfing on a television in the living room or the stadium-going ticket buyer who gets a chance to click a 'selfie' with his or her favourite star in the background.

This urbane cosmopolitan fan belonging to the new middle class of India enjoys the idea of the best international players playing for teams such as Kolkata and Chennai and relishes the prospect of an evening out with friends at an event with food, drinks, music, cheering, and celebrities. The IPL appears to have been put together with the intention of encouraging the cricket fan into embracing their other identity—that of a consumer— to be someone who is capable of switching seamlessly between one 'brand' and another, be that of commodities or indeed cricket teams.

Notes

*   This article was part of the author's doctoral research conducted at the Centre for Studies in Science Policy (CSSP), Jawaharlal Nehru University, Delhi.

i.   Interviews conducted during PhD Field Work (2013 to 2015).

ii.   In South Asia, a maidan is an open space in or near a town. The space is often used as a playground and also for public meetings and events.

iii.   A tamasha is often a show, a pageant, a theatrical performance, or even a celebration with dance, and so on. It is also used to denote a public spectacle, or even a commotion or fuss.

iv.   Kerry Packer, the Australian newspaper magnate, was the first to see the massive potential of television for cricket, or to put it another way, the massive potential of cricket for television. After being refused exclusive broadcasting rights to Australian cricket, Packer set up a break-away professional cricket competition known as World Series Cricket (WSC) in 1977. The WSC was the first cricket tournament to bring in the sort of razzmatazz to cricket that we have now come

WHO WATCHES CRICKET? 369

to accept as *de rigueur*—coloured clothing for players, cameras at both ends of the pitch, matches played at night, a personality-driven marketing campaign, and so on.

v. Giulianotti's (2002: 33) definition for topophilia states: "Topophilia involves an intense emotional attachment to a particular part of the material environment; otherwise stated, it is a love of place."

vi. Television Rating Point (TRP) is the viewership rating for any broadcast programme over a period of thirty days. Television Rating Points quantify the gross rated points achieved by the broadcast among targeted individuals within a larger population.

vii. Interview with Gideon Haigh, senior journalist and author, November 2014.

viii. Survey conducted online using Google Forms in May 2015.

References

Amarasingam, Amarnath. 2011.'Nationalism, Cricket and the Religio-politics of Sport'. *The Huffington Post*, 5 April. Available at http://www.huffingtonpost.com/amarnath-amarasingam/nationalism-cricket-and-t_b_844034.html; accessed 3 June 2015.

Cricinfo Staff. 2009. 'Lara Hopes Artistry Returns to Twenty20 Batting'. *ESPNCricinfo*, 8 April. Available at http://www.espncricinfo.com/westindies/content/story/398808.html; accessed on 11 April 2016.

ESPNCricinfo Staff. 2012. 'Shah Rukh Khan Gets Five-Year Ban from Wankhede'. *ESPNCricinfo*, 18 May. Available at http://www.espncricinfo.com/indian-premier-league-2012/content/story/565312.html; accessed on 20 May 2015.

———. 2013. 'The Cronje Chronicles'. *ESPNCricinfo*, 22 July. Available at http://www.espncricinfo.com/ci/content/story/654219.html; accessed on 17 September 2015.

Giulianotti, Richard. 2002. 'Supporters, Followers, Fans, and Flâneurs: A Taxonomy of Spectator Identities in Football'. *Journal of Sport & Social Issues* 26 (1): pp 25–46.

J.A. 2015. 'Why Cricket's World Cup Is Full of Meaningless Games'. *The Economist*, 15 February. Available at http://www.economist.com/blogs/economist-explains/2015/02/economist-explains-13; accessed on 21 May 2015.

Kanthwal, Gaurav. 2015.'Why It Took KXIP So Long to Show Up at Their Home Ground'. *The Tribune*, 27 April. Available at http://www.tribuneindia.com/news/sport/why-it-took-kxip-so-long-to-show-up-at-their-home-ground/72895.html; accessed on 3 June 2015.

Lotringer, S. and P.Virilio. 1997. *Pure war* (2nd ed.). New York: Semiotext(e).

Memon, Ayaz. 1992. *Wills Book of Excellence: One-Day Cricket*. Calcutta: Orient Longman.

NDTVSports. 2013. 'Mahendra Singh Dhoni's House Pelted with Stones'. *NDTV*, 24 October. Available at https://sports.ndtv.com/india-vs-australia-2013-14/mahendra-singh-dhonis-house-pelted-with-stones-1528320; accessed on 18 November 2018.

370 MOVIES, MEDIA AND TECHNOLOGY

Pansare, Rajesh. 2018. 'IPL 2018: Chennai Super Kings Still Getting Used to "Home" Ground in Pune, Says Stephen Fleming'. *Hindustan Times*, 29 April. Available at https://www.hindustantimes.com/cricket/ipl-2018-chennai-super-kings-still-getting-used-to-home-ground-in-pune-says-stephen-fleming/story-FrHRZ7qDxVJvZzancTzwEN.html; accessed on 18 November 2018.

Press Trust of India. 2008. 'Bhajji 'Slaps' Sreesanth, Makes Him Cry'. *Times of India*, 26 April. Available at http://timesofindia.indiatimes.com/india/Bhajji-slaps-Sreesanth-makes-him-cry/articleshow/2983882.cms; accessed on 20 May 2015.

Redhead, Steve. 1997. *Post-fandom and the Millennial Blues: The Transformation of Soccer Culture*. New York: Routledge.

———. 2007. 'Those Absent from the Stadium Are Always Right: Accelerated Culture, Sport Media, and Theory at the Speed of Light'. *Journal of Sport and Social Issues* 31 (3): 226–41.

Rowe, David and Callum Gilmour. 2009. 'Global Sport: Where Wembley Way Meets Bollywood Boulevard'. *Continuum: Journal of Media & Cultural Studies* 23 (2): 171–82.

Schilling, Chris and Philip A. Mellor. 2014. 'Re-conceptualizing Sport as a Sacred Phenomenon'. *Sociology of Sport Journal* 31 (3): 349–76.

Sen, Satadru. 2005. 'History without a Past: Memory and Forgetting in Indian Cricket'. In Stephen Wagg (ed), *Cricket and National Identity in the Postcolonial Age: Following On*, pp. 94–109. Oxford, New York: Routledge.

Srinivas, Alam and T.R. Vivek. 2009. *IPL: An Inside Story—Cricket and Commerce*. New Delhi: Roli Books.

Subramanian, Vidya. 2012. 'Cricket in the Fast Lane: Politics of Speed'. *Economic and Political Weekly* 47 (50): 21–4.

Tennant, Ivo. 2011. 'A Sport for the Fast Food Generation'. *ESPNCricinfo*, 8 March. Available at http://www.espncricinfo.com/innovation/content/story/504671.html; accessed on 21 March 2016.

Times of India. 2001. 'ESPN To Telecast Premier League', 10 August. Available at http://timesofindia.indiatimes.com/ESPN-to-telecast-Premier-League/articleshow/1964583945.cms; accessed on 17 September 2015.

Zee News. 2015. 'IPL 2015: Virat Kohli Breaks Players' Protocol, Meets Anushka Sharma during Match against DD', 18 May. Available at http://zeenews.india.com/sports/cricket/ipl/ipl-2015-virat-kohli-breaks-players-protocol-meets-anushka-sharma-during-match-against-dd_1597128.html; accessed on 20 May 2015.

Editors and Contributors

Editors

Padma Prakash is the editor of the pioneering social sciences web repository and publishing space *eSocialSciences*, and is director of a non-profit IRIS Knowledge Foundation, Mumbai, India, that works at the interface of knowledge dissemination and information technology. She also co-edits *eSocialSciences and Humanities* with Pramod K. Nayar. She was the associate/acting editor of *Economic and Political Weekly* for two decades. She has been a social and political activist in feminist and health movements, and has written extensively on sports and science and medicine in the academic space and in the popular media. She conceptualized, contributed to, and edited *State of Urban Youth, India 2013: Employment, Livelihoods, Skills* (2013), the first report on India's urban youth. She was a track athlete and hockey player at university level in the 1960s and 1970s, and a lifetime sports follower. More recently, she is an on-and-off marathon runner and has been an active participant of school- and district-level athletic clubs.

Meena Gopal is professor at the Advanced Centre for Women's Studies at Tata Institute of Social Sciences, Mumbai, India. She is a member of the autonomous feminist collective, Forum Against Oppression of Women in Mumbai, India. Her research work is largely on social movements, gender and labour, and public health. She was an all-India university record holder for Heptathlon (women) and 100-metre hurdles for women (Inter-University Games, Gwalior, 1986). She represented Madras University and Tamil Nadu in inter-state and national athletic competitions. She was also selected for the Indian athletic team for World University Games, held in Kobe in 1986, but was unable to travel due to injury.

Contributors

S. Ananthakrishnan is an independent scholar and social and rights activist based in Norway. He was formerly director of the youth programme at UN-Habitat and an active promoter of the UN sports for development programme. Currently he is the co-chair of Urban Economy Forum, Canada, and has been consulting for the World Bank and various UN organizations. He is on the boards of many organizations, including International Centre for Energy, Environment and Development (ICEED), Nigeria; Glocal Cities; and Fledge. He has postgraduate degrees in engineering from Indian Institute of Technology (IIT) Mumbai, India, and race relations and community studies from University of Bradford, UK.

Kausik Bandyopadhyay teaches history at West Bengal State University, Barasat, Kolkata, India. Prior to this, he taught at Kidderpore College, Kolkata, India, and in the Department of History, North Bengal University, Siliguri, India. He was a fellow of the International Olympic Museum, Lausanne in 2010, and of the Maulana Abul Kalam Azad Institute of Asian Studies, Kolkata, India from 2006 to 2009. He is the deputy executive editor of the journal *Soccer and Society*. His areas of research interest include social and cultural history of modern India, popular culture in South Asia, history of sport, and contemporary South Asia.

Nikhilesh Bhattacharya teaches English at Birpara College, West Bengal, India. He has been a sports journalist and a researcher of physical cultures of Bengal. He received his doctorate degree from the School of Cultural Texts and Records, Jadavpur University, Kolkata, India, and his thesis was on the role of the Anglo-Indian community in the history of Indian hockey. His doctoral research was supported by the Ryoichi Sasakawa Young Leaders Fellowship Fund (Sylff) and the IOC Olympic Studies Centre.

S. Janaka Biyanwila is a former Olympic athlete, former Sri Lanka national diving champion, and a published author with a PhD in organizational and labour studies from the University of Western Australia. He is also the author of *The Labour Movement in the Global South: Trade Unions in Sri Lanka* (2011) and *Sports and the Global South: Work, Play and Resistance in Sri Lanka* (2018).

Pulasta Dhar is a football commentator and sports journalist, with a post-graduate degree in broadcast journalism from the University of Sheffield, UK. He writes for *LiveMint* and *Economic Times*, among other newspapers, and has worked with BBC Radio Leicester, *Firstpost*, and *Scoopwhoop*.

EQUATIONS is a research, policy, and advocacy organization working on tourism and development issues in India. Its work focuses on the economic, environmental, social, cultural, political, and administrative impacts of tourism, particularly on people living in and around tourist destinations. It collaborates closely with organizations and people's movements to influence people-centred forms of tourism and policies that ensure significant local benefits and take the negative impacts of an unbridled growth of tourism into account. On the research front, it undertakes the study of the relationship between tourism (and its development patterns) and the communities and ecosystems it most affects. It supports people's struggles against unjust, undemocratic, and unsustainable forms of tourism and tries to ensure that people's experiences influence changes in tourism policies.

Raadhika Gupta is a law graduate from NALSAR University of Law, Hyderabad, India, and LLM from Harvard Law School, USA, and is a social entrepreneur. She has researched and written extensively on gender, including on gender and cricket, taxation, copyright, and disability. She has taught gender and the law at the O.P. Jindal Global University, Sonipat, India, where she received an award for excellence in research for her work on cricket and gender. She has worked on skill development programmes with the Government of India, and now works with the World Bank. She is also the co-founder of Foodshaala Foundation, which aims to build a food and nutrition secure world.

Avipsu Halder currently works in the Department of Political Science, University of Calcutta, India. His research interests are international relations theory, political economy, and globalization. After his MPhil work on sports and globalization at the Centre for International Politics, Organisation and Disarmament (CIPOD), Jawaharlal Nehru University, Delhi, India, he is pursuing his doctoral work.

S. Mohammed Irshad is an assistant professor in the Jamsetji Tata School of Disaster Studies, Tata Institute of Social Sciences, Mumbai, India. His

374 EDITORS AND CONTRIBUTORS

academic research focuses on disaster economics, risk economics, development planning, political economy of development, water governance, and history of disasters. His research examines the relationship between state and society, welfare models and its contemporary challenges, disaster loss and its impacts on the economy, more specifically the local economy, and social and political movements around development and risk.

Sabah Khan is the co-founder of Parcham, a group dedicated to breaking stereotypes based on religion, class, caste, gender. and other markers of difference to create a society respectful of diversity. She has a postgraduate degree in social work from Tata Institute of Social Sciences, Mumbai, India, and is a feminist activist whose interests are minority rights with a focus on women.

Kruthika N. S. is an associate at LawNK and a researcher at the Sports Law & Policy Centre, Bengaluru, India. She is a law graduate from the West Bengal National University of Juridical Sciences, Kolkata, India, and has three gold medals in constitutional law. Her research interests at the Centre include gender and sport, athletes' and workers' rights, and the influence of technology on sport.

Boria Majumdar is senior research fellow in the School of Sport and Wellbeing at the University of Central Lancashire, UK. He has previously worked as distinguished visiting fellow at La Trobe University, Melbourne, Australia and, since 2003, as visiting lecturer at the University of Chicago, USA. After an MA in history from University of Calcutta, India, he was awarded DPhil in history from University of Oxford, UK, where he was Rhodes scholar. He is a sports journalist, a prolific writer, and a much-cited author in the field of social history of sports in India.

Nissim Mannathukkaren is an associate professor in the International Development Studies Department at Dalhousie University, Canada. He is the author of *The Rupture with Memory: Derrida and the Specters that Haunt Marxism* (2006). His research has been published in journals such as the *Journal of Peasant Studies*, *Third World Quarterly*, *Journal of Critical Realism*, *International Journal of the History of Sport*, *Economic and Political Weekly*, *Dialectical Anthropology*, and *Sikh Formations*. He is a regular contributor to the media and his articles have appeared in English in *The Hindu*,

The Wire, Indian Express, The Telegraph, Deccan Herald, Deccan Chronicle, Asian Age, Outlook, Tehelka, Citizen, Kafila, Open Democracy, Polis Project, The Wall Street Journal, and *Kochi Post*; and in Malayalam in *Mathrubhumi, Kalakaumudi, Malayalam Varikha,* and *Navamalayali.*

Vrinda Marwah is a doctoral candidate in the Department of Sociology at the University of Texas, Austin, USA. She has previously worked with Delhi-based feminist groups Sama and Creating Resources for Empowerment in Action (CREA). Her research interests are gender, political sociology, and reproductive health. Her dissertation is an ethnographic study of Accredited Social Health Activists in Punjab, India.

K.P. Mohan is a sports columnist and writer. He was a prolific sports journalist for many years at *The Hindu.* He has written extensively on sports, and consistently and concernedly on doping in India. He is on the boards of several sports and sports media bodies.

Pramod K. Nayar teaches in the Department of English at the University of Hyderabad, India. He has authored *Indian Travel Writing in the Age of Empire* (2020), *Ecoprecarity* (2019), *Brand Postcolonial* (2017), *Bhopal's Ecological Gothic* (2017), and *Human Rights and Literature* (2016). He has also published essays in journals such as *Narrative, Image and Text,* and *Celebrity Studies.* In 2018, he received the Visitor's Award for the best research in the category of humanities, arts, and social sciences.

Frederick Noronha is an independent journalist based in Saligão in the Bardez taluka of Goa, India. He is active in cyberspace and has volunteered with several e-ventures involving Goa, building communities, and free software. His interests include studying Goa, developmental issues, and photography. He is the founder of the alternate publishing house, Goa 1556, and has been a volunteer for the Goanet cyber network for the past twenty-five years.

Madeleine Pape is a postdoctoral fellow in the Science and Human Culture programme at Northwestern University, USA. She received a doctorate in sociology from the University of Wisconsin–Madison, USA, in 2019. Her current research examines debates over epistemologies of sex and gender and how these are influenced by the actions of governing bodies, with a focus on international sport and biomedicine in USA and Canada. Prior to her graduate studies, Pape was a track athlete who competed for Australia in the 800 metres at the 2008 Olympic Games in Beijing and the 2009 World Championships in Berlin.

D. Parthasarathy is professor in the Department of Humanities and Social Sciences, and associate faculty in the Centre for Policy Studies at the Indian Institute of Technology Bombay, India. His research interests include urban studies, development studies, law and governance, gender and development, climate vulnerability, and disaster studies.

Bino Paul is professor at the School of Management and Labour Studies, Tata Institute of Social Sciences, Mumbai, India. He teaches labour economics, social network analysis, and analytics. His research interests are centred on labour market, micro data analytics, and social network analysis.

Elizabeth Pike is professor and head of sport, health and exercise at the University of Hertfordshire, UK. Her research focuses on the potential of sport and physical activity to address issues of equality and diversity, with particular attention to improving opportunities for older persons and females in and through sport. She has published more than fifty research papers/books, delivered invited keynote presentations at international conferences on six continents, and written numerous commissioned monitoring and evaluation reports. She was an invited member of an international conference which produced a multi-disciplinary consensus statement on the benefits of, and barriers to, physical activity for older adults. She is currently collaborating with Watford Football Club Community Sports and Education Trust on a reminiscence project for older adults living with dementia. She is co-founder of the Anita White Foundation, UK, which provides education and development opportunities for women leaders and scholars in sport, and former president of the International Sociology of Sport Association.

Kaveri Prakash works in the field of violence and substance abuse with a focus on women. She has also worked with the centres set up as part of the harm reduction strategy for controlling substance abuse being adopted in Canada. She has been a competitive athlete, which has prompted her interest in sports studies and the larger ramifications of doping and strategies to control it. She has presented papers at sports conferences and has written on sports as a journalist and in academic journals.

Sarthak Sood is a law graduate of the West Bengal National University of Juridical Sciences, Kolkata, India, and is currently an associate at AZB Partners.

Vidya Subramanian is an interdisciplinary scholar whose research interests lie at the intersection of technologies and societies. She is currently a postdoctoral fellow at the Centre for Policy Studies, IIT Bombay, where she studies the nature of the digital turn in India. Her doctoral work explored the influence of information and communication technologies and television on the Indian Premier League (IPL). She has a number of publications in sports studies to her credit, focusing on the impact and influence of technologies on cricket.

Sharda Ugra is senior editor for ESPNcricinfo.com and ESPN.in, ESPN's multisport websites. She is one of the earliest women in Indian sports journalism and has been a sports journalist for over three decades: She has worked with the Mumbai tabloid *Mid-Day*, national daily *The Hindu*, and *India Today* magazine before joining ESPN. She worked with former New Zealand captain John Wright and Indian cricketer Yuvraj Singh on their memoirs around Indian cricket. She has written about Indian sport in popular and academic publications across India, the UK, and Australia. In 2013, she was a fellow at the Australia India Institute at the University of Melbourne, Australia.

Index

Abhinav Mukund, 211
academies, 205
    Badmintion academies, 209–210
    cricket academies, 210–211
    Football academies, 39
adventure, 80, 81, 85
age fraud, 215, 221, 223
All India Radio, 345
Anglo-Indians, 182–183, 184
anti-doping rule violations (ADRVs), 252, 255, 262
Asian Games, 122, 205, 207, 219, 237–247, 252, 261, 327
autoethnographic, 11, 150, 153, 198
ayurvedic medicine, 257–258

beach volleyball, 61
beggars, 246
Beighton Cup, 176, 178, 179, 180, 183, 184
Bhiwani Boxing Club (BBC), 208
binary sex/gender, 114–115, 116–117, 119
biopic, 322–331
biopower, 322, 324
Board of Control for Cricket in India (BCCI), 92, 207, 211, 224, 225, 263, 341, 345
bodies, 295
    bodily cultures, 152, 157
    intersex bodies, 115, 117
    sporting body, 325, 326
    triumphal bodies, 325
    women's bodies, 295
Bollywood, 273, 301, 305, 306–312, 317–319, 322, 328
branding, 23, 237, 329
Brazil, 62, 192, 278, 283, 285, 286, 287
Brazil Medals' Plan, 278
Brian Lara, 360
BRICS, 134–135, 238
British Empire Games, 57
buccal smear test, 119–120

care labour, 19, 27–28, 150–151, 155–157
casinos, 190, 192

Caster Semenya, 9, 114, 122, 124
Chennai Super Kings, 363, 366
Chhatrasal Akhada, 207–208
civic culture, 196–197
Commonwealth Games, 12, 21, 28–29, 57, 135, 160, 209, 219, 225, 237–247, 252
Comptroller and Auditor General (CAG), 239–240
Concurrent List, 12, 215, 216, 219, 220, 221, 224, 226–227, 228, 230–231
Corinthians Football Club, 278
Court of Arbitration for Sport (CAS), 9, 114, 253, 258
Cricket Association of Bengal, 163, 345, 346
cricket pitch, 3
cultural globalization, 37, 41, 47
cultural workers, 24

Dangal, 207, 273, 301, 312–313, 318, 319
Deccan Gymkhana, 55
decolonization, 11, 20, 141, 159
Delhi Daredevils, 363, 366
Dhyan Chand, 175, 177, 181–182, 184
diaspora, 4, 41, 193–194
diffuser of conflict, 281
domestic cricket, 95, 96, 98, 100
Doordarshan, 345–349
doping in sports, 251–265, 266–275
Dorabji Tata, 53–55, 57
Dutee Chand, 9, 10, 114, 121, 122–123

elite nationalists, 52, 58
elite sports, 4, 12, 30, 114, 186, 272
emancipatory, 1, 38, 150, 151, 157
empowerment, 10, 21, 39, 51, 151, 276, 280, 283, 292, 312, 313
English Premier League (EPL), 287, 361, 362
environmental clearance, 244
ethical medical supervision, 271–272
ethics of sports, 298
Evangelical sports, 21, 27, 29, 32
Everest deaths, 70–71

evictions, 239, 244–247
expedition ethic, 78

fandom, 37, 46, 48, 357–358, 360
favela, 278
femininity, 93, 94, 118, 119, 150, 295, 296
femininity control, 119–120
feminist
    critique, 314
    perspective, 11, 125, 143, 150, 296
    politics, 300
    practice, 150
    science studies, 116
    theories, 1, 2, 142
field hockey, 178
FIFA World Cup, 281
film culture, 322
flaneurs, 358, 359, 360, 368
Flavia Saraiva, gymnast, 279
football clubs, European, 44, 45, 47, 48
football merchandise, 37, 38, 39, 40–41, 47
football, 36–39
football, global, 39, 43, 47
    globalized, 11
franchise, 138–139

Game Ethic, 54, 57
gaunkaria, 191
gender discrimination, 280
gender eligibility regulation, 11, 115, 118,
    120, 123, 124, 125
Gender-based violence, 282
Global Commission on Drug Policy, 270
Grassroot Soccer Programme, 283
grassroots cricket, 95, 98

harm reduction strategy, 13, 271
Harris Shield tournament, 54
Harsha Bhogle, 362
HawkEye, 361, 367
Hero Cup, 345, 347, 353
heterotopia, 38
hijab, 293, 294, 295, 299, 300, 301
human traffickers, 286
Hyperandrogenism Regulations, 122–124

Indian elite, 141
Indian Olympic Association, 53, 57
Indian Premier League, 19, 92, 138–139, 211,
    225, 340, 350, 357, 360–363, 366–367

Indian Railways, 66, 101, 286
Indian Super League, 44
India-Pakistan Friendship series, 348
intersectionality, 7, 10, 298

Jagdish Singh, 208, 209

Kalaripayattu, 8, 143
Kerry Packer, 357
Khelo India, 207, 228, 230, 263
Kings XI, 363, 365
Kolkata Knight Riders, 352, 363, 366

Lalit Modi, 351, 361, 364
Laura Trott, 280
legacy plan, 240
leisure, 2, 5, 11, 20, 22, 37, 38, 39, 41–42, 44,
    133, 151, 164, 269, 298, 334, 362
lifestyle sport, 71, 85, 287
local league, 95–96
Lodha Reforms, 225

Maharashtra Mahila Parishad (MMP), 294
marathon, 55, 200, 259, 371
masculinity, 7, 10, 43, 107, 142, 143
    aggressive, 93
    hegemonic, 93
match fixing, 37, 139, 223, 225, 366
media commons, 30
mediatization of sports culture, 357
mega events, 12, 21, 22, 28, 135, 196, 202, 237,
    246–247, 279
mentoring, 11, 150–152, 153–157
migrant workers, 37–39, 42–43, 45, 48
mining, 36, 190, 191, 192
missionaries, 137, 152, 191
modern sports, 1, 3, 160, 164, 271
Muslim girls, 293, 294, 297, 299, 300
Muslim women, 292, 299, 300, 301

National Anti-Doping Agency (NADA),
    251–264, 272, 273
national imaginary, 327–328
    nationalist imaginary, 305
national sports federations (NSFs), 215, 220,
    221–222, 225, 226, 230
National Youth Policy, 279
nationalism, 2, 4, 7, 51–52, 57–58, 92, 159,
    160, 305–315, 365
    muscular nationalism, 7–8

neighbourhood, 44–47, 66, 196, 197–199
Nike, 285, 286, 351

occupational hazard, 70
oligarchies, 11, 20, 24, 25, 32
Olympians, 175, 184, 185, 186
Olympic volleyball, 62–63
Olympism, 51–52, 53, 56, 58, 67
othering, 38, 91, 94, 99
outsider status, 89, 90, 92, 94, 97, 104
    outsider group, 106, 107
Oxford Mission, 178

P V Sindhu, 210
P.T. Usha, 152, 336, 339
pan-continental sport, 61, 63
Paralympic and Special Olympic Sports, 222,
    277, 278
Parcham, 293, 297, 298, 299, 300, 301
Parupalli Kashyap, 209
Patiala, 56, 154, 257, 258, 259, 260
patriarchal cultures, 27
patriarchy, 1, 300, 313–314
PCR method, 120–121
Performance enhancing substances (PES),
    266–275
physical education, 60, 152, 228, 281
Pink Stumps, 105
playgrounds, 44, 46, 48, 54, 206, 294
political economy, 1, 2, 6, 11, 37, 349, 351
political tool, 164, 283, 298
Port Commissioners, 184, 185
porter, 73, 77, 85
post/colonial, 11, 14, 147–148, 305, 349
post-fandom, 357
Prakash Padukone, 210
priests, 180, 190
private capital, 5
Professional Volleyball League, 64
profit, 23, 32, 138
public spaces, 37–38, 42, 43, 45–46, 48, 282,
    296–297, 298, 299, 300, 356
public time-space, 38
Pullela Gopichand, 210
Punjab XI, 352

racialized labour, 72, 78, 79–81, 84
racism, 9, 309, 311
Rajasthan Royals, 352, 363
real estate, 36, 42, 193, 241, 362

Reforms Report, 215
reportage, 13, 340
role models, 105, 299
Royal Challengers Bangalore, 363

sacred journeys, 79–80
sahibs, 75, 77, 78, 79, 80, 83
Saina Nehwal, 210
Sakshi Malik, 207
Satpal Singh, 207–208, 211
school sports, 5, 44, 45, 46, 54, 164
seduction, 74, 76, 77
serious games, 74–75
sex work, 246
sexual abuse, 287
sexual harassment, 81, 221, 223
Sherpa cheerfulness, 77, 79
Sherpa image, 75–76
Sherpa mimesis, 76
sherpanis, 81
social capital, 140, 182, 196–197, 198, 330
social history, 159, 161–163, 164, 165
social reproduction, 20, 28, 31–32, 157
Sonepat, 205
South-South, 284
spectator, 9, 25, 46, 65, 138, 139, 146, 180,
    356, 358, 359, 362, 367, 368
    football spectator, 357
spectators of cricket, 360
sporting glocal, 71
sporting-entertainment complex, 367
sportive nationalism, 21, 25, 27
sports administration, 12, 215, 216, 226,
    231, 341
sports and development, 21–22, 23, 32
Sports Authority, 209, 218, 221
sports based development programme, 283
sports club, 12, 24, 27, 151, 153–155, 197, 198,
    199, 201, 224, 280
sports column, 156
Sports commons, 11, 12, 19, 21, 28–32, 151, 157
Sports consumer culture, 19, 31
Sports cultures, 11, 19, 20–25, 27, 28, 30, 31,
    67, 146, 151, 160, 329
    Sporting culture, 12, 160, 196–198, 202,
        206, 228, 330–331, 357
sports diplomacy, 229
Sports Ethics, 223
sports for development, 276, 283, 298, 299
sports goods, 5, 19, 285

382 INDEX

sports historian(s), 160, 163, 166–167
sports hostels, 152
sports industry, 49, 211, 285–286, 340
sports journalist, 334, 338, 339, 340, 343
sports labour, 24–28, 32
sports labour regimes, 25
sports market(s), 9, 19–20, 21, 23–24, 27,
    29–32, 151
Sports mega events, 12, 21, 22, 237–238
    Sporting mega event, 286
sports schools, 152–153
sports talent, 206, 209, 211
sports workers, 9, 24–26, 32
    celebrity, 19
sports, global production networks of, 19, 23
sports-based jobs, 209, 210
Sportscapes, 36, 37
sports-media-industry complex, 47, 49
sports-media-tourism complex, 22, 26–27, 32
Street Child World Cup, 283
strike, 70, 77, 84
subalternity, 2, 4
supplements, 262
    Nutritional, 273
    Food, 256–257
Sustainable Development Goals (SDGs),
    276–277, 283, 287

tamasha, 2, 357, 367
Target Olympic Podium Scheme (TOPS),
    230, 263

televised, 47, 329, 356, 361, 362,
    363, 366
therapeutic use exemption (TUE), 253,
    255–256
Tigers of the snow, 74
topophilia, 360
Tour de France, 270, 356
tourism, 237–238, 241–243, 244
track and field, 114, 116, 118, 150, 151, 153,
    154, 261, 262
Trans World International (TWI), 345
Twenty20, 92, 138, 211, 360, 362, 367

urban renewal, 237

women commentators, 340
women's expedition, 81
work and play, 31, 133
World Anti Doping Agency (WADA), 251–263,
    266–275
World Cup (1983), 339
    Cricket World Cup, 66, 135
    ICC World Cup, 21
World Cup (Reliance), 336
World Cup for women, 96
World Cup, women's (2017), 97, 98, 102,
    103, 105

zero tolerance, 251
zhindak, 80